THE PARISH & THE WORKING CLASS

The Parish
&
The Working Class

ABBÉ GEORGES MICHONNEAU
Parish Priest of *Sacré Cœur de Colombes*

Foreword by
HUGH SOMERVILLE KNAPMAN, OSB

AROUCA
PRESS

Arouca Press
PO Box 55003
Bridgeport PO
Waterloo, ON N2J 0A5
Canada
www.aroucapress.com
Send inquiries to info@aroucapress.com

CONTENTS

FOREWORD

HUGH SOMERVILLE KNAPMAN, OSB
Douai Abbey

O NLY A MODERN-DAY Rip Van Winkle among Catholics would be unaware of the debate that surrounded, and still surrounds, the Second Vatican Council, in particular the subsequent implementation of its decrees. At times the debate has proved simplistic in its premises, superficial in its observations, unnuanced in its expression, and ungenerous in its motivation. The polarisa- tion that has marked the debate has led to some facile, even absurd, working attitudes: everything before the Council *bad*, everything resulting from it *wonderful*—and vice versa. At the extremes are those who argue that the self-styled "pastoral council" represents an innovation in the role of councils in the Church, rendering it at worst illegitimate, at best as having an implicit expiry date and so fully repealable. There is a third, marginally more moderate tendency which sees "The Council" as a second Pentecost, liberating the Church from more than a millennium's apparent famine of the Holy Spirit.

Essential to any reasonable assessment of the Council are an historical sensibility and a full appreciation of the Church both in its temporal manifestation (as "the people of God") and its fundamental mystery (as "the Body of Christ"). Without these the Council cannot be adequately appreciated in its full and proper context, a context that is inevitably and necessarily diachronic (across time), synchronic (at a given point in time), and exochronic (outside time; we might also say eschatologi- cal). The Church has a history that is essential to its identity and activity, a history that is still a work in progress. The Church on earth adapts to the needs of its time and place, but resists capitulation to either. Otherwise, the Church would risk behaving as a purely human institution, socially contingent, and destined—doomed—to prioritise the natural over the super‹ natural, the passing over the eternal.

To put it another way, without the guides and stays of its Scripture and Tradition, which reveal Jesus Christ to those with eyes to see and ears to hear, the Church risks running off its rails. Christ *is* the self‹revelation of God, and the Church as the Body of Christ locates God's revelation in the people of God. This truth had pride of place for the Council fathers as they gave their teaching, but one might wonder whether it has been given similar pride of place in its reception and implementation. The reader of Abbé Michonneau's works in this anthology will find in them a profound awareness of the full reality of the Church of Christ, its role in the world, and the service it must render to the people who make up the Body of Christ on earth. For that reason, and because his priestly heart was very much in the right place, and also because the pre‹conciliar pastoral prob‹ lems he sought to address are still in essence the same pastoral problems as today's, what Abbé Michonneau had to say in the mid‹twentieth century retains value in our day.

Indeed, it is impossible to ignore, no matter one's ecclesio‹ ideological stance, that the Church has been enduring a cri‹ sis since the Council. The crisis is natural and supernatural, demographic and doctrinal. Fundamental dogmatic positions, both theological and moral, are now regularly questioned even at the higher levels of the Church. Even as the Church grows in numbers globally, the active practice of, and identification with, the Catholic faith of its members is in seemingly inex‹ orable decline—at least in the global north. The inner life of the Church has become as unstable as the world around it, a world which the Church is called to be in, but not of; a world Christ sent it into to convert, not to coddle or cajole. Of course, there is in this crisis, no less than any other, a moment of opportunity.

However, to identify this crisis as essentially *post‹*conciliar, directly and exclusively a consequence of the Second Vatican Council, is to reveal an ignorance of history. It is often an inculpable ignorance, as a good deal of the relevant history has been lost to general view. All through its history, but espe‑ cially from the Enlightenment onwards, the Church has had to grapple with the missionary challenge of reconciling divine revelation with human flux, proclaiming Christ's gospel within an ever‑changing temporal reality. The Modernist crisis was a major flash‑point in this struggle, and its legacy is still in evidence in the life of the Church in our day.

What the three books of Abbé Georges Michonneau (1899– 1983) collected here reveal and reflect is that there was a pas‑ toral crisis in the Church, conceived of as potentially existen‑ tial, *before* the Council. Indeed this crisis was manifest at a time that some today see as a golden period in the life of the Church. What Michonneau, and others with him, suggest is that the apparent health of the Church was not as vigorous as it might have appeared. By today's measure, Mass attendance was generally high. Yet the raw statistics of Mass attendance often mask deeper trends. Michonneau laments the low per‑ centage of active participation of all the Catholics in his own Parisian working‑class parish, Sacré Coeur du Petits Colombes. Yet the numbers, seen today, would appear admirable, and they afforded him abundant collaborators among the laity that many, maybe even most, parishes of the global north today would be giddy with joy to have.

Michonneau, with Cardinal Suhard, laments a world—the 1940s—in which society had become predominantly pagan. Most at risk, as he assessed the situation, were the workers, often poorly educated, with little opportunity or incentive to deepen their knowledge of the Christian faith, and too vulner‑ able to the charms and blandishments of worldly ideologies, not least the ascendant voice of Marxism that now sought to build a brave new world from the ruins of fascism. The Church had become parish bound in the worst sense, too bourgeois in its priorities and accommodations. It had become insular, seemingly content to allow the masses to fall away from the Church, or at least resigned to the prospect.

In Michonneau's eyes, and in Cardinal Suhard's as the reader will see, the geographical parish is naturally the fundamental unit of the Church's presence in the world; indispensable but, alas, increasingly inadequate to the challenges facing it in modern times. Few parishioners had the training or the time to seek out the lost; too few had even the inclination. Main-tenance of the parochial *status quo* was work enough. In our parishes today, usually vastly reduced in the number of active parishioners and financial resources compared to the 1940s, this problem is even more acute. The faithful remnant are either too busy or too old to bring into being the missionary parish of which Michonneau dreams, let alone the military outpost for spiritual reconquest that Cardinal Cushing envisages in his Foreword to the first English edition of *Revolution in a City Parish*.[1] Something more was needed then, and is even more needed now.

Even in Michonneau's day hope for the "more" was directed to the laity, in the case of France to Catholic Action and the Young Christian Workers. Their role was to go to where the masses—the workers—were, to share their life, to meet them on their ground. They were to be amid the masses as a pres-ence initially, then to become a force for gentle encouragement to seek in Christ and his Church the purpose, direction, and motivation they were being enticed to find in the insidious and misguided Marxist promise of a proletarian utopia. It was not merely an apostolate of presence—of accompaniment we might now say—but of guidance. It was a properly lay apos-tolate, a flowering of the laity's mission to sanctify the world through their daily witness to the gospel. In comparison with this authentic apostolate of the laity, the roughly contempo-rary worker-priest movement, however idealistic, was naive

---

1   This is the English title of the book *Paroisse, Communauté Mission-naire* to which frequent reference is made in this new edition. Undoubtedly it was chosen by the publisher to provoke but it is not an accurate title since it also omits the word "missionary" which as one reviewer stated in 1952 "is of the essence of the Colombes enterprise."

and misguided. The Church needed its priests to be priests, to be pastors to the laity who were called to be the front-line apostles in daily life.

Catholic Action has come and gone. Young Christian Work- ers are a shadow of their former selves. Both did immense good in their day, but it seems their day has come and gone. That does not mean we have nothing to learn from them and all that they achieved. The question is: where, and in whom, will we find the Catholic Action and Young Christian Workers for our day, the lay apostles sorely needed in every age, but desperately in our own?

The lay apostolate, which has admittedly been explored with mixed results since the Council, has come to a moment of great opportunity, in part arising from the crisis of the clergy. The various abuse scandals that have emerged in recent decades have compromised the moral authority of the clergy. Their number has dwindled alarmingly. Unable now to do all they once were wont to do, the clergy need to focus on doing what they must do, what is proper to their ministry and place in the Church: the celebration of the sacraments and the pastoral guidance offered through them by Christ the Good Shepherd. The world will not be changed by the clergy. The world will only be changed—let us say it: converted—by a laity wit- nessing to the gospel in the ordinariness of their daily living, accompanied and encouraged by vigorous lay apostles. These lay apostles will themselves need to be given particular care and support by the shepherds. This apostolic laity is very much the vision of Abbé Michonneau.

What the Church does not need is a clericalised laity, just as recent history shows it does not need a "laified"[2] clergy. A cler- icalised laity seeks to "run" the Church, whatever that might

---

2   I have avoided the more obvious term *laicised*, as this is used for the canonical punishment of returning a priest to the lay state, rather than the tendency among some clergy to want to be less distinct from the laity. The neologism *laified* is the best I could think of for my purpose here.

mean, though it usually entails use of the word *power* at some point. A clericalised laity seeks power in the Church in order to change the Church, rather than to change the hearts of those in the Church, let alone those outside it. A clericalised laity inevitably, and rather ironically, thinks and works in terms of structures and institutions, rather than people and their souls.

An apostolic laity, on the other hand, seeks not to change the Church but to be the agents of change for *the world and all its peoples*, to make disciples of all nations by modelling discipleship, thinking and working in terms of communities and the individuals within them, not structures and the exercise of power within them, happy to be servants of the Church in their area, tools in the hands of Christ. Theirs would be an attractive joy that comes from a living faith in Christ, a faith whose essence has been handed on over the centuries within the Church for the sake of the world.

This is not particularly original as should be obvious, and to some extent that is precisely the point. We have heard something similar for years, but perhaps not always framed fruitfully, or articulated and delineated helpfully. What we might forget, or perhaps do not even realise, is that this is not something that emerged from some sudden revelation through the Second Vatican Council. Abbé Michonneau—as well as Abbé Godin, Cardinal Suhard, Cardinal Cushing, Maisie Ward et al—had these insights and aspirations before the Council, aspirations which very much inspired and informed the Council. After the Council these insights and aspirations prospered and developed a life of their own, a vocabulary and even a propaganda, that kindled much activity but, as it turns out, vastly less achievement than desired. Indeed the movement for an apostolic laity that Michonneau and others so zealously advocated, morphed into a momentum towards a clericalised laity that looked more to the sanctuary and the chancery than to the home and workplace. The lay apostolate has also been in great measure supplanted by a professionalised, salaried lay workforce within an increasingly corporatised, institutionalised, and bureaucratised

Church. If only financially, the Church cannot long afford this new lay caste within it, if only because ecclesiocrats—lay or clerical—do not tend to make converts or even retain current members of the flock. There will soon be too few active Catholics left to pay their salaries.

As the adage goes, it is better to light a candle than curse the darkness. Both before and after the Council it was recognised that the ordained clergy, and the religious orders, could not do all that was needed to spread the Gospel and "rechristianise" the world. It was not only that the world had become less Christian; since the Enlightenment especially it had become less religious, less open to the supernatural, and more materialistic and temporally-oriented: in a word, paganised. That said, the world has not become any less superstitious, any less gullible, though it has come to be beguiled by more secular and more technological idols.

What was—is—needed is a laity that lives and works in the midst of such a paganised world, making of its daily life and work an apostolate of witness to the eternal, the supernatural, the true: to Christ. Such a laity needs to be able to withstand the lures and temptations, the frauds and deceptions of a paganised world. Inevitably, it will require leaders from within its ranks, catechised and strategised for bringing Christ into homes and workplaces, be these hitherto familiar or unfamiliar with the Gospel. Their lead, encouragement, and support to the general body of the laity in being effective witnesses to Christ in all corners of a paganised world will be indispensable. Not every Christian can preach or teach, but all Christians can love their neighbour, whoever that might be; the preachers and teachers—the bedrock of an apostolic laity—will have to unlock this latent, too little esteemed, power at the heart of the Church in all its members.

Who might do this? Almost certainly the same people as always: people who are prepared to forego a large measure of monetary, temporal wealth in order to earn treasure in heaven, in the coin of human beings won to Christ and Christian living on earth. However, if the approaches of the past seem no longer to work, what can we do differently?

Most likely, the key will lie with the young. Not, please note, young people trained up to be a slick bureaucratic caste within an even more institutionalised, if declericalised, Church. Rather, we will need young people prepared and able to be identified as Christians, to explain the Church's teachings and resolve the usual objections to them, to be available to those among whom they live in a way the clergy cannot reasonably be.

There are intimations and beginnings of such an initiative. From my own experience I have come across the Catholic par= ishes at Bondi in Sydney, Australia. Here can be found com= munity houses of young people—men and women living sep= arately—who for minimal rent are able to live in commodious accommodation with like=minded peers. They go to their work= places during the day, but out of working hours they commit to serving the parish community in various ways. Hospitality is a strong element of what they do, with meals, evenings of talks and fellowship (including separate men's and women's events), even barbecues at which anyone passing is invited to share. The young have the energy and enthusiasm to do all this, and the attractiveness of what they do reaches not only the young. Unsurprisingly, at Bondi the apostolate of these young lay people extends to the liturgy, which is the modern liturgy seasoned by the consistent tradition of the Church, marked by reverence and beauty. The Sunday high Mass is followed by a gathering around food and drink, with the fellowship these foster. Young people, and the not so young, have been coming from across Sydney to be nourished by an expression of faith that is not ashamed to be seen and to be shared.

Still, is something else needed, something different but com= plementary to such initiatives? The Bondi project is very much consistent with the thought of Michonneau, but embraces its own local and particular advantages. Other initiatives are needed for different circumstances. One might be a variation on Bondi, involving young lay apostles willing and able to devote themselves full-time for a set period to the apostolate. Perhaps the Mormon model of youth mission has something to offer here. Young Mormons, between 18 and 25 years of age, who meet the fundamental requirements, are invited to spend two years overseas in the work of evangelisation. They go about in pairs, instantly recognisable to so many of us in their white shirts and black trousers, clean cut and clean living. Such mis-sionary service is a seen as a privilege by the young mission-aries themselves, and as an honour and joy for their families.

There is much we could take from the Mormon model of mis-sion, especially the esteem they give to such an apostolate. Life in community would be essential, communities of like-minded, like-aged young men or women. Essential would be their being based in parishes, especially parishes struggling to survive demo-graphically. Since these parishes often do not have the properties needed to house such communities, nor the finances to main-tain them, the dioceses would need to provide the necessary resources. So much has been wasted by dioceses in recent years on initiatives that are high in profile but low in results. Rather than pursue these fruitless exercises, the money would be far better spent on such communities of young lay apostles.

These communities are likely to produce vocations to the priesthood and religious life. Just as importantly, and even more likely, they will produce committed young Catholics who will marry and raise the families the Church so desperately needs. So often in parishes we hear lamentations over the absence of young people. When there does occur an event at which young people come in some numbers, the tendency is to exult over a "success," one that all too often proves fleeting and shallow. It is right that we lament the absence of the young. Yet why *do* we see so few of them now, vastly fewer than in Michonneau's day? In part it is often because their parents have wandered from the Church. In part it is because Catholics are having so few children in the first place; there is more than one commen-tator who has opined that Catholics are "contracepting" them-selves out of existence. In part, too, it is because what young people find in the worship and local activity of the Church is too often more banal than beautiful.

We hear talk today of missionary parishes, an aspiration that dates at least from Michonneau's day and is not purely post-conciliar. Yet, given the demographics of so many parishes in the global north, who would be available to do the mission-ing? Onto an ever smaller group of ageing stalwarts the burden of such initiatives usually devolves, in addition to the burden of just keeping the parish going from week to week. They cannot be expected to do it all.

If parishes are to remain the fundamental unit of the local Church, perhaps their future lies in hosting and support-ing—and being supported by—communities of young lay apostles who have committed to one or two years of serving the parish by liturgical service, and by simple human hospitality and accompaniment. Such catechised youth would attract other young people, and older ones too, who might find it easier to hear the Gospel first from those more like themselves. The older parish stalwarts would find a good deal of the parochial burden taken off them, more of a buzz about the place, more beauty and life in the liturgy, as more young people appear among them. The stalwarts would also have more opportunity to offer to the young the wisdom that comes from experience, especially of family and working life. Dioceses could start direct-ing their resources to enable such local, de-bureaucratised, rel-atively non-institutionalised initiatives which, God willing and experience suggesting, would help not only the young but all within the parish community, and beyond it. Needless to say it would require a cadre of parish priests willing and able to support, guide, and nurture, but not dominate, such commu-nities of young lay apostles.

This is what has come to my mind. When you read Michon-neau's ideas and experiences in the pages that follow, you may find other ideas coming to mind. They may be worthy of shar-ing and testing: if they are of God they will bear fruit, fruit that will last.

Of particular interest to some readers will be what Michon‑ neau had to say about the liturgy in reviving the active partici‑ pation of Catholics in the life of the Church, and in promoting the "rechristianisation" of a paganised world. Michonneau's pri‑ mary focus is not on the liturgy, but that does not mean he has little to say about it. Indeed, he has some distinctly forthright opinions, and was not averse to some liturgical adjustments in his parish. The second chapter of *Revolution in a City Parish* is devoted to "a living, apostolic liturgy." It is an important chap‑ ter not so much for the ideas he suggests as for the description of the liturgical life and practice of a not‑untypical suburban parish. His tone is not snide, but exasperated in his yearning to reach his people through worship. Reading his description, it is hard not to agree that something seemed certainly amiss by 1946. At Mass there were good numbers of bodies present, but their hearts seemed to be elsewhere.

Michonneau explains two fundamental principles for the lit‑ urgy of a revivified parish: that it must be communal and thus apostolic; and that it must be adapted to the circumstances of the community in question (in his case, a working‑class community). He does not advocate "discarding canon law or doing anything contrary to express rubrics." Rather he seeks to make the celebration of Mass "intelligible" to the people, something in which they can "participate to the utmost, and in a way suited to their mentality." He notes that elsewhere there was already liturgical experimentation involving "'terrible' adaptations." Priests everywhere, it seems, found an increasing disconnect between people and liturgy and sought in good faith, but with often poor judgment, to remedy it.

Michonneau preferred to "make the Low Mass as *high* as possible." By this he meant making the Low Mass less silent, more visible, more engaging. He saw a need for priests to improve what we would call their *ars celebrandi*, the way they celebrate Mass. He had his congregation sing the *Gloria*, Creed, *Sanctus* and *Agnus Dei*. He preferred to add ceremonies para‑liturgically than to tinker too much with the Mass, though he added things to the Mass as well. Yet he could also lament that "liturgical chant has given way to hymns by a soloist or by a choir, or even to musical renderings of a violin or violoncello."

Both liturgical traditionalists and progressives would do well to read Michonneau on the liturgy. Both groups will find things to cheer, and things to boo. More importantly, both will see that there was a growing disconnect between people and liturgy, and that pastors such as Michonneau sought to address it not by doing violence to the liturgy but by making it more engaging for the ordinary, primarily working-class, person. We might do well to assess our own practice, priorities, and principles in the light of those of a sincere, zealous, faithful pastor who valued both the tradition of the Church and its people, not least the strayed.

Reading Abbé Michonneau today is not of purely historical interest. His narrative helps explain today by revealing the realities of yesterday we might not have known, or have preferred not to know. At the same time he can make a contribution towards our charting a lively path into the future. In his work we find a yardstick to help us measure what we have got right and what we have got wrong in recent decades. He reminds us that revivifying the Church is essential for christianising the world. Above all he reminds us that the Church and its life are ordered to people and their souls, nurturing them in this world that they may be ready for the Kingdom of heaven of which the Church on earth is the living icon. The pride of ideology must be left behind; our bearing must be humble, our vision must be generous and expansive, and unashamedly faithful to the Gospel of Christ handed down to us from the apostles for the life of the world. ✢

Revolution in
a City Parish

FOREWORD TO THE
FIRST ENGLISH EDITION

HIS EXCELLENCY, THE MOST REVEREND RICHARD J. CUSHING
Archbishop of Boston

CARDINAL SUHARD OF Paris gives warm and unqualified praise to this book of Father Michonneau's. His Eminence describes the work as the outgrowth of practical experience, priestly zeal, and a genuine thirst for souls. It is revolutionary in a sense of that word without sinister con= notation. It is a sincere effort to point the way for the renewal of Christianity among the dechristianized proletariat of France.

Thoughtful men in many parts of the world can discover in Father Michonneau's work a pattern for advancing the bound= aries of the living Church everywhere, by the use of established Catholic parishes as active cells for such growth.

Father Michonneau notes that, traditionally, the parish has been the expression of religious community life. In the par= ish as it developed in Catholic Europe, practically all human beings dwelling within its confines were, by that very fact, its members. Some individuals were less faithful to their duties than others, but no man, woman, or child denied his or her allegiance to the particular unit=cell of the Mystical Body, the parish, within whose confines he or she dwelt.

Today in France, the author explains, things have become very different. New factors have introduced great changes. In many parts of France there are great masses of humanity who are spiritual drifters. A small number are aggressively irreligious, hostile to their nation's Christian tradition, not merely ignorant but malignantly misinformed on things Christian, bitter in their disdain for the priest and the institution for which he stands. The great majority, however, are merely religionless; they are not *hostile*, but are completely *ignorant* of Christian life and teaching, unacquainted even with the inside of a house of God.

3

With France's insufficient clergy, it is hopeless to seek to retrieve the lost ground by operating the parishes as in the days of faith. Instead, this unit of Catholic organization has come, in many cases, to be an outpost for spiritual reconquest. The pastor must now make of himself a captain at the head of loyal lieutenants who are his curates if he is so fortunate as to have such. His spiritual fighting force, in any case, must more and more include lay apostles, who recognize that Christ can be served best by bringing Him into the homes and hearts of every creature of God within the parish confines.

Father Michonneau notes that the "missionaries" of France must start anew to awaken a consciousness of what Christ means. Their task is quite different from, and even more difficult than that of apostles in China or Japan who announce the Christian message for the first time. In France the populace *thinks* that it knows Christianity; people have long ago dismissed it once and for all as having no practical bearing on their lives or their needs. Christian truths, ideals of Christian beauty, when presented in routine fashion, have no power to "startle" such people. "Yes, yes, we've heard all that," they mumble with a shrug, even as they continue their search for values elsewhere. The apostles of modern France must be sufficiently alert and dynamic to persuade these people that they are mistaken that the quest of man leads to the Christ of the Tabernacle.

We might well apply the findings of Father Michonneau to our Englishspeaking world. Catholic parish life, it is true, is strong in many parts of England and the United States. But all too often our parishes are far from possessing the truly Catholic concept of the term as it was used in the Middle Ages. Indeed the element of allembracingness has long since been forgotten. In the Protestant world of today the term "parish" signifies much the same to the Catholic as it does to the Baptist or Methodist. The parish is a sort of spiritual club, the membership of which is composed of chosen adherents within a given area, who live their lives together and ignore all the other inhabitants of the area.

We ask the ordinary Catholic in the English-speaking world: "How many souls are there in your parish?" He replies immediately with a figure—eight hundred, fifteen hundred, five thousand, ten thousand. And by that figure he means the Catholics alone who dwell within the parish lines. He may say that there are fifteen hundred in his parish, while in point of fact twenty thousand souls may be serving out their lives within its confines. The sense of the authentic Catholic tradition that would embrace the remaining eighteen thousand five hundred has been lost.

And so perhaps we have a lesson for our English-speaking world to learn from Father Michonneau's book on France. Perhaps our parishes must become outposts of spiritual attack. It may be time for each pastor and his curates, even with us, to organize the stronger elements among the laity for an advance that would bring the forgotten and disdained Christ of the Tabernacle not merely to those few who already find their way into our churches, but to the huge multitudes who are outside the Church—but within the parish.

Christ came for all, Christ died for all, Christ calls all, not only the practicing Catholic, not only the pagan in China to whom we send our missionaries. He desires as well the millions by our side, the dwellers in our established parishes whom we have accustomed ourselves to overlook. Here is the oldest and yet the newest of apostolates—that to our immediate neighbors. God prosper it! ✠

5

PREFACE TO THE FRENCH EDITION

HIS EMINENCE EMMANUEL CARDINAL SUHARD
Archbishop of Paris

I

T IS ALWAYS a happy experience for the shepherd of a diocese to read a record of priestly effort for the conquest of souls, and to see proposed an apostolic way of life which is adapted to the needs of a world that presents a problem of ever-increasing urgency to the Catholic apostolate. I cannot adequately express my thanks to Father Michonneau, and to Father Chéry, his editor, for their portrayal of the parish activity accomplished by a priestly unit at Sacré Cœur de Colombes for the past five years or more. Truly this is an account which should renew and guide the apostolic zeal of those whose mission it is to lead our people on the search for a life that is completely Christian and also compatible with the actual conditions around them.

This book is indeed timely. For years zealous priests have been meditating on the grave words of Pope Pius XI, who said that the scandal of the nineteenth century had been the loss of the working class by the Church. For years now, this meditation has been bearing fruit in a large number of activities to which the whole Christian community owes in great part the renewal of its vitality. And these activities, by their very success, call for a deeper enquiry into the problem of winning the common man for Christ. The religious effort itself of the last twenty years in France has raised the questions to which Father Michonneau's labours give a direct answer.

It would be a mistake to think that this volume is concerned only with finding a new clerical technique. Father Michonneau's last wish is to be an instigator of rash changes; he wants, rather, to face squarely the problem of bringing the Gospel into the lives of our people. His constant concern is to find more effective ways of re-Christianizing people, and especially the working class of our cities. Everywhere groups of active young working-class Christians have been formed, and these Christians, as they grow up, are going to found an ever-increasing number of Christian homes, which will often be admirable centers of faith and devotion. In the degree, however, that Catholic Action bears fruit, it becomes increasingly clear that a somewhat different task must be undertake—not opposed to Catholic Action, but complementing it.

We can no longer ignore the fact that these new Christians, born of Catholic Action, must face a world which is practically pagan, one in which there is almost nothing truly Christian. We cannot conceive of a spirituality abstracted from the contacts and influences of daily life, work, pleasures, housing, the common opinion of friends, the outpourings of the cinema, the press, and the wireless. Sooner or later, the problem of reconciling life and spirituality arises. And the crisis is especially marked when a young Christian marries and establishes a home. From that moment, he should be able to settle himself in a community which is Christian, and is therefore capable of absorbing his whole life and of filling it with the light of grace and faith in Christ. Because this is so difficult we have in many cases to admit failure.

We are drawn, inevitably, to the heart of the problem, which is the re-Christianizing of the life of our people at its source. Even though Catholic Action is a privileged instrument of this task, we have to admit that only the parish, the local and the universal seat of the Redemption, can become the adequate means. It is this conviction which has been directing all the pastoral labours of Father Michonneau.

Now when dealing with parishes devoted to this work of re-Christianizing, we ought to exploit all that the past can teach us about apostolic conquest, so as not to miss any possible method. Our first task must be to form again an atmosphere of religious life which can spread the message of Christ through every level of life within a particular parish. Only in this way will the masses be won back.

We congratulate Father Michonneau on this important con=
tribution to a new advance of the apostolate in France. He gives
a plan, and he also shows results. Hard work and experience
have preceded this book, which is the account of the experi=
ences of the priestly team at Colombes and of their contacts
with real life. This makes the text concrete in its thoughts, and
its realism gives even more weight to its message, which tells
of the tremendous religious longings of souls who are waiting
only to find a living manifestation of the profound holiness of
the Church, before they turn to her.

This account of such a missionary apostolate and of such
a pastoral life totally consecrated to these fundamental prob=
lems of our age cannot fail to make its appeal to the hearts
of many priests who are anxious for the spiritual progress of
their own parish. And it will awaken many questions in the
souls of those who are trying to mold and train themselves for
the ministry, and they will come to see the role of a diocesan
priest in a new light.

A few words may be necessary for those who may believe
that they find in this book of Father Michonneau things he
never intended to say. It should be evident that shortsighted
criticisms are no help to anyone; true charity is always con=
structive. It is true that the Church down through these long
centuries has explained the Redemption and the graces of the
Spirit according to the needs of each age, always with the inten=
tion of perfecting each age. Our generation should remember
that, if it now has before it such a wealth of faith and religion,
such a chance to spread the Christian spirit, it owes this to
its predecessors. They are the ones who toiled at the work of
cultivation and seeding on fields which some precipitate mod=
erns want to plough under.

A real apostle is no mere critic. He is a servant in the work
of Christ, and he knows that he is only one link in a long
chain of generations; he is eager enough and humble enough to
accept the fruits of time=proven wisdom. It may be that certain
customs and plans must gradually disappear, to be replaced

by others more suitable to our own times, but, at the same time, we must recognize that there was a day when these were useful. We must avoid the childish error that our generation is destined to settle every problem, to reconstruct everything. Even our efforts and methods, good for today, may show their inadequacies tomorrow. Let those preparing to become apostles of Christ remember these fundamental truths and refrain from criticism that is as ill-advised as they are inexperienced.

It sometimes happens that we get excited questions about whether or not Father Michonneau's picture of a missionary apostolate does not demand a revision of priestly spirituality, even to the extent of modifying the traditional form of priestly prayer — the Breviary. That was never the aim of this book. Rather, it proposes to revivify these basic practices of prayer-life by means of a constant solicitude for the work of Christ and for the sanctification of the parish. It would truly be shortsighted for anyone to think that he finds any incompatibility between the missionary ideal of a priest who keeps in contact with reality and the demands of the interior life without which the priest will soon find himself stripped of the spirituality he thought he had. The interior life has its inexorable demands; it must be sustained by intimate converse between the soul and God; it must take part in the common prayer-life of the Church, and the natural expression for this is the Breviary. There are many who, in their sincere desire to radiate the influence of Christ, find these ancient safeguards of the spiritual life burdensome. Such men are merely avoiding the problem, not solving it, when they think that they can accomplish an apostolic task without these same basic elements of apostolic spirituality, mental prayer, and the Divine Office.

The demands of this apostolate are not such as to force us to abandon all care for "culture," as some might think from reading the chapter in this book which is devoted to that problem. What is demanded is that the priest must know how to be approachable, and so he must somehow share in the "culture" of his people. It may be that Father Michonneau does not make

9

his distinctions clear enough between that illusory familiarity with the popular mind which would result if a priest were to jettison the humane culture, which is part of the equipment of a minister of God, and the true adaptation by which a priest can be understanding and be understood without thereby ceasing to elevate and spiritualize the souls entrusted to his care. The first attitude would be a deplorable debasement, and would seriously compromise the efforts of any priest. Only the second is worthy of an apostle bringing Christ back into our world.

There is no point in deceiving ourselves: the adaptation demands constant effort from all of us. We still have to acquire and use our heritage of sacred sciences, but we must avoid the error of keeping it in the abstract and academic. We must make use of secular sciences too, so as to gain an entrance into the interests of our world and make Christ known in it. In any case, we may be sure that, if people are offended by seeing priests who find it hard to come down to their level, they will be even more hurt to find in us the same common and vulgar limitations they see in themselves.

And finally, it should be clear that apostolic endeavour cannot succeed without constant obedience to the hierarchy, which has the task of organizing the whole Christian life of a given area. There are priests who think that daring experiments begun in their own parishes are of concern to no one else but themselves. Now, besides the fact that these rash undertak﹦ ings seldom produce any lasting good, these priests make the mistake of thinking that obedience to the hierarchy will stifle all boldness in the cause of Christ, all generosity in his ser﹦ vice. The reverse is true, and every isolated effort can gain real benefit from the control and support which the heads of the hierarchy, because of their greater vision, can furnish if there is submission to the overall work of Christ. As individuals we may come upon a particular solution of particular problems, but we should ask ourselves if we have sufficient vision, if our zeal is in step with the whole Christian community, which the Holy Ghost is guiding. These questions find their answers in constant reference to the judgment of the hierarchy and in constant submission to its decisions.

This does not mean that we should always wait for impetus from above; only laziness would come to that conclusion. But we certainly are obliged to submit our projects to the approval of superiors and to ask for the advice and judgment which obedience to the Church demands. There could not be, for example, any question of altering for some professedly apostolic reason, but without the consent of the hierarchy, customs generally observed in the Church. Some have asked whether or not the wearing of ecclesiastical dress may not be a liability rather than an asset to the apostolate.

One thing to remember in questions like these is that we are poor judges in our own cases; that is why we must submit to truly hierarchical authority.

It should also be evident that no apostolic effort can attain its goal unless the priestly dignity and office are upheld. A priest must grow in the esteem of his people and in the sight of God.

We cite these instances by way of example, and without any intention of making reservations in our opinion of this text, because we are delighted with the book. Our intention is merely to put things in their proper light for all those who wish to take this priestly group at Colombes as a model. May the book of Father Michonneau give rise to new developments in the marvellous Christian activity among working people, and may it shed new light on the zeal of all those who, in every corner of France, are engaged in this work.

August 1, 1946 ✢

FORETHOUGHTS

I

A SUBURBAN PRIEST MAKES a poor author. How will he find time to write? From the time of his Mass, until the end of the last meeting at night, his day is well filled with the care of his flock, visits to be made, tales to hear, business to do.

When, poor man, will he be able to undertake any writing? He has hardly found time to think of it, when his door-bell rings, calling him to solve some immediate problem.

Besides all this, his viewpoint is necessarily limited. Completely given over to this corner of the vineyard which the bishop has entrusted to him, how can he have the broad outlook or do the research that is necessary for writing a book?

And yet, if a parish priest will not speak about parishes and parish ministry, who will?

How often are we parish clergy exasperated on reading the work of some pastoral theologian, because we know that he is expressing only theoretical views. He did not live the life before writing about it. And it is so easy to make up an armchair approach to the ministry!

That is why, after much hesitation, I acceded to the request of Father Maydieu, and put down in black and white my ideas about a parish of working people. That was in "Rencontres."[1] But I did refuse to take on the editing of this work, and asked for a collaborator; and so Father Chéry has added his style, as flowing as a Dominican habit, to these thoughts.

I say now that these thoughts are "our" thoughts, for my curates and I are one. We lived this book together before we came to write it with Father Chéry. It is the result of our common experience and of our lengthy discussions together as a

---

1 *Rencontres* is the title of a series of essays and studies which began during the war when *La Vie Intellecttuelle*, like all the other periodicals, was forbidden by the Germans. This book is included in the series.

team in contact with reality. That is why, even when it is only the parish priest speaking, it is always "we," the plural of reality, not of majesty.

Let none of my fellow-priests see in this work the slightest intention of teaching them a lesson. If certain statements sound categoric and others seem sweeping, I ask them to forgive my awkwardness. A man of action is always a little precipitate; he believes in his "pet theory," gives himself to it, heart and soul, and does not worry much about the finer shades.

It was not my intention in writing these pages to compose a treatise of pastoral theology, and still less to describe a model missionary parish. I was asked about what we had done at Colombes, taking into consideration the circumstances of time, place, and persons as they are here; and this is the answer. We might have done differently in the years ahead; as I get old and have other collaborators around me, it is very likely that our methods will evolve, because, as the proverb goes, "only fools or dead men cannot change."

So let no one try to find in these pages anything that smacks of hard and fast rules. Parishes are very different from one another. The men whom Christ has chosen to evangelize them are too distinct in nature and grace, and pastoral gifts are psychological factors too diversified for anyone to presume to lay down the last word about methods.

I marvel at those who make up plans for the conversion of parishes or for the penetration of certain classes of society. The only eventuality that they do not foresee is that their plans may never work out.

There will always be a definite role for intuition to play in making plans, and even more important and more indispensable is grace. These "undeterminates" always prevent us from calculating ahead the precise value that any particular parish work will have.

And yet priests from every section of France who have come to see us or who have been asked random questions about our thoughts, have shown that they reached pretty much the same conclusions on many points. They were facing the same problems in about the same perspective as we, and seeing, as did we, the failure of the same timeworn methods, they arrived at similar solutions.

Thus it may be that our pages will have only a general interest, for we do not believe that they are saying anything very new. We only want to bring together ideas that are now scattered and unable to express themselves.

Some, more prudent than we, would no doubt have hesi= tated before putting forth certain ideas which may seem a little radical, but if anyone needs a shoulder on which to shift the responsibility for such ideas, we will gladly lend him ours.

And, in exchange, we ask our confreres to be good enough to say a prayer that the parish of Sacré Cœur de Colombes may not suffer too much from having a parish priest who deserted them for a while, so as to work on this book.

ABBÉ GEORGES MICHONNEAU
Parish Priest of *Sacré Cœur de Colombes*

II

Now a word about the editor of these pages.

When Father Maydieu asked me to work with Father Michonneau, I had no idea of the opportunities being offered me. I came to Colombes on a fine May morning in 1944; pastor and curates were together at a simple meal. In a few minutes I was plunged into a warmly apostolic atmosphere of mission problems, of priestly brotherhood, and of supernatural life. Christ was here; Saint Paul was here.

The "ideas" of Father Michonneau and his co=workers are not mere ideas; I mean they are not living by an ideology. Rather, it is actual parish experience that they have thought out and expressed. In fact, they have a dread of theory. But they are thinking while they live, and it is with joy that they see priests and lay people all over France thinking with them. They have begun to realize the "mission parish" as they see it. It is not a finished product yet and never will be. Nothing is more opposed to the very idea of completion than their missionary undertak‑ ing. A permanent evolution, a constant adaptation based on actual needs—that is the essence of Sacré Cœur de Colombes.

It is easy to see how this attitude makes for a difficult job. A plan was set up for each chapter. I took notes from a dic‑ tation that was more like a conversation. Then I would go off and make a rough draft of what had been said. At the next meeting I would read over this copy, and watch for frowns or approving nods; that would show me where I had become lost in theories: so we revised and revised. Finally, after some months, the book appeared.

This is not a complete work. It is for the reader to follow up what is said here. Let no one judge this book as though it were a text‑book of a professor. We are in the midst of life. And it is for this very reason that these proposals of Father Michonneau will reach a large and interested audience. If they provoke readers to write to us, if they occasion contacts or suggestions, they will have fulfilled their purpose.

It might even happen that the "Rencontres" collection will have to put out a new volume to bring these results to our readers.

The outline of this book is simple enough.

We are confronted, as was Abbé Godin,[2] by a pagan pro‑ letariat, by that section of France which is truly a "mission land." In this land, parishes already exist. Providentially, they are the mission centres; if they do not accomplish their end, they are failing in their vocation. And they cannot accomplish it by remaining stagnated in an atmosphere of "faithful parish‑ ioners." They must become Mission Communities. That is the theme of the first chapter.

How will they become Mission Communities? Answering that question is the function of the whole book.

---

2   Abbé Godin was one of the founders of the famous *Missions de Paris*, which have been winning back the pagans and the communists to the service of Christ in the suburbs of Paris. He has also contributed to a volume in the series *Rencontres* entitled: *France Pays de Mission?*

By a living and popular liturgy, says Chapter Two.

By the apostolate, says Chapter Three, wherein we take up the study, from a mission point of view, of the value of what are generally called "parish activities," We consider different types of specialized movements. Finally, we decide on the superiority of the "direct apostolate" by clergy and laity.

Then comes Chapter Four, with a discussion of the pastoral needs which compel us to aim at creating a stir with our parish communities in this de=Christianized world of ours, so as to make it face the religious question quite frankly.

A great obstacle stands in the way of priests who are trying to reach the mass of people. It is the "clink of money around the altar." Chapter Five tries to form the type of conscience which will end this noise, which drowns the voice of Christ.

Another obstacle, and one to which we generally pay little attention is that of our "culture." The object of Chapter Six is to get over the hurdle, especially in preaching.

What is required of apostles to the people is the theme of Chapter Seven; namely, an adjusted priestly spirituality, and a spirit of teamwork to bind the priests together and to be extended throughout the parish.

Finally, the last chapter deals with results of the whole plan as worked out at Colombes, and shows that the parish must be ready to receive "neophytes," which other apostles (e.g., the Mission de Paris) direct towards it.

We have written this book in dialogue form in order to keep the direct style of the talks which are the origin of the book, but it will be clear that the questions and answers are the fruit of careful editing.

FR. HENRI CHARLES CHÉRY, O. P. ✛

✠[I]✠
The Parish and the Missions

PLEA FOR THE PARISH

In "An Open Letter to Abbe Daniel," I read, "You seem to group indiscriminately, under the name of "pagan masses," the totality of those who do not come to church. Allow me to disagree. It is certainly clear, at least in France, that almost all these people are really Christians, that is, they are baptized persons who used to go to church, who have learnt their catechism, who know some priests and who may even have taken part in some parish activities. I will grant that such are mediocre Christians, almost apostates; but, bad as they are, they are not 'pagans.'"

❡ *Do you agree with this view of one of your confreres, a priest in Paris? Is it true that the majority of people are really Christian?*
   What we think is that all of this is mere playing with words, as regards the title of Christian. If you consider as "real Chris⸗ tians" everyone who has been baptized, or even only those who made their First Communion and had, in childhood, some degree of contact with the Church, then the problem is solved. The "mass" in France is Christian; there is no "mission ter⸗ ritory" in France. But if we wish to restrict the title of Chris⸗ tian (and we are not saying "good Christians") to those who have the Faith, to those to whom Christ is a reality, we must have the courage to stand by the opinion of "France, a Mission Land," and that the mass of the working class is pagan. Not because they do not practise the faith, but because (and the evidence is so clear on this point that we are amazed at any discussion of it), their mentality is pagan and completely foreign to the Christian spirit, indifferent to our creed and careless of the demands of our moral code. Let a child of this group make his First Communion, let him be married at church, let

him call on a priest to bury his dead (and many do not even do that), and yet, all of that does not really change him much. Behind all these appearances, behind this exterior ritualism, the heart of these people is pagan. And so we must approach them in a different way. The method must be different; it must be missionary, for this portion of our country is a mission territory.

❨ *Will this class become apostates?*

We no longer think so. An apostate, essentially, is one who denies a doctrine he once held to adhere to a new one. He leaves a Church of which he once was a member, and he is aware of this abandonment. There is nothing like that in the lives of our mod⸗ ern infidels. Our youngsters who never go back to any practice of religion after their First Communion day are not conscious of any true apostasy. Their parents, who have ceased practicing their religion, which they used to practice in Brittany or the Vendee, are perhaps aware of a certain negligence. When we realize the irreligious atmosphere in which children are steeped from their earliest years and the force of the stream that is carrying each one of them along, we also realize that it is impossible to determine guilt in the fault that they commit. Furthermore, we have to see that the mentality of their surroundings completely conquers them, after a few years of factory work, or even office work. The anti⸗religious, or rather, pagan attitude, is so strong in the factories and offices that the mentality of those who have been baptized, and whom some would like to call "real Christians," is no different from that of the non⸗baptized. The conduct of both is the same. We can consider both as pagans.

Yet there is something in the affirmation of our confrere of which we must not lose sight, not so much in his use of the term, but in the consequences which flow from it, and in the conclusions we can reach about it. Often we have dealings with people who used to practice their religion, and who used to have some contact with us. Despite what we said above, there is more than a spark of Faith left in them, and this gives us some hope that they may be influenced by the parish.

❡ *How is that?*

First of all, since the great majority of our people come into contact with us at some time or other, there must be a way of using this contact. And since the parish is the intermediary by which they get into touch with priests, it follows that the parish must play a part in evangelizing them.

So, let us have the courage to admit that:

1. Since, as things are now, the only evident result of their relations with us is that it keeps their indifference alive, it follows that our methods have to be checked if not completely changed.
2. Here and now the fact of having had some contact with priests is something that people cannot erase from their lives memories, impressions, direction of ideas, and even certain habits kept through life—all these make up a web on which the parish can work. A slender web, often invisible—Abbé Godin saw that—but it is something still there, and it is the basis of our hopes for the parish apostolate.

Here, then, our first conclusion: we have to deal with a parish which is a mission parish in a mission land.

❡ *Is that so in the section you have to evangelize?*

If we tell you that it is situated on the outskirts of the Department of the Seine and that almost all its inhabitants are workers, that should answer you. That should tell you that almost everyone here is a pagan.

In this population, there are individuals who keep up the religious practices they learned in the provinces; but these are the older women, a few men, and any children whom we may have gathered into some parish society. So it is new parish territory for us, though not as unworked as are many sections of our Parisian suburbs.

Here are a few figures. There are about 22 or 23 thousand inhabitants, and, five years ago, we used to see one thousand at Sunday Mass. Every year since, we have seen an increase of approximately 10 percent; so, in 1945, when the evacuees come back, we can expect to have from 1400 to 1500 persons in the church for all the Sunday Masses. During our district missions, in one district, we found only 40 families out of 800–1000, in which we priests knew even one member as practicing. In another district, out of the same number of families that we visited, 117 were represented at the mission on the first night; and of these 117, 82 families were completely unknown to us and had not even one practicing member. All of this means that the percentage of practicing Catholics among us is about 5 percent. You can see that we agree with Abbé Godin, whom some consider too pessimistic.

The only reason we hesitate to give examples of the pagan spirit is that their frequency and number make them common= place. Any parish priest has a stock of them; any of our visitors can cite some to you, because, being visitors and less hardened than we, they notice the paganism more. An example of this was given by the small boy who came to the priest for First Communion classes. When the priest asked for his father's name, so as to put it down in the register, the youngster inno= cently replied: "None, right now, but we're looking around for one." The same outlook is shown by many mothers who, when speaking about their children to us, never mention the child's character or disposition, but always find the height of praise in such remarks as: "How sweet he is," or, "How cute," or, "What sturdy legs he has." It was such a mother as this whom we were trying to console when she lost her child; we did our best to speak about the happiness of the innocent soul in heaven, but the mother kept moaning out her grief in terms like these: "He was so chubby," and, "What a beautiful child he was."

When people come to make arrangements about Baptism, First Communion, or Marriage, they often make remarks that show up their point of view, as if these meant nothing. "Oh, if you only didn't have to have Baptisms before breakfast!" "You know how it is. If his catechism marks are going to look bad on his report card, I'd just as soon not have him make his First Communion." "If you won't marry my boyfriend and me with= out making us wait for eight days, then we won't be married in Church." "I want to be married by a priest, but if it has to be in the sacristy, it's simply not worth the trouble."

Throughout this book we shall have occasion to cite other examples which will show the condition of the religious and moral values of our poor people. But let us repeat now, so as to make ourselves clear: there is no difference between real pagans (those who have had no contact with religion), and those semi=apostates who have been re=paganized, and who are totally different from true Christians.

❧ *Do you think that these pagans can be drawn by Christianity?*

The answer to this question is a difficult one. There is little religious sentiment in these people, and so there is a lack of adequate response to real Christianity. And yet they are not totally indifferent to religious problems, because things like the existence of a hereafter, the explanation of suffering, the person of Christ, etc., catch their attention and interest, once such things are presented to them.

❧ *Does that mean that they can easily be attracted towards the Church?*

Not at all. They will willingly let themselves be drawn by the mystical side of Christianity, but they are decidedly rebel= lious when it is a matter of practices. The positive law of the Church leaves them indifferent, even hostile. If you will forgive the use of a barbarism, we are of the opinion that they are easily "Christifiable" but not yet "Ecclesiasticable."

Two factors make the Christianization of the masses more difficult than conversions in the early ages or in savage lands. Bringing the Gospel to ancient Rome was possible partly because it was merely a question of a change. The pagans had a religion; the State had a religion; the gods were a topic of everyday conversation; and there was public, official worship.

In our days religion has vanished from the hearts of our peo‡ ple; they consider it as something outworn, dead. When we try to bring them back to a practice of it, it is as though we were recalling a thing of the past. Hence, the task is more difficult now than it was in the time of the Apostles. Besides, the pagans of Rome or the savages to which our foreign mis‡ sioners go, are people accustomed to obedience; they recognize authority and are submissive to superiors. Not so our modern Western pagan; he is a fierce advocate of equality. He does not want to obey. So, when it comes to embracing a religion and accepting two authorities—God who makes laws, and the Church which teaches in His name—there is difficulty. All of our militant Christians, and especially those of the "Mission de Paris" have spoken to us of the difficulty (which we too have experienced) of forming a spirit of obedience to authority.

How often, in the missions we were holding at the church, we felt complete agreement between Our audience and our‡ selves whilst we were talking about Christ, his social doctrine, or the moral worth of the Gospel. And yet it was always impos‡ sible, for the time being, to expect more than that. How often we have heard women, and even men, tell us that they pray at home or at work sometimes. With complete sincerity, they tell us that they are believers, that they would not dream of missing Mass on All Saints' Day or Palm Sunday; that they absolutely never eat meat on Good Friday, and so God must be pleased with them. Poor training? It certainly is. But the thing to notice is the distance between their mentality and ours; the lack of a sense of obedience enabling them to accept obligation; the resistance to "clerical domination;" and, above all, the lack of an understanding of our rites, our dogmas, our demands. There is no evident effect from our liturgy, preach‡ ing, or influence. And remember that we are speaking here of semi‡Christians, and not of the pagan majority.

Let us learn how to be patient, and how to approach this task in the right way. We always set up the standards of the Fifth Lateran Council, which determined that the norm of piety for Christians must be at least attendance at Sunday Mass and the reception of the Eucharist at Eastertide. But we must realize that that norm has not yet been attained. That standard was made for Christians who knew what Mass and Communion meant, who recognized the authority of the Church and the necessity of submitting to her laws; our people are more like those of apostolic times, when the pressing need was to show them Christ, to draw them to spontaneous gatherings, to convince and stir them, before organizing and directing them.

Our task, then, is to create an atmosphere, and this is principally a task for the parish as a whole. The parish should be full of mutual kindness and charity, devout and proud of the Christian name.

Not that that is all, because we do not mean that we have given up hope of one day attracting converts to the practice of religion. We do insist, however, that it is foolish to hope to attract them without a long preparation, without a change in their present mentality. It is false to measure their willingness to accept Christ by their unwillingness to come to Mass. Many priests make that very mistake, and consequently, we must take special pains to avoid it; it is nothing but "putting the cart before the horse" to invite to Mass people who have no Christian values. To judge the progress or failure of our efforts at evangelization by the number of people who appear at Mass is a very poor method of judging. That attendance is not only secondary (in ordine intentionis), but also second (in ordine executionis). We cannot "shanghai" these people; their participation must come from a true need of religion. Hence, our apostolate must aim, not at organizing those who already are practicing Catholics and who go to Mass and the Sacraments, but rather, to penetrate the different milieus with the spirit of Christianity, so that the need for a Christian life will drive them to Christ, who is communicated to us by the Church and the Sacraments.

Our contention that these souls are "Christifiable," but not "Ecclesiasticable," should not cause any apostle to become discouraged; it merely points out the proper approach.

*❦ Do you consider this transition from a pagan spirit to a Chris‑
tian one an individual or a collective phenomenon?*

A collective one, certainly. And for the reason that, as Abbé
Godin pointed out, and as we shall have occasion to observe
later, the majority of our people think only collectively. Only
a small percentage is capable of individual thought, and it is
these who discuss and reflect on social and religious questions.
The others, the great majority, are not aware of any personal
capabilities along such lines; they are submerged in the vague
"personality" of the group to which they belong. They think as
a unit and subscribe only to those ideas which the group holds,
whether that group is their Union, their fellow‑workers, their
political party, or their friends. Hence, it is impossible to draw
them to Christ as individuals. Either the whole group goes over
to him, or no one does. The conquest must be a collective one.
That does not mean a conquest of the entire working class
(which "class" is an entity, but not a reality), but of this group,
of this portion here and now.

We must bend and direct the mentality of this particular
group or district. If the clergy become well thought of, if parish
life and activity are brought into the light, if everyone hears
about the different feasts and ceremonies, if families really live
like Christians, if militant Christians bring to different services
people who had not even realized that such things went on, if,
in short, we use a team spirit and a network of Christian action,
then we are creating an atmosphere, and the parish is already
playing an important role. Maybe the pastor will not see any
increase at the processions, held on the first Sunday of every
month, but his people are nearer to Christ.

❦ What conclusions do you draw from all this?

It means that our efforts will proceed along two approaches.
For the small class of "thinkers," we will work on their com‑
pact family circles. For the others, the vast majority, we must
go out and win over the entire group among whom they work
and live.

❡ *Who is to make these efforts?*

Both the parish with its priests and active laity, and the "Mission de Paris," or its equivalent. We shall come back to the part the latter has to play.

❡ *So you think that the parish has a place in this conquest?*

Absolutely! A parish in a mission country must be a missionary-parish. It cannot confine itself to the spiritual needs of the Christian people. Naturally, part of its activity will be meant especially for them but only a part, and that is not the most important. Since 95 percent of our people do not come to us, we must direct 95 percent of our efforts to them. Not merely by sighs and vain wishes, but by real activity.

❡ *What do you mean when you say "the parish?"*

This is an important point. A parish may be considered as a conservative, or as a conquering force. According to whether we adopt one or the other meaning shall we be able to make our parish "missionary;" otherwise, we might as well give up the idea. This distinction seems to us to be essential to what will be said in this book, so we shall be insistent on it.

The first meaning: for some (and inasmuch as most of us do not react against routine, we usually fall into this category) the parish means the sum total of all those who come to church. "My parishioners," a priest will say. In this sum total we can distinguish several groups: first of all, the few really faithful ones who receive Communion every day or every Sunday, and who are the backbone of all parish activity; then, those who come to Mass every Sunday, and whom the priest knows at least slightly; next, the type which comes to church for the big feasts, if only to offer their pious mite of worship, because, as they will tell you, "they are on the Church's side;" lastly, the border-line group of those who are well-disposed, in a sense, to religion, who have their children baptized and instructed for First Communion, who come to the church to be married (usually), who call for a priest at their deathbeds, and who hold to church burial as to a family custom.

So according to this conception, the parish means all those who have some contact with the Church, with whom the priest has some connection—even if these relations show a great similarity to commercial ones of some special nature.

Parish life becomes the cultural life of souls such as these. Its basis is the calendar of feast-days and Sundays. Its manifestation is found in ceremonies, baptisms, marriages, processions, funerals, various meetings at the church or parish hall, triduums, retreats, and Lenten services.

The mainstays of such a parish are its societies which supply the various reservoirs on which we can depend when it is necessary to organize things for some big feast, or where we can go for help in forming special groups—such as youth activities, sodalities, men's groups, or ladies' clubs.

The clergy, pastor and curates, must divide their time between ministering to these souls according to their spiritual needs and taking care of temporal affairs. And this latter becomes more and more burdensome according to the number of the activities, and according to the prosperity and growth of the parish.

Hence, this concept means that parish and the parish milieu are identical.

In the rural areas, a parish is usually considered as being just what you have described. But in a city or suburban parish, making contact with immense numbers of pagans, "parish" surely must have another meaning.

Unfortunately, it does not. The illusion is ever easier and even more widespread in our suburban and city parishes than it is in less densely populated or rural areas. In the country a priest wittingly has to think of those who do not come to church, and to enter into contact with them. First of all, his small flock does not take up all his time; and with regard to the others, he meets them every day in the streets. He knows them and they know him. While the number of practicing Catholics in city parishes is not more than a tiny fraction of all

26

those who live within the parish, it still is a number sufficiently large to occupy all our time; and which is worse it prevents us from seeing the others who do not come near us.

In our suburban parishes, even more than in the rural areas, you will find the very essence of this parish spirit spoken of above. Parish life here, more than in any other place, is reduced to the ordinary life of the people. The smaller the proportion of faithful to the number of the indifferent, the more is this noticeable. In the country those who come to church usually represent good people of all classes. Here, since the pagan proletariat is a tremendous majority, the contrast between parish life is reduced to conform to the milieu, and the life which goes on in this particular district is more marked. A full church at Sunday Mass should not lull us into thinking that all is well; let us look at realities.

It is easy enough for the clergy to be kept busy with the faithful flock. The church will look full enough, and services and activities will be well attended. The priests will think that they are reaching the masses because of this large number, and they will think that they have here the real reactions of the people; in reality they are reaching only the "parish milieu." They will think that they are succeeding because their ministry is bringing them satisfaction. In reality, they have no contact at all with the masses.

Another factor clouds our perspective. We tend to judge the parish by the contacts we have in the church or sacristy, with those who come about their children, or to arrange a marriage. We are wrong. Those who come to see us especially if they are ordinary folk come with an attitude of inferiority, even servility. They talk like us; but they do not think like us. And the real hardened cases never come to see us. How often, in our visits around the parish, we have been conscious of that complex of servility in families who had a child in our catechism class. We could see it in their very welcome. We realized that we were to give the decision whether or not their child should be admitted to his First Communion; they were flattering us. They would not dream of contradicting us in whatever we might say.

Besides all this, another enormous difficulty in parishes like ours is knowing our parishioners and remembering their names, let alone trying to look for them in church. And hence it is an easy step to begin to misconstrue their attitude, to make no effort to understand their mentality, and even to forget about those whom we no longer see around the church. Evangeliza≠ tion here is a terrible problem. It hurts us to think about those whom we must reach; forgetting about them is easier.

❧ *What about the other meaning of a "parish?"*
The other concept consists in this. Having studied a map of the parish, or better still after having made a walking tour of the whole place, we say to ourselves: Our parish is this entire territory; all those living inside this section are committed to our care, without any exception made because of nationality or immorality or hostility to the clergy. Nothing can free us from the obligation of caring for their souls. Hence, all those who do not come to us, and whom we will never get to know unless we go to them; all those we meet including Algerians and Chinese they are all our parishioners. We have to say to ourselves, "We, their priests, have the care of these souls."
Our parish life should inform the life of all these people; the spiritual life of those who have any (and how can we tell if a spark is not still there, even in those who seem most dis≠ tant?); their workaday life; their life at home, at rest. That life is made up of the very air that they breathe, the things that occupy them, the joys and sorrows they have known, the influences which play upon them, the influence of the doctor who tends them, of the paper that interprets the world for them, of the leaders who direct them, of the public house at the street corner, of the theatre which sees them more often than the church does.
Our parish . . . we see it at noon, when the factory lets out its workers; at mid≠afternoon, when the children get out of school; in the morning, when buyers line up outside the shops; in the evening when the suburban trains roll in with wave after

wave of our people; at night, with the young fellows and girls on the corners.

This is our parish, and we must recognize that fact, for souls are at stake.

¶ *Does not every priest feel the same way?*

In theory, they do. In practice how many act according to the logic which such a theory demands?

We have not reached the point of reversing the numbers given by our Lord in the famous parable; that is, we do not say that ninety-nine sheep have left the fold, and one faithful one remains. And yet, we remember a saying of one of our professors in the seminary: "We do not go after the lost sheep any more. We let them run off to the hills, these ninety-nine lost ones, while we argue about who is going to be allowed to fondle the one that is left."

This comes about because we confuse in practice the Kingdom of God with our own kingdom—the advance of God's reign with our own influence over a flock. What does it matter if it is small, as long as we have it well in hand?

¶ *Still, is it not Utopian to be forever thinking about those who do not come near us, and forgetting those upon whom we can count? Is not the old proverb true which tells us first to conserve what we have, before we try to conquer anything new?*

No! Open the Gospel. Whether we want it so or not, however hard or impractical it might appear, we are only obeying Christ when we busy ourselves more about those afar off; and, if we let ourselves forget these separated ones while we tend the faithful little flock, there is nothing evangelical about us. Maybe the Gospel is not practical; maybe it is a little idealistic sometimes. I remember a parish priest saying to me one day: "My dear friend, we can hardly expect to apply the Gospel nowadays." And yet, was it not by purely evangelical methods that Saint Paul and the other apostles transformed the world? Might it not be by our too reasonable methods that we are running the risk of letting this world perish? Anyhow, it is not so certain that we do have to abandon the faithful in order to run after the lost sheep. It may well be a matter of getting our faithful to be with us and like us in the pursuit of the others. We shall come back to this point too.

What is certain, and what we really want to emphasize, is that the way we think of a parish is of paramount importance in deciding its part in the missionary movement.

If the parish is no more than a central rallying point for Christians, a place where the faithful gather for services and meetings and activities, then, whether this attitude is based on theory or a mere acceptance of things as they are, we have to admit that the parish is not capable of attracting the 98 percent, of the working class which does not know Christ. We will have to leave it to specialized missionaries to take up work among them.

But if, on the contrary, we strip off routine and turn boldly to new forms of the apostolate, the parish becomes a living cell, destined to propagate itself over an entire district. Then we can see that it has its role to play in this missionary endeavour.

❨ *Do you think that the parish can play this part?*

Without a doubt. Firstly, because it is already existing. Whether it plays its role or not, hic et nunc, the parish is a fact. It is, by right, if not in reality, that tiny cell of Christianity, of the Incarnation, about which we are talking. Whatever be its future, the parish is, right now, the one concrete element of the task of evangelization.

If we look at a whole territory like France, or even just Paris and the suburbs, we have to admit that the network of parishes is admirably suited to the task ahead of us. Every community has its own. Not even the civil government is as well organized, for many a district has several parishes. One of our pet ideas is that there are not enough parishes, that we must multiply them; and the building of new churches has shown clearly that parish organization is not only a fine framework, but also a supple one, which can be enlarged indefinitely.

So it is something that the parish *is* and that there is no question about its existence, or right to existence. It is no small thing to know that something is, when others have to figure out what is going to be. It is no small gain that the parish is recognized, solidly rooted, instead of being a novelty which could be attacked.

And that is not all, for a parish is equipped. It has its priests, and parish clergy have always been the mainstay of the Church's force. They are the ones who always have borne the brunt of the burden, wherever the bishop might send them; they represent the Church in the eyes of the people. They live in the midst of those whom they are evangelizing. They are, or can be, or should be, in permanent contact with their people. They are the ones whom everyone sees in the streets, whom everyone greets, knowing very well that they alone have the authority to carry out the chief functions of common Christian life.

And if, besides considering the number of these priests, we realize the actual set-up in each parish, we shall see what power and influence these parish priests and curates—all occupied by the same sort of problem, and all striving in different places for the one great goal of the apostolate—could wield. Unfor-tunately, we say "could" and not "do."

A scene from the J. O. C. Congress of 1937 comes to mind here. Seeing the crowds of youths surrounding their chaplains, the secretary of the Socialist Youth Club leaned towards Abbé Godin and said: "You certainly have the chaplains. If we had as many men who would dedicate themselves to making militants of the rest of us, you would see us get somewhere."

And parish priests are even more numerous than are these J. O. C. chaplains. Add to them the number of nuns who work in parishes (more than 5000 in the Archdiocese of Paris!); add to this the number of lay persons who are entirely occupied with different parish activities. Then the question is not, "What can the parish do?" but, "Why hasn't it done more?"

And this is not all. Every parish has militants in all sorts of movements—marvellous Christians, whose influence is enormous. And it has all the faithful, who live in the midst of the ordinary people and whose lives could be and should be lived round the parish life.

Materially speaking, every parish has its church, and that is no small advantage. Here is a reality which even the most uninterested can hardly ignore. It may well be that many a person has never set foot inside the church, but it is more probable that most have, at one time or another. In any case, it is there, for all to see, as a witness and symbol of something which they are ignoring, or, worse still, misunderstanding. For all, even confusedly, it means something.

A parish has some sort of a hall or meeting-place, too, and God knows how much energy has been expended these last fifty years to build them up. Maybe they are never filled; maybe they are, in the minds of many, places to stay away from. At least they are a means of gathering some people, and perhaps they could be made to appear different from the rest.

A parish has revenues, no matter how small or how large, how steady or how sporadic.

It has means of expression—magazines, bulletins, announcements, and the pulpit is always available.

Above all, it has official recognition as the instrument of missionary work in a particular sector. It is a continuation of the Christian communities which the Acts of the Apostles tells us were established everywhere that the apostles went; and it is to this community that new converts in the area are joined. Hence, if a parish abandons, theoretically or practically, the task of announcing Christ to the mass of men in its territory, it is failing in its mission, it is betraying the mandate it received. Let specialists come in, if they are needed; that is normal enough; but to leave the infidels to these specialists and concern oneself only with the faithful—that is thwarting the will of Christ. And if these special helpers are not being used, the obligation of aiming at these infidels rests even more heavily on the parish.

To sum it all up: the parish is like a mother-cell, the source of all apostolic work. In the future—supposing the task of conquest is over and won—it is to the parish that all the new cells must be joined in a common life. Let us imagine, for a moment, a splendid catechumenate (and we have much to say on this point, too): keep it as distinct as you wish from the body of the faithful, and yet it will still be necessary, once the catechumens are ready, that they should join up with the faith= ful. Strictly, they probably can find the necessities of spiritual nourishment outside the parish but for official acts like baptisms, weddings, funerals, where will they come but to the parish?

From this flows the duty and urgent need that the parish be ready to welcome new converts. We shall come back to this.

A parish must be ready to accept any aids which may come to it; there should be a place offered to any person who comes forward to assist in the work, no matter where they come from.

However generous or forceful or ingenious may be special= ized methods, it will always be the parish which represents the main strength of the attack, like the infantry of an army. Like the infantry, it will be beaten if it fails to use new armaments and tactics, but it remains the indispensable means of winning and holding any point of attack.

PARISH MILIEU OR COMMUNITY MILIEU?

Do you think that the Parish can play the part you have indicated?

Yes, but only if it undergoes a bold transformation.

In what sense do you consider this transformation necessary?

The chapters to come will give the details, but for now we would say this. First: everyone must take an active part in the work, because none of the proposed reforms, taken by them= selves, can succeed; it is teamwork which will bring victory to the parish. Secondly: the whole point can best be expressed by the formula that "the parish must cease to be a mere parish milieu; it must become again a community."

What prevents a parish from being a missionary power?

The fact that it is now reduced to the parish environment, which envelops and stifles it; it gives the illusion of vitality, but it is false, or at least, circumscribed, vitality. What will make the parish a missionary force again? Only the fact of its becoming a community again.

¶ *What do you mean by all that?*

Read the Acts of the Apostles; it describes a crisis in the new-born Church which is amazingly similar to that of our own times.

What do we read there? As the Lord had commanded, the Gospel had been preached to the Jews first; the first of the "brethren" were from the synagogue, and naturally, they kept to their customs, their attachment for the Law of Moses, the distinction of clean and unclean foods, legal purifications, cir-cumcision, etc. They made a synthesis of their normal way of living and their new-found faith in Jesus Christ. But soon the pagans were attracted by the preaching of Christianity and entered into the new communities. Saint Peter baptized the cen-turion, Cornelius, at Caesarea; the Hellenistic Jews at Cyprus made conquests among the pagans of Antioch. Then Saint Paul arrived to spread the movement, from Antioch into the whole of Asia Minor, Greece, etc. Immediately there arose the difficulty of how and under what conditions to receive these new Gentile converts. The diehards among the Jewish Christians, not being able to dream of any salvation without some connection with the Chosen People, wanted to impose the Mosaic observances on all. A more moderate group was willing to omit this condition, but insisted that they themselves should keep the observances. Even Saint Peter, at Antioch, got up from the table of Gentile converts, to eat with the converts from Judaism, so as not to offend the diehard group. It was Saint Paul who corrected him, and so forcefully proclaimed the "liberty of the children of God." If the Law of Moses is going to be foisted on converts from paganism, we might as well abandon preaching the Gospel. Faith in Christ is enough; the Christian way of life is enough. If, furthermore, the distinction about foods is going to be kept up, the destruction of Christian unity will result. Saint Paul won

34

the day, and at the Council of Jerusalem, it was decided not to burden the Gentiles with a load they could not carry. As Msgr. Batiffol put it, "The world would never have become Jewish." For quite a while, the converts from Judaism were to keep their customs, but soon, being a minority, they were absorbed into the majority of pagans who were being converted. Then there arose communities that were simply Christian, in which all elements were fused. The world was to become Christian.

❰ *Why did you bring up that crisis?*

Because it is the prototype of all the other crises which the Church has ever experienced and especially of the one we are now going through. We, who live in the midst of the common people, can transpose Msgr. Batiffol's words into "the world will never become parochial" at least not in that sense of "par- ish," which we have just been developing. There would be an incompatibility, an incongruity in it. Either the parish would remain enclosed in what we have called the "parish milieu," while the rest of the world stays outside; or else the parish is to blossom out into a true "community." Then there will be another crisis, caused by the difficulties, protests, and tugging of dead weight and routine. However, if Saint Paul carries the day again, the people will become Christian.

❰ *What do you include in this "community" you talk about?*

Remember those first Christian communities! What were they? Merely groups in which charity and simplicity reigned. Tent-makers dwelt along with doctors; servants with ladies of high society. As Saint Paul put it, there was "no longer Greek or Jew, slave or free," for, while each lived according to his own station, they were "all one in Christ Jesus." Everybody used to say "Brother," and they really meant it, for they had "but one heart and one mind." They used to come together for fraternal meals and the "breaking of the Bread." By the sheer strength of their faith and constancy under persecution, but most of all by the love they had for each other, they were real witnesses of Christ whom they professed. They were not recognized by the "culture" in which they lived, but by the love with which they loved one another, in the love of the same God. Since they were all recent converts, they were dynamic and convert=minded. These Athenian philosophers, these old leaders of the synagogue, these people from the lowlands of Corinth or Ephesus—they all were formed into a completely new sort of unity. As Father Lebreton wrote:

> The Church took to itself all these recruits. Once baptized, they all were but one Body, the Body of Christ, no matter what were their origins. This is what gave the Christian community its deep unity, its essentially religious character. Birth did not give it, nor education, nor the free choice of human attractions; it came through faith, by which the neophyte, being joined to Christ, took unto Himself all Christians, His members.

By this faith and charity they were like a leaven in the old pagan world. An unknown apologist of the third century could say, "As the soul is to the body, so Christians are to the world." So effective was this leaven that, in three centuries, these Chris= tian communities had invaded and overthrown all the levels of society in all the Roman Empire.

❦ *Are our parishes no longer communities like these?*
  You have but to observe our parishes for a while, especially one in a pagan environment.
  Come into a church on any Sunday morning for the parish High Mass. What do you see? Children, a few nuns, a few women and old men, and a group of choir girls. How many adults between the ages of twenty and fifty? How many men? How many of those who are at the prime of life, and who are really "alive?" At earlier Masses, who are these pious ladies you see at Communion? What standing do they have in their neighborhood, in their family, at their work? What enthusiasm do they have? What influence? What natural qualities? How about the late Masses, around noon, and the people we see there? At these, the situation is reversed; there are plenty of

men and women who are in the prime of life but what sort of Christianity do they profess? What interest do they have in the Gospel? What do they represent to the common folk; they are individuals of another class and type, who happen to live amongst the masses of this quarter?

We must not exaggerate. We do know of parishes where young people and entire families are really alive to the natural and supernatural values in life, and they put their Christian vitality into action. But such are extremely few. More often the parish means nothing, and they think of it along lines which we have already mentioned. Other communal groups have given them vitality, but they do not find in the parish that spirit of early Christianity in which they can expand. If (and we do not mean to be unjust, for we realize the spirit of the times) the parish does mean something, and if the efforts of the clergy have been directed to this goal, that same clergy will be the first to lament over what we are lamenting, and the first to rejoice where we rejoice. After all we ourselves are parish priests, and we know that many a priest thinks just as we do. As a matter of fact, this realization led us to publish this book.

Whoever has preached a special sermon for Christian mothers knows the discouragement which comes over us, as we look out at the great number of grandmothers who willingly come to hear us; but we look in vain for the women who might find some profit in the words so carefully prepared for them. And the Christian fathers! Where are they? We see these men, or at least a minority of them, during the three sermons of the Easter retreat, and approximately the same number of them at the back of the church for Mass on Easter Sunday—but when will we see them again? How can we capture them? What are we going to do about them? How many do we never see, retreat or no retreat!

The parish milieu! The Children of Mary, in their veils and blue ribbons, the catechism children, the ladies of the League, a few of the "good" young people, a few of the men of one sodality or another! In middle-class parishes the fairly large number of fine families which do turn out hides the absence of the great majority which does not come. In the "working class" parishes, there is no such deception; we see the absence.

❰ *Faithful followers of Christ are always a minority. These numer≠ ical comparisons are no true indication.*

Granted! Especially on certain feast days, and we are happy in the numbers. Even if we grant, for now, that it is all right to be happy about this, let us go further, and ask a few ques≠ tions. What is the worth, as Christians, of this crowd that we see in church? Do they love one another? Are they a unified element of the community? Do they even know one another? Once out of the church, what ideas will they exchange, what influence on one another will they have? Do they have the idea of belonging to one and the same living Body, of being mem≠ bers of one another? Has the ceremony they have just come away from united their minds and hearts in the one, identical hope and thought? Do they go out with the burning desire of making Christ fill their lives and of seeing him reign in their environment? Did they come to fulfill an obligation for their own salvation, or did they come to strengthen and feed a life which they want to spread? What kind of an example are they going to be to the great mass of indifferent souls among whom they live? Will they be a family recognized for its charity, loy≠ alty, faith in Christ, confidence, joy, courage under hardships? Or will they be pretty much like everyone else around them, except for a weekly habit peculiar to them? When others look at this band of the faithful, will they have a mind to become Christian? Is it not more often just the opposite, "If that is being a Christian! No thanks. Not for me!"

Let us go a little farther. Take the hypothesis of a conversion. I do not mean the conversion of some intellectual who has come to accept Christianity; he would be accepted with open arms. What I mean is the conversion of some militant Communist, who had been a zealous anticlerical or the conversion of some streetwalker who had been a public scandal. How would they

38

be welcomed? Oh, we accept Mary Magdalene, because she is in the Gospel, but I should like to see her walk into one of our meetings! We read about the reluctance with which the Christian Jews of Jerusalem received Saul the persecutor, when he appeared before them as a neophyte, and we find their attitude astonishing; I should like to see him drop into one of our men's groups! And if this Saul were to multiply himself by ten and invade this parish mentality, causing havoc by his strange attitude—what a disaster! "Things are not what they used to be in the parish." Is it not true that the attitude of Catholics to a convert is, almost instinctively, the attitude of the elder brother to the prodigal son, who has finally come home?

¶ *It seems to me that you are forgetting the Jocists.*[1]
No, we are not. The question—is how have they been welcomed in certain parishes? Were they supported? Are they recognized as a model of what Catholics ought to be: concerned about life, about the atmosphere around them, about their relation to Christ? Or is it not more true to say that they are considered as an unusual type, as people to be tolerated because of their evident goodwill and sincerity, but hardly in step with the parish.

¶ *But why do Catholics, taken as a whole, lack this Christian vitality?*
Unfortunately, it is our fault! We are not overlooking the tremendous influence exerted by the materialism and sensuality which have spread through all our institutions, all our lives; but we are responsible for the weak fight that our faithful make against these influences. Have we not reduced our parishioners to the status of being mere listeners to the sermons, even in organizations where *they* are supposed to do the talking? Are they not obliged to bear with our proposals, advice, commands,

---

1   *Jeunesse ouvrière chrétienne* (Young Christian Workers) founded in 1924 in Belgium by Fr. Joseph Cardijn [made a Cardinal in 1965] and receiving papal approbation by Pope Pius XI in 1925.

without a chance of showing their own ideas? Do we not act more like superiors than guides? We complain about their pas‍sivity, but where in the world could they get any ideas of activ‍ity? Even those who are very active and successful in their own fields and on a purely natural plane have become, because of us, people who, when they are around the church, merely receive, preserve, and sometimes defend, the teachings of Christ. They do not give anything; they are passive beings. The parish has become the business of the clergy; it is of no concern to the faithful. They are asked to give money often enough, but never given a say in the use which is made of the money. What is worse, they are kept barred from the apostolate. Yes, we tell them — since Pius XI said so they have a duty of undertaking Catholic Action, that they must be apostles. But what means do we give them to this end? What initiative do we encourage in them? What part of the work is deliberately and systemati‍cally given to them? Sometimes youth movements do blossom out, but our timidity in allowing them to do so is something to see. We are a hindrance where we should be a help. Besides all this, think of the many who are not engaged or interested in any of these movements; what are we doing for them?

❮ *You are summing up the reflections made by the youth of the Church.*

That is correct. Maybe you also read the article, "Has Chris‍tianity softened mankind."

Evidently the answer is "No," if it is a question of the Chris‍tianity of Christ, but, alas! What distinctions will we have to make, if it is a question of the kind of Christianity which we all too often present, who can deny that there is some truth in quotations like the following, taken at random from the above article: "We might compare the Church to an over‍anxious mother, who, lest her children fall into some gully, keeps them at home, in a state of childishness or pseudo‍innocence, which prevents them from becoming adults." "It is all too evident that a certain kind of religious education has produced, especially

among the so-called "upper classes," a weak sort of man, scru-
pulous and even timorous, scared by his own shadow, too thoroughly tied to the apron strings of the Church." "It seems that,
generally speaking, everything connected with Catholicism has
to shake off that heavy, enervating atmosphere which has succeeded in watering down its great truths, weakening their sense,
hiding their deep and health-giving reality. Thanks be to God,
Catholicism is not always expressed by Sulpician imagery, of
which the least we can say is that it shows neither strength nor
character, but rather a tendency towards an inoffensive neutral-
ity. We must not let Saint Thérèse become a sweet and timid
young thing; we must stop misusing phrases like "a good little
child," or "a fine young man." Spiritual directors are not firm
enough, and do not know how to get rid of the old ladies and
old spinsters who clutter up the sacristies, and cause priests
to lose so much precious time."

Why continue quotes like these? Everyone who thinks a
bit and is honest must agree with them. Even though splendid
exceptions can be shown (and the ones we know give us hope),
it still does not detract from the value of the whole argument.
The parish atmosphere is not that of a community; it has none
of the dynamism of early Christianity; it has no power to cut
into the pagan world in the midst of which it vegetates. Some
individuals have left their natural environment and have come
into this artificial one—this colorless and lifeless thing we call
the "parish milieu;" they have been given a sort of "ecclesiastical tinge," which amounts to their becoming bourgeois. But,
if they were already bourgeois of a "high class," they will not
feel at ease with this tinge, for they fancy themselves somewhat superior culturally. If they were of the working class, they
do not feel at ease either, but realize that they are on foreign
ground both here and in their former milieu. What do they
find here? The type of person who is engrossed in "pious
works," devout and willing enough, but absolutely useless for
the apostolic conquest or for the infiltration into the masses of
the pagan proletariat which is our chief concern.

¶ *Well? How can the parish become a community again; how can it become the early Christian type which is necessary for the missionary labor it must do?*

That is the problem, and it is tremendous. We do not pretend to have found the solution; we realize its urgency, and we know that thousands of priests and lay people are asking themselves the same questions that we are. In the following chapters, we will attempt a modest presentation of the ideas which came to us; but we repeat, and will continue to repeat: it will be useless for anyone to attempt any of the reforms which we propose, if he goes at them as though they were text-book lessons or exercises. There are plenty of suggestions which can be made; we only hope that this book will stimulate some. May these other suggestions, joined to ours, provide a practical course of action which will enable the parish to work as a unit, come right out of its shell, and become again a conquering community. ✠

✠[2]✠
A Living, Apostolic Liturgy

❡ *Anyone who assists at services in your church can see that you go to considerable effort to get the people to share in the liturgy. Do you think that the prayers of the people have any great importance from a missionary viewpoint?*

These are tremendously important. The Christian life to which we are trying to attract souls is not, we realize, merely a way to pray; but since it is the life of Christ, and since Christ lived to give praise to the Father, we can say that the Christian way of life is principally a worship of God. Our goal is "to make our brothers Christian," but it is obvious that they will not suddenly start coming to Mass or to devotions; they will come only by degrees, impelled by the growing conviction that Christianity is a complete way of life. It is only at the last stage that we shall have to worry about assimilating them into the praying, sacrificing Church.

But in the meantime, it is essential that we give these pro-spective converts the kind of Christian worship that will con-tinue to attract them, that will keep them coming, once the first breach is made in their paganism. Also, we must use it to teach them, and draw them gradually along to a full realization of the Christian mysteries.

As a matter of fact, almost the same could be said for the Christians themselves, especially the young ones. If we want to keep them in the Church, we must let them share her life and not be mere spectators. If we want them to become dynamic apostles, our ceremonies must help them to become conscious of the meaning of Christianity.

❡ *That is not usually the case.*

Unfortunately, it is not. It takes no prolonged survey of our parishes to see that the way in which our ceremonies are usually conducted is far from edifying. More often than not they are boring, empty, meaningless. An unbeliever who went into a Catholic church to see for himself what Catholic services were like would almost certainly come out yawning.

❡ *Nevertheless, strenuous efforts are being made to vivify the Liturgy.*

Indeed there are, and we are grateful for them. Certainly we do not think that this book is a pioneer, nor that we are the first ones to set down or to try new ideas. Rather we realize our position as a part of a growing stream, in which we are carried along more by the efforts of contemporary apostles in every line than by our own. The liturgical movement is growing, but it is still too weak, too little understood. Our contribution will try to make it less so.

❡ *What are the major weak spots in our Liturgy, such as it is?*

The description of a Sunday*morning Mass is the most dev* astating answer we can think of. Let us take a look at a typical scene.

The Low Mass is going on. A few men are standing up at the back of the church and gazing around. Further up, the church is pretty well filled, with women mostly; some are saying their beads, to the accompaniment of clicking and of audible "Hail Marys." Some are reading prayer books or missals. Some are seated while the rest kneel; for no apparent reasons, there are periodic reverses of position. Only during the reading of the Gospel is the whole church in the same position. At the altar, the priest moves back and forth, reciting words that no one beyond the front pews can hear; he turns round from time to time for a *Dominus vobiscum*, to which only the altar boy answers. Obvi* ously he is isolated, cut off from the people behind him. Obvi* ously the people in that Church are not a community, but a mere collection of individuals, praying individually as best they can.

At one point contact between priest and people does seem to be made. A priest mounts the pulpit and makes the parish announcements (often poorly read), and talks on various subjects (often on money). Then comes the sermon (of which we have much to say later on), and it seems to be made up of a collection of cliches that are completely foreign to the ordinary, daily prob= lems of this people; anyhow, they have heard them all before.

After the sermon, the Sacrifice begins again, and the col= lection begins too. Everyone starts looking in their pockets or pocketbooks for their offering, and the ushers give change as they go along. Then, those who are trying to follow the Mass settle back and try to find out where the priest is now. At the Elevation, a hush comes over the church. Some of the people bow down; others look up at the Host and the Chalice. Immediately afterwards the collection continues, beads start to rattle again, mingled with the sound of turning pages, and so to the Communion.

At the Agnus Dei, those who want to receive start towards the altar=rail, and, pretty soon, the aisles are choked with men and women coming and going to and from the rail. Everyone gets back into place, despite the usual lack of cooperation from others in the same pew, and settles back in thanksgiving.

Ite Missa est, and some are already on their way out to join those who left after the Communion; the better ones wait till the Last Gospel is read. Well, that's over!

We have just assisted at the most solemn act of the Christian community at prayer, the offering of Christ to the Trinity by His Mystical Body, the Church.

At the High Mass, it is a little different. The priest at the altar is more prominent because he is chanting. But the church is only a quarter filled. Present are those who "must" be there—school children, duly watched over by the nuns, and bored by the whole proceedings; they have to keep quiet, and all in all find the service far from appealing. The nuns are there, partly to watch over the children, and partly to "give a good example." The choir is there. Scattered here and there through the church are a few adults. That is the cross=view we get of the parish at the official parish Mass.

The people who are present do not sing at High Mass; they listen. For the most part, they do not understand either the Latin or the meaning of their missal translations; because to understand, they would have to have had explanations and training, and no one has given them that. So they are bored too; bored willingly and without resentment, but still bored.

A proof of this is found in the way our people avoid the High Mass; nobody wants to come to it. Who can blame them? It is difficult for anyone to see in this uncomprehended expression of worship the solemn and official prayer which the Church is rendering to God. It is not the community at prayer. In fact it is even less so than the earlier Low Mass we observed, since few, if any, go to Communion at this one.

Look at the last Mass on Sunday. Liturgical chant has given way to hymns by a soloist or by a choir, or even to musical renderings of a violin or violoncello. The working families have given way to the more prosperous members of the parish, because working people in their less stylish dress would feel out of place in this crowd.

❡ *At least they come, and that is something.*

What good is it, if we do not get them to pray? Surely we cannot be so blind as to think that the mere material perfor= mance of the obligation of Sunday Mass is pleasing to God! Surely we cannot be so legalistic as to think that this is all that the Church wants!

❡ *What have you to say about services other than Mass?*

Some parishes still keep up the practice of Sunday Vespers, mostly for the principle of the thing; almost no one comes to it. We have processions, too, straggling things that have no other purpose than to let the parish priest feel comforted in seeing his "parish" around him, and as Father Ramillieux said, "to give illusory satisfaction to the Heart of Jesus." At these things too, our deadly and ever=present enemy boredom is present. No one knows quite why he is walking around the church.

46

Then there are the months of Saint Joseph, of our Lady, of the Sacred Heart, in which the clergy can preside over tiny gatherings of the same faithful souls and at which they can continue giving Benediction of the Blessed Sacrament. No one seems to be any better off for them; at least they do not show any more Christian vitality or apostolicity. Meanwhile, the "others" are still staying away, because these affairs have no connection with their daily lives.

Is it not strange and sad that we satisfy ourselves with all this, when we could organize ceremonies which would be understood, which would be pointed to the lives of non-Christians, and which would help win them to Christ? Strange and sad, too, is the fact that we seem incapable of opening or closing any service with anything but an "Our Father" or a "Hail Mary," which everyone repeats automatically, thoughtlessly. It certainly seems that there is no realization of a community at prayer. Even in the morning or evening prayers that some parishes and schools keep up the words are hurried, the formulas are not understood.

❦ *How do you explain all these difficulties in the celebration of Christian worship?*

The explanation is simple enough; we have let ourselves fall into a lazy spirit of "conforming." We misapply the words of Saint Paul, who told us to guard the deposit of Faith, and we hold on for dear life to traditions. Over and over again we repeat things "the way they are done in this parish," and make no effort to adapt them to the needs of those who are our parishioners, whom we are neglecting. It seems to be a cherished illusion of us priests that the faithful who are present at services are getting some good from what we give them; in reality, they are politely bored. They shift for themselves, and manage to pray as individuals and in their individual ways. The attendance at ceremonies other than Mass frightens us sometimes, and we make appeals, trying to get more to come, "to give a good example." Or we try the other approach, and thank those who were good enough to come. The truth is, and we know it, that they will not come in any increasing numbers until we change our methods.

¶ *Your criticisms are valid, and most priests will admit that. The question is, what changes can you suggest? How do you manage things in your own parish?*

The answer to those questions involves so many factors that we must beg for time to explain. Everything that is done at Colombes flows from these two basic principles. First, that the parish is a community, and its prayer must be communal; second, that our parishioners belong to the working classes, and so our collective prayer must be adapted to their lives. Going one step further, we distinguish two fields of action. The liturgy as it exists now is the prayer of the faithful, and it must be celebrated with the "Old Christians" in mind, even though we try to think also of the new converts present, and also of the pagans who may, occasionally, be present. On the other hand, there are "para-liturgical" ceremonies, usually at night, which are pointed directly at those outside the fold, even though Christians, too, may benefit from them.

Permit us to explain the two basic principles we gave above. Our liturgy must be communal if it is to be living, apostolic. At first glance, that phrase may seem trite, but yet it is the key to the revolution of the parish. We priests must convince ourselves first of all, and then convince the faithful, that the parish is a unit, a pocket-size edition of the ONE Church. This parish has its prayer and worship to render to God, not as individuals but as a collective and social unit. Church services are meant to be group prayers. Mass in the parish church is the Sacrifice of Christ being offered by this part of His Mystical Body for the whole Body, and there is no place for personal peculiarities of prayer in this act. All this must be meditated upon, explained, repeated, because it is the very cornerstone of our program; until this is grasped, there can be no further building. No leniency can be allowed for any opposition which would endanger the communal character of parochial prayer; that includes personal, direct opposition by any of the parishioners, and it also includes the type of parishioner who likes to frequent chapels or parish churches other than his or her own. Coupled with that, we must do our best to organize our own ceremonies in the best possible manner. That will be easier in working-class parishes than in ones where wealthier people predominate, because workers are less individualistic and, generally, more co-operative.

The second principle is that the liturgy must be adapted. That does not mean discarding canon law, or doing anything contrary to express rubrics; the Church can decide about changes which involve either of the above cases. We limit ourselves to what is here and now permissible, and will give some examples of what we mean later on; for the time being, we will explain some of our general principles. As long as Low Masses are celebrated as they are now, our task is to see that the people participate to the utmost, and in a way suited to their mentality; what the priest is doing must become intelligible, and its relation to their lives must become apparent. Instead of this, we see all around us the spectacle of souls left to personal piety, to Rosaries, or to hymns that have little or no connection with the supreme Sacrifice going on before them. The ones who worry about the laxity of ecclesiastical authorities in allowing adaptations aimed at making the liturgy more understandable should rather marvel that the same authorities have done so little to prevent a tragedy such as the above. It seems to us that these "terrible" adaptations are preferable, by far. In making them we must see that they permeate everything connected with the Church hymns, prayers, translations. We must see that they mean something to the people for whom they are intended. We must not make them for our own satisfaction, nor to show our powers of expression, nor to show a mirror of our lives. They are the people's, and they are meant to revivify them.

❮ *How do you go about applying all this?*
The Low Masses celebrated at Colombes are a good example of what we mean; the parish Mass—a High Mass—can be

treated later. First of all, a word of warning; we make the Low Masses as high as possible. This means that, in accordance with the rubrics, we say everything allowable in a tone which can be heard by everyone. The faithful have a right to hear the Mass, and we have the obligation of ridding ourselves of the habit of mumbling in such a way that the server can hardly hear us. More than that, we have the obligation of letting the people see Mass, and of grasping the purpose behind our movements. A young priest remarked once that it was only when he was actually learning how to say Mass himself that he discovered that there were Signs of the Cross made over the chalice at different times; he had served Mass often enough, but he had never realized that the sweeping movements he saw priests making were Signs of the Cross! A good many of the faithful can say the same thing. Our people have learned to answer the prayers of the priest together, to say the Gloria, Credo, Sanctus, Agnus Dei. They have learned to stand together for the Gloria, Credo, Preface, and Pater Noster; to sit together for the Epistle and after the Credo; to kneel together from the Sanctus to the Agnus Dei. Before Mass begins we always give an understandable summary of the *Ordo* for the day. A dream which we have not been able to realize yet is to have the Epistle and Gospel, at least, read in the vernacular. Some day that will come, using laymen trained for this purpose.

¶ *How well do the people follow these directions?*
They are completely co=operative about answering the prayers, but not quite as much so about posture; a few pious souls still insist on kneeling throughout the Mass.

¶ *Tell us about the parish Mass.*
Sometimes, but not ordinarily, it is a High Mass. We are of the opinion that High Masses should be chanted by the entire congregation, and, until that day can come, we are sparing of them. If they are chanted by a choir or a schola, the faithful become mere spectators, and that is not the purpose of the liturgy.

In a mission parish like ours we cannot do all the things that a completely Christian one can. High Masses will come gradually.

Here at Colombes the parish Mass is at eight o'clock so that the faithful may receive Communion at it. We try to have the whole parish proportionately represented youths, adults, parents. All the priests are on hand, to greet and seat the arriv= als. There are no reserved seats; the first to come fill up the front of the church, and so on till it is full. Every pew has the same type of missal in it, and the people leave them there after Mass; they can own a copy if they wish, but every other type of missal or prayer=book is mercilessly prohibited. The reason for this is so that all may be together, page by page.

Our people have become an active community when at Mass through their collective responses to the prayers. Mass is fol= lowed attentively, and what was once a serious innovation has become the accepted thing. In addition to the responses in Latin, sometimes there are prayers or hymns expressive of the different parts of the Mass. We have no regular schola (choir); the whole congregation takes up the prayers and hymns with their priests in their midst.

Quite often Mass is celebrated on an altar which has been moved out near the congregation. On the big feast days it is set up on a platform in the middle of the Church. These occasions are still the exceptions, and Mass is usually said in the usual place. On Sunday the bread and wine are placed on a table in the body of the church, and at the Offertory the priest brings them to the altar as a more obvious symbol of the fact that they are the offerings of the people.

❧ *What about collections?*

The collection, please, for we have only one. Payment of pew rent has been replaced by a quarterly donation which is given when the people are leaving the Church. The regular Sunday collection is taken with a minimum of distraction by the priests or laymen during the Credo. It is over by the time the Offertory ends.

REVOLUTION IN A CITY PARISH

Do you have any special ceremonies for the major feasts?

Here again we try to adapt according to the conditions we face. You have doubtless noticed that the Holy Week ceremo= nies are more mysterious and removed from the people than is the ordinary liturgy; that is because the liturgy itself was made up when all work was halted for a week, so that every= one could concentrate on worship, but the pattern of life has changed, and we are in a mission land.

What a chance these days are to announce Christ to our people! What beauty and solemnity in these feast=days! As far as the Church is concerned, they should be as they always have been the most moving, the most welcome days, and we have tried to keep this note in any adaptations we made.

Since we were just talking about collections, we should like to emphasize the fact that we never take one on days like these. It works to our advantage, from an apologetic angle, and it is a real aid to the devotion of the faithful.

On Palm Sunday, it is wise to do something which will make an appeal to as many as possible, because many of those at church on that one day are just the ones we want to win over. The ceremonies have to make an impression; the triumph of Christ must be portrayed. We cannot afford to let this day be merely one when palms are to be brought home for cemetery decorations, or for good=luck charms. So we have adapted and translated almost all the liturgical texts, which the congregation is supposed to say or sing.

Naturally, we have kept the official services of Holy Week, but because their very length makes them impossible for most to attend, we thought it wise to give an explanation of them at evening services. We have symbolic representations of the next day's Gospel performed by the young people, translated hymns sung to Gregorian chant by the whole congregation, choirs to say the prayers adapted from the liturgy of Good Friday, transla= tions of the Reproaches (which have become almost meaningless to the majority, because of their lack of biblical knowledge). The result of all this has been that, besides the fifty or sixty adults

52

present for the morning Masses, we have been able to get five or six hundred to pray at night during Holy Week.

At the parish Mass on Easter Sunday we have a ceremony based on the blessing of the new fire, while the "Exsultet" is sung in French. We have tremendous crowds at this service, whereas there is but a handful present on Holy Saturday morn‹ ing. After all, our people have to work for a living. In 1945, despite the fact that we are in a pagan district, there were 1400 at church on Easter Sunday and 1250 of them went to Communion.

For Christmas we utilized a long‹standing custom here, and put on a real Christmas Eve celebration, with old carols and plays, and a good crowd turned out for that. A large number of those present were ones we wanted to convert, and the good feeling caused by the party did much to put them in the proper frame of mind for the Midnight Mass which followed. In 1944, we used a choir which portrayed four scenes: "The world needs a Savior" (in our homes, our work, our hearts); "The Saviour is born" (carols); "Those who welcomed Christ" (the people, shepherds, workers). All of these take place on a raised platform, where Mass is then celebrated. The success of this venture was encouraging: about 1800 persons stayed for the whole ceremony, and many of them were certainly not church‹goers.

❨ *I understand that you have special ceremonies for some new feasts?*

Yes, we use them to bring out the point of a sermon, or to support some program we have under way, or to capitalize on some legal holiday, or for a representation of a liturgical season.

For example, we decided to profit by the popularity of Moth‹ ers' Day, so as to sanctify it and recall its meaning to families. So, for that day, we reserve the main aisle for mothers; a cradle is set up towards the front of the church, as a symbol of their devotion and their maternity. At the Offertory, the mothers come up, and have photographs of their children placed on the altar. In the afternoon, we bless the cradle and the moth‹ ers at Benediction; and after this very moving ceremony, the children bring to their mothers the magnificent bunches of flow≠ ers they have been carrying before the Host. We also have a feast called "The Christian Joys of Mothers." For this, there is also an afternoon service, with a choir chanting a special "Litany of the Family;" during this, there is a procession of young mothers with their newly≠baptized children in their arms, then the first communicants, followed by young men who have just become engaged, carrying their engagement gift for their fiancées. Bringing up the rear is a young priest, accompanied by his old mother. The ceremony concludes with the blessing of the new priest, first to his own mother, and then to all.

To bring home our preaching, we also organized a "Feast of the Gospel," preparing for it by plenty of propaganda about reading the New Testament and by instruction on this subject in the catechism classes. For the feast itself the church was decorated with symbols of the evangelists and with murals depicting scenes in the life of Christ. The Gospel of the day was chanted with special solemnity. At night, a deacon chanted answers taken from the Gospels in response to the terrible questions of our own times: a good crowd was present and most of them were unbelievers.

In the same way, a "Feast of the Mass" was used to illustrate and clarify a series of sermons on the Mass, and also to help make clear our constant effort to make the Mass "everybody's Mass." As a crowded church watched, men of the parish brought forward three benches: these were to be the altar. An altar boy carried in the altar stone. Skilled and willing hands had made the crucifix, candelabra, the altar cloths and vestments, and even had written and designed the missal. As all these were brought forward, a priest in the pulpit described each article. To make the Mass more personal, everyone brought up, at the Offertory, an envelope containing a list of his or her own special intentions. The children each bring up a piece of coloured glass; when the pieces are fitted together, the phrase, "The Mass is the centre of our lives" is spelled out. As each child comes up with his piece, he says aloud, "This is to make my Mass mean more."

The evening service is used to develop the same idea. Up to the altar are brought the tools of the workmen, household objects, school-books, children's games, and bread and wine. Meanwhile a long chanted prayer fits all these things into the harmony of Christian living and unites all the crowd in an inspiring prayer. The ceremony closes with veneration of the altar-stone.

In a more or less similar fashion we have started a feast of the Missions, of the Cross (during Lent), of the Apostolate (with a blessing of the parish quarters and a development of our plan of conquest), of Baptism (together with the baptism of a group of elder children), of Catechism, etc. We are not saying that every parish priest should do all this, but we are pleased that many priests asked us to compile a handbook of such ceremonies.

We insist on the necessity of creating and developing a catechumen-directed liturgy which will not supplant our tra-ditional liturgy, but yet which will be useful in evangelizing a people who are woefully ignorant and who learn more from participation than from listening. It amounts to a use of the modern ideas on "active educational methods" among people who are only children so far as religious knowledge is concerned.

❡ *Have you done anything like the above for baptism, funerals, etc.?*
From a missionary angle, these services present the best opportunity to us, because of the presence of so many persons who, ordinarily, never come near a church. We all know how ceremonies like these are so often hurried through, and how the group concerned stands around, laughing and whispering totally unconscious of the tremendous mystery taking place before them. At baptisms, the only time they crane forward to look is when the priest puts the salt on the baby's tongue. At marriages, the only interesting thing is the costume of the bride. Even funerals which could be such a marvellous occasion for touching the hearts of the people remain cold and meaningless to our people. Surely there is nothing to prevent us making these important Christian ceremonies live, and using them as powerful tools of evangelization.

At our place everyone who assists at a baptism uses a leaflet in which are translations of all the prayers and simple explana= tions of the whole service. One priest performs the rite, and another one describes each step; in this way, it becomes clear that here we have the gateway into Christianity, the mystery of incorporation into Christ. We use this opportunity to remind the parents of the obligation of a Christian upbringing for this child. The liturgical Pastoral of Vanves (January 1945) expresses a splendid proposal of having collective Baptisms every Sunday, publicized so that a good crowd will attend. Honestly, it is hard to understand how this most important sacrament—the one by which the Christian community grows—has come to be an individual, almost clandestine, ceremony. It used to be a communal act. The very purpose of Lent is a public retreat for all those preparing to receive Baptism. Since we are again a mission land, it certainly seems possible to bring back this idea to our own times, at least to some extent.

⁋ *Class=distinctions must be a big obstacle for you at marriages.*
Not at all. While it is true that we have not officially done away with these "classes," we still avoid them. When anyone comes to arrange for a marriage, and mentions "money," we answer "sacrament," "prayer," "preparation for marriage," until they get the idea that money does not interest us and that the stipend will be normal. If they insist, and demand the frills which involve expense, we give in, but such a case, however, occurs not more than once a month. We think that the best way to discourage these class distinctions is to restore, with all possible religious solemnity, the liturgy of the nuptial Mass and to have the whole congregation pray at it. In this way the "smartest" marriage will be that at which the people prayed with the greatest devotion, namely the marriage of good Christians, whose many friends prayed wholeheartedly during the Mass. We have a leaflet for use at weddings; in it are all the words and prayers of the Nuptial Mass in French, together with the text of the Blessing and various other prayers made up for the

occasion. As at baptism, a second priest explains the ceremony and leads the people. Experience shows us that friends of the young couple are more than willing to say these prayers, and the custom of receiving Communion at the wedding Mass is becoming more common. In such cases, the bride and groom bring up the host and the wine, while each of the other partic⹀ ipants brings a small host. We never neglect a chance to speak about the Christian ideal of marriage and of the family during the customary brief sermon. Besides weddings, we have also celebrated Engagement Masses, with adapted prayers and chant.

❧ *What do you do at funerals?*

They are one of our best opportunities to reach the people. When we think of pastors who organize celebrations in the parish hall, just to be able to say a little bit about religion to those who never come to church, we are astounded that they should miss their chance at funerals when the same type of person is sure to be present. At such times, these are sure to be better prepared to listen to teachings on religion than they would be at some parish hall "get⹀together." Why not make the most of it then?

Some do, but only to utter some general exhortations, or to praise the deceased. We let the liturgy give the sermon. When the body is met at the church, the celebrant gives a brief outline of the ceremony and its lesson on eternity; then everyone is invited to pray for the dead person, using the leaflet provided and its rhymed translation of the *De Profundis*. During the Mass another priest reads the translated Introit, Collect, Epistle (itself a good sermon), etc. All recite the Pater Noster. Chants are used too; for example, the paraphrased Kyrie of the Requiem Mass. At the Absolution, some of the prayers are said in the vernacular. When a whole group of families is seen in this sort of prayer, the effect is moving. More than that, the scene itself preaches a sermon which no one can ignore.

Many have come back to God because of it.

It is easy to see that the distinction of "classes" no longer seems so important, with funerals like these. The emphasis is

57

shifted from the organ and the decorations to the expression of a common heartfelt prayer. A typical expression of how our people feel is found in what one of my parishioners told me: "I was at a fourth-class funeral in Paris the other day. Can you imagine? They didn't even have a prayer-leaflet in the seats, nor any priest to lead the people in prayer!"

When the funerals take place in the afternoon (as about half do), we begin as we do in a morning service at the meeting of the body; then the Epistle is read because of its tremendous lesson; some paraphrased Psalms or liturgical prayers are then chanted, and we finish with the absolution. We announce a Mass on the following day for the soul of the deceased, because we always celebrate a Mass for every deceased member of our parish.

❧ *From all you have said, it seems that you have very little con= fidence in the liturgy as it is, in Latin Gregorian chant, etc.?*

The answer, as always, is that we are in a mission land. We could, of course, adapt the liturgy in a strictly traditional sense; that would be even easier for us. We could certainly find some young people who would be willing to take a course in Grego= rian chant and form a schola. Under a musically-minded curate (who would probably be changed in a few years) we could have fine liturgical chant, to tickle our aesthetic ears. We might even reach the point of having the whole congregation sing at High Mass, as we actually do sometimes. We could do all this but we should be missing our goal. We should satisfy the little group of the faithful, but we should leave everyone else as indifferent as they now are; we should be limiting still further the deadly parish atmosphere. If we were dealing with completely Christian parishes, then we should do all these things. Look at it from the mission viewpoint, and see if such a procedure would make for growth, or for stagnation. Our job, like that of most parishes in this year of Our Lord 1945, is very different. Our people have everything to learn. We think (and shall develop this idea under the heading of "Culture"), that our people can be influenced only by community action, by which they can live their praise of God, and live the life of Christ. After all, what is the liturgy, but the collective life of the whole Christian community "through Christ, with Christ, and in Christ," directed towards the Father? If we can realize this, we are fulfilling our task, provided we really reach this end.

All our liturgical efforts are meant to form a warm, living, dynamic community. We are building neither an ivory tower nor a monastery but an active community which will attract others because they find it attractive, which will stimulate its members because it is alive.

❡ *You have mentioned chants and hymns quite often. I should imagine that you would not care too much for such things.*

We realize that the word "chant" or "hymn" has a bad con-notation. We often hear people regretting the passing of the "good old hymns," even though most of them are products of the last century. Most of them are trash, with words so sweet and sickly that we would be ashamed to ask normal adults to sing them; even the melodies are generally affected and dreamy. Look through a hymn-book and criticize its contents from the triple viewpoint of doctrine, taste, and realism; see how many will pass this test. To call Our Lady "O, Our Only Hope" is a terrible exaggeration, for that title is Christ's. To use phrases like "Languid Glances" is mawkish. To call Jesus in the Taber-nacle the "Divine Captive" is heresy. To ask anyone to sing after Communion "O, Ineffable Sweetness," or "I Taste the Sweet-ness of Holy Love" is to ask of them what a saint might feel once in a lifetime. Certainly it does not correspond to the feeling of most communicants, and it only serves to make them think that they are not as they should be. That is wrong! Furthermore, we should not insist on expressions like, "Christians, Raise Your Banners!", because they do nothing but cause laughter.

But that is not the worst part of it. The really regrettable thing is that we are making the people use words which are meaningless. They certainly do not profit much from using words like "Cherubim," "the Sanctuary," "a holy transport," "a transgression," "a foretaste of heavenly joys," or a "safe haven." All these words are in the dictionary, but not in their vocabulary. Consequently, they connect these words with unearthly, illusory things and that is what does harm. Because these hymns do not sound true, because they cannot feel these sentiments, because they express things completely foreign to life, it too often follows that the religion which uses them must also be untrue, unfelt, foreign. Too often that very conclusion is reached by many an adult whom we have brought up on such stuff. We only hope that teachers and priests will notice this.

Equally false is the longing for heaven which we try to make our people express, when they know only the things of earth. "Oh, how bitter and tasteless to me are earthly joys!" "Would that I could fly like a fugitive dove to heaven!" The notion that the service of God brings nothing but joy is almost as bad: "Let me always taste Thy secret sweetness," or "All sadness turns to Joy in Thee."

We firmly believe in a merciless eradication of such unhealthy, unsafe hymns. When we talk about hymns at Colombes, as you remarked, you can be sure that they are not like any of the above examples. It certainly is possible to compose splendid vernacular hymns, with words that are simple and prayerful, with tunes that are neither dances, marches, nor wails. We could mention a few that we had made up over the last five years, but we do not wish to set them up as models. We tried to express real Christian sentiments in words that can be understood; anyone can do as much. They are powerful and moving, when a whole church is singing the Liturgy of a particular ceremony in terms that are exact, and yet familiar. In this sense, then, we do believe in the use of hymns.

❡ *Do you think that we should do away with Latin and Grego=rian chant?*

Never! Latin must remain the liturgical language, for several reasons. The liturgy is the prayer of the Universal Church, and it is good to pray in the same tongue that our brothers of old used, and our brothers throughout the world still use. Also, Latin, because it is beyond the stage of change, serves as a fine basis for varying modern translations. If we had a French liturgy based on the language spoken in the days of Froissart, it would be incomprehensible by now and would need translation as much as Latin does; there would be a constant necessity of bringing such liturgy up to date. For example, read some of the prayers which Fenelon wrote for use at Mass, and see how unintelligible they are now. Experience proves that real Chris= tians, and converts too, once they are integrated into Catholic life, find no repugnance in the use of Latin, as long as good translations are available. When we say "good" translations, we do not mean transliterations, because such are as mysterious as Latin itself. There is no point in translating *"qui sedes super Cherubim"* into "Who sittest above the Cherubim." What we need are translations which keep the Latin sense and still mean something to the ordinary people who read little more than the newspaper. That is not easy to do; we know, because we have tried. But it is absolutely necessary. If we have such translations, our people can easily sing or say parts of the Latin ordinary of the Mass, and easily follow the rest of it. In time, the people can even sing some of the better known Gregorian melodies.

So — for the Christian community, Latin which is well trans= lated, adapted, together with some vernacular ceremonies; also Gregorian chant, but together with some vernacular music. But, for the pagans, French that is modern and yet keeps the spirit of the liturgy, without symbolisms which would not be under= stood anyway.

❡ *Do you not find that the different levels of society and of culture among the people make a real difficulty?*
No, because in a parish like ours we deliberately try to create a workers' atmosphere. Now that may be surprising, because the church should seem to be hospitable to all classes, without any distinctions. At Colombes we began, five years ago, to stress what would appeal to the working class, even though,

61

now, you would not especially notice any such emphasis. We had to, because it was necessary to put the workers at ease in the church, and also to rid them of the notion that religion was "a middle-class affair;" moreover, if we expected them to make prayer a living part of their lives and sorrows and joys and needs, we had to bring in references to their factories and work and homes.

In a working-class parish, you must use working-class language.

Likewise the people ought to be able to find things with which they are acquainted, in the decorations of the church, in the feasts we made up. Naturally there can never be a question of admitting the use of anything that is trite or in bad taste.

❧ *What do your other parishioners — the lawyers, doctors, and the like say about all this?*

Some protested, and some still do, but it is because they still do not understand. What can we do? We are so sure that we have to take a firm stand. By leaning a little more to the workers' side we know that we can bring back the balance which should be in our community.

Gradually the ice of our stiff middle-class is breaking, their formalism is bending, and we do not have to insist as much as we used to on the working-class direction of our common prayer. Once a worker feels "at home," feels wanted and loved, the need of such insistence on our part disappears. Little by little the balance comes back, and all can pray together.

❧ *What do you think of the use of children's choirs?*

For one thing, we are sick of hearing people tell us things like this: "Oh, I used to love the prayers and the ceremonies; you see, I was a member of the choir until I was seventeen years old." Every priest has heard this sort of thing a hundred times — often from those who are bitter opponents of the Church.

Because that is so often the case we ought to think a bit. If the result of organizing children into a choir is going to be adult apostasy, we would rather not have anything to do with it. We realize that many apostates use their childhood memories as a mere cloak to hide the real reasons why they left the Church, but we do not want to provide even the cloak.

One of the chief reasons for this unfriendly attitude is that, too often, we pick only the "good" children for our organizaⸯtions. Too often, the ones we pick are those who seem incapable of anything very bad or very good, either; they are deadⸯheads, as far as the other children are concerned. We were speaking like this to a fellow priest one day, and he was cynical enough to answer: "True enough, but our prospective vocations come from them." That must not be! The members of the choir must not be "little saints" and "sissies," "culture" in which we find vocations. We have had fifteen members of the parish enter the minor Seminary in the last five years (not to mention the belated vocations to the Major Seminary), and these fifteen were not grownⸯup choir boys of that type.

It is easy to make a closed group, a little caste, out of the altar boys or choir; easy, because the fact that they have been specially picked, have special meetings, have special knowledge of the rites and the Latin, tends to set them apart and above the ordinary Catholic. We must not let this happen. Nothing does more to take possible apostles out of their own environⸯment; nothing does more harm to their sense of conquest for the cause of Christ. It may make us feel good to see children who know the ceremonies of Holy Week inside out, who know all about High Masses, even Pontifical Masses but what good does it do them? What good will that sort of knowledge be in their lives as workers? What good will it do for the prayer life of the family to be founded one day by these young Christians? We have given them an ecclesiastical tinge, and nothing more. After all, it takes but an average memory and ordinary poise to sing or serve at Mass. It takes much more to get in with one's fellowⸯworkers at the shop, so as to win them over to Christ. That is the hard task, and a thankless, often unsuccessⸯful one. Consequently, if the only special service we demand of the talent of our youth is a little memorizing of words and gestures and the necessity of showing up for different functions, we cannot blame them for stopping there. We cannot blame them for losing their apostolic zeal.

❡ *Aren't you exaggerating?*
We wish we were. Let us give you but one example of what we mean.

In our parish (and remember that we are deliberately a mission-minded parish), we put a layman in charge of the altar-boys, to train them in Latin, ceremonies, and general smoothness. It seems that this layman went a little beyond our commission, and he gave the boys a real course in liturgical functions. Still, what harm in that? However, one day, when we had planned to have a High Mass for some special feast, something happened, and we decided to have a Dialogue Mass instead. Do you know what the result of that was? Our altar boys were peeved, and said that they would not serve any more in a parish that had so few Solemn Masses! We had a job on our hands trying to convince them that it was a case of the general good, that we were a mission parish, etc. It did not seem to matter to them that we had to have a general policy of adaptation according to the needs of our parishioners, that there were souls to save, that everyone had to make sacrifices of personal tastes in order to bring Christ to the parish. Only one thing mattered to them; they had taken the trouble of learning the ceremonies of High Mass and they wanted to put them to use. Their satisfaction came first; that was that.

❡ *What do you suggest then do away with Choir and Altar Societies?*
No; after all, we do have to have ceremonies. We should, however, think of the souls of these children rather than consider their usefulness to us. We should not have the same one serving two or three Masses in succession, for example.

A better system is that at Notre Dame d'Esperance, where they have no special groups for the choir or for serving Mass. Every boy of the parish is invited to serve, and the system is succeeding so well that the poor priest is forced to make a choice of candidates thronging around him before every Mass; he looks over the eager faces and the outstretched arms and picks out the one who seems best-disposed and most worthy on that particular day. In this way no elite is set up, no break is made between servers and non- servers, and much of the formalism which can affect altar-boys is avoided.

We should be able to see that many young workers have no liking for ceremonies. We should realize that putting on a cassock and surplice compromises a young man—even a Jocist—in the eyes of his companions. Such an attitude is understandable, and should not make priests resentful; rather, it should make us discreet about whom we ask and how and where. Some will serve Mass, but grudgingly and merely because we asked them; others will do so willingly, but without realizing that it may be unwise for them. We want to preserve their influence; we should not risk their losing it.

By way of conclusion to these ideas on the liturgy, we should like to point out that, while this subject is an important one, it is by no means the most important part of our concept of a mission parish. We say this because many priests—to judge from their conversation when they come here for a visit—seem to think that the liturgy holds the answer for any and every pastoral problem.

We wish that it could be as easy as all that! It is vital that our Christian communities be given a real and communal spiritual life, but liturgical adaptation is but one among many answers to the many evils which we are facing. Seeing the wretched condition of so many souls, we are driven further by our zeal for conquest, and we must find ways that will be even more useful, even if more difficult to put into practice, and these, in turn, will intensify the common life of prayer of our people. ✛

⊹[3]⊹
A Missionary Apostolate

I. THE PROBLEM OF ACTIVITIES

❡ *It is, of course, important to restore or re-establish a living liturgy for the sake of the apostolate, since we want to be able to offer to new converts a form of worship which will attract them and show them the way to God. But our first problem is more fundamental, because these converts must first come to church before they can share in its liturgy. And they must be contacted before they can be converted. What approaches do you have in mind for that?*

We agree that this is the fundamental problem. It is also a very difficult one, and one requiring a great deal of discussion.

First of all, we ought to look at what has been done in this field.

Over the last hundred years, a vast amount of energy has been expended in this apostolic task, and has been expended with devotion, zeal, and intelligence, as anyone who made a study of our parishes would admit. Usually we lump all these varied forms of apostolic energy under the classification of "activities" (Oeuvres). The Church in France, especially since she realized the spread and might of the de-Christianizing forces, has set up a network of activities in almost every parish, and this has done much for the vitality of individual parishes. So much so that when a priest says that he has flourishing parish societies, he is equivalently saying that his parish is active, and that he and the curates are kept busy. Looking back on the parish of former years, when priests were more numerous, one cannot help but wonder what priests did with their time in those days, and what contact they had with non-Catholics. Nowadays, it is practically impossible to conceive of a parish without also thinking of its many and varied societies. Priests who ought to know say that these are the mainstays of parish life.

❨ *Is that your opinion too?*

For the moment it is, because doing away with such activ= ities would mean, in most parishes, the end of any apostolic endeavour. Here, in this chapter, we are not advocating their suppression, and we ask the reader not to misunderstand us on this point. We want to outline all the good factors of these activ= ities not with the malicious intent of making later criticism more telling but wanting honestly to see good where there is good.

The danger in them is a real one, because they are so integral a part of parish life that they tend to submerge us in a round of activity which we no longer stop to analyze and appreciate correctly. We are like workmen who are so busy using their tools that they will not stop to sharpen and align them. In the years that we have lived as curate and pastor, we noticed certain defects and shortcomings, and we should like to point them out now.

❨ *For a beginning, would you say that some line of demarcation must be drawn? We lump too many things under this vague title of "Activities" everything from recreational projects to the Jocists. Maybe we should be more scientific, and limit the extension of the term.*

Absolutely. Otherwise, we shall seem to be criticizing things we do not intend to include. When we talk about "activities," we certainly do not mean specialized Catholic Action groups, like the Jocists, despite the inability of some priests to see the difference. They add the Jocist Movement to the already large number of parish societies, and see no incongruity in such an attitude. Later on more will be said about these distinct movements, such as the Jocists, the Catholic Trade Unions, which are professional and not parochial, and hence, should not be so classified.

What we do mean by this term are the institutions which have grown up, in and around the church, for the education of our children and young people: recreational centres, parochial summer camps, Scouts and Guides, parish athletic teams, choral groups, etc., etc. Also, we mean the charitable endeavours as exemplified by the St Vincent de Paul Society, by soup kitchens, nurseries, and the like. Last of all, we include propaganda activity, such as the parish bulletin or plays.

❡ *You have mentioned so many and such varied things that it is going to be difficult to analyse them.*

We will treat them separately, but a general consideration makes for a logical beginning. Everyone knows what all these activities have done for the "restoration" of the Church in France, especially since the separation of Church and State. Everyone admits that they have stirred up the flame of Catholicism, united priests and people, and manifested the life of the Church to an indifferent world.

Where parish activities are well organized, the faithful can satisfy almost all their wants within the parish boundaries. Children come there to play; older boys and girls for their sports and music. The whole family can relax at parish plays or cinema shows, the men have their card games, there is a library, the poor are helped, the sick are cared for. No wonder, then, that this complex activity gives the impression of strength and vitality, and that it brings satisfaction to the hearts of priest and people alike. Truly, all these activities are the mainstays of the parish, and we cannot imagine what would happen if they were not there.

❡ *Does it seem to you that activities which are so complex will result in completely absorbing the priests' time and the parish's resources?*

It certainly is true that they cost a great deal, in time, in strength, and in money; as a matter of fact, it would be true to say that they will consume as much as we are willing to put into them. Think of how much it costs to put up the necessary buildings, to keep them in repair, to engage the necessary staff, etc., etc.! Once a priest has become involved in this sort of tilling, he might as well be prepared to face continual worries about money, about organizing all sorts of things to support his plan, about bazaars and raffles. The sermons that he preaches will reflect this preoccupation.

If he should be so fortunate as to get all that he needs, his worries are still not over, because success itself lures him on, with dreams of bigger and better and still more activities. The plans and schemes and ideas become even more complex, and he is caught up in a round of more plans, more financing, more administrative work. What was intended as a means has become an end. Worse still, these activities are a terrible drain on his priestly abilities. Ask any priest how much time he has to spend on organizing and running his programs, the purely material side of his parish. The answer will show you that practically all his time and energy are being consumed by one phase; very little is left for the other.

True enough, the results are not small. He has, by almost herculean effort, bridged some of the gap between priest and people. The cassocked figure of the priest has been seen often and almost everywhere, and a certain amount of sympathy and understanding has been won. People have come to see that a priest's life is not such an easy one; they have grown from active hostility towards priests to a sort of kindly indif= ference—if that is a good result. The network of co=ordinated Church programs has even given us a national prestige; even anti=clerical governments have had to admit that the Church was a living, progressive actuality. The influence of our activi= ties has gone out to those not of the Faith, and has, over the past forty years, contributed much to the training of a youth which has been subjected to some degree of Catholic training. Better still, it has been the cause and occasion of a spiritual elite, separated and molded to think and live as Christ would have us do. Thousands upon thousands of young men and women have, thanks to these activities, known what it was to talk to a priest, and to receive spiritual direction, such as they never would have gained from any number of Sunday sermons. Much of the vitality of certain parishes, much of the close relationship of priest and people is due to this same influence. It has done much to keep by our side "tomorrow's generation."

❧ *Everyone agrees about the good results of these activities. What about the often unseen dangers in them which you mentioned a while ago?*

In apostolic, as well as military strategy, it is most important not to deceive oneself. Marshal Foch used to say that he wanted to hear the truth and not just favourable reports. We must not be content to maintain, but also to examine, our position. In the light of present conditions there is no place for us priests to applaud one another for the great good we have done, nor to congratulate one another over the Church we have helped build in France.

What we want to say, we shall try to say simply. We are going to tell the results of personal observations, and try to rea= son back from them to reasons for failures or thwarted advances. All we ask is that no reader should see in our remarks a prej= udiced view of any particular activity or person.

❧ *All the oratorical precautions that you are taking seem to indi= cate that this must be a very delicate subject.*

Like anything else, it is capable of quiet discussion or of heated argument. We want to avoid the latter, and at the same time avoid a vain and empty discussion, such as in political analyses in the papers. Our purpose is to inspect what has been done — not so much to point out defects as to adapt the methods to changing needs.

Since we are talking about things as complex and elusive as the affairs of everyday life, we do not hope to mark out a complete, all=inclusive program. Even the maximum that our efforts might attain will affect but a small part of the evil to be overcome. Anyone who opens a debate on the subject of "meth= ods" simply to force everyone else to accept "my" method can be certain of a sterile, useless, possibly dangerous discussion.

It is always difficult for anyone who has given himself, heart and soul, to any particular activity and who has known hours of sweet consolation from it, to stand back and force himself to make a cold and rigid examination of his cherished project. Why risk discouragement by looking at its shortcomings, when we know that it is doing some good? How can a man of action find the time or the patience necessary for such investigation? Plenty of people are more than willing to cool our ardour, to cast suspicion on the way we are doing things, without our doing it ourselves. This explains why directors of activities are so notoriously hostile to "new" methods or "new" ideas. It explains why parish priests often expect their curates to use the same approach "which they themselves used when they were curates." We are not saying that they should not be wary of any sudden and radical changes, or of the inexperience of young priests "who like nothing better than change," and who destroy before they know how or what to rebuild. Our point is that there exists a tendency to become afraid, actually afraid, of initiative. Curates will tell you that they dread getting a parish priest who has some pet work which has succeeded, because they will be expected to use no other method than his. He was a revolutionary twenty years ago, but not now! There is a great deal of truth in this sarcasm. If we would only remember that generation succeeds generation in an ever-increasing tempo, especially in our times; needs and conditions are constantly changing. What was successful twenty years ago is not necessarily so today. A blindness to that fact accounts for parish priests making their curates endure the same rebuffs that they experienced when they, as young priests, dreamed dreams and saw visions.

(*Despite all that, we still should be able to reach an objective judgment on this question of activities and methods.*

The human factor we spoke of in the previous paragraph is an important one, unfortunately, but there is a more concrete one to be examined. This one is even more harmful to a priest's perspective. Usually it takes the form of one of two tenden= cies in the apostolate; we either become "saviors of souls" or "builders of Christianity." We shall try to explain what we mean.

The first group sees the salvation of individual souls as the most important goal, and it uses whatever means it may to ensure its contact with young and old. The thing that mat= ters is the number of souls saved on the Last Day. Fish with nets or fish with a line, provided the maximum catch is made for Heaven. The tormenting, saddening, sobering fact is that so many will not be caught, so many are swimming towards eternal ruin.

The others see the validity of this first viewpoint, but they are more disturbed and haunted by the thought of the "King= dom of God," which must come. They are more communal in their thought, and their solicitude is directed more towards affecting in some way society as a whole.

❨ *In practice, it seems that both viewpoints reach the same end.*
Not at all. Each sees the same goal, and no true apostle can exclude either aspect, even though his preference may bend him towards one or the other approach, but there is a difference.

❨ *Explain what you mean by this, as regards parochial activities.*
If I am preoccupied by the salvation of individual souls, it is clear enough that I will try to attract as many of the faithful as possible by the activities I sponsor. I will want to have as many children and young folk as I can in catechism classes and recreation periods. I will want to kindle at least a tiny flame of truth in the greatest possible number of my people. If critics want to say that these young people will leave me soon and end up as indifferent Catholics, I say that even the indifferent ones will keep at least a tinge of Christianity from their youthful contact with us, and, some day, they will come home again. Maybe it will be at the hour of death, but they will come back. What can we say to such priestly solicitude?

It is a tender, moving thing to see, and we take no pleasure in the criticism we are going to make of it later on.

The other group, the builders of Christianity, does not look at the numbers engaged by our activities, nor does it find such consolation in the semi-indifferent product it sees coming from them. According to this second perspective, society is not a mere mass of individuals, but an organism which requires insti-tutions and leaders; and Christianity itself is something more than a mere ticket to salvation, God's plan for our salvation is built on the nature He gave us, rooted on the humanity with which He created us. Consequently, if some souls can be saved today in this pagan society, then many more can be saved tomorrow in a Christian one. This plan says that we must build for the future, even though our work will take years upon years.

In any case, we need not discard one viewpoint for the other; they are not mutually exclusive. But, as Abbé Godin formulated it, the mass of men think as a group, and they will be converted only as a group. We favor this attitude, and will adapt it for our criticism of activities.

❨ *Are you saying that these are practically useless for individual conversions?*

We are not. Over and over again we have met or "reclaimed" souls who were approachable simply and solely because they had been altar-boys, or had been in some parish society as children. We should be the last to scoff at the value of such contacts.

That is why this chapter intends only to present one phase of a much bigger problem; neither here nor elsewhere do we pretend to be giving solutions. We are looking for them, just as many others are, and we shall keep on looking. At the begin-ning of this book we said that our only purpose was to evoke interest and provoke thought on all these problems, and such remains our purpose.

Our aim is only to establish a "mission parish" among "ordi-nary" people. From this point of view we are going to criticize parish activities, because we think that too much emphasis has been placed on them, that they have been expected to produce more than they can produce. We should like to see an end to such complete dependence upon them, and an end to the purpose they seem to have, namely, the attracting and keeping of persons who already go to church. We are afraid that they have grown to be obstacles, and not aids, to the apostolate. That is the problem.

❡ *It is about time that you began your criticism.*
All right, we shall. For the purpose of discussion, we are going to group our thoughts under three headings:

   1. Recreational activities
   2. Educational activities
   3. Charitable activities.

1. Recreational Activities

❡ *What do you include under this heading?*
Especially all athletic and gymnastic teams, but also any activity which has no other purpose than the occupation of children's leisure time; in other words, anything which amounts to a "nursery" for boys and girls of varying ages. What we say here will apply, in varying degree, to any other project which, even though it may not have this end in view, obtains the same result.

It is just as well to admit at the outset that we are going to be very hard on these purely recreational groups. In a country parish, or in one where Christianity was flowering, a priest would be wise to organize his young people in this way; in the old days of anti-clericalism, they probably served a good purpose, because they brought priest and people together. But here and now, in our day, Catholic Action is the answer to modern needs, and we find it hard to see how a priest who is hard pressed for time in our huge city parishes can give so much of his energy to athletics. At our parish we did away with them, because we had seen the meagre results they bring and the great amount of time and work they consume; judging by our experience, the return on such an investment was not proportionate. Moreover, they do not seem to be apostolic. Sad to say, they even seem to harm, sometimes, the very ones we are trying to help.

I remember one Sunday when our parish teams won many of the events at a field day. I had not seen one of them at Mass that morning, but they were there in full strength that afternoon. When the games were over, one of them said to me: "You should be proud to be the head of our club, Father. We won everything." "Proud? I feel more like crying."

All the priests with whom we have talked on this subject have seen the same results and come to the same conclusion.

❡ *Is it really so difficult to explain these facts? It seems that we are in error, when, in this age of materialism, we foster the cult of muscles and physical strength.*

Do not misunderstand. We are not condemning sports or athletics in themselves; we are disgusted with sports that pre= tend to be "religious," or claim to be good religious propaganda. Whether we intend it so or not, many of the youth who come to our gyms or games=fields think that they are taking part in something religious.

I recall a man telling me one day, after one of the parish teams had been poorly represented numerically at some game, that I spent too much time on non=athletic activities, that I should get more of the young men into the teams. He reasoned that, if a fel= low joined a parish team, it was a sign that he was a pretty good Catholic, and that I was foolish to be using other approaches.

Actually a great many young men think that way. If they kick a "Catholic" football, or hit a "Catholic" tennis ball, they are serving the cause of Catholicism; if they win a game, the Church is advancing.

Oh, I know. You will say that sport is only a means, and that it is merely a matter of knowing how to use that means correctly, and of demanding at least a minimum of spiritual activity along with it. But the necessity of being obliged to make such demands while using such means is precisely what repels us, because we have so little confidence in this approach. It is putting the cart before the horse. We are fooling ourselves when we depend on methods which have nothing to do with Christianity; we are fooling our young people when we let them think they are really Christian, whereas they are not. Some: thing is wrong, because both we and our youth go at this thing for different reasons; we for their spiritual advancement, and they to have a good time. The diversity of purpose gives rise to necessary conflict, or, at the very least, a frittering away of apostolic opportunities.

It is probably necessary to say again that we are not opposed to sports in themselves. This is not the place to go into a dis: cussion of physical culture. The stumbling block here is the lack of religion in "Christian" athletics, precisely because boys in church teams think that they are performing an act of religion by playing games.

True enough, these teams do provide fine opportunities for individual spiritual instruction. What we are saying is that there is a disproportion between the results and the effort involved in attaining it, especially since that effort could have been used elsewhere. Take the picture as a whole, and you will see that nothing is accomplished for the community. Nei: ther faith nor morals are appreciably better; Mass is no better attended; the sense of what it means to be a Catholic is not any keener. Possible anti:clericals or enemies have been changed into indifferentists of a vaguely sympathetic nature. That is not much to boast about. Even the good Christians in these groups are not trained for the apostolate; their spirituality is not enlivened, stirred up, brought into action.

❬ Yet, if they cannot find their amusement under Church auspices, they certainly will go elsewhere for it.

This is a frequent reply, and it is a valid one, up to a point, for many activities besides athletic ones; we have made this argument a yardstick for our use of a social club. Many a priest has come to the point where he wants so badly to have the young around him that he unashamedly lets the club become nothing but a welcome relief to parents who are more than glad to be free of the care of their own children.

We have let our people become so used to this that it is not unusual to hear parents complain when the recreational facilities are not opened immediately upon the completion of the school term. We are really performing an anti-social function. We are encouraging mothers to neglect their children when we are so willing to take them off their hands.

Concerning this, there is an excellent little pamphlet by a Chartreuse Father entitled *A Reculons*; it is old, but still revolutionary. In it the author shows that many of our parish activities aggravate rather than alleviate the evils which they are supposed to combat; they miss the roots of the problem, and they are carried along in the general disorder.

Because we wanted to avoid this pitfall, we refused to open any regular clubs in our parish. It was just as well, for, if we had wanted to look after the children during all of their free time, we could have had a huge task during the irregular school periods of the war. Instead of that, we have the club open at different, stated times, for the different age groups. That leaves a priest time to perform priestly functions, and it makes parents keep an eye on their own children for a change. Some mothers have even had to give up their jobs.

You will say there is a danger of the children growing up in the gutters. We say that such an outcome would be a shame, but let us look at the question before us. Is it our job, as priests, to amuse children and keep adolescents occupied? Our task is one of conversion, preaching, educating, and distributing the Sacraments. If the children are in the gutters, so are the adults, and in a more harmful manner. While we are trying to keep the youngsters happy, their father is in a bar-room, their mother in a cinema, and their elder sisters and brothers are God knows where. Certainly it is a shame to see children being neglected, but it is still worse to see adults being ruined, families being de-Christianized. It is better for us to bring them Christ directly. If we could do everything, then we certainly should not neglect any aspect of bettering their conditions. But, since the task is so complex, we cannot expect or be expected to do it all. A choice must be made, and it seems to us that the best choice is the one which takes us directly to our function as priests.

We have stopped clubs at Colombes, not merely to rid our-selves of the job of taking care of children, but especially for the reasons which we shall develop in the section of this book devoted to educational activities.

Anyhow, even if we did believe that our aim must be the protection of the young, consider what that would mean! We want them to have their recreation under our auspices rather than see them go elsewhere. Let us be logical. If they go to some swimming pool, does that mean that we shall have to install a pool? If they go off for winter sports, does that mean that we must find a Catholic mountain? How can we expect to compete with all the current fads of hostels, swimming teams, camping trips? If we are going to keep up with every new organization and hobby that the modern world can produce, we must expect to be perpetually in action. Every innovation of State or national authorities in the field of recreation will mean more worries for us. It is better to keep in mind the wise statement of men who know how far afield these activities can take us, when they tell us that we cannot hope to compete with any secular force in the field of recreation. It can offer attractions which are completely beyond us.

❡ *Are you trying to say that we should abandon our young people to the evil influences around us?*

Of course not. It seems to us that, instead of trying to orga-nize and reorganize, it would be more sensible for us to try to Christianize what already exists. Secular organizations are not our business, and neither is their administration. On the other

hand, it is our business to try to fill individuals and organizations with a Christian spirit. That opens up a tremendous field
to us, and it is a field where our temporal resources, or lack of
them, will not be a constant problem.

What we really would like to see is organization of the
patronage-type done by Catholic lay people themselves. For
example, the Catholics of a neighborhood could band together
in order to ensure decent entertainment at the local cinema.
Or the mothers could work out a system of taking care of
one another's small children on different days. The young
men could organize themselves into a Catholic sports group
which would be open to non-Catholics. Little by little, as we
Catholics begin to realize what our Faith means, things of this
sort will spontaneously arise. A priest's task is to encourage
them, keep an eye on them, but never to be himself the artificial cause of their existence. Most of all, he should never
isolate our Catholic people from the men and women living
around them.

We are everlastingly trying to organize life and society as
though we were in a majority! The fact is that we are a very
small minority. Our attempts to set in motion all sorts of Christian activities are really nothing but superficial efforts. We may
as well admit that we are in a pagan world. Did St. Paul, for
example, try to channel the recreation of his new converts
into Christian lines? If we can stimulate men to become solid,
ardent Christians, then the social institutions will take care of
themselves. As it is now, all our toil is doomed to failure for
lack of fighters; paganism creeps in as though by osmosis. But
that is another, later problem.

What we have said against the nursery-patronage was meant
only for those which are nothing more than nurseries. To be
honest about it, that means, or did mean, the great majority of
them; it takes no great acumen to see that most of them are
doing nothing for the formation of the children. Small wonder
that we question what good, if any, they are doing towards the
rearing of future apostles, working-class apostles.

2. Educational Activities

❰ So much for activity that has no other purpose than the direc=
tion of leisure time. It certainly seems that the educational type
should be different.

The first thing we want to say is that serious and scientific
study has done a great deal to improve methods in the course
of the last fifty years. We have moved from purely recreational
to truly educational activities, thanks to the work of capable
men in the field of child education.

Considering what has been done, and realizing the great and
tireless zeal of the apostles engaged in this work, we are most
anxious for all to understand that our criticism appreciates
these things, and that we know and admit that a great deal of
good has been accomplished.

But our aim is to see how our parishes can become mis=
sionary parishes, and therefore we have to question whether
or not these activities have any special apostolic influence on
the mass of working people; not whether they are doing a little,
but whether or not they are influencing, changing, shaping that
mass. Two possible answers can be given to us. Some would say
that they are forming leaders who will, in their turn, transform
the people amidst whom they live. Others would say that they
were having a direct influence on the more important element
of the working class.

To limit the debate, we shall consider only the activities
which deal with children and young people. There are two
questions to be answered:

1. Are they giving the workers the leaders they need so
badly?
2. Are they reaching into the lives of the workers?

❰ I certainly can see no difficulty in the first question. Our edu=
cational system has no other purpose than the training of an
elite, which will, in turn, become the leaders of their generation.

I agree with you that that is their purpose, and we sincerely admire the many men and women who are wholeheartedly devoted to this task. They are always on the look-out for new methods, new findings. Hence, it is not a matter of their good intentions, but of their results; good intentions are fine, but, as in any other kind of warfare, they are not enough. What we have to say is not intended as an attack on anyone, and we hope that it will not offend or discourage anyone, despite the seeming harshness of some of our statements.

The first question we want to treat is whether or not we are really producing the leaven that St. Paul talks about. After all, we do have to form and insert the leaven which will spread through the whole mass around us: that is our vocation. And, if we are going to give so much of our time and of ourselves to this task, we should be able to procure proportionate results. They will come only when we do mold men and women capable of becoming sowers of the seed, leaders, magnetic Christians. A necessary condition for this result is to see that the leaven is in contact with the group which needs leavening; it must become an integral part of the group it is to influence.

Look around, and see what sort of leaders most men are ready to follow. Admit that they are willing to be led, but admit also that they refuse to be herded. At least that is the case with our French people. They will recognize leaders who rise out of their own midst, but they scorn those imposed on them by an alien authority. That is a fact, whether we like it or not. Look at those who have become, practically speaking, dictators over some of our factory workers, principally because they are "like" the other workers, and because they know how to dominate without domineering.

With us the opposite is true. Much of our educational pro-gram seems more intent upon giving us commanding officers than it does upon fashioning real leaders. We get our youth so accustomed to precise commands, to military orderliness in thought and action, that the apparent disorder of their own surroundings bewilders them when they return to it. The result often is that "our" young people are unwelcome, to say the least, among their fellows; they do not know how to adjust themselves to the needs of their apostolate. We have more to say about this in our section on "culture;" all we want to do now is simply to point out one of the reasons why we are not shaping the kind of leaders that working people will be willing to follow.

Another error, as we see it, is our regular practice of with-drawing potential leaders from the milieu to which they belong, and doing this at the immature age of twelve or so. It takes no great experience with youth to realize that many of our young hopefuls do not or cannot become what we once thought they might. How can we pick out a bright boy of twelve, let us say, and act as if we knew for certain what he would be at the age of twenty or twenty-five? The facts are against such a policy. No, an elite is not to be picked out ahead of time, nor can it be developed in circumstances completely foreign to the group it is supposed to lead. We must look for it in the element that produces it, youth leaders among the youth, worker-leaders among the workers. If we insist on trying to raise them our-selves like hothouse plants, we should not be surprised that they have all the weaknesses of hothouse plants.

❡ *That is only a comparison. Are things really as bad as all that?*
It is more than a comparison, and things are as bad as all that. Look at the youths and adults we have trained, and see how out of contact with the mass of people they are. Their Christianity alone is not the cause of this separation, but their tastes also, their reactions. We might say that we have brought forth a semi-ecclesiastical caste with leanings like our own; they are somewhat at home in our circles, but really belong to no social class. Every day the truth of Abbé Godin's observation comes home to us. He said that our young people are fairly good, but that they have no influence over their companions.

At the beginning of this book we referred to the question of whether or not Christianity has softened men. The answer is that Christianity, real Christianity, does not and cannot, but our training can and does. We think that we are moulding an elite-corps; we are actually producing docile, conformable men and women.

Look round and see the youth we have formed. They are recognizable in any neighborhood on any job. Of course this is partly because they are Christian; they cannot behave just like those around them, because they realize that many things are forbidden. Also, we see in them a smile, a charitableness, a goodness that results from Christ being in their hearts. All that is good. The sickening part is that they are so often prim and mincing and artificial, like puppets turned out in our shops. They behave in a superior way compared with their poor benighted neighbours and seem to have lost the ability to be natural. That is the result of our training. As if it were not bad enough that this should be the unconscious result, some of us even aim at making Catholic Youth aliens among their own surroundings.

Once, when I was a young priest, I had charge of a girls' group. One of these girls worked with her sister in a factory. The nun who was organizing the girls came to me one day and told me that she was going to start giving this particular girl a course in typing and shorthand, so that she could get a better job, and get away from that terrible factory. And yet, at the factory, she and her sister were the only fervent Catholics, the only witnesses to Christ in that hotbed of modern paganism. The nun had her way. The girl did leave that terrible factory; within a few months she had also left the organization. She had gone up in the world, and her sister, her family, her old friends had become distasteful to her.

Everything about our training seems pointed to a final prod-uct which will be polished to a bright middle-class lustre. In the face of this we express surprise when our graduates are unwilling to go back to their native working class. We have made this practically impossible.

I remember a young girl I talked to one day. She came from a very poor family, and her father was a communist; without the girls' group she would have found it very hard indeed to persevere in the Faith, especially now that she was working. I asked her if the work was very hard, and he said that it was; she found the days long, and looked forward with longing to the nights, when she could come to meetings and activities with the Catholic group. I tried to explain that God meant her to work and to influence others at her work by means of the Christianity He had given her; it made only a slight impression. So then I asked her if she had joined the Jocist Movement, because that group was more pointed to the apostolic work she could have a chance to do. Yes, she had joined, but the games and good times of the girls' club meant more to her; that was not so bad, for she was young. But her real reason for clinging to the first group was a dangerous one. She kept away from the Jocists because "factory-girls" went to that!

Consider how serious are the three self-betrayals contained in this girl's story. She is dissatisfied with her work, with her apostolate, with her own class of people. And this is no exception; it is more typical than anything else. Even though this girl was good and unusually intelligent, this was the result of the training we had given her.

A few years' experience with real apostles among the working-class will clarify the difference between the young people we produce and these militant young workers. Any chaplain of Catholic Action will admit this as an obvious fact, but parish priests do not seem able to see it. The reason must be that the latter are so engrossed in their parish activities that they do not realize how different real life is.

❡ *It seems strange that, if our organizations can produce Catholics who go to Mass and support the Church, they cannot also produce militant apostles.*

Sometimes they do. Many a boy and girl from out of our midst has become a fine Jocist, better than average in fact, because of the background of good habits gained. But this only happens sometimes; it is not the general thing.

Some priests will tell us that the Jocist girls have been lucky to be able to use already existing parish activities as a recruit-ing source for themselves. On the contrary, it has spelt ruin for entire Jocist units. It has resulted in a loss of zeal, in an unconcern for the workers they are meant to convert; it has resulted in little groups around the priest, with no thought and no capabilities of influencing the very ones to whom they should bring Christ. Our modern pagans instinctively shy away from this sort of Catholic, and when ex-Jocists of this kind do try to approach the non-Catholic workers, to speak their lan-guage, the attempt is artificial, forced. Instead of real, accepted apostles who could transform their whole group, we see Cath-olic gadabouts, worried about this or that social function. They have become hothouse plants.

It is evident that our young Catholics are not sufficiently concerned with the conquest of their pagan companions; they have no burning zeal to make Christ known to the Gentiles. Why?

That is the difficulty. At the risk of exasperating our readers, we are going to be honest, and say that we have not the answer. The defects of the parish activities, as we have described them, are an almost inevitable accompaniment of the good features in them. For those who did not see the defects because of the apparent good results, we wanted to clarify the issue; that is something in itself. Beyond that, we can answer the question we raised, only by these two reasons.

One is that our youth becomes accustomed to and familiar with our tremendous religious truths. It is a glorious thing that they have prayed, gone to Communion, and lived Christian lives from childhood, but it is also true that they have become so used to these mysteries that their grandeur, their greatness is dimmed. A new convert will realize better than they what the Christian life and sacraments are, because a bottomless void has been filled in his life, whereas the Catholic youth has never been conscious of this emptiness. We have raised them in an atmosphere where, unlike the world outside them, everyone thinks and reacts as they do. That means that they cannot grasp the urgency of the need of bringing Christ to the world. They are not haunted by the vision of a rejected Christ because they do not realize, concretely, that He is being rejected. They have not had to find the pearl of great price for themselves, and so, they do not feel impelled to call others in to rejoice with them. They cannot quite imagine themselves as apostles.

A good example of this attitude came up at a recent Jocist meeting. Some of the members were converts, and these were discussing, with great animation, the progress of their aposto= late in a certain neighbourhood. Another member, from a group which had gone to Catholic schools and societies since child= hood, lamenting the fact that her group was so timid, asked the others how they went about this process of explaining Christ to non=Catholics. None of the converts could answer, because none of them had thought of such a problem; it was a matter of spontaneous words, based on the individual situation they were facing. The others felt lost, because they needed plans and procedures; this was one result of the marshalled formation they had been given by us.

The second reason we can bring forward for the lack of apos= tolicity in our own youth is the excessive concern for their own salvation and perfection which we have drilled into them. We tell them that their own soul is the most important thing in the world, that they must not go with anyone who might endan= ger their salvation, that there are persons, places, and things which they must avoid for their own good. Everything that we tell them seems pointed to that question of personal salvation. Everything is accepted or rejected according to whether it will advance or retard this. On that basis it is hard to see why we should be surprised at their lack of zeal for the conversion of the mass of men. We have given them instead an instinct for spiritual self=preservation. Add to this the tendency already in us to do what is easier, to stay with our own rather than break into a new circle, and you have the development of an "ordinary" Catholic. We talk about those "outside the Church" as ones to be pitied, to be prayed for even, but without a serious thought of going out to them and bringing them to Christ.

Being in contact with so many groups, we have noticed a great many things. One of them is the difference between Jocist members and members of parochial societies. The latter, when they are teased or scorned for their "religion" tend to find solace with others of their own kind. The former, on the contrary, take such reversals undauntedly, and get into lively discussions about how to break down the opposition. One group shrinks; the other thrives on this sort of thing. That does not mean that the youth we have trained are useless, nor that they have no concern at all for the apostolate. That is not so. But the striking thing is that this concern was always an individual phenomenon; it was always a case of working on one prospective convert, one who seemed better than his pagan companions. And the method was almost always the same, namely, getting him to come round to the church for some activity or other. It is very difficult for our youth to see that influencing others does not necessarily and inevitably mean getting them to do something "religious."

One way in which we can improve the formation and edu= cation of young Catholics is to associate the older boys and girls with us in the task. This explaining to others will help them learn Christianity better themselves, and they will be more capable of presenting it to non=Christians. However, in this association we must make sure that they avoid a serious pitfall; we must make sure that they do not cease to be mili= tants precisely because they have become "leaders" of others. Often it happens that working for the betterment of those who are already Catholics softens us when it comes to the battle for the non=Catholics, as we have seen. If we withdraw a really zealous apostle, so that he or she can be a stiffening influence on younger Catholics, we run the risk of letting that apostle become content to work among his own, and to neglect the ones who need his fervour even more. In a parish which has comparatively few apostles from the working=class, and which has a great proportion of pagans, it would be a serious mistake to withdraw such firebrands to any great extent. I have seen such mistakes made. One case comes to mind, that of an eighteen-year-old factory worker who had been given charge of a group of boys of twelve to fourteen. When the curate suggested to him that he would be able to do better work in the Jocist movement, he said that he preferred to stay where he was. An apostle was being wasted, at least to some extent.

Choosing these helpers in the work of training the boys and girls is no easy matter. We have to decide whether they are going to be taken from student groups or from among the workers. If we pick students, it is almost impossible for them to prepare the youngsters to live as they must live, in surroundings which the "better-class" teachers do not know. And if we pick workers, we are retiring choice campaigners from the field in which they can do most good; besides, as we saw above, it often means that such workers lose contact with the ever-changing problems of their own milieu. The dilemma is still with us, but at least we can see some of the difficulties in our way.

Too often we priests fall prey to the temptation to use those who come forward to help us in a way very distantly related to the direct apostolate. We press them into service as typists, messengers, stage-hands. That may be good for the parish budget, but it is hard on zeal. Worse than that, it can compromise, in the eyes of their fellows, the very persons who could reach the non-believers; if they come to be considered as the "priest's right hand man," their influence is definitely impaired.

One other important danger that most of us have not avoided is being honest enough to realize that the programs we launch "grow old." We have all seen this happen. A new curate comes in, starts a movement that goes along for years and does splendidly, but the young people who were foundation members lose their youth. Still, we hate to replace them with new leaders, because those are so sincere and so devoted. Before we know it, the organization is stagnated and the youngsters consider it as something for the "old folks." What began so well has outlived its usefulness, even though it continues to exist.

❝ *That failing is an inescapable factor in every living thing.*

It certainly is a natural failing. A solution is not easy to find, and we certainly do not recommend the suppression of all activities just for this reason. What we must do is to rec= ognize the limits of our organizations, especially as regards the conquest of the non=Christian world around us. We cannot go on telling ourselves that we are forming the elite of the future, and be satisfied with that. Seeing the danger will help us avoid it. It takes courage to keep on measuring and calculating the exact worth of our programs; it takes more courage to keep on making the necessary adjustments.

❝ *Still, even if our parish activities are not giving us the leaders which we should have, they do at least console us when we see the great numbers engaged in them. And, sooner or later, if the children continue to come to us, we shall have conquered the pagan world. Even if we do not succeed in transforming it here and now, we certainly shall.*

We have heard all this before. It is true that our work has had good results and that children have grown up and founded Christian homes precisely because of our parish activities. That helps a great deal. We said at the beginning of this chapter that the network of parochial work of this sort has done much to strengthen and invigorate the Church in France. Without meaning to disparage past praise, we still are compelled to say that there is another side to the picture.

For years, for generations, we have been told that our control over the children of today means the support of the adults of tomorrow. For years we have heard newly=arrived priests say that they were here to make a fresh start in the parish. Some= how it seems contradictory that, after fifty years of "controlling" the children, we still have to dream about the support of the adults, and every new priest has to go on making fresh starts. Something is wrong.

A young socialist told me, a long time ago, that he supposed we were satisfied to have so many children around us. But he went on to tell me frankly that that was no proof of any great strength, because he planned to send his children to the parish club until they were about fourteen; then, he would take them back and make good socialists of them. The years in between the Church could have; it was easier for him and his wife that way.

We must find the reason for these spasmodic, perpetually spasmodic, efforts. Some of the fault lies in the fact that we lean too heavily on parish activities, and especially on those dealing with children, in our attempts to advance the kingdom of God. We work with children too much, and not enough with families. A child is yet to be formed; he is plastic. More often than not it is his anti-Christian family which has the preponderant influence upon him. In a later chapter the question of the apostolate to the family will be treated at length; all we want to do here is to show the connection with our work among the young.

Part of the fault is found in the fact that our clubs have to have rules and regulations and supervision. The children are kept well in hand. Obviously not all of these rules have anything to do with Christianity, but a confusion does arise in the minds of the children. Consequently a great many never really enter into the spirit of what we are trying to do; their lives and the intended formation of our guidance remain in two distinct spheres.

⟨ *Surely there are enough varieties of organization to contact and influence every type of person,*

That is questionable. However, the primary aim of any orga-nization of ours should be to instill Christianity; whether that is done by camping, by study clubs, or by any other sort of group is secondary. One important point to remember, lest we tend to develop blind faith in groups and clubs, is that many Catholics do not care to join any of them. This type of person, too, merits attention, and the fact that they seem not to cooperate should not be misconstrued. It does not necessarily mean that they are less Catholic than those who come to parish functions. When I came to this parish, my predecessor handed me a list of names of persons who, he said, were "not active:" as a matter of fact, a good many of them were exemplary Catholics, and they did respond, when given a chance to be apostles. They had not joined the ordinary type of parish activity simply because their family life and religious security had made joining unnecessary.

The conclusion is this. We must not delude ourselves into thinking that parish societies are everything, and that anyone not interested in taking part in them is nothing. We can, if we do not check ourselves, reach the stage wherein we think of non-cooperators as selfish, apathetic Catholics, and treat them as such. In reality, they often are very much the opposite.

❧ *Looking at this situation from another angle, is it not an inspiring sight to see young priests so zealously engaged in the care of all the associations usually present in our parishes? It must be a providential outlet for their fervor.*

It is inspiring, and we would be the last to dampen their zeal, or to say, from our ivory tower, that they are not accomplishing any real good. That would be most displeasing, to say the least, to many an old priest who has given his whole priestly life to just such work. No, it would be wrong to deny that they are doing good, and that the work is doing them good. In connection with this, we would like to make one issue clear. When we say now, and again later, that we favor the suppression of these parish activities, we do not mean that we advocate this course because such a suppression is easier for us priests. Young curates who are quick to take our advice often support us simply because it will mean less work for them, or so they think. They are wrong on both counts.

In the apostolate, it is most unwise to destroy what we cannot replace. Hence, if we have no substitute, we should keep things as they are until we get one. When we talk about doing away with children's groups, the reason is so that we may devote our time and abilities to the adults. That general norm must be believed in and followed.

Once that is understood, we should like to go a step fur=
ther, and expose a very real danger. When young priests come
into a parish, they are usually given charge of the youngsters;
very seldom are they given any other type of association. It
seems to be generally agreed that the purpose in life of young
priests is the formation and guidance of everyone in the parish
under eighteen years of age. What does that mean? Simply
that we are channeling the most powerful stream of priestly
enthusiasm into the solitary outlet of the youth apostolate.
Besides depriving the adults of at least some of this benefit,
we also are encouraging these new Levites to fall into the old
misconception about the children of today equaling the adults
of tomorrow. And the adults continue to be neglected. If a
young curate is assigned to take charge of children's groups,
as well as being asked to preach, hear confessions, visit the
sick, etc., he can hardly be blamed for having no time left over
for the grown=ups.

The fact that the clubs and leagues take up so much time
is not as serious as is the fact that they also consume our
interests, our dreams. We become almost incapable of seeing
any other means of advancing the reign of Christ; we become
almost unconcerned about the progress of the parish as a whole,
provided our club or our group is doing well. Even seminari=
ans are infected by this outlook. They all seem to have ideas
about what they plan to do for the boys and girls, once they
are ordained; very few have done any intensive thinking about
the parents of those children.

Surely there must be a way of reaching both young and old.
This is a hard thing to say, but it almost seems that we priests
are consoling ourselves at the loss of the men and women by
turning to the boys and the girls. When the men lost interest in
religion, we concentrated on women; when adolescents began
to abandon us, we made intense efforts to keep the little ones
around us. They are easier to handle, more receptive. Woe to
us, though, if we narrow the limits of the kingdom of God to
the point that it includes only the little ones!

❡ *You mentioned, a while ago, the danger of being too ready to suppress all parochial activities. Is the opposite danger, namely, to be too engrossed in them, equally wrong?*

We think it is. It leads us, among other things, to the smug attitude of mistaking the following out of a program for a really worthwhile result. Péguy mentioned this when he wrote about the tendency to be satisfied with what has been done rather than with doing things. He meant that we call a group together, draw up a constitution, make a program, and then sit back. True, we keep trying to make the meetings interesting, but we look upon the task as more or less completed. We are, unconsciously, in the process of losing the realization that there are others to be gained for Christ, outside this tiny circle. We can honestly tell ourselves that all our strength and ingenuity is being expended, and that we are not "taking life easy." The first statement may be true enough, and the second too; but we are not doing enough once we let this one field satisfy and absorb us. We are coddling ourselves. Rather than seeking out the others, the ones who will not come in, we have established our sway over relatively easy subjects. Most of us will deny the truth of that conclusion; in fact, most of us do not realize that we are doing just that, because we are in good faith. The fact still remains.

There are, of course, many priests who have established a balance in their work; they do reach both young and old. Many more have been rendered practically useless for the adult apos= tolate by their excessive preoccupation with the children. It is much easier to talk to a group of impressionable youngsters than it is to preach "Christ before those who might ridicule us." Gradually, imperceptibly, we grow soft, and the easier ministry becomes our total ministry.

❡ *Another evil feature of our times is the fact that priests, though few in number, are compelled to do so many things which are not properly or necessarily priestly.*

We agree with you. A modern priest, more than ever before, should be free to exercise his priesthood to the utmost, and not be bound down to merely temporal and material tasks. The activities that we have been talking about do much to bind him down, because a priest engaged in them has a thou‹ sand worries about how and where to find the resources to keep them going, and about drawing up their programs or organizing their celebrations. Go into the room of the average curate, and see the proof of this for yourself. You will see a room cluttered with bazaar posters, lists of names, program notes, publicity placards, and a host of other similar things. It is a pity that successive generations of priests have been and are being forced to limit the possibilities of their priesthood in this fashion.

❨ *What is your conclusion from all that you have said about educational activities?*
Adhering to the principles we stated when we began this book, we will draw no conclusion. Everyone who reads this work has problems which are locally, psychologically, and spir‹ itually, different from those we find at Colombes. Hence, every reader must make his own conclusion, based on his own situa‹ tion. All that we can say is that, while these activities do seem to be a necessary part of the modern apostolate, they were not always so. The time seems to be approaching when they will no longer be so. Good judgment and true zeal will indicate when and how changes can be made in each corner of the Lord's vineyard, and also how these changes can be improved upon as the times continue to evolve around us.

❨ *Would it be a correct conclusion to say that you are against the types of activity about which we have been talking, and that you favor their suppression?*
Not at all. We should, we admit, be deeply interested in the work of a priest who found the courage to replace all these groups with a program of intense direct apostolate. It does seem to us that such boldness would be rewarded with more success than meets our present efforts, but we have not the courage

to take such a stand ourselves; nor could we, therefore, advise it to anyone else.

Looking over the history of the Church in the last fifty years, and it was during this time that the system of parochial activi= ties grew up, two facts stand out. One inspires us with confi= dence; the other is disturbing. The first shows a gradual growth from the material to the spiritual. For example, the club used to mean little more than a nursery; nowadays, it is becoming concerned with the formation of the young. Another example is the evident growth from groups interested only in providing athletic facilities for boys and girls to our present concept of study clubs. All of that is good. The other, the disturbing factor, is the tendency which all these groups seem to have, namely to settle into a routine. Zeal, especially for those outside one's particular circle, is all too easily lost.

One certain fact is the need for a change, for a renewal of spirit. The ardour and magnanimity and apostolicity which inspired the beginnings of all these activities must be rekindled. It is not enough to be concerned only with the smooth running of what someone else started; it is definitely not enough to be enmeshed in details and administration, and thereby to lose sight of the purpose of these details and this administering. All that we do for God must be touched by the eternal youth which the Holy Ghost will give the Church.

3. Charitable Activities

❡ *What do you have to say about the works of charity?*

Here we have a really integral part of the Church. Like Christ before us, we must be concerned with the misery of mankind, and find in it a means of bringing men to know and to love and to serve Him. Ever since the time of the Apos= tles, the Church has been helping the poor and caring for the sick; until the Revolution in France, the Church bore almost the whole burden of these works of charity. Since the Revolu= tion, the State has taken them under its wing, but the Church must continue doing what she has always done. It is a logical consequence of the command to love our neighbours, body and soul. Unlike the State, we act from a motive of supernatural charity; the government can give money or clothes or food, even as we do, but only the Church of Christ can give His love.

Over and above this general picture, there are certain peculiarities to be remembered in the exercise of charity in a working-class parish, when that charity is meant to have a missionary purpose. One is that this need not be intended as propaganda; despite the apparent contradiction here, the statement is absolutely true. The very fact that we love our neighbors will be a more powerful witness to Christ than any attempts we might make to capitalize on it will be. If our motive for practicing charity is to draw others into the Church, the recipients will shy away; they will realize that there are invisible strings on our gifts. If, on the other hand, our motive is the love of God, that love will shine through the gift and through the giver up to the very source of the love; we need not worry about that. When we help anyone and then try to get that person to come to Mass or to approach the Sacraments, he cannot help but recognize our mixed motives; and, usually, he refuses to be bought by our aid.

In a parish which is predominantly pagan, the distinction between "saviors of souls" and "builders of Christianity" must be kept in mind. We want the non-Christians around us to be forced to see and acknowledge the love which animates the Church of Christ. Those whom we serve must be able to see Christ in us before we can expect them to draw near to Him. The sight of Sisters of Charity at work can do more for propaganda than any clumsy exhortations we might try to foist on the poor or the sick.

In connection with this, we would like to say that charitable organizations are best conducted by nuns and lay people rather than by priests. The basis for that opinion is found in the Acts of the Apostles, for they ordained deacons to do that sort of work and to leave themselves unencumbered in the preaching of the Gospel. If the clergy take up the direction and administration of charity, they are using time which could be better spent on more direct apostolic endeavours, and they are jeopardizing the results of the charity. Everyone knows that priests are Christians; there is no need of laboring that point. Moreover, they will give the whole program a clerical aspect, which is, as we know, most undesirable. For the good of the mission cause we should prefer to see priests staying out of this field.

One more thing. The very generosity we show to the needy may, and often does, lead people to believe that we are wealthy. Anyone who knows the limits of our wealth and the hard task we face in raising it, will smile at such a thought; but, for the mass of men, that belief is more evident than the Gospel we preach. They see "the Church" giving away money and food, and they come to the conclusion that, somewhere and somehow, she has an inexhaustible supply of money. So they are willing enough to help relieve us of some of our excess wealth, and the good which our generosity intended to do is destroyed. The answer to this difficulty lies, we think, in placing the control of charity directly in the hands of those most interested in it, namely, laymen of the same social and economic standing as the majority of the parish. The Jocists or the family groups which exist in most parishes would be ideal directors. They are among the people and of the people; they know better than we who really needs help, and what form it should take. Moreover, they will not be suspected of "clericalism." Hence they make the best witnesses of Christ in the dispensing of His charity.

PROPAGANDA

❮ *You mentioned propaganda activities a long while ago, but you have said nothing about them.*

No, because we wanted to keep them for a special section. They, above all others, are specifically missionary, and we include under this heading any and every movement which has as its sole purpose the spreading of Christian truth. The only exception we make is the spoken word, because we want to leave that to the section devoted to the question of preaching. Here we mean the written word, the stage, and the cinema.

❝ *Are they such an important part of the mission movement?*
Indeed they are. An especially noteworthy fact about them
is that most parishes use them. Like everything else, they are
delicate instruments, and we must make sure that they are not
so mismanaged as to hurt the cause.

The press, first of all, is of primary importance. By the press
we mean anything printed, ranging from pamphlets to newspapers. The printer's ink will reach out to those who will not
come to hear our words; it provokes thought where our personality or presentation might be an obstacle; it answers questions
which men would not have the courage or the inclination to
put to us. Consequently, a "pagan" parish which neglects this
avenue is losing golden opportunities. There need be no fear
of using it too much; notice how secular and other far-seeing
groups make use of it! By it we can reach those whom we want
to attract, and whom we cannot hope to convert by speech.

Now for the precautions we must take. Knowing how our
people love to classify everything, we must be wary in our
recommendations of any particular paper. The one we do recommend or permit to be sold in the church becomes, in the minds
of the parishioners, "the" paper of the Church. We can protest
as much as we like that people should realize that we are not
giving complete approval to anything and everything that the
newspaper may say. The fact remains that the ordinary person
does not and will not make such distinctions. We cannot go to
the absurd opposite and refuse to praise any newspaper, because
the good ones do deserve our support; discretion and investigation of the ones we approve is the answer. One of the chief
reasons for the gulf between the Church and the people is the
widespread opinion that the Church has become the property
of the "upper" classes. Consequently it is not difficult to see
the harm we can cause, if we act as agents for a publication
which gives support to that false conviction by its attitude.

The wealth of truly Catholic newspapers makes our support of the smug, intransigent ones all the more senseless.
There are so many which deserve all the backing we can give

them that it pains us to see a parish priest praising them as "anti=communist," "anti=Protestant" papers. Of course, even the best of them does not speak officially for the Church, but they are doing a tremendous work in bringing Christ back to the souls who have seen Him only in caricature. We must do what we can to gain support for them, but, in so doing, we must not endanger the good they are doing. By that, it is meant that no one should be able to see in our recommendation a basis for calling these newspapers "clerical." Let them do their own advertising.

❡ *What do you think of the value of a parish magazine?*

It is a powerful weapon in the missionary conquest we are striving to accomplish. In it the priests of the parish can air their opinions freely; by it the news of the whole parish is cir= culated. The magazine can continue where our Sunday sermon left off. All of these things it can do and more, if we really use it as a mission weapon. That means sending a copy to every family, and not just to those who pay for it; the ones who pay for it are already convinced, and have less need of the Physi= cian. The ones who are convinced can be persuaded to help by paying for the copies sent to the others. Another cardinal principle is that we direct its articles, its tone, its approach to the non=believers, because its prime purpose is a missionary one. While it is good for parishioners to see their name in print and to read about the different social functions of the parish, such a carefree attitude is out of place in our circumstances at least, as a main purpose. Nor should it be "pious," because sugary spiritual items will repel the audience for whom these bulletins are intended. Its style, too, should be watched, so that the articles will be direct, unaffected, and friendly in tone. A good thing to remember is that people who read relatively little read very carefully; students or educated men fall into the habit of swift reading, and the retention of only the main points. But the average working=man is a thorough reader, and he attaches more importance than we ordinarily would to the written word.

Hence the care that we take to present truth in a telling way may be rewarded by the return to Christ of our readers.

Many parishes use a syndicated magazine which is made up elsewhere, and intended to be general enough to interest the average parishioner anywhere. That may be cheaper in money, but it is more costly in souls for anyone who plans to use the publication as a propaganda agent.

The format and coloring and the use of cartoons, etc., are important, but we have found that they are not worth too much trouble; the contents are more vital than the dressing. Our audience seems to have a higher regard for the pure newspaper type, rather than for the illustrated papers. As long as we keep forever before our minds that this publication is intended for the non-churchgoers, we shall avoid making it a social paper, a humorous magazine, or a purely "parish" bulletin.

❡ *You also seem to be avid users of pamphlets and notices of all sorts.*

Indeed we are. It seems, sometimes, that we consume almost as much paper as the *Propagandastaffel*[1] did in its heyday. We are staunch believers in the power of the printed page when it can be easily read, and when its few main points are highlighted.

We have formulated two classifications for these placards and pamphlets; one is used to attract people, and the other to provoke thought. For us, the first type is more sensible, because our purpose here is to let everyone know that the parish exists, and that it exists for everybody. When we can give the impression that these notices are practically personal letters (and that often happens!), so much the better. As long as we refrain from putting out too many, too often, they retain public interest. Another practical point is in their distribution. Instead of mailing them or slipping them under doors, we have found that the best method is to have a militant put them in the hands of the recipients. The personal touch is

---

[1] German propaganda service in Paris entrusted with the control of the French press and publishing during the Occupation.

heightened, greetings are exchanged, and an invaluable contact has been gained.

Naturally, tracts which are being used to spread ideas and cause comment can be distributed much more often than can the invitation type. They can be made into a graphic apologetic vehicle, not with a "defense complex," but in a positive, confident way. Different seasons of the Church year, like Easter and Christmas and Pentecost, are natural occasions; incidents or problems of the neighborhood also can be utilized by an intelligent editor.

Even billboards, of a striking nature, can be pressed into service. We have several regular spots scattered around the parish, with placards that tell the time and nature of services at the church; besides these, we put up special ones for extraordinary events, like a mission, a feast day, etc. At least they show the vitality of the parish, and publicity of this sort is especially needed today, when we tend to relegate religion to a forgotten corner of our individual worlds.

❡ What do you think of parish cinema shows?

Frankly, not very much. As films are now, a parish priest is out of place when he acts as a distributor for them; unless he means to present only religious pictures, he is, to say the least, wasting his time. Our fond hope is that soon Catholics can have some good historical films produced on subjects like the beginnings of Christianity, Joan of Arc, and the like. To try to use the ones circulating now is an impossible task for a priest. We could go into more detailed reasoning, but it hardly seems necessary. Any energy that we want to spend on films would be better directed to getting the lay people to make sure that the cinemas in their neighborhood are not showing objectionable films.

❡ And the production of parish plays—what do you think of them?

These are not, of course, as dangerous as films, but they are not much more useful as missionary tools. The time consumed by them is hardly proportionate to the results. Most of us have been subjected to enough parish plays to agree that they are pretty tiresome, and that they involve so much delicacy in assigning roles that they often end in animosities, not Chris= tian charity. Sometimes, of course, a really good production is staged, but this is more the exception than the rule. No, a priest with a missionary goal cannot afford to waste the time and talents which these plays consume.

SPECIALIZED MOVEMENTS

❈ *Is your approval of the specialized movements as qualified as was that of the other types of activities?*

On the contrary, we have nothing but praise and support for them. These organizations, like the Jocists or the family groups, have a completely praiseworthy purpose and result; they are meant to instill Christianity into particular groups and places, and they are doing that splendidly. They represent the apostolate of "like to like," as the Popes have asked; they are made up of fervent apostles in action at the factories, offices, and in the neighbourhood.

By this truly Catholic action the transformation of entire classes has been begun. Religion has come out from the sanc= tuary in a very real effort to sanctify the world. Jocist and sim= ilar groups realize that men will not answer appeals to come to Mass, but that they will listen when Christ is brought to bear on their social, industrial, and individual lives. Rather than stress the happiness of heaven, a solidly Christian attempt is made to better present circumstances. Scoffers and doubters are shown that the Gospel is not ethereal, but real and practical; apologies are replaced by proofs of an ideal way of life. The very men and women now engaged on this work are proofs of what can be done and of what is being done, because most of them are drawn from former scoffers and doubters and bewildered souls. We cannot say enough to show how highly we regard this manifestation of the apostolate especially in a working=class parish like ours.

❡ *And yet the general impression seems to be that movements like these are engaged in by "Revolutionaries." They are respected, but treated with a certain reserve, as though they had a different purpose than the parish.*

What you say is, unfortunately, too often true. Basically, such an attitude is founded on the idea that a parish means only those who come to church; we discussed that at length a while back. If anyone does hold to that idea, he will logically see the Jocists, etc., as "non-parochial." A priest who wants to hold processions and services for his "regular" parishioners will not be overly pleased when the Jocists do not show up at them; they may be off for a day of recollection, or engaged in an apostolic effort but they should be at the church or in the procession or so the priest thinks. Recriminations and questionings follow, and ill-will is established. Our Catholic lay apostles are human too, and very often discouragement and bewilderment result from this attitude of the priest.

❡ *Are the results of this type of apostolate as impressive as is sometimes claimed?*

There is no denying that they are impressive. And yet, after approximately fifteen years of toil, the Christian Workers' Movement is still in a spasmodic state, with the expected results still distant. Before criticizing the apostles engaged in this work, we should look nearer home for the blame. We priests have supported them but poorly, and have preferred to keep around us and around our more petty concerns the young people who could have become valuable recruits to the cause. We have been negligent in making ourselves efficient and useful directors of consciences for the Catholics who especially need us. Anyone who has talked to these militants knows how poorly we have fed them with the spiritual substance we are supposed to dispense; they want to taste the things of God more than we make it possible for them or so it seems. How then can we point an accusing or a self-justifying finger at them, when we have made ourselves obstacles to their fervour? The

REVOLUTION IN A CITY PARISH

time we could give to forming and directing these hungry souls we prefer to spend in other ways.

Even when there are efforts to form and guide these apos= tles, the misconceptions of a priest can be almost as harmful as positive neglect. It is a serious business to undertake, this guidance of modern apostles. Any priest who does enter into it must grasp that he is to help them see Christ in all the affairs of modern life; he is to fan an already brilliant flame. For that undertaking the priest cannot be mediocre himself. He cannot fall back upon shopworn cliches; he cannot preach at these men and women who ask to be guided. They have questions to ask, problems to clarify, and listening to a one=sided sermon will not aid them. A priest who sees in their inquiries only impudence is woefully wrong. A priest who would like to see these young Jocists more orderly, more systematic, more demure, has missed the eagerness for Christ that is driving them on.

Another mistake is the opinion that a combined "study and formation circle" is the ideal way to guide groups like the Jocists. In them Christian doctrine can be discussed and applied. While the idea has its good points, it has defects also. The meetings, once or twice a month, are too far apart for a sustained and profitable study. The ready=made explanations of our teachings are too abstract and too general to help its members apply them to existing conditions. Last but not least, such study clubs often wean the apostles away from the real problems that surround them to theoretical study of principles. Connected with these defects, it is not unusual for a priest to ask that a Jocist unit become more "integrated" with the parish. Since he means by that that the unit is to devote itself to strictly parish activities, the net result is the collapse of another Jocist cell. Tangled in a maze of parish functions, the unit loses both its appeal and its internal fire; those "outside" are gradually forgotten.

We must keep our hands off movements like these, and permit them to remain what they are intended to be: lay move= ments. True, the priest must guide them in doctrine and in spirituality, but, instead of trying to make them clerical, he must leave them free to exploit their peculiar appeal to the non-believing world. Let us never give place to the absurd idea that laymen and laywomen are no more than our messengers, sent by us to persons and places we cannot reach ourselves. They are infinitely more than that. As members of the Mystical Body, they, too, have their mission to accomplish; they, too, have a duty to preach Christ when and as they can. Paternal-ism or kindly toleration from us will stamp out the spark of apostolicity that God has given them. All of this we have done, but we must change.

❡ *So far, you have spoken as though the clergy were entirely to blame for defects in the specialized apostolate. Are there no faults on the other side?*

Of course there are. Not infrequently laymen fall into a certain snobbishness, a feeling of self-sufficiency; they neither need nor want any interference from the priest, and they let that be known. The final result is, of course, a lessening of the good that each could do by cooperation, and a loss of the supernatural character of the priesthood. Lay Catholics must realize as indeed almost all do that the priest holds a sacred trust from God, and that He is essential to their sanctification. Without that source of holiness, they are incapable of bringing Christ to others, and their very purpose is defeated.

Another weakness is the ever-present danger of becoming so involved in the struggle to make better working conditions and family life that the original purpose of making Christians of these pagans is forgotten. We are not saying that the Jocists or similar movements should not try to improve these human factors, because that is an important means of bringing men to Christ; but we are saying that Christian apostles should not degenerate into mere humanitarians. Our starting point and our goal must be supernatural, or we shall never make Christians of them. Better, happier human beings, maybe; but not Christians.

There is another, more subtle, defect to which these partic-ular organizations fall heir. In their zeal to convert the great numbers outside the Church, they falsely think that they must attract great numbers. That will come, but not immediately. Sometimes, when the meetings or entertainments they sponsor are crowded, it looks as if their work were succeeding wonder= fully and therein is the worst part of their error. Numbers have dazzled them. Instead of realizing that many who came, came to pass the time, and many will not come again, our Catholics see success in the offing. In such a concept the fundamental principle of contact with Christianity has been swept away. If Catholic Action is to be "successful," it will be a matter of influencing individual souls, of drawing them to the stage where Christ will become visible, desirable, attainable. The fact that a meeting is "mammoth" is not, in itself, a good thing. A few pages back, when we discussed educational activities, we tried to bring out the point that such activities were not defeated completely by the presence of mediocre Catholics, because the very nature of the work protects its participants from serious contamination by alien influences, even the lukewarm Catholics were more or less safe. However, in work such as the Jocists do there is no such protection. Two harmful results will follow from this mass contact. One is that the Jocists themselves will be affected by the pagan majority to which they have come. Secondly, if mediocre Christians only are put in contact with non=Christians, there is certainly little hope that enough of the spirit and love of Christ will be given off to draw those who know Him not. In either case the results are lamentable.

It does not follow from this that we, as priest=guides, must forbid all large=scale contacts, nor that we leave the task of meeting pagans only to the real apostles. The first is not nec= essary; the second would spell the death of the zeal of many an embryo=apostle. What we must do is to indicate the possible dangers underlying this type of action.

The last weakness we shall mention is also a widespread one; it consists of the transition into administrators of those who began as magnetic Christians. Routine, excessive paperwork, ritualism—these are shoals to be given a wide sweep. Only by work in the market places, only by a quenchless thirst for souls will the working apostle find his place in the Mystical Body.

¶ *Going a step further, do you think that such activities as these have a place in parish life?*

Positively. In any parish they are a priceless testimony to the place of Christ in everyday life; they are living teachers of what it means to be a Christian. As such, they are infinitely more important than the parishioners who come for Vespers, but do not manifest God to their neighbors. We priests must grasp this, must see the peculiar value of their work, and must not try to measure it according to the usual parochial standards. We have grown used to placid, docile followers; we must become used to this new species. If they seem rough and hasty, part of the appearance is due to our own excessive gentility. Instead of being horrified at their outspokenness, we might well learn to speak more of their language. Instead of letting our dignity be offended when they plan a celebration without consulting us, we might well take fire from the sparks of their impetuous zeal. Instead of threatening to disband these anarchic Christians, we might learn to rid ourselves of the moss of routine grown up around us.

Someone told us about a pastor who became infuriated at the Jocists in his parish because they were so casual towards his position. He mounted the pulpit of the church, clad in surplice and stole, and delivered a terrible denunciation of the group. Waving his stole, he cried, "Here I am in command, and you must obey me; this is the symbol of my divine power." Since no one knew the symbolism of the stole, his climax drew more titters than feelings of awe.

It will be easier for us and for these lay people if we realize that they are tremendously conscious of the necessity of making Christ known; they cannot rest under the weight of that consciousness. That explains much of the apparent carelessness we see in them, and it is a motive we disregard only at the risk of displeasing our common Lord.

Consequently, we ought to direct their efforts into the mission-effort of the entire parish. Some parishioners will object to working with them, either from haughtiness or from fright; we priests must show these Pharisees that no one can be a Christian who refuses to be an apostle. Anyone who feels supe= rior to these young workers, because of being better educated than they, or because of belonging to some one of the "bet= ter" parish societies, is not worthy of them. Such a one needs instruction, and needs it badly.

The actual direction of their efforts can take different forms. Here at Colombes one of the priests is the director of the Jocists; he enables each of the different committees within it to keep in touch with the priests who have charge of separate sections of the parish. In this way, the whole set-up is coordinated and informed on the needs of the whole parish. The ideal would be to have a complete Jocist movement in each of the portions of the parish, but the present plan is the nearest we can approach to this ideal. A better picture of how these lay=apostles actually work will be given in our treatment of the "direct apostolate." All that we say here is that there is a very definite and very valuable use for these movements in any parish.

❡ *How do you attain unity among such diverse activities, so that each of them is truly parochial?*

That demands care. Obviously, not all are suited to the same kind of work, nor could all of them work alongside one another. We have to find a place for each. One way to attain this unity or rather, to prevent disunity, is to make sure that the really diverse ones have their own places to meet; if the Jocists had to assemble at the parish hall, the reaction might not be so good. To avoid clashes of background, it is a good idea to have something like a clubhouse or meeting room for the Jocists away from the parish hall. Besides the other reasons given, it enables them to do more good, since they are not "around the church." Hence, in realistic ways, we try to find the place for each movement, where each can do the most good for the whole parish=mission.

THE DIRECT APOSTOLATE

¶ *All that you have said sounds impressive, but it also sounds rather strong. Even though the activities you have criticized do have many defects, they are, at least, functioning and doing some good. What would you substitute for them?*

Please understand us. We are not negative critics, and we are not so much interested in the exactness of our criticism as we are in the hope that some good may come of it. We priests are few in number, and the work at hand is overwhelming; the days when we could worry only about our own churchgoers is past. Somebody has to call for a change in attitude and approach, and we have tried to do that. Like every other priest we have made many mistakes since the day we came from the seminary, and we are still making them. We are not setting ourselves up as examples, but we have come to the conclusion that a direct apostolate is more efficient and more valuable than the indirect activities we were analyzing. What we have said was not meant to tear down other men's work, but to help to clear away mis= conceptions, and to show why we came to the conclusion that there must be a better way to bring Christ to this world of ours.

¶ *Tell us how you reached that conclusion.*

It was a gradual process, made up of the mistakes we made and the thinking we did. At the risk of boring you, we will try to give a short description of the road we travelled.

As far back as we can remember, the effect of militant Cath= olics upon unbelievers astounded us. We used to be afraid that their new=found zeal was too direct, too brusque, that they would repel the pagans they contacted. Instead of that, we saw that they were respected even by those whom they could not convince. After noticing that fact for years, our slow mind finally saw the light. This was one of the answers! By contacts here, we mean personal ones, and not mass meetings; although it is easy to draw crowds, it is difficult to reach the souls of individuals in them. Incidentally, speaking of mass=meetings, there does seem to be some value in those such as the Salvation

Army holds. Over and over again, we have heard it said by people watching them that at least the Salvation Army had the courage to profess what it believed. Maybe we could use something similar to good advantage.

Apart from that, our observations were of personal conversa-tions, of words said with confident conviction to a neighbor or a fellow-worker. The resulting conversions are amazing. Con-sequently, it seems only reasonable that this man-to-man way ought to be considered; it does produce results, and it certainly goes directly to its goal.

Nearly all of us will admit that the modern adult needs to be given a reason for living. His confusion is crying for an answer, and that answer must be true and inspiring and spir-itual. It used to be said that we only had to let them recall the religion of their youth and they would come back to its practice when this confusion came upon them. Not so now, because this generation knows nothing about religion; we can-not remind them of mysteries they never knew. And yet they need something, disillusioned as they are by the hollow claims of progress. They know they need something, and they will grasp at spiritual values, materialists though they still are. They are weary of *ersatz*, distrustful of glowing promises, and more or less convinced that happiness is not here. Religion, because it will be a new experience for most of them, has a splendid opportunity at this very time. What Christ is offering will be revolutionary to these jaded revolutionists, and their souls will open up to his warmth.

❡ *It sounds as though you would like to herd them into our ranks.*

Not quite. The day when priests could herd souls is gone, and we are not lamenting its passing; as a matter of fact, because that day has gone, we need the direct apostolate all the more. If we tried the old system of starting a "movement" to r-Christianize them, they would stay away in droves; they have had enough of "clubs" and all the rules and regulations which accompany them. Here in France we saw that reaction after the Liberation. In their minds there already exists the idea that the Church is nothing but another "movement," another organization that wants a lot of members, and wants them for its own selfish reasons. There is no point in approaching them in such a way that their false opinion will be strengthened.

Our goal now should be to show them a spiritual, disinter-ested Christianity that is "lived," not "joined." We must show them Christ, in all His love, all His grandeur, all His beauty, so that they will come to Him, and make Him the source and the end of their daily lives. That is our goal.

❡ *How shall we do this?*

Not by activities, but by our words, our deep convictions, our unglossed presentation of his gospel. One of the most telling ways of doing all this is to have one soul in contact with one other soul; to have the believer tell the non-believer exactly what happened to him. The doubts and fears that were washed away, the experience of what it is to know Christ told by an intense believer—this is what will win our modern pagan proletariat. We priests cannot achieve this by our old willing-ness to "enroll;" it is not a matter of getting members, but of transforming the unbelievably dreary spiritual lives of these people. We cannot do it merely by opposing error and false doctrine, but we must show them the way, give light to their paths, and something positive to their lives.

Nor shall we do it by our text-book apologetic arguments. Some, of course, will be interested and even convinced by them, but the mass of men are not swayed by our well-reasoned argu-ments; they heard so many errors so well expounded during the war that they believe it possible to prove anything. So, when we try to prove the truth of Christianity from historical or social or philosophical premises, they are unmoved.

❡ *Well?*

We shall do it only by showing them what Christianity is and what it demands. That sounds over-simple, but we believe it to be the answer. It is what our militants do; they never hesitate to state what this religious transformation entails. They explain the personal nature of this call of Christ and the necessity of a personal reply. Unlike most modern priests, they are not slow to speak about the last ends of man, not of the fire and brim= stone, but of the fact that an end does exist and that it must be considered. They make the after-life sound like a personal problem of the one they are trying to win, and, more often than not, it actually is. Personal, individual adherence to the Christian way of life is what militants work for, because it is the only real conversion. Despite what we said about the neces= sity of working on the mass of men, and on social or economic groups as a whole, it still remains true that we must win each member of those groups as individuals. We are so convinced of this that we consider it the very essence of our priestly work.

So, it seems, did St. Paul and the other apostles. We like to go back to those cornerstones of the Church and find in them the answer to our present problems. Somebody wrote somewhere that Paul, if he were to come back to our world, would become a newspaperman. Maybe so . . . However, there is no conjecture about the fact that he did convert his prison guards, that he did talk religion to people he met in the public squares, that he did gather acquaintances and strangers together to talk to them about Christ. We know that he did win people to Christ, and in these ways. Why not, we ask ourselves, use these same methods today?

People will not be surprised if we bring up the subject of religion; they accept that as our "job." Hence, it seems fool= ish to take roundabout ways for something they expect us to do. Since priests are so few, it is foolish to burden them with complicated and indirect approaches to possible converts (as we said so often in our section on activities), when a simple, direct avenue is open to us. We simply cannot do everything, and if, as we have found, the direct apostolate brings us more souls than we can satisfy and guide then it certainly is impossible for us to give time to anything less immediately apostolic.

Another reason why we are boosting the direct apostolate is the fruit of much reflection. We have seen priests who "suc‑ceed" in the ministry, because they are good choirmasters, or athletes, or theatrical producers. Without sarcasm, we came to the conclusion that such men could not have been given Holy Orders simply because of the possession of these natural gifts; while it is helpful to have them, they certainly have no necessary connection with the priesthood. They certainly are not intended by God as the basis of a fruitful ministry; nor does He con‑demn all those not possessing any such natural endowment to mediocrity in His service. It seems to us that Christ, who calls and picks His priests, must send them to a work which will be possible for them simply because they are priests. To say that he measures the worth of his anointed servants by any other standard than the love that impels them is more than absurd. And so, from that conclusion, we say that the direct apostolate is the one form of his service in which his love suffices, no matter how ungainly a priest may otherwise be. He loves the souls which God made and redeemed, and he wants them all to come in; they, in turn, respond to this single‑minded, selfless motive, and they will come in. At least, they will come in more often than they do through our present oblique efforts.

❡ These arguments sound fine, but we still want to know how you go about applying this direct apostolate.

First of all, we shall try to explain the priests' part in it, because they are the foundation of the whole structure. Later on, we will tell you how the parishioners are mobilized and what weapons they use.

In the course of a priest's day he makes a great many contacts with souls. Here at Colombes, all the priests consciously try to use these meetings, these incidents, as stepping‑stones towards winning a soul for Christ. For that, the human side of the priest is very important. Lest we seem to be contradicting what was just said about the sufficiency of the priesthood itself, we hasten to explain that we never said that human qualities had no importance; we were talking about the false opinion which makes these accidentals more important than the priesthood itself. With that understood, we can proceed. Because we are men, we must use our humanity to draw our fellow-men, just as Christ took on our nature in order to make it possible for us to come to God. Hence, the priestly character within us must manifest itself in human understanding; Christ must be visible in our poor flesh. We have to use little things, like smiles and handshakes and friendliness, just as he would have done in our times. We priests will admit all this, and we have heard it repeated in one way or another since our seminary days. It might help us to see whether or not we are living this truism.

Allow me to project myself into all this, to bring out what I mean by using little things. I have a wretched memory and cannot remember whether I met this man or where I met that woman. It has been terribly embarrassing many, many times. To avoid such embarrassment I have got into the habit of greeting everyone by a wave or a nod or a smile. At first the people were astonished to have the parish priest greet them on the street or in stores, but, after a while, they got used to it, and even liked it. Now they greet me and the other priests first; everybody does it. In fact, a priest friend of mine says that he can tell when he is in Sacré Cœur parish by the fact that everyone starts saying "hello" to him. Maybe a story like this seems to over-simplify the apostolate, but it has been my honest experience that the step from a greeting to a conversion is not very long.

There is no appeal here for priests to become back-slappers and hail-fellows-well-met. All we advocate is a natural, casual way of talking, an ability to make small-talk. "Weeping with those who weep and rejoicing with those who are joyful." We want everyone in the parish to feel that we are with them, that we are theirs. That is not easy, as indeed we know. We have a different background, a different vocabulary, different tastes. I remember a young priest who tried to strike up a conversation with a mill-worker. In an effort to break the ice between him and the old man, he mentioned that his father had been a mill-worker too. "Is that so, Father? I never would have thought so." What was intended as a polite compliment contained a lot of bitter truth. We tend to become artificial when dealing with men and women who work for a living, and they, in turn, are uncomfortable in their dealings with us. Whether we actually are or not, we act and sound like people from the "other side of the tracks," and that handicaps our efforts in the direct apos-tolate. To overcome such drawbacks we have to make intense efforts to know our people, their jobs, their troubles; a good beginning for us is to stop them in the street and chat a bit, or to stop at a doorstep and exchange a few words with a family. There is no great value in accepting dinner invitations, and there can be great harm in them if we go too often to one house, or if we go only to the more comfortable ones.

❨ *Chatting in the streets or doorways sounds like very inadequate contact.*

There are better ones; for example, the ones with people who drop into the sacristy for one reason or another. That drab little sacristy can be a haven of peace for many people who come in for some "business" purpose but find there a priest who is interested in their life and troubles. Too often those who do come to arrange for a baptism or wedding feel awkward and bothersome; they are not asked to sit down, nor is there any evident pleasure in the priest's face or manner. The sacristy has the atmosphere of a city hall office, and the priest acts like a hurried and tired clerk. How foolish we are to miss these opportunities! Here we have a chance to talk with parishioners we rarely see. We have a chance to show that the marriage or baptism they came to arrange is no mere ceremony, but an integral, essential part of their lives; we can make Christianity, immortality, grace come down from the realm of the abstract so that these intangibles will fit into these lives. These sacristy visits are precious opportunities ... But we are in a hurry to get back to the priests' house and read the paper; so, according to our temperament, we growl or joke our way through the interview, and the opportunity is lost. It would be foolish, of course, to believe all the reasons that people give for their abandonment of religion, but so many of them say that it was due to some sort of upset with a gruff priest that we should be most careful not to give anyone a chance to blame us for his loss of God. It is a question of fact, not of logic. We know priests that we are afraid to approach, and we can imagine what his parishioners go through. We know Catholics who have gone through a civil marriage rather than go back to a parish priest who ranted and raved when they went to him during their engagement. These are small things? We are not so sure.

Other good contacts can be made at the time of the chil= dren's First Communion. We always meet the youngster's par= ents, and always manage to get across the idea that it would be a wonderful sight to see the father and mother receiving our Lord on that morning too. Many parents had not even thought of that; when reminded, many do receive. Again, when somebody stops us to bless a medal or a rosary, it never hurts to stop and talk a while with them. I recall one young girl who asked me to bless something one afternoon, and simply because the priest stopped and talked with her, a tragedy was averted in her life. Or again, in the confessional we can do incalculable good for the cause of Christ. It honestly seems to us that a priest could make an apostolate of staying around the church, and talking with as many people as he could, those who come in for a visit, to pray at a statue or to light a candle. Even though he could not and should not start a conversation with everyone, his time and effort would be rewarded in the tears he dried, the worries he calmed, the doubts he answered.

All of these examples are commonplace, and purposely so. They prove that even "routine" ministry is filled with oppor= tunities for the direct apostolate if we want to look for them. A priest who is awake can find many such—provided he is willing to "waste" time with people who are half=way willing to talk to him. He can be a brusque official, or he can be a priest.

One thing to remember is that all our other efforts will fail unless we are kind and sympathetic. We may have grandiose and clever ideas about liturgical revivals, about sermons, about all sorts of activities but they are as sounding brass and tin= kling cymbal. Unless we are loved by the ones we are trying to win, and unless we love them, we shall most certainly fail. The greatest of these is charity still.

❡ *I suppose that you encourage people to drop into the priest's house when they want to talk over something?*

Yes, we do; and since we do, we try to make sure that nothing in our house is going to make visitors feel uncomfort= able. We are in a working=class parish, and so we try to have our furnishings and their arrangement simple and ordinary; if they are luxurious, none of our people will feel at home. If they do not feel at home, they will not come back, and we shall not be able to influence them as we might have done. Abbé Godin advised priests to make their rooms fit the type of person they were trying to attract. For example, young stu= dents would feel at ease in a somewhat disorderly, cluttered room. In any case, our quarters should never be sumptuous and ornate, for our lives should be a reflection of Christ's and not a denial of it.

❡ *You seem to be restating Maritain's slogan about "being one with your people."*

Exactly, for it is our purpose in life to become Christ to this portion of His inheritance. We are not meant to be kings, but commoners; we are to be neighborly, friendly, sympathetic, and kind, so that it becomes almost second nature to us to "feel" with our people. During the war we did our best to be like this to everyone around us, and it was noticed and remarked upon by many persons who never came inside the church door; we had a chance to bring Christ to souls who once would have scoffed at the idea that they would talk to a priest.

¶ *Besides all these more or less accidental contacts, tell us about the ones you deliberately make.*

As we shall explain, we make systematic visits to every home in the parish. For a parish priest, no other function of his min⸗ istry is so pressing, no other function is so suited to reaching the great numbers who are his parishioners despite the fact that they do not come to church. The Curé of Ars believed this, and practiced it. The immense size of city parishes makes it much more difficult than it is in country towns, but organized teamwork by pastor and curates can accomplish it. We cannot expect to find everyone at home, but we always come back, like insurance men. All this takes up a great deal of our time, but it is time well spent—better spent than it would be on something less directly connected with the preaching of the Word of God.

Lest we be misunderstood, let us make clear here that the purpose of our home visits is not simply to pass the time of day, not simply to hear the family gossip; we come to talk about religion, and that is what we do. As a matter of fact, we firmly believe that we are expected to talk about God and His affairs, and that we scandalize people when we carry on a completely secular conversation with them.

¶ *How do you go about these home visits?*

There are several possible ways. One is to go from house to house and from street to street until the whole parish has been covered. This method (if such it is) takes too long, and produces little fruit; we might start a few children coming to catechism, and we might get a nodding acquaintance with a great many people. Never much more than that.

Another way is to use the information that our militants can give us about different families in their neighborhood, and to use the publicity that they can give others about us. It helps, when we come into a house and know a little about the family; we can understand better the reception they give us, and we can stress what we know will interest them most. More about all this later.

Still another method was suggested by a priest in Nice, namely, the idea of home-meetings. Basically, it is the same practice as that used by the apostles, for they used to gather the faithful in someone's private home, and there preach to them. We arrange with a militant Catholic to come to his house on such and such a date; he and his wife tell the neighbors, and invite them over. Of course, many refuse, but enough always appear to make the meeting lively. On the appointed night, one of the priests drops in and gets the
conversation round to the subject of religion, gradually or abruptly. Since everyone present has come for that very purpose, it is not a hard subject to approach. Once the awkwardness and novelty have worn off, the questions come thick and fast, and the evening is all too short. The priest leaves fairly early, but the hosts can easily prolong the discussion after his departure; it is an excellent occasion for them to do their own type of apostolic work and to wield an influence over their own kind.

The above description is not meant as a typical one, because these home-meetings have almost infinite possibilities; we can get neighbours together, or parents, friends, members of the same nationality or workers from the same factory. They are not hard to organize, because our militant Catholics are proud to work on them, and people seem to want them; their timidity vanishes in the sincerity of the questions they want to ask. Because of the great interest in some particular matters, it may be advisable to start a home study-club, so as to treat the subject more satisfactorily, especially since we can be quite sure that the interested parties are not likely to come round to the church for their answers.

❨ *Even your routine ministry must furnish occasions for "follow-ups" at homes.*

It does indeed. When somebody comes to the rectory to arrange for a funeral, we always drop in at the house to express our sympathy. Before or after baptisms, we have a talk with the parents of the child. At marriages the priest who has charge of that section of the parish visits the couple. Before All Souls' Day, the families of those who have died during the past year receive a personal invitation from us, asking them to come and pray for their dead. Every feast day of the Church provides similar opportunities.

❡ *What kind of a reception do you receive?*

Generally, people are surprised to see us, but most of them are friendly enough; there are plenty of exceptions to this, but they are, after all, exceptions. What does not surprise them is that we bring up the subject of religion; they really expect that of us, even the non-churchgoers. Our own timidity is more of a barrier than any hostility from the people, because, strangely enough, we priests do feel awkward when we talk about Christ to individuals—especially to men. It does take courage, and a little persistence, too, because men usually tell us that they will call in their wife—as though religion was her concern. So we have to bring them around to see that religion is not a strictly feminine preserve; usually it is not too difficult, once we gather the courage and the skill for the correct approach.

❡ *Yours must be a satisfying and absorbing priestly life.*

Honestly, it is, precisely because it is priestly work. It starts from God and ends in Him. Remember, too, that it is the work of a "team" of priests, who pray and work as a closely knit spiritual unit. Because of the size of our heavily populated parish, we have split it up into sections, each one in charge of one member of the team but not mathematically nor exclusively. By that we mean that the division is not made by dividing the number of priests into the total population, nor by making each priest "king" of his own territory only, with no concern for the rest of the parish. Rather, each is given a "district" as his special field, but with the understanding that his section is an essential part of the whole parish, and must be so considered.

❡ *Do you think it would be a good idea to make parishes smaller?* Yes, we do. It is a physical impossibility to know our people in these oversized parishes; consequently, Christianity no lon= ger reaches the "excess" population. In the Middle Ages, when our cities were much smaller, and our Christianity much more real, there were many more places of worship. Nowadays, we have one church for 25,000 to 100,000 parishioners—and we wonder why the worship of God is not a reality for all these souls. How can it be? When Cardinal Verdier[2] started build= ing city=chapels, he acted on the theory that the more places of worship we have, the more Christians we shall have; the results have proved him right, and his plans merit expansion. These chapels should be parishes, and not mere absorbers of the overflow from the main church, because we are firmly con= vinced that worship must be a community function. Connected with the number of parishes is the number of priests assigned to them. As things are now, assignments are made on a basis of how many practising Catholics there are; one parish will have ten priests, while another will have four even though the total population of both is about the same. Naturally, there are more confessions, Masses, etc., needed in one than in the other, but we are thinking of missionary work. Surely that cannot be con= sidered less important than the "routine" demands on priests.

In any case, it is usually possible to use curates more effi= ciently. Instead of giving them some particular activity for their personal charge, as we sketched further back, we think that it is more practical to give each of them a part of the parish as his mission=field. When every curate is concerned only about his own little groups, how can he be expected to see the parish as a whole? How can he be expected to reach those who are not a part of his group, or of any group? When, on the other hand, activities are cut to a minimum, and each priest is a part of a team that concentrates on the entire parish, it is possible for him to be a real priest, a real missioner. Over and above

---

2   Jean Verdier (1864–1940), Archbishop of Paris from 1929 to 1940.

the practicality of such a plan, it has the tremendous advantage of making a new curate feel that he is wanted and needed, and not merely "assigned." He can develop his talents and his gifts to the utmost, in union with the rest of the curates and the parish priest. He has a chance to know his section and his people intimately, and he can develop and direct militant Catholics on the spot. He can live his apostolate.

In a set-up like this the pastor has a delicate role to play. He must know how to direct without domineering; he must encourage initiative without creating jealousy; he must realize that a young priest can see and accomplish possibilities that are beyond his own powers.

However, despite all the good that this decentralizing process can do for priests, this is not its sole purpose. It also stimulates the life of the parish as a whole. As Cardinal Suhard said when he came to the diocese, "The whole parish must become a mission field, and it can be this by becoming a community."

❡ *Explain how you go about convincing your "regular" parishioners of the missionary purpose of the parish.*

First of all, we have to drive home the idea that a Christian has to be an apostle! Never delude yourself into thinking that this is an easy matter. If you try to preach this to the stolid, respectable, "Sunday-Mass" Catholics, you will know what we mean. It takes time and repetition, by sermons, conversations, pamphlets, until the churchgoers begin to see what we mean. It takes time and repetition. An example of what we mean can be seen in two very different reactions to what happened at a Midnight Mass here a few Christmasses ago. One man—a pillar of the church, by the way—complained because he and his family were unable to get good seats. The church had been packed by persons not seen at Mass from one end of the year to the other, and he thought that preference should be given to the regular churchgoers. Another parishioner happened to speak to me about the crowded condition of the church, but this one was glad about it. She admitted that she had not been able to see the altar, but seeing strangers in there meant more to her than her own satisfaction.

I mentioned these two opposite reactions to the congregation in the following Sunday sermon, in order to help impress them with the fact that we are more concerned about "outsiders" than about our faithful flock. Gradually they come to understand; gradually the vision of the thousands around them who know not Christ becomes a reality to them too. We stress the impor= tance of the Pope's statement that all Catholics must take part in Catholic Action, so as to help them see that their apostolate is an essential part of their Christianity, and not "something extra." Once that concept is grasped, the Christian community unconsciously becomes more of a community; its concern for those outside the Faith draws all its members together in love and in labor.

The second stage, following upon their conviction of the necessity of becoming apostles, consists in making apostles out of them. Many of them will confuse Catholic Action with the apostolate, as indeed do many priests. Many of them will think that they are meant to round up children for catechism class, to talk couples into having their marriages "fixed up," or to persuade those that have lapsed to start coming to Mass or Novenas. All this is good, but it is not what we mean or what we need. We are not trying to patch up the ills of the world around us; we are trying to rebuild it completely. For that we need real militants who will fill their surroundings with the spirit of Christ, so that men and women will want to know and follow this Christ. We are not interested in gain= ing recruits for our church services, but we are passionately interested in gaining recruits for Christ. The creation of this new and revolutionary Christian atmosphere depends on the common efforts of each and every Christian; it cannot be left to the members of the specialized movements we mentioned a while ago. Every man has his own little world to influence, to change, to Christianize. That is what we must do as united individuals.

Convincing people of this necessity is difficult, because most of us would rather be apostolic in some easier way; we would rather face the shamed embarrassment of lukewarm Catho= lics than the possible scorn of non=believers. To put across the proper persuasion we use every possible means — talks, meet= ings, personal conversations; in the district meetings, the priest in charge constantly emphasizes the influence we should have on some particular point. Maybe this particular street has such a bad reputation that we must have a militant family living in it; maybe the corner barber=shop needs instruction on the kind of magazines it provides for the customers; maybe the daily line=up of people waiting for rationed food is a good place to discuss Christianity.

Every Sunday we announce the special meetings to be held in the different sections of the parish, and we try to make every single Catholic feel invited to them. We want every man and woman to take part in them, and we also want to prevent the growth of the idea that only certain persons are charged with the carrying out of the Christian revolution. We cannot afford to permit the "let=George=do=it" attitude to take root. Some, of course, are actually unable to do much active work, and these we try to impress with the necessity of earnest prayer for the program. Apart from these few exceptions, every single member of the parish has a role to play, according to the tal= ents and the circumstances that God has given him. There is a diversity of gifts, just as there was in the early Church; we do not expect the same results from varying abilities. All that we are trying to convince them of is that each of us has a definite and responsible work to do for Christ; no one is excepted.

Any attempts to organize this apostolate are dangerous. Per= sonal zeal is what we are after. Once a priest erects an organi= zation, with officers and meetings and by=laws, zeal will suffer; that is a proven fact. By some strange quirk in our minds we seem to believe that the founding of an association is equiv= alent to the success of that organization, and we stop trying to do what we joined together to do. No, we need a group of apostles who will be in a constant state of change, because their work demands constant change; we want apostles who will see the work as never done, because what we are trying to do is, actually, never completed. Consequently, we avoid regimentation, lest zeal die. The place of a priest is to guide, to point out possibilities, to talk over results; he is not supposed to rule and dictate, by means of an organization that he, and not the Holy Ghost, brought into being.

❡ *Will there not be confusion and overlapping between what the parochial and the specialized militants do?*
There will be overlapping, but that does not necessarily imply confusion. The Jocists, and the like, can reach and affect where parochial apostles cannot. After a little experience, each group finds its proper field.

❡ *Once you have convinced and trained your parochial apostles, what concrete missionary work do they accomplish?*
We have to provide the tools and the occasions, because most of them need more than their original first fervor. They can use the parish magazine that we mentioned previously as a source of ideas to talk about; that is one reason why we insisted above on the magazine's being a propaganda weapon, and not a mere social sheet. They can bring up for discussion some one of the adapted feasts to be held in the parish church; when prudent, they can even invite some interested non-believer to attend, knowing that he will be able to understand it. Every detail of our parish life, because it is directed to the winning of the "outsiders," is built on and for the apostolate, and a convinced believer can be shown how to use it as propaganda.

❡ *What part do you assign the family in your apostolate?*
It has a primary place; we hope to bring that out as we proceed. It is our firm conviction that past efforts in the apostolate have been disappointing precisely because they neglected the family as an object and a means of conquest. Somebody would

do well to make a study of this; here and now we can say only a few words. It seems to us that we should be preparing our young folk for Christian marriage, and helping young married couples to make their homes Christian. These new families are our real source of strength for the immediate future, and we should exert our influence on them. Catechisms, for example, should be so written as to have some value for parents, as well as children; to do that we can expand and supplement the ones now in use. Our ceremonies, too, should leave the family together. There is no point in separating a family as soon as it comes in the door of the church, sending the children to one part of the church, the father and mother to others. Our entertainments should not split up a family either, but could easily be directed to the entire group. One of the most valuable aspects of the direct aposto= late, with its home meetings, is that it definitely tends to bring families, as such, closer together; it unites them in a common cause, in direct reaction to almost everything else around us.

❧ *Do your lay apostles really have the time and the ability to carry out all these ideas?*
That is a difficult question to answer. Instead, we should like to put forward an idea of which we are fond, one that we have thought about for a long while. Why should we not have a Congregation of Sisters who would devote themselves solely to the direct apostolate? As things are now, we have flourishing Orders doing almost every conceivable kind of work, ranging from orphanages to hospitals. Not for one moment would we even hint that this work is not valuable; it is indeed, and we would be lost without it. But, if there were a Congregation which would devote itself exclusively to a door=to=door preaching of Christ, without any secondary motive, we believe that a tremen= dous uprising of Christianity would result. Everyone accepts nuns and respects them. In lay or religious dress, they could be the Christian equivalent of social workers, or the Western equiv= alent of mission catechists; better still, they could provide the Catholic equivalent of the evangelical zeal of the Salvation Army.

¶ *It is time you gave us a concrete example of your experiences in the direct apostolate.*

All right, but remember, we are not setting ourselves up as models. What we say will show our failures as well as our success; being ordinary, and not learned men, we have learned as we went along. For whatever it is worth, we will give you a summary of the past five years' work in the direct apostolate.

We began by a month of intensive preaching on the apostolate itself, and kept referring to it all during the year. At the end of the month we called a meeting for all the faithful of the parish, and explained our ideas on decentralization. To make the notion understandable, we split the meeting up into groups based on our division of the parish into districts; the priest in charge of each told them that they were each to sit in a special part of the church at next Sunday's Mass. The majority expressed doubts that enough people would come to fill each section, but, thanks to advertising, the doubts were not realized. Merely dividing up the seating arrangement in the church is no great feat. The important fact is that it made the people conscious of their own districts, and convinced them of the possibility of influencing it. That was the beginning. That year was spent in trying to find out how to go about holding meetings and making visits. One of the curates tried the door-to-door system, but it was impossible; another hit upon the one we now use, namely, letting the militants in the neighbourhood direct us. We tried mass-meetings in the different sections, but they involved more entertainment than apostolicity, and we abandoned them.

The second year we spent in organizing—dull perhaps, but very necessary. By the third year we were ready for home-meetings. At first, we simply mentioned the idea, and waited for reactions from the people; there was no point in forcing our plans on them. It took two months before anyone invited us to hold a meeting in his house, but, from then on, they spread rapidly and are commonplace now. As a matter of fact, the lay people did far more than we to make them succeed;

they know each other so much better than we can hope to that they adapt the discussion to the audience with remarkable skill. During Lent of that year we held thirty-four such sessions; of the average ten or twenty persons present, normally only three or four were practicing Catholics. We started with themes like the Church's attitude to Nazism or the problem of deporting workers into Germany; gradually we shifted to the reason for wars, the problem of suffering, the Providence of God. The questions we were asked gave us clues as to what to talk about, and they also revealed the torment in the souls of the questioners.

By the end of that third year, we got the idea of district missions, and began to plan for them; during the fourth year, we started to hold them for two weeks in each section of the parish. The first week was spent with all of the priests trudging from street to street and door to door in that particular section, as directed by the curate in charge there. We went into every home and we talked about religion, frankly and proudly and lovingly, and usually we were more than welcome. Some came back to Christ on the spot. In our talks with them, we emphasized that this mission was for their neighborhood, and that we thought they would like to take part in it, as the personal appeal and the localized setting made a good impression. At night, we held home-meetings all over the chosen area, and they were very well attended. For the last part of the second week we held services at Church; a sermon reviewed the general principles we had been stressing, and then we acted out the Passion. After each tableau, during which a priest chanted the Gospel story in the vernacular, the preacher outlined the main points of the scene; we ended with an appeal for a return to God who made and saved us. The audience was impressed, we know. They were not immediately, nor always, converted, but, for many of them, it was the first time they had heard the word of God. That was something. We had taken down the names and addresses of all present, and we followed up this contact.

Unfortunately, we could not keep up the pace we set for ourselves, and now we hold one or two such missions a year.

Together with these, we have what we call the "Journey of the Blessed Mother," just as many another parish has had before us. On Sunday night we bless one statue of our Lady for each of the parish sections, and give it to a militant from each one of them; he is to see that the statue goes from home to home, staying one day with each family. Most families wanted to keep it longer. As a matter of fact, it has stayed as long as two weeks in places where we had thought no one would welcome it! Along with the statue goes a little leaflet of prayers to be said before it by the family every night. This "Journey" has some marvelous advantages. It gives us an occasion for visiting every family which keeps it; we bring a little memento of the incident, and we talk about what it means. Also it enables the militant in charge to gather all the families together on the last night of the devotion; the priest comes over, too, and explains our Lady's place in our lives. Only two or three houses closed their doors to the Blessed Mother, and many who took her in were complete strangers at church. She is loved, and she will help those who do not realize that they need her help.

All that we described here is but a fragment of the sum total of possibilities in the direct apostolate. Whoever tries it will find new and different approaches, based on local circumstances. The field is inexhaustible.

❡ *I do not want to quibble, but there seems to be some inconsis-tency in the fact that you used Lent as a special time for these missions. Lent has no meaning for non-believers.*

We agree with you, but, remember, these were not ordinary Lenten Devotions; they were an offensive during Lent. We chose that time because the Church means those forty days as a special time of grace; all the mortifications and prayers of Christians are calling down God's help in a special way during this season. Moreover, it is a time intended for effort and for reflection on what it means to be a follower of Christ. That is why we chose this season. If we had done no more than gather together those who already believe, your protest would

REVOLUTION IN A CITY PARISH

be valid; but, since we made every effort to draw those who do not believe, and tried to make the service appeal to them, we have to justify our choice of time.

What results can you show?

For one thing, there has been a steady increase in Easter Communions. One Easter Week we were approached by six adults who wanted to receive Baptism or First Communion; what they said to us shows that it is the cumulative effect of our work that counts and not the individual conversations or meetings or services. One of these men told us that we had visited him several months ago, but that he had received us coolly, because he was not then interested in religion. Later on, he heard us speaking at a funeral, and he realized for the first time that we evidently believed what we preached! Still later, he accepted an invitation to a home-meeting, and was forced to think seriously of the message of Christ. He came to Mass for Palm Sunday and Easter; the sight of everyone going up to receive Almighty God made him realize that he was an outsider, and he was determined to ask for Baptism.

The story is an unadorned fact. It is a proof of the gradual penetration of a soul by repeated and varied approaches to Christ. It is a testimony to the worth of the direct apostolate.

Still, everything that you have been doing is for adults. Are you completely neglecting the children in these plans?

We were wondering how long it would take you to get to that. It is usually one of the first objections put to us by fellow-priests. There seems to be some necessary connection between priestly labors and the care of the children. Despite the impression which our section on clubs may have given, we hasten to assure you that we are looking out for the children too. It is possible to be concerned about both young and old without neglecting either. You see, we are more interested in evangelizing the youth than in educating them; we are not meant to relieve parents of their responsibilities, and we do not intend to do so. We try to give them a meaning of Christianity which will be suited to their age and will also be real and personal. After First Communion, we group them according to districts, and put them in charge of one of their own members, under the eye of a militant lay-person from that section of the parish; their work is that of the junior members of the Jocists.

By a development of their own life with Christ these young people can make him known to their own age group in a peculiarly effective way. They become little Christian communities in their own right, and they bring the influence of their convictions to everyone whom they know. Naturally, they have games and programs for themselves, under the direction of laymen and laywomen. Most of all, they are made to feel the meaning of communal parish life, its unity and community. We do not expect these children to be present in herded groups at every church service; we want them to be apostles, and not mere attendants. During the year there are special feasts for them, and they come willingly and eagerly. They are young and are still to be formed. We are content with forming them. ✢

✢[4]✢
Dynamic Christianity

❦ *What do you think of the idea that we must have a Christianity which startles people, a Christianity which is dynamic?*

The idea appeals to us very much, even though these phrases are rather objectionable. This idea is founded on the undeniable truth that Christianity is static. It no longer causes any surprise or scandal or admiration or imitation; it has become classified, labeled and forgotten, just as any dull subject is dismissed. When it is discussed, the comment is about its ceremonies or diplomacy, and not about its meaning. It has become part of the order of things, exactly as teachers and judges and doctors have, and it has ceased to conflict with the lives of the mass of men. Christianity is here, but we can forget about it.

Why should this be so? Partly because our Christianity appears to the outside world only as a ritualistic system which does little or nothing to change the men and women who practice those rites; partly because we have ceased to be an influential community; partly because Christianity has reduced itself to attendance at Sunday Mass, without any evidence of the vital nature of Christ's teachings. The modern pagans who notice us do not see in us the striking characteristics which caught and held the pagans of ancient Rome. They see only that we are not very different from themselves, and unfortu‹nately, they are correct. We go to Mass, and they do not; that is the extent of the difference for most of us. Christianity has ceased to be "dangerous;" it involves no risks, no sacrifice, and it hardly causes a flurry in the affairs of the world.

Consequently, it is understandable why non‹Catholics should not be interested in investigating the mystery of our Faith, for they see no evidence of it. Nor is it strange that they should be untouched by the burning love of Christ, since

His professed followers fail to transmit the effects of His love. We are not obviously anxious to communicate his love, but rather appear to be satisfied with the untruth that each man's religion is his own affair. We are content to leave the rest of the world in its unrealized misery, nor would we dream of startling them by the Cross of Christ, which we bear about in our bodies.

¶ *Who is to blame for this?*

Partly the people, because they should know better and should do better. The greater fault is ours, we priests, because we have substituted ritualism for the pentecostal flames. We do not demand enough of our people. That statement does not mean that we are too easy with individual weaknesses. We should be "too easy" with particular failings, just as Christ was before us. We mean rather that priests do not ask enough of the Christian community. Instead of transforming our parish-ioners into a living, united group, we feel that it is enough to get them to come to services. The more we have, the better we are satisfied, as if it were enough to have the name of Christian and nothing more. We administer the sacraments, but make no effort to instill into our parishioners a sacramental life. Like the thousands of sects, we want to increase the number of our adherents, while seeming to ignore that we must make God live in man. Even Catholics have lost the meaning of our rites and our outlook, and so people think of them as some sort of "hocus-pocus."

¶ *What is the reason?*

It is obvious. Think of how easy it is to become a Christian. We put a little water on a child's head, and the parents go home to celebrate their offspring's redemption with a pagan feast. Later on, the lad will come for a few years of catechism, ending in a touching ceremony, a sermon that makes all the mothers weep, and the inspiring sight of boys and girls going up to the altar rail for First Communion, the "church" part of the day is followed by a celebration long to be remembered. Still later, this typical Christian comes to arrange for marriage, and to pay the priest. After this ceremony a new Catholic family begins its existence, without a single distinguishing feature to set it off from the neo-pagan families around it. When the time comes to die, a Christian burial is a matter of course; with it ends the life-span of a "follower of Christ."

There we see an ordinary example of Christianity—the reli-gion which once turned the whole world upside down.

When we hear radio orators declaiming about our "struggle for Christianity," we cannot help but wonder what that phrase means to our Catholics.

❡ *How would you suggest establishing these dynamic communities?*

Before we offer our suggestions, for whatever they may be worth, there are a few qualifications to be made. When we put down our thoughts on this subject, it is done because we feel that we are obliged to share our conclusions with the findings and hopes of many other priests and lay-people. However, when we put them down, it is with the understand-ing that the Church is the final judge of what is to be done or not done.

The first reform should begin in our conduct of parish life. The manner in which we conduct the routine affairs of the parish should reflect a burning thirst for souls outside the family of Christ. It should be so evident and so sincere that our parishioners will come to share it. Particularly, we should administer the sacraments in such a way that the sacramental life we talk about will be understood and realized. In baptism, for example, we must make sure that the meaning and conse-quences of this fundamental sacrament are understood.

Parents bring in their children for baptism much as they would for vaccination; it makes no difference that they them-selves do not practice Catholicism, nor that they have no intention of rearing this child in the Faith. Baptism is sim-ply one of those things that everyone goes through. It is an important social function. You know how it takes place. Most of the men present have anticipated the celebration; every= one crowds around to watch the curious ceremonies, and the godparents know that they are in for a teasing if they get through the Credo and Pater without a halt. Worse still is the common practice in maternity hospitals around Paris. The priest walks into the ward and announces that he will baptize all the babies whose mothers are willing. Nothing is known about the mother, less about the father, and yet we pour the saving waters on one and all who ask for them.

It makes our blood boil to see abuses like these and to be the agents of such a farce, and yet the people would think we had lost our minds or our religion were we to rebuke them for their ignorance. What are we to do? It is a terribly hard thing to refuse baptism to a helpless child. And yet the teaching of the Church, as expressed in canon law and elsewhere, is that children of infidels should not be baptized except in danger of death, unless a Christian rearing is reasonably guaranteed. The qualifications required of godparents is another proof of the attitude of the Church. Moreover, when we baptize so freely, we rob the sacrament of part of its meaning; it is intended as a sign that this person is now a member of the Christian community, with all the accompanying obligations and privi= leges. Remember that our Lord said "No one, unless he believe and be baptized, will be saved," and he gave us no permission to forget the first part of that statement. Yet the children we baptize will find it hard to believe and to practice that belief, in the face of daily, practical disbelief on the part of their parents. We are bringing into the Church of Christ souls over whom the Church will have no influence.

Consider the common practice of missionaries concern= ing baptism. They are severe on this point. They have to be. Because they are, the meaning of baptism is caught and the new Christians are fervent; their faith means a great deal to them and has a great influence on their pagan neighbors. The same practice, and the same result, was true of the early Church.

❦ *Still, refusal of baptism would drive a family outside the Church forever. There would be absolutely no hope of priestly or lay apostolic influence on them.*

That objection bothers us too. However, we cannot permit this very real abuse just to avoid displeasing people. If refusal did become a general practice, the growing generations would have a chance to see Christianity as it is, instead of accepting it as an uninteresting, uncomprehended part of their lives. This is a delicate problem, and we do not pretend to have answered it, even though we did bring it up here. A thing like this cannot be solved by any individual priest, and it will not be solved by anger and tongue‑lashings. The old adage about honey rather than vinegar is still true. At every baptism, we must try to explain the importance of this step. All of our efforts come back, as we said so often before, to the education and winning of the adults, the parents. Until the parents have come to understand Christianity, we are at an impasse.

❦ *Despite your gloomy picture, it is true that most of these children are sent to you for catechism and First Communion instructions.*

They are, but what does that prove? About eighty percent of the children we baptized come back to us for religious instruc‑ tion, but that fact is little comfort to us. If the preparation were not demanded, the youngsters would not be sent for it; the parents would be satisfied with the celebration only. To show what we mean, there is a classic case in our parish files. There was a lad who had told his mother, over a period of two whole years, that he was a member of the catechism class here; as a matter of fact, we had not even seen the boy once. By chance his mother discovered the fact of his deceit on the very afternoon of the Confirmation ceremony after two years of unbroken absence! Fortunately all turned out well, and that boy is now one of our leading apostles. However, the incident does prove that parents, even friendly and practicing parents, have almost no concern about the religious training of their children.

They send them off to catechism, just as they were once sent off, and that is the end of their problem. The motive is not so much to ensure that their sons and daughters will know and love Christ as to keep up an old family tradition.

When one or another of the parents is positively hostile to the Church, the situation is worse, as anyone familiar with the appalling leakage after First Communion will agree. Sometimes the religious training we give to these children of anti-religious homes serves as an oasis of faith; sometimes the youngsters do persevere beautifully. Yet we have to admit that something is wrong. The Church has had charge of almost all the children of France for the last hundred years and yet most of those children have left her fold. We might honestly call First Communion day the day of Solemn Apostasy and be done with it. Without exaggerating, we can say that eighty percent of these new communicants will have ceased receiving the sacraments within three or four years. Yes, we have children just as we have had every year for the last century; every year we have the same hopes, and every year the same disappointment.

❪ *Maybe the blame rests on the catechists?*

It is easy enough to shift the blame around, but it is hardly fair to the catechists. If they are at fault, so are we pastors; if we want to cast aspersions on their teaching ability or on their knowledge, we must admit that we have the primary responsibility. While we are on this subject, we wonder why a body of salaried catechists could not be trained, just as is done on the foreign missions. Furthermore, we wonder why our catechisms have to be so abstract and so ponderous and why the language has to be so theological. Anyone who thinks that the children understand or retain very much of the "religion" we teach them has only to question a class about last year's matter; the answers are informative, even if discouraging! Somehow, and soon, we must find a way to teach the truths of our Lord Jesus Christ in words and examples that modern children can understand. A good teacher can supplement the defects of the catechism, but we should still be able to provide all the teachers with a suitable manual.

¶ *Some of the blame certainly rests on the careless parents.*
No one will deny that. The formation of an impressionable child is begun and completed by the parents, more than by any other influence. If the father and mother are indifferent or hos‑ tile, our efforts will, ordinarily, be counteracted, and the hope we had of forming a new Christian vanishes. Consequently, we repeat that it is absolutely necessary to win over the adults of these pagan times. Without the conquest of parents, our dreams for their children are vain and bitter delusions.

¶ *But, until the parents are won over, what are we supposed to do?*
We will answer the question gradually. First of all, think about our manner of teaching religion. Here, in de‑Christianized cities, we act as if we were in completely Catholic surroundings; the books used are the same. If anything, the priests of the Catholic sections demand more of children who really know their faith, while we are easier on those who know almost nothing about it. We forget that really Catholic youngsters need only to have their firm background supplemented, while the other children need a thorough grounding.

If we did go about the establishment of a catechumenate, we certainly should plan it for an age group older than our present catechism class age. Since we mean the training of the cate‑ chumenate to result in a life‑dedication to the cause of Christ, it is absurd to ask such an outlook from ten or twelve year olds. In the first place, they can hardly be expected to realize what we are asking of them; secondly, they are so much under the influence of their non‑believing parents that our training is usually of little lasting value. By the time they are twenty‑five, their only recollections of religious training are hazy notions that no one really believes; by the time their own children come along, they hand down the same unbelieving attitude, and the cycle is continued. Consequently, our emphasis must be on the slightly older children who are beginning to mature. Even our best efforts towards adapting the catechism and improving the teaching of the younger boys and girls will not bring us a comparable result. Between the ages of fifteen and twenty, they are beginning to realize for themselves the possibilities we are trying to uncover for them.

Bear in mind that we are not presuming to change diocesan regulations. It is a matter of speaking our minds on a subject we have observed for a long while, reaching the conclusion that the present catechism set-up produces more indifferent Christians than it does Christians. Fewer boys and girls would come to our classes if we succeeded in starting the idea of an adolescent catechumenate which would end in a more or less solemn dedication to the apostolate two years later. Despite the falling off in numbers there would be other more important gains. We firmly believe that subsequent apostasy would be decreased and that the spirit of communal Christianity would be much more firmly rooted. If our only concern is to be for numbers, we ought to resign ourselves to the present state of spiritual stagnation.

❮ *Your statements seem to be in direct contradiction to the teach= ing of Pius X on Children's Communions.*

This objection was expected, too. In reality, there is no contradiction, because the Pope was certainly talking about children of Catholic families, and not about our neo=pagans. He meant youngsters who had grown up in religious surround= ings, who had imbibed the faith with their mother's milk, who had breathed the spirit of Christ all the days of their young lives. Surely, no one would make such a case for the spiritually undernourished children we know.

❮ *What about the Sacrament of Matrimony? Surely you cannot disregard existing custom, and refuse the nuptial blessing to couples who may not be model Christians.*

Unfortunately, we cannot. We get cases like the young lady who came here to be married, even though she had never made her First Communion; she wanted to be married "at church," and that was that. Another girl honestly answered "yes" to our question about whether she believed in divorce, and we explained that it would be impossible to marry her under such a condition. The next day, her mother came in, breathing fire, and complaining about our cruelty to her daughter. We get cases similar to these every week, and they baffle and sadden us.

❴ *How can we continue to assist at the marriage of persons whom we know to be incapable of receiving the Sacrament of Matrimony?*

Our dogma and moral theology teach us that the validity of the sacrament demands the intention of binding oneself before God for the rest of one's life, or at least demands the absence of a contrary intention. But what do the average couple want? The sacrament? There is no point in pretending that they are interested in anything more than the external ceremony, the pomp and social setting. It is wrong, absolutely wrong, for us to be accomplices in this sham, and to make one of the seven sacraments a mere social affair. One of the worst features of the whole picture is that we priests have become servants to those who can pay for costly weddings. Later on, in our chapter on money, we will go into the question more thoroughly; it is enough to say here that our ceremonies, by some perverse twist, are more accessible to rich pagans than to poor Chris⹀ tians. It hurts to admit it, but everyone knows what kind of a wedding the average working girl gets, at the side altar, and as brief as possible; while a wealthy girl has the main altar, even though it often is the first time she has stepped inside the church for years.

Leaving aside the injustice of the situation, we are doing pos⹀ itive harm when we assist at the marriage of these neo⹀pagans. They do not believe in the indissolubility of marriage, and we are binding them to it! We explain the Church's position, and

we put them in positive bad faith! We get them to make prom=
ises which we and they know to be lies! By the divorces which
ensue we cut them off from the Christian community! Feeling
the way they do, it would have been better for them—and for
us—if we had let them contract a civil marriage.

❡ *In practice, how do you handle these cases?*
First of all, we have to be certain that couples understand the
Church's teaching on marriage; a careless explanation will not
do. Usually they are so receptive at this tremendous moment
of their lives that we should have little trouble. With tact and
zeal we can find the proper approach. Furthermore, we ought
to solemnize the marriage in proportion to the Catholicity of
the prospective partners, so that the whole parish can offer
prayers for their future; for indifferent Catholics, the absence
of solemnity will emphasize the Christian attitude. This is a
delicate matter, but one better solved by Christian principles
than by money or social standing. If a couple cannot accept
the Church's teaching on marriage, it is better to let them go
than to take part in a practical sacrilege. Then those who do
believe and those who do not will see that Christ's doctrine
is a reality and not a matter of form. We will begin to "shock"
and "startle" them with our application of what we believe.
    Even if we ourselves cannot take the first practical steps in
this matter, it is still a subject which should be considered by
the competent authorities. Moreover, it should be weighed by
every priest to whom the good of the Church is more important
than personal position. Thought and prayer and decision are
badly needed.

❡ *No doubt, you feel the same about funerals?*
Even more so, because no sacrament is involved here. As
matters stand now, the degree of honor which the official
Church pays to the mortal remains of Christians is determined
by money, and by nothing else. There will be more about this
later, too. From the point of view of what can be done by way

of example to the Christian community, there is much to com⸗
ment upon. We have seen priests who were furious because
lay apostles failed to accord them the degree of respect they
demanded; we have seen those same priests hold a first⸗class
funeral for notoriously non⸗practicing Catholics. Under those
conditions, how can we honestly say that religion is a "way
of life" and not a mere business? In spite of what canon law
says about ecclesiastical burials for public sinners, we seem to
be honored by a request for a funeral, no matter who asks us.
Some of us even think that we are doing the Church a service,
since another civil funeral is forestalled; we are being charitable
to a poor dead sinner. Maybe so, but our charity should have
started sooner, with instructions about the meaning of "Chris⸗
tian life." Consequently, we think that the funerals of sincere
Christians should be as ceremonious as possible, so that the
whole community may see our attitude; negligent Catholics, on
the other hand, should receive a minimum of public attention.

❛ That seems unjust, because a negligent Catholic needs prayers
more than does an exemplary one.
   But we are not talking about prayers, but about the pomp
and ceremonies accompanying the Mass. Every deceased mem⸗
ber of our parish has a Mass celebrated for the repose of his
soul, and we remember them in special prayers. Certainly no
one is going to be deprived of spiritual benefits simply because
the catafalque was not the best one, or because the Mass was a
low one. These additions are for the survivors, not the deceased.
The purpose of the difference is to bring home to our people
that the Church feels differently about loyal children.

❛ Maybe your people will understand, but the others—the
non⸗believers—will not, and will complain.
   That statement is a revealing one. It shows that we have
grown accustomed to doing unapproved, ambiguous things
simply because we lack the courage to explain the correct
state of affairs to our people. We are afraid they would not

understand or that they would be offended, and so we go on with non-liturgical practices. Rather than do what the Church asks and what the spirit of the liturgy calls for, we prefer not to offend our people; rather than lead, we find it easier to fol= low. If our ceremonies are meant for those who are not Cath= olic and who do not understand, then there is a reason for deviations, where such deviations are allowed; but, since the Church intends her ceremonies only for her baptized children, we should keep them as they have been given to us. That is the difference between liturgy and para-liturgical functions. That is why the Church had the dismissal of catechumens in the Mass. Once a zealous lay-apostle told us that the Mass was not meant for everyone; despite the apparent heresy, she was right. Essentially, it is the assembly of Christians at prayer, offering again the Sacrifice of Calvary. It is not supposed to be the setting for a musical concert, nor the background for a public patriotic rally; those who come for the music or for the civic function only are among those for whom the Mass is meaningless. It is absurd and dangerous to expect a practical pagan to find inspiration or benefit from attendance at Mass. It is not meant for him, and his confusion or boredom is natural.

A more logical and more practical attitude is needed. We ought to distinguish between missionary liturgy and Catholic liturgy. The former will be purposely intended to draw and hold the uninitiated, while the latter will be the official worship of the signed and sealed followers of Christ. Naturally, we do not plan any police methods to ensure the Christianity of everyone who comes in the church door, but we should try to work out a program adapted to all stages of spirituality. It is not wrong to ask people to come to church for ceremonies other than Mass. When they are present, community prayers or chant can be used in a great variety of forms, and with a great deal of profit.

One last thing in connection with this. Somehow it seems paradoxical that we should prepare children so carefully for First Communion but do almost nothing to prepare them for assistance at Mass. We insist upon their attendance at Mass, but this only leads them to think that the Mass is a pious exercise which precedes Communion, without any intrinsic connection between the two. We forget that they are catechu‹ mens, and that they need special training before they can be expected to offer the central mystery of Christianity. A child looks forward with anticipation to the day when our Lord will come to him in Holy Communion; he should, and could, also long for the day when he can join with the whole Christian community in offering the Sacrifice of the Mass.

* * * * * *

Foreign missioners have told us that they could never build up a living Christianity in pagan lands with the system we use at home. This is a powerful observation. Everyone knows that there are important differences between their problems and ours, but still we ought to be able to see the necessity of adopting some of their methods. To do so demands courage and ingenuity, but the prize is precious. All that we have written or shall write is done with that prize in mind. ✠

✠[5]✠
The Clink of Money Round the Altar

❡ *What would you say is the chief obstacle in your attempts to bring Christ to the people around you?*

Without any hesitation we should say that it is the firmly-rooted belief that religion is nothing but a business affair. Our apologetics course, back in the seminary, made no mention of this objection; but it is by far the most powerful barrier to Christ in our day. Almost everyone believes that priests are after money, that religion is a "racket."

❡ *Do you think it wise to treat this question in a book intended for the general public?*

We bring it up deliberately. Any lay-people who read this book will understand that we want to change this scandalous element in the life of the Church, and they will rejoice. Instead of being scandalized, they will feel relieved. After all, they are not fools; they have eyes and ears, and they know what is going on, and they are waiting for someone to be honest enough to admit our common shame. Sometimes it seems as though we priests were willing to ignore this money-abuse. The laity are not. The faithful Catholics do not complain to us, because of excessive respect for our priesthood, but they do complain among themselves about the intolerable burden they are made to bear. When we brought up this matter in discussion with lay persons here at Colombes, we could not miss the relief that was evident on their faces. At last a priest is willing to admit that this problem exists!

Some readers may fear that frankness will only serve as ammunition for the Church's enemies. The truth is that any-thing and everything can be used against us by those in bad faith, and we are not going to worry about that eventuality. We hope that what we are going to say here will be proof that the priesthood is not a "racket." We hope that lay apostles will be able to use this text as undeniable evidence that priests want to change the financial set-up, even to the extent of suppressing sources of revenue, so that they may be more efficient spiritual servants.

¶ *Most of those who raise this objection about money are not serious about it. It is table talk, and means nothing.*

On the contrary, they are serious, and they do believe it. It does no good to tell them even if we could that we priests could have found more lucrative positions if our purpose in life had been the making of a fortune. The faithful realize this, but not the "outsiders." To the majority of men we seem to have a profitable calling, as officials in a huge organization; we are seldom now mistaken for apostles.

We say that this is a potent objection, because we have seen it as such. At every step along the road to the Church the question of money keeps cropping up. Even when a non-Catholic thinks of investigating the claims of the Church, his incipient faith is almost always killed by the unshakeable general opinion that we represent a tremendous money-making scheme, and nothing more. If a non-Catholic can withstand this overwhelmingly unanimous opinion and investigate for himself, he will see differently; but human beings do not usually oppose majorities. Everyone says that priests are interested only in money, and it must be so.

A few incidents will show you why we put so much stress on this matter of money; the examples could be multiplied easily.

I remember a house that I stopped at during one of our district missions. The woman who opened the door did not even give me a chance to say why I was there; she immediately said that she had already contributed. To my shame she said it loud enough for passers-by to hear. That was how zeal for Christ was mistaken; I was trying to speak the word of

God, and she was answering "money." Standing there on the doorstep, I convinced her that I had not come for a collection, and she let me come in; before long, the message of Christ had touched her heart, and she said she would come to the mission. Despite the fact that I had expressly told her that money was not my object, and despite the fact that we had been talking only about religious matters, she tried to force some money on me as I was leaving. The connection between priests and money was deeply rooted. She insisted that I take it, "for the poor;" I told her that she could do that directly herself, and went off, leaving the good woman in her astonishment.

Another stop was at the flat of an old couple who had been away from church since they left their country home. It was fairly easy to get them to promise that they would come to some of the services, but I noticed that they were exchanging embarrassed looks while I was talking. Finally, the old lady let it be known that they were not able to afford to give much, because the pension they received was just enough to live on. When I explained, emphatically, that no money was expected, that no special clothes were required, the relief on their faces was good to see!

How do you account for the fact that this prejudice is so widespread?

Good Lord, put yourself in the position of an ordinary working-man! Of the few contacts he has with priests, very few do not involve money; it is almost inevitable that he should come to consider religion as a financial question. We never demand money for Baptism, but a contribution is certainly expected. We never demand payment for preparing children for First Communion, but the seats in church are paid for on that great day, and the candles the children hold have to be paid for and returned to the sacristy after the ceremony. The clothes the children wear accentuate the difference between the rich and the poor. None of this is simoniacal, and, in fact, none of the money usually goes to the priest himself. However,

it appears to, and the ordinary person will not make any investigation or distinctions; as far as he is concerned, the priest
gets the money, and that is that.

When working-people are married, do you think that they
are blind to the class distinctions we foster or permit? For those
who can afford them, we furnish a bedecked high altar, music,
carpets; for those who cannot, the side altars and silent plain-
ness are good enough. Can we blame them for their bitterness
and their cynicism? We try to tell them that the sacrament is
the same, and that all these external trappings mean nothing;
they ask us why we permit and receive payment for what we
say is vanity. They ask us how we can preach our Lord's words
about wealth, how we can say his "Blessed are the poor." We
can talk all we want, and make as many distinctions as we
want, but the evident facts are against us. In religion, as in
everything else, you pay for what you get.

Ironically enough, we cannot hope to become rich on these
tiny sources of revenue; we have acquired a reputation, but not
wealth. Still, it is that name, that stigma, which is blocking our
efforts to bring Christ to our world. The clink of money round
his altar makes it impossible to hear his words.

❡ *Funerals are a good example of the inequality you mentioned.*
Unfortunately they are. We have to admit it. Even when a
person is dead, his money (or lack of it) determines the honor
which the official Church is willing to grant her child. We
have a regular scale of prices for different kinds of Requiem
Masses; sometimes those who cannot meet even the lowest
price have to be content with the priest's blessing! Even in
the hour of their death we consecrated ministers of God deny
to His children what He most certainly intends them to have.
Part of the fault lies in the fact that we have stepped into the
background, and have let funeral directors arrange matters with
the bereaved families. Nowadays the undertaker sees the family,
finds out what kind of a Mass they want, and tells them how
much it will cost. We have permitted this important part of a

person's life to become a mere business transaction — so much Christian worship for so much money. Naturally, our people are bitter about it.

The shameful part of all this is that everyone considers it as normal. Those who can pay for honors will receive them; those who cannot will not. That is the rule. What a tragedy! What a travesty of the teaching and the life of Christ, whose followers we claim to be! And yet we have to admit that the Church has adopted secular standards, in practice, until the stage has been reached where wealth buys this honor which belongs only to those who earned it by their Christian lives. We ought to thank God that He cannot become hypocritical, as we do; He searches the heart of man, and knows each of us for what we are. We tell the people that God is merciful, and that He will apply the merits of Christ where they are needed, but it takes a great deal of faith for anyone to see that we believe that. According to the way we act, the Solemn High Mass for the rich man is more efficacious than the simple absolution we give a pauper. What are our people to believe?

¶ *Usually these class distinctions are made on account of merely external trappings. Is it not just that those who want them should have to pay for them?*

It is meet and just; they cost money and they must be paid for. Even a working-family could pay for them, because their wedding receptions, for example, cost twenty times as much as the Church fee which they complain about. But, here, we are not worried about what is just or legal; we are concerned, like St. Paul, about what is expedient. The mission cause is at stake in little things like these. If we are going to give scandal, let it be the kind of scandal Christ gave when He consorted with sinners and the publicans; at least, let us stop the oppo-site scandal, which our present attitude about money is giving. Because the world seems to have lost the idea of selfless service of others, we ought to give proof that the Church and ministers of Christ are here for just that reason. Because the modern world believes that "you pay for what you get," we ought to show them that their principle does not hold true in the Catholic Church. We are not after tips; we are after their souls.

It is bad enough for a priest to live in luxury, and to enjoy personal comforts which the vast majority of his flock cannot afford. But it is worse, far worse, for him to expose the gifts of God which he administers to scorn and cynical contempt, simply because he practically demands money for them. We are not tradesmen, and it is time we stopped acting like tradesmen. Until the world sees that we are servants of Christ, with proof from our attitude towards money, they will laugh at our apostolic schemes. And it would be difficult to blame them.

❡ *You seem to say that our present system of collections and seat money is unjustifiable.*

Taking things as they are, we say that no one who believed that priests were obsessed by money would find any reason for changing his mind were he to attend a church service of any kind. The collection (or collections) begins at the Credo and lasts till the Communion; it is taken up by priests who might better be occupied in helping the people to attend Mass intelligently; it is preceded by a sermon composed of lengthy appeals for a thousand different parish needs. Small wonder that people think as they do about us.

One afternoon I was out walking with a friend of mine. Even though he was indifferent about religion, he remarked that the church we were passing was the parish church of his childhood, and he spoke of all the memories it brought back to him. Naturally I seized the opportunity and persuaded him to drop in for a visit—his first visit to a church for many years. We were hardly inside the door when an usher sidled up to us and whispered, "Ten cents." Without taking him too seriously, I whispered back that we had dropped in for a moment only. His voice became more stern as he informed us that he was not concerned about the length of our visit; the price was ten cents. My friend had been standing by during this conversation, near an old priest who was walking up and down, saying his Breviary and oblivious to all the commotion. This was too much for a man who had lost the faith, and he turned to me and said, "Let's get out of here. This trafficking is shameful, and it is always like this." My ears burned at that last phrase, at the terrible condemnation it contained; and I thought with sorrow of all the men and women of good will who are being kept away from Christ because of petty scandals like this.

What do we think our people are? Week in and week out we preach money to them—appeals for the Holy Childhood, for the school, for fuel, for everything. We are not saying that these are not worthy causes, but we are saying that we ought to give our people a rest, and permit them to hear the untainted word of God. A sentence or two can tell them about the nature of an ordinary appeal, and we can devote most of the sermon-time to the sermon.

Besides the financial sermons, we disgust our faithful with the custom of paying for seats in the house of God. They come to pray, to worship God, and we take advantage of their love of God to collect a few more cents. True, the money is not intended for our pockets, but that is not the point. True, the money may be needed, but that is not the point either. We are talking about the ceaseless and irritating demands for money; regardless of their purpose or their need, they do estrange our people. They are a scandal and a stumbling block, and should be treated as such. Ask any lay apostle what he or she says when they are taunted with the charge that the Church is a business organization. Try to think of an answer which would satisfy a non-believer who saw with his own eyes, and not the eyes of faith, what was going on every day in almost every Catholic church in the land. Honestly and frankly, how can we expect a pagan world to believe that we are apostles with a supernatural commission?

❡ *You are talking childishly. Do you think priests like to keep on asking for money? Do you think that the parish is going to live on hot air? Our work demands money, and how shall we get it if we do not ask for it?*

We realize that priests hate to be forever begging, and we realize that parish needs are always pressing. Just as in other points of this book, we are not laying any claim to have found the solution of a torturing dilemma. We are not setting our‑selves up as models to be followed; like many, many others, we are trying to find an answer to this perplexing problem of money. Moreover, all our observations are made from the per‑spective of priests engaged in the conversion of a semi‑pagan parish; they will not, consequently, apply as aptly to a parish of true Christians. It is a difficulty we all face, to a greater or lesser degree, and we can only hope that our words will be taken (as they are meant) in a spirit of fraternal and constructive criticism.

In practice, we try to keep two aims in view. One is to reduce as far as possible the amount of money we need; the other is to regulate our use of the money so as to dissipate any prejudice about priests and money which may be lurking in the minds of our own parishioners. If you recall what we said about parish activities, you will remember that one of our objections to them was that they cost too much for the results they obtained; also, they make us appear wealthy, even though we are far from that. Hence, we favored the direct apostolate, both for economy and for results. Even for that we need money, of course; but it is much less, and can be raised without per‑petual appeals or parish bazaars. Usually spontaneous gifts take care of our budget for the ceremonies and literature, and a few wealthy persons can always be approached in case of real need.

Before going on to the six principles about money which we, with deference to better ideas, are going to enumerate, we should like to point out two errors which a great many priests commit.

One is in connection with building. Frankly, it seems that some parish priests have a passion for building—churches, schools, parish halls, trail in their wake as they move from parish to parish. Some of them are needed, but more of them are the fruit of personal pride. And what happens? The parish is burdened with debt for years to come, and the endless cycle of appeals for money is put in motion. Besides that, many of the buildings become completely useless, as our city population moves around. It would be far wiser to restrain the building impulse until a case of actual need arises, and thus to spare the people a heavy debt and a legacy of ill-feeling between the parish and its future priests. Just in passing, I should like to quote a witticism made by a priest-friend of mine. We were being shown, through a new hall which one of these "building fathers" had just erected, and my companion, after remarking about how well it had been built, how spacious it was, etc., said, "Now all you have to do is fill it."

The second error is the belief that, because we actually do expend most of our income on charitable causes, we are help- ing to break down the prejudice we have been describing. As we mentioned in the section of charitable activities, such is normally not the case. Understandably, the recipients of our charity get the idea that we must be very wealthy, and a city population, especially, has no compunction about relieving us of a part of it. This is not to say that we should put an end to our charity. We simply want to clarify the point of view of those who think that, because we help with the money we receive, people will therefore understand why we ask for money. It is not as easy as all that.

⁋ *Granting all that, we still should like to hear your six suggestions.*

Here they are then. Just as everything else we have written or shall write, they are subject to the official decision of the hierarchy, which is in a far better position to see the whole picture than we are.

1. Talk less often about money from the pulpit. The con- gregation have come to hear the doctrine of Christ. If we let it be known that we shall deliberately refrain from the subject of finance, we can be certain that they will give more generously than they did for our long- winded appeals.

2. Never give the impression that money is of primary importance in the advance of the Kingdom of God. Our priestly purpose must never be swayed one way or another, simply because the one we are called upon to serve is rich or poor.

3. If possible, do away with seat-money. Here at Colombes we have a quarterly collection for that purpose, and everyone seems pleased with the elimination of the weekly unpleasantness. At the evening services that we described in the section on liturgy, there is never a collection for any reason.

4. Have as few collections as possible, and make them as inconspicuous as possible. At Mass, the Offertory collection is a part of the liturgy, properly understood, and it should be kept in that sense. Never prolong it. To help show its connection with the Mass, one pastor whom I know has the baskets placed upon the altar during the rest of the Sacrifice. Outside of Mass we never take up a collection; it is wrong to capitalize on the goodness of our people every time they step inside the church door.

Some priests will say that such an attitude towards money is idealistic; like a pastor I know, they are firm believers in the old system where the parish priests pass the basket with a knowing eye on every member of the congregation. To such we can only say that a deeper trust in the providence of God is never displeasing to him. Let us tell you an incident that happened to us; it is not a "miracle-story," but it does demonstrate what we mean. Five years ago we decided to do away with the traditional seat-money and candle-offering that goes with First Communion. After we had taken the resolu-tion our faith wavered; thinking of our parish budget and the disastrous consequences our foolhardy step would have upon it, we asked God for a sign that we were doing the right thing. Just as He did for the weak Isra-elites in the desert, He did for us; within a few days two unexpected and anonymous gifts of considerable size came to us. Since then, similar incidents have occurred again and again. Knowing that our parishioners are far from making a habit of this sort of thing, we marvel and we thank God. To some these happenings may not pro= vide any evidence of any connection between our plans and God's pleasure; we can only believe that they do.

5. Eliminate as far as possible the distinctions now in vogue at weddings and funerals. Show, by word and deed, that we do not look upon these occasions as sources of revenue. Make a real effort to enter into the joy or the sorrow of those who come to arrange matters with us, so that they can see in us their priest and not an official of some organization. Talk to them about the Sacrament they are going to receive or the help they can give the deceased by their prayers; keep away from every reference to money. Many of the pres= ent differences will disappear when our ideal of a united and praying community is realized.

6. Put charitable activities in the hands of lay apostles. That will rid our people of the false notion that we are inexhaustibly wealthy; also, it will make for more effi= ciency in the distribution of charity, and will cause our laity to be active in this important part of Christianity.

❦ *Have you anything to say about the practice of personal poverty on the part of the clergy?*

That was a rhetorical question, we are sure. As a matter of fact, poverty is the most telling proof of the Gospel we preach; unlike our personal chastity, our poverty can be demonstrated. It will prove that we have left all things to follow Christ, and that He is sufficient for us. Many a priest does give this testimony, especially in rural areas, but it is by no means universal. Often our failure in this regard is not due to avarice, but to a lack of understanding about the power of this proof, and to a forgetting of what we are. And even when we are not rich, but simply comfortable, we do not realize that our standard of living is superior to many of our parishioners; our furnishings and table and pleasures are out of the reach of their income. In itself that is not necessarily evil, but neither is it good when it results in a feeling that they are "beneath" the man who was ordained to serve and guide them. Sometimes it is a mixed blessing never to have known want or hunger. For one thing it makes it difficult for a priest to tell his parishioners to bear their sufferings patiently, when they are hungry or out of work, and he is well-fed and has money in his pocket. It makes it difficult to go into homes where your parishioners are cold and ill-clothed and try to tell them of God's love for those who bear crosses patiently, when their eyes tell you that they know you are warm and well clothed.

All of this may sound harsh. We know that many of our confreres do not fall into this category, because they do know what want is, and they do give of their very sustenance to those who are poor and hungry and naked. We also know that many do not. Think what it means to live in insecurity, to be uncertain about next week's food and rent and clothing. Realize that that is the ordinary lot of most of our working-class parishioners. Then think about our own lives and our own security, and we shall see what a gulf there is between our people and us, even when we are far from wealthy ourselves. By gradual, unconscious steps, we grow into a state of mind which looks for personal security more than for apostolic results. Even our clerical parlance betrays us, for when we speak of a "good parish," we mean one which provides a good living for its clergy; when we talk about promotion in the ranks of the clergy, we mean that the priest in question has gone to a wealthier parish. Something is wrong.

In any case, the result is that we have no close sympathy with our people, nor they with us. We cannot even hope to have the irresistible influence of the Apostles, of St. Martin of Tours, of St. Francis, of the Curé of Ars. In our churches there is heard the clink of money round the altar. ✠

✠[6]✠
Clerical Culture

❧ *Surely you are not going to say that our culture is an obstacle to the evangelization of our people?*

Strange though it may sound, we do say that. It will take a great deal of explaining before you will see what we mean, but we shall do our best to prove our point. Lest you cite examples like Abbé Godin, who was certainly a cultured man, and who yet succeeded remarkably in his apostolate among people who were far from refined, we say that he succeeded because he knew how to overcome his own gentility.

❧ *Please explain what you mean.*

We mean that our influence upon ordinary people is not what it should be, partly because we are so different from them; we think differently, live differently, speak and act differently. In other words, we have a different culture. Our seminary training in the classics, philosophy, and theology has put us in a class apart. Properly speaking, we are not like any of our parishioners, but we seem more "middle-class" or "bourgeois" than anything else. What is the result? Usually it means that we feel compelled to surround ourselves with those who will understand our thought and our speech, and who have tastes like our own. One of the reasons for the rise of the "parish atmosphere" we spoke of at the beginning of this book is found in the priests; we tend to move among and work with people who resemble us—it is easy to do so. In fact, it is wise; that is the basic principle of Catholic Action expressed in the formula of "like to like." Our objection comes from the consequent forgetfulness of the great mass of men who are not like us. Our concern is about the consequent inability to meet ordinary people, to talk to them, to make them feel at home in the "catholic" Church we represent. Even when we do attempt to make contact with them, we use terminology which is completely foreign to the ordinary working-man; more than that, we take for granted the fact that they already accept the basic ideas of Christianity, even though they do not. What we are trying to say to them goes against every principle of modern pagan life, and yet we bliss-fully assume the very things we must prove and demonstrate. We are living in another world, a tidy clerical and philosophical world. It is time to come down to earth!

¶ But is our culture so completely foreign to the average working man?

Our answer is an unqualified "yes." If anybody wants to debate whether or not he is capable of absorbing it, that is another matter. However, as things are now, we say that our culture is completely foreign to him, so much so that he dis-trusts it. Briefly we will outline some of the more obvious dif-ferences between our world and his.

Cultured or educated men reason out their actions, and they live by a set of principles which their intellect has come to adopt. Ordinary men, on the other hand, act through sentiment or through principles accepted by their neighbors; most of their rules of action can be reduced to eminently practical and com-pletely materialistic proverbs. Everyone has heard them. "Make hay while the sun shines." "Make the most of a good thing while you have it." "If you don't take care of yourself, who will?" The same thing can be seen in the usual attitude of parents when their child tells them that he was in a fight at school; the first question is always whether or not he fought back, because the greatest shame of all is to let someone else take advantage of one.

Another difference is in the critical spirit of educated men. They will discuss and dissect whatever is proposed to them, sometimes simply because they are unwilling, in principle, to follow the herd. Again, the mass of men are quite the opposite. They take as their own the opinion of the majority, and they act collectively upon that opinion. This is not the result of a lack of personal courage, but, rather, a poverty of ideas; it is not so much an unwillingness to find objective truth as it is satisfaction with the ideas which their own milieu has provided ready made for them. Personality is swallowed up in the group. Such men will be firm enough in expressing their opinions, but they fail to realize that their conclusions are not really their own.

Cultured men base their judgements on certain criteria out-side themselves, but the ordinary working-man's standard is less exacting; generally, he is satisfied with the creed which begins: "t's all a matter of opinion." Since school days, he has heard innumerable contradictions of every fact and dogma under the sun; radio, films, and magazines pour over him more con-fusion than he can handle. Consequently, a knowing cynicism becomes his practical philosophy of life, and even his power of judgement is swallowed up in the common attitude of his class.

❝ You sound like one of these superior sociologists who say that the "laboring classes" are incapable of thought.

We do not mean to, because we are not sociologists, and we definitely do not feel superior to the working-class. At the beginning of this book we touched upon this whole subject; we said that, until they have begun to find themselves again in their family circle, the majority of workers would not think for themselves. That was why we stressed the importance of group-apostolates, and the importance of family life. Our cities do something to a person; they strip him of his individualism and personality, principally because they make normal family life so difficult. Hence, we must help them to find themselves, their traditions, their self- respect and honesty, by trying to restore that family unit. Then they will think and act from principle rather than from group-compulsion.

❝ What would you consider as the cause of our radical difference from our people?

One of the main causes is certainly our theological training. We need it, of course, and need it badly; we are supposed to know as much as possible about the mysteries of God, His ways, and His plans. Without that knowledge we cannot lead others to him, since the blind cannot lead the blind. However, we have learned it bookishly, not vitally; we have left it in its intellectual dress, and have not made it a part of our lives. Our highbrow attitude about the things of God is alien both to our people and to the Gospel we are supposed to preach, and we are failing both. We think that people are rejecting Christ when, often, they are rejecting only our bloodless and unreal presentation of him. Our talks and sermons may be chiselled to grammatical perfection and formed from the most orthodox of sources, but they mean nothing to our hearers. We need the gift of tongues. Besides that, we need the ability to listen, and to let others talk to us about their spiritual discoveries; we may and should know more about theology than our parishioners do, but many of them could teach us about God and about how to present Him to our flock.

That is one of the best features of the study-club—everyone gets a chance to talk, and then we are forced to listen. The effect is good for them and for us. It is much more real to hear a man or woman tell about his or her contact with God than it is to listen to a logical, but unreal, talk based upon a scholastic syllogism.

Someone told us once about an English priest who brings the daily paper into the pulpit, reads some article to the people, and proceeds from there to a Christian demonstration of the subject. No doubt he scandalizes a great many parishioners. Scandal or not, he is more attuned to the needs of the times than are those super-scholastics who get up to talk about the Omnipresence of God, for example, and who start: "My friends, God is everywhere, by His Presence, His Essence, His Power. First, by His Essence . . . ". Christ did not talk like a scholar. He was of the people and among the people and His language and metaphors and examples are immortal in their appeal to the common man. He, who is God, knew that the humdrum affairs of everyday life are what every man knows and what every man must learn how to use in his approach to God.

If we wish to make a show of our great knowledge, the con‑ gregation cannot prevent us; neither can they assimilate what we are trying to say. When we soar, we soar alone. The average person is more interested in the fact of Christ's presence in the Eucharist, for example, than he is in the mode of that presence. The same is true for all the tremendous dogmas of our Faith. Our people are eager to be able to put them into practice—in the life which God has given them to lead; the historical and philosophical background of these truths does not interest them. Most Catholics are unconcerned about their inability to answer objections made by unbelievers, but they are concerned about their own service of Christ. Before an intellectual, reflective audience, our technique would change, naturally, but it is the height of folly to suppose that such an audience is the usual thing. Most men want an external expression of their internal faith, and our cold presentation frustrates them. We might as well learn now to accept and use human nature as it is. If we doubt whether man can live by rational bread alone, the suc‑ cess of innumerable public expressions of faith should convince us. At some of them, here in France, the most indifferent and anti‑religious souls have been moved to return to Christ, and we are not a peculiar people in this regard; the same principle underlies our liturgy, all our shrines, and pilgrimages. And yet, Sunday morning sees us treating these same souls as though they were angels and not men.

One winter we held a study club on the "Our Father." It was easy to see that the study made far less impression than did the attempts to reduce the meaning of our Lord's prayer to the scenes and problems of their own lives. That was what they needed, and that was what they did.

❧ *In your efforts to escape formalism in religion, you are running the obviously equal danger of de‑spiritualizing it.*

A very true observation. We do have to be careful, because we can be misunderstood and give occasion for superstition. As a matter of fact, that tendency was responsible, to some extent, for the success of our experiment with the passing of the statue of the Blessed Mother, which we described in a previous chapter. Some families took part in it simply because they felt it would be unlucky to break the chain. What can you do? We see the danger, and we try to be sensible in our material approach to religion; it would be absurd to shy off from it altogether, just because of the possibility of its abuse. For every external act of devotion there must be a corresponding explanation of the interior meaning. Since we are body and soul, and the soul cannot be reached directly, the material side of man must be the approach to the soul, and we make every effort to use such an approach. Superstition is one extreme to be avoided, and disembodied, intellectual spirituality is the other. We have tried to find the middle course.

What do you think about the literary tastes of priests?

If they are an obstacle to our ability to bring Christ to his people, we say, "Get rid of them." When we try to present him to uneducated audiences in language and phrases and literary devices that we borrow from the "great" books we read, we are wasting our time as well as the people's. Our subtleties of style are lost on them. This sounds very harsh, we know; if the Gospels were not so simple and matter-of-fact, we should hesitate to advance this opinion. But, with Christ on our side, we feel more sure. His audience was much like our own, and we can see how He talked to them.

Honestly, it is hard to follow you. Do you mean to say that the good education we have received must be considered as a stumbling block to our apostolic work?

Of course not. We warned you that this question was a difficult one to understand and to explain. When we cry out against "clerical culture," we mean the way in which priests tend to make use of their training. We do not seem to realize that everything we learned and absorbed was meant for the souls among whom we would labor; instead of that, it has become clerical property. When we give it out, its dress is clerical, and its wording, and its meaning. A "class" culture has arisen, even though that is contrary to our very purpose in life. Even our manners are so very different from those of other good Christians that they have come to be caricatured by the term "churchy manners" — meaning a mixture of unction, pomposity, and caution.

That is why we object to our education, or rather, to its results.

It need not be so. We can be educated to the finger-tips, capable of appreciating art and music and letters, and yet be simple, approachable men. There are plenty of proofs of that in the ranks of the clergy. Until we shake off that unwarranted dignity, our work will suffer. There is no reason in the world why a priest cannot strive for the real, unalloyed dignity of his calling as a fisher of men, and learn how to adapt himself to the code of his people. Instead of being offended that a man should presume to talk to us with his hat on, or with a cigarette in his mouth, we should realize that no offense is implied in these acts, according to the social laws of the man's circle. Instead of being mortified when someone shouts a greeting and carries on a conversation with us from the other side of the street, we should be able to see that friendliness, and not contempt, is being shown. Our "churchy outlook" on life needs overhauling.

We are different, and should remain so, but the difference is far more spiritual than material, or should be. When we pre-serve this difference by clerical pomposity, we are wrong; when we try to rid ourselves of it by being patronizing or by being too much like a lay person, we are equally wrong. The balance is found in a burning love of Christ, which expresses itself in unaffected simplicity, solely because we love these people whom He has given us to lead to Him; any other forced simplicity is a sham, and will be quickly seen as such, for our people are keen judges of their fellow-men. This is the balance which Don Bosco found, and the Curé of Ars, and countless other priests of Jesus Christ. This is the balance St. Paul defined in the Epistle to the Hebrews, when he said that a priest was a man "taken from among men, and ordained for men in those things which have to do with the service of God." Because of this passion to bring Christ to the working-classes, whose loss we lament, some priests, like Father [Jacques] Loew¹ in Marseilles, have even begun to labor with their hands at the docks and in the mines.

Even though some may consider this an extreme, it is, at least, a testimony to heroic priestliness; it may prove to be a very practical, and even necessary, part of the training of future apostles to the working-class.

¶ Are there any other obstacles?

Yes, indeed. One would be our personal likes and dislikes, in so far as they are carried into our priestly work. We are not so lacking in understanding of human nature as to think that we can ever rid ourselves completely of these personal preferences, but they must not be left unchecked. When they make us avoid certain people, or make certain people avoid us, they are a definite obstacle. As much as possible we must try to be all things to all men, so as not to hurt and alienate other human beings. We are priests, and we are ordained for all men, not just for those we like. People are sensitive before us partly because they realize, dimly or clearly, our exalted office, and partly because they feel inferior to us in one way or another. Learn their likes and dislikes, and then make use of them honestly, for the cause of Christ. Forgive this personal note, but it is such a striking proof of the perception of our people when they see that a priest loves them unashamedly,

---

1   Fr. Jacques Lowe (1908–1991), a Dominican priest, believed that the only way to reach the working class was to share fully the experience of the industrialized masses. Pope Pius XII placed severe restrictions on the worker-priest movement after a great deal of labor unrest and some priestly defections. These restrictions were relaxed under Pope Paul VI. Abbé Michonneau recognized the danger that a priest could become "too much like a lay person." He could hardly have seen so early the consequences of this movement.

that I feel obliged to tell it. One Christmas Eve, at Midnight Mass, a curate overheard two working-men at the end of the sermon I had just preached on Christ's love for the poor. One of them said to the other, "He is one of our own, that priest!" Ignoring the fact that the compliment was a personal one, it does show what we mean. When we actually do love them all, they sense it, and respond to it; we become, as we should be, an avenue to Christ. When we permit personal caprice to direct our apostolate, we become obstacles.

❧ *Yet we are supposed to be leaders. You seem to say that we should be merely friends and helpers.*

Remember that we are working among non-Catholics who have no reason for following us; it is utter folly to consider oneself as a "leader" in their eyes. Unlike the Pope and the Bishops, we have no *ex cathedra* authority, even over our own faithful flock; we, like them, follow the directives of the hierarchy. What power we have should be used sparingly, because the dictatorial attitude affected by some priests is an intolerably obnoxious quality. It is more in keeping with the office of a priest to draw his flock to love the same divine things which he loves, to influence and attract them to the beauty of Almighty God. To some, this will sound like weakness. If it meant that we were to be benevolent in a sickly fashion; if it meant that we were to utter nothing but platitudes; if it meant that we must avoid hurting anybody's feelings, then we would agree. It is none of these things. We do have a commission to preach, and that assignment necessitates telling the truth; we do not intend to advocate anything less than that. But there are various ways of fulfilling that commission. To our mind, harsh words and bitter tongue-lashings are not the way of Jesus Christ, any more than the other extreme of colorless, watered Christianity is. One who loves his people will under-stand how hard it is for them to fulfil the duties of their state in life, and will try to help them find the most practical means of doing it; he will not shout at them, nor will he lay down a penal code of fire and brimstone.

We must enter into the hearts and minds of our people, so as to be able to convince them that the law of God is really for their own good; and even though difficult to fulfil, He will help us all to comply with it. This is not weakness, unless love be weakness. If so, we do not know what to answer to our Lord, who said: "You know that those who are regarded as rulers among the Gentiles lord it over them, and their great men exercise authority over them. But it is not so among you. On the contrary, whoever wishes to become great shall be your servant; and whoever wishes to be first among you shall be the slave of all; for the Son of Man also has not come to be served, but to serve, and to give his life as a ransom for many." And what will you answer to our Lord, since he said to all of us that he would no longer call us servants, but friends? Even the communists know this much. Their leaders are "comrades," and great care is taken that their popularity be preserved, and their identity with the struggling masses be never obscured. We priests of God seem to have forgotten both the command of Christ and the psychology of human beings.

Part of the reason for this is, as we said before, the natural result of our training. We are separated from ordinary people during all the years of our intellectual and cultural grooming; when we emerge, it is into a strange and crude world. Naturally we tend to avoid crudeness and to move in the circle most like the delicate cocoon which hatched us. Unfortunately a priest cannot afford to act "naturally." We must—and it is impossible to overemphasize this—go out to the ordinary people, mix with them, know their wants and hopes and feelings, love them, and thus bring them back to Christ who died for just such as these. They may not be as polite as we think they should be; they may be ignorant and prejudiced and ungrateful; they may even be unwashed, noisy, and vulgar. These are the ones whom we avoid and who avoid us, but no more! They may be less obviously unpleasing, and be simply smug middle-class bores but these, too, are woefully in need of Christ. We must stop limiting the Kingdom of God until it includes only those who resemble us; we are meant to love all men without exception. It is hard, dreadfully hard, to love without shame and without reserve, when the beloved is so unappealing. It takes sanctity, and sanctity of a special kind. Despite the prevailing attitude, priests are not exempt from the obligation of acquiring that sanctity, that heart of Jesus Christ.

❨ *You reduce the difficulty to the fact that, we have let our culture make us strangers to our own people. Is that correct?*

Precisely. Our conversation, our manner of thinking, our choice of friends are alien to the common understanding and the common good of the parish as a whole. The natural preferences we give free rein to, color our sermons, make our choice of examples, determine what families we visit. A dangerous road for a priest to follow! Our priestly influence becomes narrower, and our priestly hearts become less Catholic. Simultaneously those outside the Church are given a false picture of her; they naturally come to believe that she is interested in the churchgoers only, and not in the spiritual "down-and-outs."

The niceties of polite society are not to be scorned, but neither are they to be confused with the essence of Christianity. This whole problem is a more profound one than mere concern with social conventions in the life of a priest, but these do illustrate, concretely, what is meant by our statement that we have become strangers to the working-class members of our flock. The heart of the difficulty lies in this, that we have enclosed ourselves in our own little clerical world, and that we have tried to make the outside world conform to that pattern. If it will not, we avoid contact with it; if it will, we feel that we are accomplishing something. The truth is that we have failed in the role of an "*alter Christus*" and are playing the part of an "alter ego," dressed in clerical robes.

❨ *Would you expand a little some of the passing references you made to the subject of sermons?*

We would not miss this chance for the world. The special feature of sermons, as far as we are concerned here, is the problem of adaptation to the audience before us; like so many other difficulties brought up in this book, it is easy to talk about, but very hard to solve. For example, I listened to two sermons on the subject of "The Fatherhood of God," given by two of the newly-ordained curates here. Both were zealous, aware of the need for adaptation, but neither of the talks fitted the audience in that church. One of the priests compared God to our earthly father, rising from earthly love and solicitude to the divine; the other described the death of his own father with telling emotion, and drew his lesson from the loss he experienced. These were good sermons, even excellent ones but, I repeat, they were not adapted to our parishioners. During the sermons my gaze wandered around the church, and I saw a girl whose father had driven her from the house, and told her to earn her living on the sidewalks, the way her mother had done. I saw another girl whose father perpetually abused the girl's mother. Do you see what I mean? If those young preachers had known the difference between the world in which they had been brought up, and the world in which these people live, they would never have used that approach to the fatherhood of God. These young workers, generally speaking, have no consciousness of pride and love for their parents, because they so often have no reason for love or pride in them, at least not along the lines pointed out by the priest in the pulpit. For this audience the talk was unreal, romantic, even fantastic.

¶ *Do you receive any criticisms of the sermons from parishioners?*
Very many, especially since we deliberately encourage them to let us know how the sermons affected them. There is hardly any better way to find out how to preach to this particular audience. From what they tell us we know that they sense when a sermon is poorly or hurriedly prepared; when sincerity is lacking, when a preacher is more interested in fine phrasing than in Christ's doctrine. One thing especially striking is the

comment that the Gospel itself is often easier to understand than the preacher's explanation of it! The people tell us about words or expressions which we are always using without realiz= ing our fault, and which detract from the force of our message. All of these things are told in a spirit of mutual charity, from a desire to help and to be helped. There is nothing unkind or sarcastic about them. As a matter of fact, it is a marvel= ous advantage to have them tell us what they think. Most congregations have no chance to express their minds, and so they sleep all through the sermon, lulled by the drone of our voices and by the unreal truisms we are mouthing. And yet we have a divine commission to preach the Word of God! To us is given the task which the Apostles began! We are indeed unprofitable servants when that glorious task is carried out hurriedly, insincerely, verbosely, or professorially.

Too often it happens, as we have seen and heard, that the Sunday sermon is a tissue of magnificent words which no longer mean anything to the people. They will understand the words, of course, but the meaning, the background, the implications are lost on them, no matter how well known these same expres= sions may be to the seminary=trained preacher. The meat of the sermon is missing. When the people go home they bring with them no nourishment for a week of work and problems in this present world. What they heard may have been beautiful, but it was as useful as a description of some Roman ruins. One writer compared the contents of the usual sermon to the vestments that the priests wear at Mass; they are used only at Mass, and then put away and forgotten until the next religious service. A bitter comparison, but not an untrue one.

Where is the familiar, powerful language of the Fathers of the Church? Why are we so unlike them? One reason is that we are afraid of offending our people; we feel sure that they would take offense, and depart, never to return. We might well be wrong about that, but, even if some did leave, we firmly believe that many more would come in, to find out what Christ is saying to our day and age. Another, and more fundamental, reason is that we *think* we are *talking to men and women who already are real Christians.* Hence we use Scriptural quotations, theological terminology, and scientifically exact Christian lan= guage. We sound eloquent. We are orthodox. Most of all, we are satisfied with our sermon. As we come down from the pulpit, and the thought crosses our mind that what we have said will not change our people very much, we brush away the misgivings; either the Devil is trying to ensnare us or else these people are incapable of grasping the majestic heights of Christian revelation. Next week we go through the same pro= cess and the same misgivings, and the week after that, year in and year out.

Somehow it seldom occurs to us that the fault may be ours, and not theirs. We would realize that, and we would say *"mea culpa,"* if we would but stop for a moment and consider the souls who are listening to us. Certainly we should know by now that most of them have little or no religious background, less knowledge of doctrine, and still less familiarity with our theological vocabulary. Having grasped that, we would mount the pulpit in a different frame of mind and with a different approach. We would be changed men, and so would our people be. With stereotyped phrases abandoned, the awful truth of Christianity would stand revealed to these people, perhaps for the first time; with Christianity presented according to their present problems they would find the answer to the doubts that gnaw at the souls of those whom we now think of as "Christian."

One possible way to get that proper approach is to realize that we are talking to neophytes, to catechumens, to pagans who simply happened to drop into Mass. One priest told us about the comment that a non=believing friend of his made, after he had heard his priest=friend preach at a parish mission. He told him that the sermon had been well delivered, but that it was obvious that the priest had intended to talk to people who were already convinced about the truth of Christianity—and only to them. He went on to say that if the church had been filled with men and women in his frame of mind, the sermon would have been useless.

We are not trying to say that every time a priest gets up to preach he should talk only on the ABCs of religion, and that in the most simple manner. Evidently there is need of progression, especially during a mission or even in a series of parish sermons. We do, however, mean that a priest will be much more effective if he is constantly aware of the necessity of speaking to those who know little and believe less about Christianity. Instead of taking for granted that everyone in the congregation is a firm believer, he will remember those whose faith is weak or lost. Instead of assuming that the congregation can follow and understand his technical Christian concepts, he will remember those who sit in darkness, even in these Christian countries of ours. Instead of presenting Christ's doctrine as a completely spiritual and unworldly matter, he will try to reach out to these souls by being more realistic, more concrete.

❧ *It certainly should not be difficult to be concrete in preaching.*

But it is. It could be easier, if we would but remember certain principles, like the following. Keep in mind that we are talking, not to an "audience," but to men and women of flesh and blood, with particular and pressing problems of daily life. Keep in mind that "suffering" and "evil" are not abstract terms to them, but that these words have a definite, actual, and personal association. Remember that "love" calls to their minds concrete persons, and individual longings; that "justice" has a vivid connection with their jobs; that the "destiny of mankind" means the longfelt answer to the confusion and helplessness of men and women in this modern age.

Realization of the intimate connection which must exist between what we say and to whom we are saying it will keep us from much of the pompous, meaningless verbiage which is the scourge of our apostolate in the pulpit. For every priest and for every parish, the needs, and the consequent adaptations, will be different; by trial and by prayer, and by common sense, we shall find our own proper approach. Unless we make that effort we shall go on with our torrent of words, signifying noth= ing. Our responsibility is overwhelming. We are the only ones in the whole of God's world who can give a meaning to life, who can answer the torturing doubts and despair of the con= fused twentieth century; without the message of Christ which we were ordained to spread, nothing can halt the growth of self=destruction. We must do it, for no one else can. In order to do it, we must be truly apostolic. We must be apostolic preach= ers. If we speak the word of God from routine, or because we were assigned to preach on this particular Sunday, we are failures. If we speak that word merely to hear ourselves talk, and to enjoy the cadence of our own polished periods, we are failures. It takes a man of God to preach the word of God. It demands a passion for souls, a great sorrow at the ills of mankind, and a burning consecration to the task of bringing Christ back into this world around us.

How to find out exactly what this particular locality needs is not easy, but it can be done. Know your people, and find out what they are thinking, and make your entrance from there. For example, it was natural to use the barbarism of Buchenwald or any of the Nazi camps as an illustration of what can happen in a world without God; our people could see that, because some of them had existed under that barbarism. Similarly, we talk about "love" when instructing a couple for marriage, because that term and that concept is certainly a common one in modern life; we use that approach to the dogmatic and moral teaching we are going to give, instead of rushing into a logical, but unreal, demonstration of textbook arguments about the Sacrament of Matrimony. Instead of decrying divorce, we try to show that it means the death of that love which these two young peo= ple experience so vividly at this moment, and which they are about to consecrate before God. These are little things, but they change religion into a personal, important, even dominant, part of a person's life.

(*What is your opinion of the "Sermon Series" which some par=*
ishes or dioceses establish as the program for a whole year of
preaching?

Some sort of planning is necessary, certainly, but it is very
important to see that the program is not a waste of time. It
sounds logical, and it is logical, to treat the Creed one year,
the Commandments the next year, and the Sacraments during
the following year. It is logical, we repeat but that does not
necessarily mean that it is a wise procedure. Life does not run
along according to strict a priori regulations. Some points in
such a program as the one above demand full treatment here
and scanty mention there; this year sees the disappearance
of what was an important problem last year. Consequently, a
ready=made plan has its drawbacks.

Here at Colombes, we priests discuss and decide on a year's
general subject matter; the decision is made more according to
the needs as we see them than according to good order. The
first year here we had a general aim of making the faithful
conscious of the necessity and possibility of "conquering" the
world around them for Christ. So we emphasized the personal
apostolate during October, shifted to a treatment of the Mass,
and came back to the meaning of their "membership" in the
church. The overall theme stayed the same, but the particular
treatment varied as we realized the needs and wants of this
parish. That same principle held true for all the subsequent
preaching programs, on matters like the family, work, the Sac=
raments, the Gospels, social doctrine, etc.

Undoubtedly there are plenty of defects and deficiencies in
the treatment we give to any or all of these themes. Somehow
we would rather be guilty of defects in this attempt to preach
the Gospel than to be guilty of the failing which he commits
who spends a year preaching against the errors of the Gnos=
tics, or in proving the authenticity of the four Gospels! We
would rather commit possible sins of omission in our efforts
to stress only the needed doctrines, rather than doggedly and
unendingly expatiate on each and every point listed in a year's

schedule. Any defect, if defect it be, conforms quite closely to the example of the great Fathers. When Augustine saw Manicheanism and Pelagianism around him, he bore down on those errors; when Athanasius faced Arianism he laid stress on the doctrines which were being attacked. Humbly, but in like manner, we are trying to fit our people to face the two great modern heresies, namely, materialism and Marxism; what is not directly suited for that fight is left reverently to rest in the deposit of Faith. Back in the seminary it was good training to refute Luther and Arius; here in the parish, the same refutation is ridiculous or it would be ridiculous were the times not so critical.

As you admitted earlier in the book, the ones who come to hear us are usually those who are steeped in what you called the "parochial atmosphere." That seems to make our concern about adaptation unnecessary, to say the least. We did admit that, because it is true. And yet that fact cannot excuse us from trying to adapt the Gospel to modern needs, nor can it permit us to go on with our monotonous cliches. The pres= ent dormant state of most parishes is the result of just such an attitude; because we no longer try to awaken our people, they go on in their smug provincialism, their self=satisfaction, their pharisaical formalism. We priests are the cause of all this. Even if there were not millions around us who do not have the Faith, we still are obliged to teach the faithful flock according to the teachings and spirit of Christ. Before we can hope to stir them to a conquest of their pagan neighbors and environment, we must help them rid themselves of all these evil aspects of the so=called "parochial atmosphere." Just as some of the strongest words of Christ our Lord were directed against the same parochial self=righteousness, so must ours be.

Sometimes it seems as though we were afraid to tell them the truth. When we do present basic Christian doctrine we take great pains to assure the congregation that we do not intend to include them in our words; we always mean these truths for the "others," who are not there to hear us. We go out of our way to increase their already dangerous self-esteem by thanking them endlessly for whatever they may have done, even though what they did may have been nothing exceptional. We thank the Women's Guild for their cooperation, the Scouts for their generous efforts, the Men's Clubs for their fine atten= dance at Mass. This is not a question of politeness, but of unwarranted praise to a people who need a sense of shame for what is not being done. There is no point in treating adults as though they were children, and yet this is what we are doing by our sugar=coated treatment.

Our Lord asked the rhetorical question about what can be used to savor salt that has lost its savor. Claudel's sad reply to this was, "with sugar." Our sermons and our general attitude would seem to make his answer reasonable. We are not virile enough; even our congregation realizes this. When they try to serve God they know that they are far from perfect; yet, because we constantly laud their efforts and everlastingly hold them up as models for those "outside," they begin to think that they must be better than their consciences tell them. And so they rest, and preen their feathers, thanks to our own lack of vision. They need a change, and we must be capable of giving it to them.

(*When a parish has a mission, some of that blindness is corrected.*

Not necessarily. When you talk about a mission we pre= sume that you mean the occasion when special priests come in for two or three weeks to hold a series of conferences for the men, the women, and the children. Such an effort does not infallibly guarantee results, because the times have changed since missions were first begun by St. Vincent de Paul and others. In the old days, even up to the turn of this century, missions attracted people who seriously wanted to examine their conscience, or people who realized that they had been doing wrong, and wanted to check themselves. The faith was there, even when morals were bad; the spark could be easily rekindled. Nowadays, missions draw only those who are already

Christian; the mass of our population is unaffected despite our efforts at publicity.

Consequently, our times demand a change in technique. The notification from the pulpit or by leaflets that a mission is going to be held at such-and-such a time must be reinforced by house-to-house invitations. The talks in church must be replaced by talks in the parish hall or school, because the people we want to attract are really unwilling to enter the church. The subject-matter must change from the traditional Four Last Things to a treatment of doctrine which is especially apt and appealing to this particular neighborhood. We would even go a little further, and express some ideas of our own on this subject of missions. It seems to us that they would be a great deal more useful if laymen and women were a part of the mission-band, as the Company of St. Paul is in Italy. Instead of two weeks they would spend months or years in one locality; they would cover less ground, but they would cover it more effectively. When it came time to leave a section there would be a renewed and growing community behind them, and that includes the parish clergy. Some sections of the diocese might be left neglected, but the ones on whom an all-out effort was concentrated would soon be able to make up the loss to their uncared-for brothers. It seems more practical to emphasize the apostolic work in definite parts of the diocese, and so produce real and lasting good, rather than to spread the labour and the labourers so thinly as to effect no permanent results.

❡ *Would you put down for us your conclusions on this chapter?*
Certainly. We hold that all the traditional tactics of the Church are, of course, sound, but that they need revision. Missions must be publicized and conducted somewhat along the lines we mentioned, although we do not pretend to utter the last word about this. The congregations which regularly preach missions must discover again the purpose for which they were founded; they must think of themselves as apostles, with a special apostolate, and not merely as secondary aids

of the parish clergy. We parish priests must make a special and intelligent effort to bring our preaching into line with the preoccupations of our people. To do that we shall have to strip off the usual coating of clerical culture which covers our words and thoughts, and which renders them unintelligible to the ordinary man and woman of the present century. The principle underlying much of our activity here at Colombes is that we can best reach the minds of our listeners by appealing to their senses. The reader will see in this nothing but a restatement of an old scholastic maxim. Consequently, our sermons and services leave room for participation by the congregation, by hymns, processions and similar activity, as was developed in the section on Liturgy.

In whatever we do we try, little by little, to reach the mind and heart of the average man, and to bring him to Christ. Since our background proves to be an obstacle, we do our best to change; since our expression is unsuited, we work to correct it. All of this involves trial and error, and we know that we have made, and will continue to make, many mistakes, but we are trying. Convinced that we have been ordained for the people, and for no other reason, we work as a team with the parish, so that all of us together may best reflect Christ in a world that needs Him so badly. ✛

⊹[7]⊹
The Equipment of
Modern Apostles

I. A REAL AND PRIESTLY SPIRITUALITY

❧ *Your views are interesting and appealing, but there still remains the difficulty of finding men who can put them into practice.*

That is our whole trouble. That lament is made by everybody with whom we have discussed the problems and exigencies of the latter day apostolate, whether they be priests or lay people. Fundamentally it is not so much a matter of having good methods as of having good men to apply and use them. More important than any other qualification for the priesthood is the apostolic spirit, the alert zeal which a man brings to his people, and by which he can hope to transform them. To paraphrase St. Paul's words in the thirteenth chapter of First Corinthians, neither intellectual nor artistic abilities will suffice, although they do help.

❧ *You are simply restating the maxim we heard so often in the seminary: "Be saints, and you will be successful priests."*

We are, but we want to point out that this saying is a much misunderstood one. There are saints and saints. Sanctity is practically as varied in its forms as are the individuals who possess it, because gift differs from gift, and calling from call‹ ing. What we are leading up to is this: since we priests have been called to a particular apostolate we hold that this same apostolate must determine and create our particular spiritual‹ ity. This life is our path to God, and so we must fit and form ourselves to the holiness which this life both supplies and demands. Hence, we feel that the proverb you quoted needs explaining, not because we feel qualified to speak as masters of spirituality, nor because we aspire to be the founders of a new spiritual school. We are simply telling you the conclusions we have reached.

As far as we can see, not all types of sanctity are useful for an apostolate to the modern pagan; in fact, some are positive drawbacks. As we go along we shall try to explain all this in our development of two principles:

1. That the apostolate demands an interior life capable of developing a priestly spirituality, properly so called.
2. That the apostolate itself is our proper means of sanctification.

❦ *What connection are you trying to establish between the apos= tolate and our spiritual life?*

A necessary one, as you shall see. A little while ago, when we were writing about that thing so close to our hearts, the direct apostolate, we said that priests must share the richness of Jesus Christ with souls who know Him not; that the love inside us must spread to all who come in contact with us. You may call that a truism and tell us that the same purpose has been the fundamental reason for all the Church activities of the last fifty years, and we should agree, with qualifications. That purpose was there, but it took an apostle of unusual personal attraction to make the system fulfil its goal; for most priests material concerns connected with the activities killed zeal and obscured the original end.

Almost the same thing has happened to our doctrine. Par= adoxically we have learned a great deal about the Trinity, the Incarnation, the Redemption, and but comparatively little about Christ. In the section on preaching we tried to show that we have become better at handling abstract ideas in scholastic form than we have at delivering the message; in our hands, Christ has become less of a living Friend and Savior than the Gospels show Him to be. At this point someone will certainly accuse us of belittling the Sacred Sciences, so permit us to explain. We are not saying, nor even hinting, that our years of philosophy and theology were wasted ones, because we unequivocally believe in the necessity of a firm intellectual basis for anyone trying to bring the Truth to this error-ridden world. What we do say is that these abstractions of the schools tend to chill our fervor and check our enthusiasm; it is simply a matter of finding how to put a greater stress on emotional conviction than is now done.

Similarly, spirituality has been affected. Our background tends to make our union with God a stiff and formal thing; we make it a part of our day, but not a part of our lives. Because it is a ready-made affair we find it that much harder to correlate with our attempts to bring others into union with him.

When a young man enters the seminary he dreams of conquering the world for Christ; when ordination comes, he is less idealistic, but he is still unswerving in his ambition to be a real priest. He comes to his first parish with ideas and ideals, burning with the desire to transform this little corner of the vineyard. We, who are here before him and over him, must make sure that this enthusiasm does not flag because of us. It will not—and this is our main point if, as a seminarian, this young priest became convinced that his passion for souls will make him a saint. Convinced of it ourselves, we could never understand the attitude of those who regularly dampen the zeal of new curates, who feel that every young priest must be "cooled off." Instead of profiting from their sincere example, we older priests, from a secret sense of shame or from some perversity, do more to eliminate that example.

Even back in the seminary that "cooling off" process was begun. We remember our superior giving a series of talks on zeal; the main theme of every one of them was that we must be prudent in our exercise of that zeal. Good Lord, what was he afraid of? He should have known that internal defects like pride and self-consciousness would do enough to temper the spirit of even the wildest of us. He should have played upon that ardor so as to have us make the most of the seminary years. He should have warned us about the day when our thirst for souls would grow less keen, and when we would be satisfied with much less than our original dreams demanded. If he had showed us that our love for Christ must grow without limit, simply because of the souls that were to find Him through us, we might have learned to lean on our zeal, rather than mistrust it.

❆ *In other words, you say that there should be at least as much emphasis on spiritual preparation as there is now on intellectual?*

Exactly; the only source of a fruitful ministry is a living and vibrant spirituality. Some seem to think that it depends on a special sort of temperament, especially for the direct apostolate to adults which we have been championing. If they mean a compound of physiological and psychological gifts, fired by a certain natural boldness and poise, we do not agree. True, we have to be bold; but that can be fought for and won in battles with our native timidity, and it need not be innate. We repeat that this is a matter of spirituality, not temperament.

In the concrete this is what we mean. For a priest to set out on door=to=door visits, with no assurance whatsoever of a kindly reception, a serious internal disposition of soul is required. Here at Colombes, everyone of us is willing to admit that he would not have the courage to do this sort of thing, except for the teamwork we have established. As proof we shamefacedly tell you that each of us spent the first three years here in every other sort of activity, simply and solely because we were looking for excuses not to have to begin this phase of the apostolate, even after we had agreed upon it. As further proof of our thesis, we know of three young priests who asked permission to spend their vacation working in an almost completely de=Christianized section of the country. They had had no practical experience, but they went to that place and talked about Christ to everyone they met; souls came back to Him in remarkable numbers, in spite of the fact that everyone thought they would fail. All that they had was an intense love of God, after the manner and example of St. Paul; we should not be astonished that this love infected others. I say that these young priests are fortu=nate, for they are beginning their priesthood by contact with individual souls, and with the determination to do anything to make Christ known and loved by men. We are the unfortunate ones, we who have grown up to look upon our ministry as a mere round of activity, of things to be organized.

Still another proof is found in what militant lay apostles have told us about their efforts to win souls for Christ; their simple unaffected stories have brought unsummoned tears to our eyes. We marvel at their faith, their courage, their selflessness, and are ashamed that we, though ordained for that very purpose, should be less eager than they in the cause of Christ. The reason? Simply that they have made their spiritual life a cause and an effect of their convictions and we have not. We lead two lives where they have integrated theirs.

❨ *Your view, then, is that there is no opposition between the "spiritual" and the "apostolic" life?*

Precisely. As a matter of fact, we would go further, and declare that there is a necessary connection between them. Those who agree that the apostolate demands deep spirituality should also see that the apostolate itself can promote and sustain the spiritual life.

If we were to believe some authors, there seems to be a fundamental opposition between the two, so much so that any attempt to combine them demands a great skill and greater prudence. The spirituality they write about is a thing apart from the grossness of the world; the seminary's purpose, as they see it, is the frantic building up of a reserve of holiness against the day when we shall have no time for spiritual exercises as we know them in the seminary. Once ordained, may God help us! Then we shall have to try to save what we can of our fund of spiritual strength; we shall have to steal a few moments out of each day's whirl of action in order to find God again. So they say.

Remember this. This sarcasm, if such it be, is not directed against the value of the familiar spiritual exercises. We are objecting only to the narrowness and the inaccuracy of those authors who teach this outlook on life in the priesthood.

We believe that our spiritual life becomes infinitely richer and fuller when we build it upon the touchstone of the active ministry, namely, our passion for souls, our apostolate. Rather than consider prayer as my contact with God, as my duty towards him, it seems less egotistical and more beneficial to see it under this light; namely, to offer it in the name of all those who are not loving God and who are starving without him. This is an expression of the purpose of my priesthood, and will be acted upon soon after I have said my prayers. The alleged danger in this is supposed to be that some of us will fall into an excess of external zeal, and will emphasize too much the active life. Possibly, but looking around at the waste of priestly energy, and at the compromise we have to make now, we are not too concerned about this eventuality. More wings are clipped by prudence, criticism, and rationalizing than by any excess of zeal; more young priests are in enforced idleness than in intemperate apostolic activity. We see more sophisticated priests than overzealous ones. There is a great deal more verbiage on sins of commission than there is on sins of omission, and yet the latter are chiefly responsible for the present condition of our people.

We know priests who are good, and even holy, men; and yet these same priests can preserve an astonishing tranquility of conscience even though faced by the vision of thousands of souls who live and die around them without the faintest knowledge of Christ, and even though they themselves have been chosen from among men to bring him to such as these. We are astonished and saddened. We know that these priests are regular in their prayers, that they keep up a daily schedule of religious exercises such as they learned in the seminary. Maybe they are too rigid; they are certainly unreal in their spiritual life.

❧ *I find it impossible to believe that a priest's contact with God would weaken his apostolic ardor.*

We do, too. It can only be that the type of spirituality we have just criticized does not afford real contact with God; the actions are empty, formalistic routine. Such men think that they have done their duty when they have put in the required time or said the indicated prayers; they cannot pretend to have met God in their prayers. Their duty has been carried out to the last detail, but it profits them nothing, at least as regards the vision of souls separated by ignorance and by sin.

It is sad that a priest can arrive at such a state and still consider himself as a "good" priest. The problems facing the Church demand the full effort of every priest, and yet this man of personal piety is doing nothing for anyone except himself—if, indeed, he is doing even that. It is ridiculous and dangerous to describe a priest as "good" simply because he is tidy and punctual and steady; part of the reason for these qualities is that he is too selfish or too blind to be unsettled by the gigantic problems, collective and personal, which he should be trying to solve.

Such a man does not reach this state because of his spir= itual life; it is the result of a lack of one, or the possession of a misguided one. The one he has is not spiritual and not priestly; it does not know the meaning of *caritas Christi urget nos.*[1] Somehow we cannot see as an ideal that priestly career which sidesteps the troubles and tales of the people he is sup= posed to sanctify; some priests do, however. We remember one old parish priest who took it upon himself to give some advice to a deacon just before his ordination; the substance of it was that the priest had reached his present enviable position in charge of a wealthy parish simply because he always was smart enough not to waste time listening to people's woes. One of the seminarians present whispered to me: "Just like St. Paul!"

What an ideal! It is nothing but that of a petty official, of a soured civil clerk. Among priests it is almost a blasphemy, for we are supposed to be other Christs, living and teaching His Gospel. Again we say that such an attitude could never have arisen except for the prevalent divorce between the spiritual

---

1   2 Cor. 5:14

and the apostolic life we are supposed to lead. It is under-standable, though not forgivable, only in a man who does not realize that his sanctification is necessarily bound up with his ministry, that his union with God must come from and return into his work with souls. Please God, priests everywhere will come to think on this.

❧ *You did admit that some forms of the apostolate were opposed to the spiritual life.*

We did, but they are the forms which are least recognizable as being either apostolic or priestly. They include things like athletics, plays, bazaars, and administrative details; these are, properly, the function of lay people. Accidentally, they may sanctify us on account of the patience and self-denial they involve, but, in themselves, they are a distraction, a dissipation of priestly energy. If the spiritual writers mentioned above had meant only this sort of activity, we would most certainly agree with their conclusions.

On the other hand, the direct apostolate is quite another matter. Its source is a thirst for souls; its practice is a constant occasion for seeing and a constant motive for correcting our own shortcomings. We are stimulated to perfect ourselves precisely because we are obliged to see that our defects are an obstacle to others. A priest may easily become discouraged, doing things that have only a remote connection with his priesthood, such as begging for money, or supervising a play; he is less likely to become so when he spends his days and nights in trying to make our Lord known to men. The confidences he receives, the grace he almost creates in the souls of sinners, these will keep alive the grace that was in him on the morning of his ordination; these are natural steps to the feet of the Master. We all know that long hours in the confessional have made us better priests; we all know that talking to and with militant lay Christians has made us realize better the meaning of our priesthood. Our preparation for sermons has shown us what it is to meditate. All of these things make us live in a Godlike atmosphere, and they are perpetual goads to do better and to be better. They may not be the best thing for a life of absolute monastic con‑templation, but they are the stuff that makes up the essence of an apostolic life. We can even quote St. Thomas in our behalf on this particular point, for he taught that the so‑called "active" life has a close connection with the cloistered one; the reason he gives is that the apostle is handling and distributing the gifts of God, and finding his joy therein, in a way similar to the monk's enjoyment of God. We agree with the Angelic Doctor.

❆ *Please explain a little more fully what you mean by saying that the apostolate is a spiritual life in itself, and that it is our fundamental means of sanctification.*

Our position is based on the idea that our apostolate is not something extra; for us it is a vocation, a state of life. Conse‑quently, we hold that we shall not become holy without fulfill‑ing that state of life; nor conversely shall we fulfill it without becoming holy. With every state in life go graces which enable us to perform its necessary duties, for God, who wills the end, also wills the means. Remember that this vocation is a special one — one demanding every ounce of our love and energy and intelligence. Do not confuse our terms, because we do not mean to leave the impression that the apostolate is similar to a job, as the use of the overworked phrase "state of life" might seem to imply. We are not men who can satisfy the demands of our vocation by putting in a certain number of hours, or by perform‑ing a certain routine of activity. We have not taken on a job; we have embraced a life. And that life will take from us all our thoughts and all our passion; it will force us to find problems everywhere; it will make us understand, almost automatically, what could be done for Christ in this place or in that situation. No part of our existence, no corner of our minds or hearts is exempt from this drive to break through the path we have been chosen to make for our Lord. If a mother is absorbed by the cares of her family, so are we for the children of God; if a businessman is constantly planning new programs, new products, so are we for the things of God. We must try to live what St. Paul said in his words about "whether you eat or drink, or whatever you do . . . ".

A priest who is deeply and completely absorbed in this vision of the City of God has already achieved a deep and lasting spiritual life.

But spiritual writers always include the idea of mortification in any outline of holiness.

And we do, too. A priest who is living his parochial aposto‑ late because of zeal for souls need never worry about the fact that we did not mention mortification; he will see that there was no need to develop the obvious. But for the priest who sees in his ministry only a set routine of duty, we hasten to point out to him that the occasions for self‑denial are many and great. We can only wish that spiritual writers would begin to outline the practical and ascetical value of the active ministry.

In general, every virtue demands self‑denial from those who would practice it; specifically, and in this life of ours, certain ones are more prominent. We shall try to give a brief picture of some of the outstanding sources of the mortification, whose apparent absence some spiritual theorizers might deplore.

The first is obedience. Not that abstract, though actual, gift of our wills we made to the bishop on the morning of ordina‑ tion, but the stark, concrete handing over of one's self to the demands of time and place which this life demands. It requires us to accept, without murmuring, the corner God has given us to evangelize, and to see in it the people who are destined to make saints of us while we are trying to lead them back to him. There is no room for disillusionment, no time for wishing that we were somewhere else, no slackening of our fervor because of rebuffs. By the same token we are not to neglect individuals or groups simply because their poverty or ignorance or crudeness is distasteful to us. We have been sent to all, and we must obey.

Connected with this obedience is the spirit in which we must meet the demands on our time. If we are rigid in allotting every minute of the day and refuse to alter that program, we are failing in the true giving of ourselves. Unexpected visits and often endless talks are a necessary part of our lives; instead of letting ourselves be annoyed and out of sorts, we must learn to accept these things as a routine part of our apostolate, and use them as such. We have made a gift of ourselves, and we will not take it back. We are willing to continue with some activity in the parish, even though we cannot like it; we are willing to live a life made up of countless tiny and unimport= ant events, with none of the dreamed=of fanfare of our youth. Neither monotony nor lack of success will cause us to forget why we are here; nor will they reduce our resistance to the point where we shall have let ourselves become social workers or sociologists but not priests. There is an obedience for you. It never lets us go our own way or force our own ideas, but asks that every priest should accept the situations, the needs, the people—the warp and woof of our consecrated labour.

The second virtue we might mention is detachment. Abbé Godin brought out the fullness of this at a talk he gave to a recollection=day group of Jocist girls. He asked the girls if they should love the Jocist movement; they cried out that they should. He asked them if they ought to love their individual cells, and the same reply came back. Much to the astonishment of all, Abbé Godin told them that they were wrong, that they should be attached neither to the Jocists nor their particular part of it; the sole object of their devotion should be the souls of the workers whom they were trying to bring to Christ. He analyzed their feelings, and showed that the love of one's own cell was nothing but a disguised self=love which could hinder the apostolate. He pleaded with them to love souls, and to forget themselves, their group, their organization.

While he was talking we could not help thinking of the par= ish apostolate, and of the application of this great priest's words to our own work. He made us reflect on whether or not we loved our parish. Should we love our parish and our special activities so much? Not to do so, and to think only of souls requires almost an heroic degree of detachment; it asks us to ignore our own success and prestige while we make the welfare of men our sole concern. A little examination of conscience about this virtue could run along lines like the following: if I loved souls and not my own reputation, the knowledge that some of my parishioners go to neighboring churches for Mass and devotions would not disturb me; my grief would be much better spent on those who go to no church at all. If I loved souls and not my own little kingdom, the absence of militant apostles who felt a greater need for a day of recollection than for the parochial procession I had organized would not infuriate me; I should rejoice at the greater good done to the cause of Christ. If I loved souls more than my parish, the news of an impending division of the parish territory would not make me feel cheated; I should rather be glad that greater attention could now be paid to the tremendous number of souls already in my care.

The same principle will apply to others, as well as to the poor priests against whom so much of the tirading in this book seems to be directed. Sisters and teachers and all the "official=dom" of the Church might well check up on their own disin=terestedness in the service of Almighty God. I remember years ago, how indignant one nun was when I asked her to arrange a mass meeting of two rival groups; she found it impossible that I should be asking that "her" girls would be expected to share their plans and assets with the other and inferior group. Even when I gently reminded her that we were all working for the same Master, her amazed and hurt expression did not change.

If we would only realize that it matters not who preaches Christ, as long as Christ be preached! St. Paul, who said those words, could scarcely approve of our jealous departmentaliz=ing, of the careful respect we must show for the boundaries of another man's field. Until we reach the stage where St. Paul would be proud of us, we are obstacles to the cause he preached, and a scandal to the faithful.

The temptation to go from detachment to poverty is too much for us, so please allow us to say a few words on this too.

Wait a minute! Only religious are expected to keep the vow of poverty.

We know that, but the spirit of poverty is certainly expected of all Christians. We think that there could be and should be an ideal of priestly poverty as a goal for the secular clergy; it would be a marvelous means of mortification as well, and would be far more meritorious than great fasts or the discipline. Speaking very practically we are convinced that this poverty is an important element of the priestly spirituality we are trying to outline.

Above, in talking of money, we spoke about the people's opinion of our middle-class way of living; without repeating all that here, we do want to emphasize the fact that a lowly stan-dard of life is essential to the apostolate among working-class men and women. That means that we shall have to begin to do without many of the luxuries we now enjoy. A seminarian, or a young priest, would not be appalled at the prospect of living simply, but we older priests are. We might admit that poverty in practice would be beneficial to our work, but we can summon a thousand reasons against any drastic change in our position; we, who are settled in this life of comparative ease, are quick to call upon the virtue of prudence and to counsel, sagely, against being too hasty. Our wisdom and our prudence are sadly in need of guidance.

What is asked for is more than a giving up of material lux-uries, because more is demanded of a priest who goes to the working-people. As we said previously, we must give up the cultural, artistic, literary delights of our own lives in so far as they hinder us in the work; that they will hinder us, if not closely controlled, is obvious to anyone who knows the aver-age man and also knows the average priest. Please notice that we are not saying that a priest must completely abandon his hours of intellectual and cultural pleasure. Absolutely not! We do say that he must not carry over those tastes in a ministry devoted to men and women who find such things completely foreign to them. We mean that a priest must be willing to work with the dullest of the grammar-school children as well as with the brightest of the high-school age. He will chat with the most unlearned parishioner as readily as he would with his intellectual equals. He will be ready to spend an evening at a Jocist meeting without letting the noise and slang and confusion weary him—at least, not too much.

Such a priest will not spend his time on those who can appreciate his repartee simply because they do appreciate it. His literary gems will be saved for the proper time, and that does not mean all the time. In brief, we are trying to demon-strate that an apostle who is honestly poor in spirit will try to do everything for the good of his people, and nothing solely for his own satisfaction. There is a thorough, unending gift of one's self! By sanctifying the duties God has given us to do, we can come to a total acceptance of His will in our regard.

❡ *That sounds more like humility than poverty.*

Most virtues resemble one another, but we want to thank you for giving us an occasion to say a little about humility. Parish work could be a splendid source of that virtue for us, but, unfortunately, it often produces the opposite effect.

In this age of contempt for things sacred we are obliged to stress the grandeur of God's priesthood more than ever before. The subsequent danger is that we begin to transfer the maj-esty from our spiritual position to ourselves; the dignity of the priesthood and the vanity of the priest are closer than most of us realize. A cure for incipient or full-blown pride is con-tact with ordinary men and women, those who know nothing about the sublimity of the sacerdotal state, and who care less. The ignorance and consequent offhandedness of these people are a tonic to our overweening self-esteem; whether we like it or not, we have to admit that they are not going to let us lord it over them. Knowing that, we have a broad field for the practice of humility, in accepting rudeness, in being pushed into the background, and in the general lack of regard for us. It will do us good.

If we knew how workers despise the pompous and dictatorial air we so often assume, we would fight any such tendencies in ourselves. Rather than speak and act imperiously, we should try to imitate more closely the Son of God, who was misunderstood and scorned by the men he had come to save. When we make a morning meditation on humility, we can be sure that the day ahead of us is going to offer plenty of chances for practicing what we prayed; our spirituality is given flesh in every circum‹ stance of our lives. Looking back, we are sincerely regretful that our seminary training did not prepare us better for the daily concrete exercise of a tremendously important missionary vir‹ tue. The abstract talks on humility were offset, in real life, by the caste system around us in the seminary, by the emphasis on dignity and dignitaries; the same atmosphere carries over into the priesthood, where pious ideals are so easily buried under the weight of existing conditions. We expect and even desire ecclesiastical honors; sometimes, we come perilously close to the pharisaism castigated by Christ Himself.

It would be humorous, if it were not so tragic, to see the petty things that cripple our apostolicity. An insulting name or a rebuff or a flippant remark is enough to change us from apostles to angry, uncharitable mortals! What a pity! At the cost of souls we defend our wounded dignity, to the sorrow of the faithful, and the scorn of the infidels. The value of our self‹esteem relative to that of the salvation of a non‹believer makes our attitude all the more pitiful.

Another help in overcoming ourselves in this matter is a deliberate intention to seek and accept the criticisms of parish‹ ioners. We are, after all, here for them not for ourselves; and they can see much more and much better than we. Somebody told us about one of the cardinals of France who asked a Jocist what the people in his surroundings thought of him. Naturally the lad was embarrassed, but the cardinal pressed him; so the young man told him frankly that people thought that the car‹ dinal was just as smug as most Catholics were. There was no outburst of rage, but a quiet and sincere request to the Jocist to come back every month and report on how the working-class felt about him. That cardinal was a great man, and a humble one. We, who claim that the position of the Church would be compromised by permitting laymen to offer suggestions, might well think of and imitate the example of this prince of the Church. We might also think on the passage in the Gospel where Christ spoke of the Pharisees who loved to be called "master" and to be saluted in the market-place.

There is no profit in trying to find this spirit of constructive criticism in those whom we might call "priest-worshippers;" it takes no great sense of honesty to realize that not from them shall we receive truly helpful advice. And yet we can be easily tempted into thinking so, and led to the pathetic lengths of the parish priest who produced two thousand signatures as proof to the Archbishop that his proposed transfer was unwise. If we want to be incensed at the altar and away from it, we can be, and we will be; but it is far better for us and for the apostolate if we know how to take fair criticism and use it to our advantage. That needs humility and simplicity.

❧ *Do you know what the most common reproach leveled against clergymen is?*

It is what some like to call "prudence," even though they actually mean a sweet sort of decorum and aloofness. That mixture of unction, reserve, and self-satisfaction has come to characterize—or caricature—the so-called "ecclesiastical" art and mannerisms and life. That this should be so is a real trag-edy, because it is this very attitude of ours which makes us so repellent to souls longing for frankness, for truth. They reject our polite circumlocutions; they want the doctrine of Christ or they want nothing. In any case they do not want our deli-cateness. We are wrong to give the name of prudence to such a state of mind, for prudence is a strong weapon, whereas we are indecisive and timid. The people and the times demand stouthearted leaders to point out and lead the way to Christ, and to do it in such a way that our contemporaries will find a fullness for the vacuum they now experience. If we do not do this for them, no one else will or can.

The truth of the matter is that most of us retreat to this mis-named prudence simply because we fear rebuffs, simply because we do not want to have our tranquil lives disturbed. A truer spirituality would realize that these rebuffs and this disturbance are an incalculable source of profit to us and to the souls we are supposed to be directing. What is needed is not haste, not foolhardiness, not brute force, but a pro-found sense of courage, based on the love of God and man. There is so much to be done.

❬ *This seems to be a good place to talk about the spirit of team-work which you have used with such good results.*

We would rather develop that idea a little later on; just now, we will mention only the part that it can play in our spiritual advancement. Our experience in the priesthood has led us to two conclusions with regard to teamwork. One is that the mod-ern priest is very definitely called to work as part of a team, not as an individual. The other is that seminaries do not lay enough stress on the formation of flexibility in our character. Seminarians still have their Orders held up because they smoke or talk in violation of the rule, but we do not know of any who are so treated for their haughtiness, bad temper, or anti-social attitude. And yet we have seen men in the priesthood who were practically useless just because of these qualities; their moral and intellectual endowments were splendid, but no one, priest or layman, could get along with them. Nowadays, per-haps more than ever before, we need the social virtues as an essential part of our priestly character, both because of the type of person we are trying to convert, and also because of the necessity of united action by the clergy.

In any case, we need the "community" virtues. The efforts we have to make to acquire them, so as to be a productive member of a team, are immensely valuable to our interior life, as mortifications and as steps towards union with God. Adopt-ing another man's ideas at the expense of one's own, dropping a cherished, personal program so as to support someone else's, takes greatness of soul. It is a very vivid application of St. Paul's words about stripping off the old man.

❡ *You would condition the whole life of a parish priest, his prayer, virtues, asceticism, by the parochial ministry. What are you going to leave him for his own, his Mass?*

True, we do not leave him very much, but it is better so; there is no reason why any element of his own spiritual life should be foreign to his priesthood in the parish. Even the Mass, that prime source of interior strength, receives a new and valuable quality from his concern for souls. A Mass which is celebrated with devotion and with exactness has an immea‑ surable apostolic worth, for a priest is never more a priest than when he is offering the Sacrifice. Here we are other Christs, other High Priests, in an obvious way, going to God for our people, and returning from Him laden with graces for the par‑ ish. When a priest thinks of the Mass as an act of his private devotion, his spirituality is warped—not to mention his dogma. Essentially the Mass is the worship of the whole Church, of the complete Mystical Body of Christ; in it the faithful are joined to the priest in one communal act of adoration through Christ.

Believe it or not, this incident happened only a few weeks ago, and not in the last century. At a clergy conference, one of the venerable parish priests summed up his opinion of Dialogue Masses and para‑liturgical ideas by saying: "at least they should let us say our Mass in peace!" Another priest of our acquaintance forbade his curate to allow the thousand children gathered in the church for a Dialogue Mass in honor of the Blessed Sacrament to utter a single audible sound; he was saying the Mass, and he did not relish being distracted or disturbed at his prayers. These things really happen, lest anyone tell us that every priest realizes that the Mass is not merely his own act of devotion.

If, on the other hand, we have a deep and lively sense of being the chosen representatives of the faithful, we shall want and expect the congregation to participate; our celebration of the divine Mysteries will be for them and with them. The richness we are bringing and distributing will make us one with them, and they with us, and all of us one in Christ Jesus. Both our apostolate and our ulterior life are progressing by leaps and bounds. Paul Claudel imagined the feelings of a priest at the moment of the Offertory in words like these:

> The Lord is with you, my brothers. I pray you, be with me.
> Here is more than the paten, more than the chalice and the wine;
> Here you are, my little ones, held and supported in my hands.

If we could say that and feel that, in our own way, what priests we should be! We could not help but be different men, and the souls we most want to attract would be drawn by Christ in us, the whole community would be joined in prayer to him through us. There would be no more of those mum-bled, twenty-minute scandals, no more of those meaningless and unmeant gestures. Our own souls and the souls of the people would grow in our common approach to the likeness of the Lord.

Surely you understand now why we are pleading for a syn-thesis of spirituality and life in the apostolate. One cannot exist without the other. If we had remained sub-deacons for life we could find sanctification in reciting the Office and avoiding sin; as it is we are priests, parish priests, and surely God meant us to find Him in the work He has given us to do. Instead of the false idea which would have us flee the field of labor for the strengthening of our souls, we ought to realize that here, in this parish, are the steps that will lead us to him. The more perfectly we realize and use this knowledge, the holier we shall be. More and more, in the seminary and in the ministry, we should use the apostolate as the starting-point of all our spirituality. Our fitness for Orders and for a particular parish should be judged by our zeal for souls, by our love of Christ; and not as often happens, by our administrative ability and our ecclesiastical air. We are not ridiculing or discarding the standard exercises of piety, which are of great value in and out of the seminary. But we plead and will continue to plead, for that attitude which sees the demands of the ministry as our fundamental and effective source of spirituality, and which admits of no opposition between the two.

2. TEAMWORK

All the structural reforms you have been explaining are certainly beyond the strength of even the most courageous priest.

They are not intended as the work of any one priest, but of an entire parish team; without that team, none of the ideas proposed in this book can be accomplished. The word "team" is not satisfactory because we mean so much more than that word implies. We have in mind something more than mere cooperation and coordination of the activity of the priests, because the attainable ideal here is a union of the clergy and the people in a single, concerted, and militant warfare for Christ. No one is to be neglected, no one is to be outside the group action.

The key to this plan is, naturally, the unity of the parish clergy; unless they are a bloc, it is silly to expect a more complex union with the faithful. If we priests here in this parish had not been closely knit together, what we have accomplished would have been absolutely unattainable; what each has done, all have done. Because of that we can face future difficulties with confidence, trusting in the cooperation we knew in the past to see us through the days ahead. This is not boasting, believe me.

In our times the task we face is so overwhelming that we cannot conceive of anyone trying to face it alone. Without stretching the imagination too far, the onslaught of modern paganism can be compared to the invasion of France by the German Army in 1940; our enemy is even stronger, swifter, and infinitely more aggressive. Just as it would have been the height of stupidity to oppose the Nazi army by local and unorganized opposition, so is it more stupid and more costly for us in this latter day. We need an organized counter-offensive which will use every weapon and every Christian according to a long-range and universal plan of attack. Without that, we are beaten at the start because of our scattered strength, and because of the delusions of victory which most certainly arise from success in isolated sectors. In the rest of this chapter we shall try to explain the concrete details of our proposal, without any further dependence on military metaphors.

At the beginning of a project like this, we need to expect no bouquets from anyone, least of all from the average parishioner. They, more than most classes, would rather face death than a change in the life they have always known; the parish may be but half-alive, but this type of parishioner likes it as it is. Love for so-called tradition is equalled only by fear of being disturbed. That is why we had to face the complaints of many an outraged member of our flock, especially in the early days; it took time and firmness and unity on the part of all the priests before the most doubtful Thomases were assured of our good intentions. It was an uphill struggle, and one that never could have succeeded if either the parish priest or the curates had let dissenting parties grow up around them; every denunciation, every criticism, had to be met by the solid unity of all the clergy. In this way not only were meddlers checked, but the enthusiasm of the whole parish team began to be communicated to the die-hard group.

Under conditions like these a man can work, and work without fear of being considered foolhardy, or of having his ideas discarded peremptorily. The responsibility and errors are everyone's, just as the success is. Failures or mistakes are met with honest but friendly and fraternal correction, and there is no stigma accompanying the errors or the advice. You can see how this makes for peace of soul and strength of effort. Unlike most priests we do not have to face discouragement alone, because we are now bound together in mind and heart and will, in the work of Jesus Christ. Difficulties and criticism are faced together, and "my work" has become "our work."

In this way the isolation that most of us have known in our priesthood is eliminated. We do not have to plan alone, and wonder whether we are right or not; we do not have to be afraid to approach other priests for their ideas. Most important of all, there can be no cleavage between our assigned activity and the advance of the whole parish. Even when things go wrong in our part of the work we are not obliged to face the difficulty alone. The others notice our downcast look, and bring us out of it either by their joking or by their actual help. Before long we really begin to think and act as a team, so much so that we instinctively lean on and support one another.

Even if this solidarity did no more than this, it would be worthwhile; merely ridding rectories of rivalry and ill-temper is a glorious result. But, over and above this, it touches and transforms our apostolicity with the lighthearted zeal most of us have not known since seminary days. Passing beyond the walls of the rectory, it reaches out to the people, and infects them too. Some readers may smile at this, but one member of the parish actually told one of us that he enjoyed visiting the priests' house, simply because it was such a pleasure to see how well the priests got on with one another. There must be some reason too for the increase of vocations from the parish; and, since we have abolished most of the parish activities, the reason must be found in the evident spiritual joy of the priests. Certainly the words of the Psalmist mean something, and he sang about *quam bonum et quam jucundum*.[2] Nor was Christ joking when He told us that wherever two or three were gathered together in His Name, he would be in the midst of them. We live and work, held together "in the Name of Christ," and that unity is the source of both efficiency and grace for us, and for the whole parish. We know that the faithful notice scandal and discord in their clergy, but we seem to forget that they also notice and imitate our single-minded spirituality.

¶ *Could you give us some sort of a definition of this teamwork?*

If not a definition we will give you a description. In the first place, it involves work; it does not mean simply a common

2   Ps. 132:1

dwelling-place, nor a certain amount of mutual understanding. The team part of it includes all these factors: that the men involved in it are to think the same thoughts, and want the same things; that they better themselves and the work as a unit, by mutual help, correction, and compromise.

❰ *That is too complicated to grasp. Please explain what you mean by "wanting the same things."*

We start with the idea that there is to be agreement on certain principles, which are to be the norms for all to follow. This does not say that we lay down a definite program or method from the beginning; only that all of us agree on the angle from which we are going to face problems as they arise. It is something like fixing a destination before the beginning of a trip. Logically the parish priest should determine these principles, but with the comment and judgement of the curates. They are not to be hard-and-fast rules, because it is almost a certainty that some of them are going to be discarded voluntarily as the work progresses.

In this parish we all did some reading before deciding on the perspective we were to take. If some of Abbé Godin's books had been written then, we might have been spared a lot of reading. Our dinner-table became a round table of ideas; to it we invited priests and laymen who were familiar with the problems and spirit of the working people. Partly for the fun of it, and partly for our own good, we decorated the dining room with placards, on which we printed different slogans. One was Pope Pius XI's, "We think so much of traditions that we do not hesitate to create new ones." Another was from a letter of St. Francis de Sales: "Popes are generally willing to let custom authorize things which would be awkward for the popes themselves to authorize."

Once the important overall principles have been agreed upon, it is essential to convince each one of us that our individual efforts and thoughts are needed. We cannot succeed without each other. That must be understood and acted upon in practice.

Even when we cannot see eye to eye on particular points, we still realize that the total plan depends on all of us. We used to joke about our "Five Year Plan," but we knew that each of us would work together, through thick and thin, to see that task fulfilled. We wanted to bring this entire parish back to the feet of Christ. We all wanted that.

When it comes time to decide upon details it takes the good-will and intelligence of all of us. There is no place for personal goals which would split the team into factions. We have our own particular assignments, but not to the extent of resenting the intrusion of one of the other priests, and not to the extent of believing that we can handle our share of the work without the cooperation of all the priests. It may sound as though we are fond of chaos, but let the reader be reassured. Each man is complete master of his particular task, but he does not have to assert his independence by jealous irritation in order to prove it. He has reached the stage of conviction where he sees himself and his function as part of a bigger and more important whole. We have willed to work together. Essentially, that is what we mean by "wanting the same things."

¶ Still, being human, you must encounter difficulties in the prac-tical application of this common will.
We should, if it were not for the fact that we "think the same thoughts." We said that both the goodwill and the intelligence of each priest were necessary for the realization of our overall plan. The curates are not simply the errand boys of the parish priest's preconceived ideas, but they are meant to give them-selves totally to the task confronting all of us. In a discussion anyone may raise a question, and all try to answer it; no one is to insist on the correctness of his own view, because then the driving force of the team would vanish. Everyone is to be heard, no matter how rash his views may be, but everyone is expected to be willing to face the opinion and decision of the majority. Once settled, the idea becomes common property, and opposition is put aside, without bitterness by the opponents

and without gloating by the defenders. There is plenty of room for differences, but absolutely none for contrariness.

Our experience has been that we grow closer together as we go along; being so close together we think as a community almost by second nature. At the beginning of each week there is a special meeting to decide upon pressing needs, but, for the most part, we find ourselves working and thinking together without adverting to it. Honestly, it has reached the stage where we hesitate, in a sense, to act without consulting our confreres. By this time a parishioner no longer shows surprise when the parish priest says that he wants to talk over the proposal of the parishioner with one of the curates before deciding upon it.

At first glance such an attitude on the part of the priest may seem harmful to good order, to authority and obedience. Somehow it does not work out that way. Everyone realizes that the parish priest has a better general knowledge of the needs and capabilities of the parish, and that his experience in the priesthood is fuller. Quite naturally it devolves upon him to decide the general directives, and his position and experience are enough to settle any discussions which threaten to be inter- minable. Obedience to him, too, is all the easier because it is free and not forced; it is given to him willingly because of the sacred task of all the priests in the parish. He is not a dictator, but a leader. He himself is bound to obey and submit to the demands which the common good lays upon all. Consequently, obedience becomes not a burden but a joy. No one is asked to be a slave, but all are asked to make a complete consecration of themselves. Parish priest and curates alike are involved in this, and each is given chances to understand the peculiarities of the other. In our opinion the issue at stake here is infinitely more important than any secondary considerations, and our first concern must be to ensure the basic need, namely, the trans- formation of our parish by the cooperation of all its members.

Another result of excessive preoccupation about authority and obedience is that it may well prevent a curate from speak- ing his mind when he should do so. This is especially true of a newcomer, who will fail to catch the spirit of the team and will get the idea that he is neither wanted nor needed unless he is made to understand that he will not be treated as a child when he does speak out. His opinions must not be met with sarcasm or mere indulgence. It is the privilege of the young to make mistakes, precisely because they are young and visionary and enthusiastic. We need that vision. If the emphasis is placed on authority, the teamwork comes to a full stop; instead of developing and building apostles, we shall have discouraged and cynical priests on our hands. That is no pleasant prospect.

❆ *It is easy enough to think along the same lines, but it must be much more complicated when each one takes up his assigned work.*

It is, but our convictions and principles remain the same. Even though each of us has a definite assignment we still act as a unit. You see, we think of what we are doing as the work, and not my work, even to the logical conclusion that none of us feels free to take time off, as long as one of us has some≠ thing to finish. But since we are men, not angels, we have to take precautions against hurting one another's feelings, because common sense and bitter experience have proved sensitiveness to be the number one enemy of teamwork. This means that it is difficult to divide up the work; it prevents a man who spots an oversight in someone else's plans from correcting the mistake. However, if we have to watch our every word with one another for fear of giving offense, if we have to wonder and worry about the reaction of the others, we might as well forget about cooperation. Unless we know for certain that each of the others will not object to what we do in good faith, unless we are sure that all the others think and will as we do, our labor is in vain; we are not a team. We are no longer striving for the advance of the Kingdom of God in this parish, but for our own reputation or satisfaction.

All of this involves sacrifices. The end in view is so important that sometimes we have to curtail some particular phase of it for the good of the whole; such a decision has to be taken graciously by the priest affected. Murmuring or insinuation or becoming a martyr can ruin the spirit and the very existence of our common work. When a man can take such reversals in his own field of endeavour, he is practicing a most profound mortification—one of inestimable benefit to himself and to our work. Such a man is well on the way to conquest of self, and he has found the real meaning of obedience.

❡ *Tell me, what is the meaning of the charts and graphs in your rectory?*

They are there as proof of the advances and the failures of our teamwork. Once a week we have a meeting to discuss the past week's accomplishments; the results are traced out on these graphs, which show the picture of five years of effort. We comment on the findings, on the attendance at services, on our sermons, etc. No one is spared, not even the parish priest. It is easy to see the advantages of such a system. For one thing, it guards against routine; every one of us is stimulated and cor=rected, whereas we should almost certainly become dangerously self=satisfied if left to our own tender goading. Everyone has a chance to speak aloud the words that we should otherwise say behind one another's back, to the loss of charity and to the detriment of our work.

Do not imagine, though, that these meetings are completely negative. Besides the failures, there are also the individual and common successes to be talked over, with encouragement and renewed fervor for all. That is equally important. But the chief value of such meetings is the concentration of many single=minded hearts and wills on problems common to us all. Where, alone, we might have been satisfied with a vague uneasiness that something was wrong, here, in the bonds of charity, we try to find out just where we have gone wrong, and then put it right. Two heads are better than one, and we pro=ceed accordingly. We try to use to good advantage that deeply rooted tendency of man which makes him see the mote in his brother's eye before the beam in his own. Everything that we do is fair prey for this criticism, and we are better men and better apostles for it.

Most young curates are agreeably surprised when they find such a system. It relieves them of that dread of doing the wrong thing and not being told about it, for new curates can find themselves in very awkward positions simply because no one told them about their mistakes. We try to ensure against both the mistakes and the anxiety, while the good-natured spirit of the meeting forestalls even the trace of a persecution-complex. Moreover, the newcomer does not have to face the jaundiced barbs or the paternal condescension of individuals; this is a mutual task of like-minded men.

What parishioners say about us comes up for discussion too, and this is especially valuable, since it shows the reactions of the very ones we are trying to influence. Without these meetings and this team-work the value of parish reaction and comment would be lost, for it would take a rash man indeed to tell a confrere in private what the parishioners are saying about him! As it is now, the comments can be revealed, since we take them as applying to all of us.

We are personal too. We are ready to discuss our ministe-rial work, our temperament, character, and deportment. Every year, just before the annual retreat, we take advantage of the spiritual mood which comes upon us, and gather around for an old-fashioned chapter of faults. Each of us, in turn, is sent out of the room while the others pick out traits to be conquered or developed by the one in question; as he leaves for retreat the next morning, he is handed a sealed envelope, to be used during the week as food for examination and meditation, by a chastened retreatant.

This includes the parish priest. In this way we actually do help one another; the steps along the way to our perfection as priests and missionaries are marked out for us. Each of us knows in his heart that all the others are with him, that their criticisms are sincere and unmistakable manifestations of love and support.

❡ *What did you mean in your definition of teamwork when you spoke about compromising oneself?*

Maybe an example will show what we mean, because an abstract explanation is extremely difficult.

Supposing a parishioner approaches a curate with a complaint about the parish priest. For the sake of example, let us even suppose that the parish priest might very probably be wrong in this particular matter. Now three possibilities are open to the poor curate. He may condemn his superior and justify the parishioner, which seems unwise, to say the least. Or he may listen patiently to the long explanation, try to illuminate the reasons for the parish priest's decision, while keeping himself completely out of the argument. Or he may refuse to accept any rebellion, any swerving from the decision made by the parish priest, in such a way that the parishioner cannot help but see that the curate identifies himself with the decision.

At first glance that last possibility may seem to be sheer stubbornness. At second glance it may still seem stubbornness; however, we hold that, taking things as they are, a parish team must follow such an attitude wholeheartedly and unswervingly. We know that complaints are going to come, and we must prove to the opposition that we are a solid and convinced bloc; once we let the wedge of individual adherents enter into our common life as priests, our cooperation is lessened or lost. There must be no little group around Father So-and-so, no devotees of Father Such-and-such at least, not to the extent of putting a particular priest outside the team. After a while people will see that our inflexibility in this matter is meant for their benefit. It asks sacrifices of people and priest, but it is an immensely important part of our program.

❡ *It seems to me that your little community is a happy one, judging from what I observed in the time I spent here.*

It is, as a result of another principle of ours, namely, that we enjoy ourselves; when we need relaxation we try to relax together. Basically it is the same idea as that which underlies the granting of holidays in a seminary. When the students show signs of tension a free day makes new men of them. Also, we try to be a little family unto ourselves, and so our jokes and teasing are very much like the ones we all knew in our own homes. It is difficult to describe, just as the humor of any family might well seem strange to an outsider. We have found our own ways of relaxing together and of enjoying one another; any other group can achieve the same in its own way.

❧ *You must have a high opinion of community life.*

We most certainly do. Not that we confuse it with the religious life, its vows, of poverty, chastity, and obedience, its rules and spiritual exercises. Rather, we have in mind a kind of community life which will be possible for secular priests. Such a community involves a minimum of being together physically, for we hardly see each other in the course of a day; spiritually, though, we are together as much as possible. "Living together" is nothing else but adapting ourselves to one another, according to the particular and peculiar gifts of temperament, character, and grace, which are given to each of us. The very diversity of these talents is a treasure which we must uncover and use. As a matter of fact, it is a good thing that others are not like us, that they have a different standard of values, see things that escape us, and are rich where we are poor. Even our defects are to be accepted, for they usually are, but the excess of our good points, and we can help each other in their correction. Maybe one of us is a little too boisterous and noisy and disrupts the community life a little; maybe he is the type who sings in a loud voice while we are trying to write up a sermon . . . but it is he who makes us rock with laughter when everyone else is gloomy. Perhaps another one of us is a trifle too meticulous and precise, but it is he who keeps order in our accounts and records.

Living together necessarily creates a certain community feel≠ing; just what that will be depends on the individual commu≠nity. It is made up of this one's speed and that one's slowness; of vision and of solidity; each plays upon the other, until the rhythm is found—like oarsmen in the same boat. The parish priest must temper the rashness and check the exuberance of the quick, and make sure that the less dynamic are appreciated.

❡ *Does this community life extend to the supernatural sphere?*

Indeed it does, for we are not merely propagandists; we are also and especially priests, members of Christ, the High Priest, intermediaries between God and man, appointed to bring the divine life to men. A vocation such as this is a stronger reason for mutual support and collaboration than is the mere organiza= tion of apostolic tactics. We must be a team in the supernatural sphere, so as to climb together, and so as to raise the spiritual level of the whole group. We must give the best that is in us, as God has given to each, and try to profit from the best that is in everyone else. We must pray together, not by any scheduled "exercises," even when that would be possible, but by a union of hearts in prayer.

Take the question of prayer. A necessary preparation for it is this very state of being united. Its first requisite is that the charity of Christ be spread among us, raising our hearts to the Father. If we were to examine our distractions at prayer, we should find that many of them are caused by bitterness and rankling left from some little quarrel. In a community which is not united, we could say that most distractions come from difficulties in adapting ourselves, from "fraternal" collisions; the greater part of our spiritual forces is expended on defending charity against these onslaughts. If we were united our prayers would, at least, be free of this care. So much for the negative side. Positively speaking, if we were each as greatly concerned over the spiritual level of the whole team as we are over our own spiritual progress, if we were anxious to open up and give of our best to the others, we should not hesitate to express our personal opinions about prayer, or about the little helps that we have discovered. This is a difficult thing to do, and conse= quently, it is rarely done. We are ready enough to exchange views on an intellectual plane; it is only with real friends that we can exchange experiences on what we feel down inside us. Yet something like this must be reached in our priestly teams, because priests who live the same supernatural and priestly life should be friends. We cannot be bashful if we want this teamwork to succeed, but we must be willing to express our= selves without waiting for somebody else to begin.

Why not have spiritual reading in common? Not the formal kind, when the parish priest imposes a book of his choice on everyone, but the spontaneous type, where a member of the team reads a passage that caught his fancy. Even better, there could be a subject proposed for everyone to discuss and where everyone can read what he found of interest or of value on the subject. That is how we often do it at Colombes. The result is far richer than would be obtained from listening to one man's ideas.

The same is true of all spiritual exercises. If we keep watch before the Blessed Sacrament, it is in the name of all; if there is a parochial offensive under way, all are joined in prayer before the Tabernacle. When we recite our Breviaries, it is spiritually "in choir," for all of us are ordained for the praising of God. When we celebrate Mass, we "concelebrate" in spirit with all those whose task and privilege it is to offer the Sacrifice of Christ in the name of and for the benefit of the parish. Even though, canonically, the Mass *pro populo* binds only the parish priest, we celebrate it every day, as a share of all the Masses offered by all the priests of the world. When one of us has some special difficulty, it is natural and easy to get another one of us to meet for prayer with him.

This common prayer is a great boon to us. It is—as it must be—really fraternal, and really in harmony with our lives.

❈ *This life as a team certainly must be a tremendous source of strength. But it must also involve a considerable degree of mutual consideration.*

It does. Living as a unit is a good purifying agent, to use the terms of spiritual writers. It involves detachment, submission to the trials of daily life, a constant struggle against pride and jealousy. We have to forget the "ego," give up many of our own little likes, value the good opinion of others, and accept the others, so as to catch the rhythm of the team. There is a crying need for simplicity, but you know as well as we how difficult it is to attain it. And yet, once we have begun the struggle to make it a part of our lives, a new peace and a new joy are ours; the interior and the apostolic life are enriched and increased. It involves mortification, but the type of mortification which is proper to our priestly lives, and it eliminates other unnecessary or incompatible ascetic approaches.

From conversations or letters we know for a fact that many young priests would like to unite with their fellow curates and with their superior in this sort of team. It could be done, more easily than many believe; we sincerely hope that it will be. As conditions are now, diocesan authorities seem more preoccu⹀ pied with particular local needs than with the possibility of assigning priests to rectories where they might find men who would be both willing and able to work as a team. We are not being critical, but we do long for the day when a long⹀range vision will inspire the appointments of the clergy; and we pray for the day when a priest will be sent to a certain place, not because the parish priest needs another curate, but because this particular priest will fit well there.

❡ *What advice could you give to a newly⹀formed team?*

Our first advice, if such it is, would be to have each man firm in his determination to make the union of minds and wills work, even though other members of the team may be slow in forming the necessary attitude.

Coupled with this must be what might be called "perpetual motion." By that we mean a ceaseless fight against slipping into a routine; a new routine, to be sure, but one that can solidify as quickly as the old one did. We must have the same revolutionary spirit that led us to come together as a team, and the first fervor and freshness must be maintained by a healthy dissatisfaction with the results that we have obtained and by a continual seeking for new outlets. It is not enough to have a few novel ideas at the beginning and then to sink back into lethargy and routine; for the existence and for the fruitfulness of our work there must be unending adaptation to the changing problems of our ministry.

❡ *You mentioned getting the whole parish into this team. How do you go about that?*
The priestly team must be no more than the nucleus of the parochial one. The latter could not exist without the previous priestly formation; but this, in turn, must include all the active elements of the parish from every corner of it.

After all, why not get the parish interested in its own wel‑ fare? When we talk about a parish we certainly mean the peo‑ ple more than the priests; they were here before we were, and will, no doubt, be here long after we have been sent to some other post. We are no more than go‑betweens for them, and so should get rid of the mental confusion which makes some parish priests say, "I am the parish."

What a pity, when the faithful confuse the parish with the priests who direct it. Because of this attitude they no longer think that it is their affair too, and that they ought to be inter‑ ested in it.

It will always be difficult for some to join in any united effort. Many priests, realizing this, ask no more than that the faithful should do what they outline for them. We say that this is not the way to form virile, stalwart characters which the Church needs so badly.

To join priests and people in one team means more than sim‑ ply calling meetings and setting up committees with no more results than a vague feeling of accomplishment. We must so act towards our people that they may be really and completely united to the life and progress of their parish.

We have lay‑movements; let lay‑people take charge of them! Let them realize that this is their movement, and that they do not have to be constantly worrying about what the parish priest will think; outside of questions of faith, morals, or things touch‑ ing the welfare of the entire parish, they themselves should be capable judges. We must leave them alone in their organizing, in their formation, so that they can acquire a necessary sense of responsibility. When they are needed for some development within the parish they should be treated as adults, not chil‑ dren. They should be asked to help, and given reasons why they should; they should be allowed to see the end in view, and not be asked to follow our commands blindly. Especially should they be encouraged to speak to us, spontaneously, about their ideas and desires and grievances, and to let us know the criticisms which occur to them or to their neighbors.

More than one splendid suggestion has come to us in this way at meetings of militants. We should get them used to feel‑ ing free to speak to us, without fear or flattery. They ought to know that we are sufficiently mature not to resent reproaches; they ought to be able to see that we can tolerate their holding an opinion contrary to our own, without our claiming that they have insulted our priestly dignity.

Every member of the parish, whether he or she belongs to any of the specialized movements or not, should feel wanted and useful. More commonly in our parishes the whole bur‑ den of any apostolic attempts that may be made falls on a few "directors;" everyone else accepts this fact, and even welcomes it. The truth is that for any movement the great majority of people are "followers" than we realize. However, we want to see everyone progressively more and more interested, personally, in the advance of the cause. Nothing more harmful to such progression could be conceived than the custom, as it prevails in too many parishes, of having periodic meetings of these "directors," so that the parish priest can give to them tasks that he has drawn up for them. They are changed into agents, whereas they are meant to be leaders. Imagine for yourselves how a Jocist group would feel if the leader were to present them with a set of ready‑made objectives, which he had dreamt up, and which they must somehow harmonize with the purpose of the group. Surely there are better ways to awaken and sustain the zeal of our people!

One better way is to outline the task and objectives to the whole body of the faithful when they are present at Sunday Mass; then they can feel their unity and participation. From that same pulpit we can give them an up=to=date outline of the work of the whole parish, of failures, successes, mistakes and advances, and of things yet to be done by all of us. Sometimes the best sermon that a parish priest could preach is precisely this sort of outline.

Since the parish is not only a place of activity, but also a family, it follows that the parish priest should be a father, and that his simple speech and evident sincerity should be directed to training his children to react properly to the demands of the family's common goal.

It is essential that this spirit of generosity and vision enter into every single heart and join it to every other member of the parish, so that all may grow to full stature in this mission atmosphere. ✣

✢[8]✢
A Glance at Results

❦ *The logical question now is: Do your ideas and methods pro⸗ duce results?*

That question is a perennial one, but not necessarily logical. After all, spiritual realities cannot be measured by a slide⸗rule, nor should proof be demanded to determine the value of apos⸗ tolic efforts. Results, in the kind of work we are doing, may be barely visible, but God alone is the competent judge of the worth of our efforts. What is begun with a great fanfare may easily end in silence; and what begins quietly and perhaps inauspiciously can just as easily grow and be successful. God gives such increase. It is almost impossible for anyone to fore⸗ see all the factors which are going to play upon any particular missionary scheme; and the men and women involved in it, the political and social trends surrounding it, all have an influence upon its apparent success or failure. In work like this it is prac⸗ tically impossible to judge results fairly and accurately. Even while we use statistics and charts (as we do), you know as well as we that statistics can prove almost anything. Even when people begin to acclaim any particular activity as "remarkable," "eminently successful," we still do not have any proof that the results they acclaim are being accomplished. God knows, and we would rather trust in Him than in mathematics or publicity.

The figures that we have kept show a steady, unspectacular growth over the last five years, and we will put them down here for whatever they may be worth.

Attendance at Sunday Mass was as follows:

1941	1,000 (average)
1942	1,100
1943	1,200
1944	1,100 (Evacuation of Paris)
1945	1,300

Attendance at the Easter Retreats is more encouraging:

	Boys	Girls	Adults
1941	75	80	135
1942	70	90	150
1943	100	100	170
1944	85	135	230
1945	135	165	230

In a large parish like this it is extremely difficult to compute the number of those who made their Easter duty. As far as we could determine, these are the figures:

1941	850
1942	930
1943	1,070
1944	1,250
1945	1,375

A rough estimate of daily Communions shows that, in 1941, there were 19,000 hosts distributed; in 1945 the number had grown to 42,000.

We put down these records without trying to deceive our‐selves or you about their value; all that they prove is that we have a great deal of work yet to do. Over these last five years we have won a considerable amount of sympathy and interest, but we cer‐tainly have not changed much of the pagan atmosphere around us. We have begun, though, and the attendance of non‐believers at para‐liturgical or simplified ceremonies is frequent enough to make us believe that the beginning is a good one.

❈ *Could you give us any estimate of the converts you have made?*
The majority of those whom we have received into the Church are lapsed Catholics, whom the grace of Lent or a mis‐sion has brought back to the fold. Besides these there are some new adult converts every year, but the number is small, and the obstacles to their perseverance are great. As Abbé Godin pointed out, the modern parish has practically no influence on the mass of irreligious or indifferent persons inside its territory.

That truth partly explains the scarcity of conversions, and it also leads us to the two conclusions that:

The Mission of Paris is a strict necessity;

Parishes must aim at the conversion and at the perseverance of non-Catholics.

Consequently, it is not enough to make a parish missionary-minded and then to consider the battle won; we need every possible means of evangelization that we can lay our hands on to supplement and support the overall effort of a mission-parish. All that we have written in this book about the gulf between clerical and popular mentalities, about the "collective" mentality of modern man, is meant to drive home the lesson that we must bombard and overpower non-believers by the very ceaselessness and diffusion of our efforts. We need men with ideas and with courage to pioneer where the rest of us may be able to follow; and we, who lack the vision and the strength to vary from the traditional paths, should give thanks to God for raising up such men in these times. *Dum-modo Christus annuntietur!*[1] When love of God and zeal for souls are the occasion of a man's mistakes, we should do better to imitate him than to laugh at him.

THE RECEPTION OF CONVERTS

❡ *Why is the perseverance of adult converts such a serious problem?*

There are many reasons; sometimes such apparent ones as the fact that a particular conversion was not completely sin-cere, or was made only to make a marriage with a Catholic partner easy. In any case, we are faced with the spectacle of non-Catholics who took instruction, received Baptism and First Communion, and who now are outside the Church; that specta-cle is frequent enough to make us want to do something about it. Certainly the power of the Gospel has not waned, nor is

---

1   *Provided that Christ be proclaimed.*

Grace lacking to strengthen and confirm converts to the Faith. And yet many fall away.

The principal natural reason for this type of apostasy is found, we think, in the failure of the Christian community to receive and adopt these newcomers. Few of us can stand alone in any= thing; we are not made that way. Fewer still are the modern persons who can break with their old religious or social group and persevere in that decision, unless their new group imme= diately and completely absorbs them. Hence; we must make special and practical efforts to fill the gap in the lives of recent converts and make them a real part of the new community ourselves. That is why we have written so much about the communal nature of the modern parish, and why we believe so strongly that every parish should be a religious family, with every neighbourhood and street united by the one parish bond. Our times need a community of souls, of interest, of worship.

If the parish to which an adult convert comes can offer him that support, he is no longer alone, no longer isolated both from the community he left and from the community he joined. On the other hand, if his new=found comrades in the Faith are not themselves bound together in interests and worship, he is very likely to drift off again. He was hungry, and we did not take him in.

❡ *Making converts a part of our community will, then, guarantee their perseverance?*

Not in itself, but it is a very important part of that guarantee, naturally speaking. Above and beyond that, there are certain "dos" and "don'ts," which we ought to observe in our welcome of converts. The list that we include here is taken from the recommendations made to us by a young man who was himself recently received into the Church.

1. Most converts go through an intellectual and emotional battle before they enter the Church, and her doctrines and ceremonies are completely new to them. Remember

that, and try to understand the enthusiasm and the curiosity they manifest.

2. Realize that the material side of Catholicism, such as collections, stipends, etc., can scandalize the exalted motives of new Catholics. Make allowances for their attitude, and try to reduce the occasions of such scandal to a minimum.

3. External manifestations of religion, such as the Sign of the Cross, genuflections, etc., do not come easily to most converts, because their background was so different from that of lifelong Catholics. Try to put them at their ease.

4. Give a convert some outlets for his new-found zeal. Introduce him to activities or circles suited to his inclinations, and help him to meet Catholics who will edify and sustain him. Remember that "ordinary" Catholics are going to be a stumbling-block to his ideals.

5. Make him feel wanted and accepted, in every way possible, for he has made a great sacrifice for the great treasure he has won.

All of these points could be enlarged upon, but we have touched upon them often already. It is up to the priests of every parish to apply them according to local needs. We are priests in order to bring Christ to the world and to find the sheep that are lost; the ninety-nine whom we leave behind (even though the modern proportion is considerably less) will understand our preoccupation for the lost members of the flock. They will come to see why our sermons and ceremonies are directed to the outsiders, and they will even come to agree that we should prefer the lost to the found. Before long, the faithful will be as mission-minded, as convert-conscious, as we are.

This process works in a circle. The converts we make by our communal effort continually strengthen and enliven the very community that helped to make them Catholics. They are both the fruit and the fuel of the labor of the whole united parish. Provided that we do not enervate them by any fool-hardy attempts to "ecclesiasticize" them, nor repel them by the scandal of our indifference or materialism, these converts are the greatest source of energy that any parish can hope to have. They are the new shoots grafted on the old vine, and we can well use that new life. ✠

CONCLUSION

A T THE BEGINNING of this book we resolved not to paint the picture of our work here as though it were a masterpiece and a model; now that we have reached the end, we cannot help but wonder how well that resolve was kept. Poorly or well, we still mean it. The examples and details given here are not intended for reproduction, because, for the most part, they belong only to this setting. Our hope is that no one will make that mistake. Our intention was, and is, to stimulate the missionary apostolate, and not to praise our own version of it.

Let each parish strive to make its liturgy splendid and full of meaning. Let each parish make of itself a real community, devoted to the conquest of souls, and united within itself for that single goal. Let every parish priest avoid the pitfalls of money, of "clerical culture," of remoteness from the thoughts and needs of his people. Let all, priests and people, be anxious to find new ways of bringing Christ to those who do not know him, and capable of following those new paths. That is our message. In giving it we could not help but localize our realization of it, but we did not mean to limit it to our abilities or to our results.

If anything that we said seems revolutionary or wild-eyed, it was not meant as such, and, in reality, it is not. Our inspiration was from the Gospel, in which all may see that Christ meant us to be united, meant us to make Him known to our fellow-man, and meant priests to be priests, not clerks, nor organizers, nor officials. Péguy described a revolution as an appeal from a less perfect tradition to a more perfect one. Because we agree so heartily with him, this book came to be written.

May it be an inspiration for a rebirth of apostolic zeal! ✛

The Missionary
Spirit in Parish Life

PREFACE

WHEN *REVOLUTION IN* a *City Parish* was in the making, one thought was a constant source of uneasiness to us. It was this: Could we trust our brother priests to take these "conclusions of five years' experience" for what they were, without trying to find in them what they were never meant to contain? Would our brother priests see that there was much more to them than a collection of recipes and ingenious devices to be used, adapting them as well as possible, to transform their parishes? Were we putting enough stress on the main thing, the thing we were really interested in—the priestly life, the missionary spirit? Without it, no method, no matter how good it is, will have any apostolic effectiveness; with it, no matter what the methods used, it is possible to succeed in doing God's work.

This uneasiness has continued to haunt us, to haunt us in a direct ratio to the favor *Revolution in a City Parish* has met with. Our book broached many problems; it had to, since we were concerned with the whole question of a "parish policy." But now the time has come for us to set aside concern for both methods and experiences and go right to the heart of the problems, speaking to the priest only. Such is the aim of this new book. ✤

✤[I]✤
The Missionary Problem Is Primarily a Priestly Problem

W HAT CHANCE TO succeed has the missionary effort now being undertaken in France?
The more one reflects on this subject, the more
convinced does one become that it is the caliber of the men
undertaking it—or, more precisely, their value as priests—that
will decide. This is an elementary truth, even truism. And
there has never been a seminary rector who has not been convinced of it. But it is one thing to come to such a theoretical
conclusion, as you meditate on the four gospels, the Epistle to
the Hebrews, the tract on the priesthood, and the Pontifical's
admirable monitions to the ordinands; and quite another thing
to reach the same conclusion every day through listening, in
grief or wonder, to lay people pour out the secrets of their
hearts, or through seeing with your own eyes, in the parishes
you visit, how the spread of the gospel is affected by the kind of
priests you find in them. During his years of training, when as
yet he knows but little of the outward conditions in which he
will have to practice the virtues that are preached to him, every
normal seminarian has his mind occupied with this thought;
but when a priest has seen the principle work out, it becomes
an obsession with him.

Good priests, thank God, are legion in France. Pious, regular
in their ministry, faithful to their duties, devoted to their parish
activities, they certainly deserve the esteem generally accorded
to them. Why, then, is their influence so limited? Why do the
parishes over which they preside appear lifeless, static, and
dormant, as is unfortunately so often the case? Could it be
that the priestly virtues have, in view of the needs of our times,
been imperfectly grasped or incorrectly reduced to practice?

Try asking Catholic Action Leaders, or, without asking them, keep your ears open for what they have to say. Learn to pay attention to the remarks of those who do not go to church. There are some, of course, who have an ax to grind, and there is no need to bother with them; but the rest, what do they say? What do they look for and expect for a priest? Only the virtues a priest ought to have. What do they complain of? Only that we are not sufficiently priests! They have a very high and splendid ideal for us, but one which is truly the ideal of the priesthood. They do not expect us to be artists or scholars or administrators or businessmen or specialists. In the final anal-ysis, they ask nothing from us that is foreign to our mission. Even the intellectuals do not expect us to dazzle them with our erudition or to be clever at juggling with theories. They ask us only to give them some solid food, because they want to avoid malnutrition if they can.

The laboring man will not necessarily give his trust to the priest who affects the way of the working class. He will per-haps think the priest a good fellow; but unless he senses some-thing more than that in him, it is not to that priest he will go when he is really in need of help, but to another, to one whom he feels to be a man of God. The case is no different with the professional man. He will be glad to invite to his table a "dis-tinguished" priest, whose fine manners, polished conversation, and literary culture will charm his family and his guests; but when he runs into troubles of conscience of family difficulties, it is to a true priest that he will go for help, even though the true priest may lack all these attractive qualities.

We ourselves know of a parish in which the practicing Cath-olics are predominantly middle-class and in which the busiest confessional is that of the assistant who is least middle-class. The "bourgeois" complain of his sermons, saying that he is a demagogue. The more refined people smile at his clumsy lan-guage. And the young ladies of the parish often make fun of the somewhat careless way he dresses. Yet at his confessional you see lines of young ladies and intellectuals and "bourgeois" as well as Jocists. When it comes to going to "the priest," people forget everything else.

What does everyone ask for? First of all: for apostolic priests, who do not look on visitors as a matter of indifference, much less a brother; but rather as a human beings, each of whom has a life all his own life to live, and as a children of God, to each of whom the Father desires to show His love.

A young man has just died, killed in the Paris Resistance. His sister, who loved him dearly, has been brought up, like him, without religion. Yet in her distress she goes to visit a priest. She is not a totally unreligious person; on the contrary, she would like to hear something about that other world to which her brother has just gone. The priest gives her the titles of a few books—excellent ones, no doubt, for the purpose. But she goes away disillusioned, and will never come back. It is not a book she is looking for, but the living words of one who was touched by her suffering, the echo of Him who wept at the tomb of Lazarus.

A working man comes to ask for a baptism—a skilled worker, very good at his job, and not at all stupid. But he cannot read or write. How will he be able to learn "the catechism?" The priest sends him away. Does he hope the man will get down to study the alphabet and come back when he can make out, "Who is God?"

Another man (one who knows how to read) comes to ask for instruction preliminary to baptism, and immediately the priest says to him, "Fine, my good man. I am going to turn you over to the sister . . . " Later, it is true, this might be the normal thing—and yet . . . But at this first contract had the priest noth=ing more that he could say?

And then this other man, who is having a very hard time leading a Christian life and goes to confession in the hope of finding some help—what does he hear from the confessor? Only the nice title ready=make sermon which did service for the pious lady before him and will do for the child after him as well; but he receives nothing personal, nothing to make him think that the confessor even grasped what he told him. And in the end, he grows tired of it, for he feels that he is all alone; it will be four years before he has recourse to the sacraments again, and then only when a lay friend of his brings him to a priest who is happy to "lose" an hour with him.

A pastor sees a man enter his confessional just after leav= ing the confessional of the first assistant, and this is what the man tells him: "Father, I have just been to confession to your assistant, and there is something I want to tell you. It has been forty years since I have been to confession, and he had nothing to say to me."

If these were an isolated case, we would not even mention them, any more than we shall mention the few unfortunate priests who abandon their vocation. But the truth is that sad incidents such as these are happening every day. There is some= thing missing. Call it the flaming zeal of an apostle or a kind of passion for souls; but whatever you call it, it is something that makes a man act and look and speak in a way that sets him apart from the mere conscientious official who does his assigned task efficiently. There is lacking that freshness of outlook which enables us to be just as much struck by every case that comes our way as we were on the first day, just as much moved by the last secret entrusted to us as we were by the first. Yet it is just such a fresh outlook that we need, because the last soul we will be called upon to assist in our ministry and the last individual whose spiritual anguish is laid bare to us will be just as important as the first. To the man who comes to see us, it makes no difference that others like him have preceded him. To him, his case, his grief, his disquiet, his joy are altogether new and full of interest.

At a meeting held in England for the purpose of study and exchange of views, we recently had the opportunity to listen to laymen from twelve different countries express their opinions. On one point they all agreed: "We lack priests able to under= stand us and help us." And it was possible to read between the lines and glimpse a situation far more painful than their words expressed.

Our laymen also ask for priests who have eyes to see not only the real problems that exist in the parish but also those that concern the nation and the world. It is not, of course, rev= olutionaries or agitators that they want, but priests unshackled by routine, priests who will make the effort to discover the real work that has to be undertaken over and above what has always been done. The laity of whom we are here speaking are obviously those individuals who are deeply concerned for the spread of the gospel—not the old guard, whose one worry is fear of change, whether it be the time of the Mass or their seat in church. The former, whose concern for the spread of the gospel is laudable, may well be scandalized when they hear a priest exclaim, "We've had enough reforms, give us some rest!" Péguy would answer, "the saints were not men of rest." The new form of charity which St. Vincent de Paul was incessantly inventing disturbed the rest of a great many people, and very often officials must have said to him, "That's enough; give us the chance to breathe!" St. Vincent, however, with his even pace, which never outstripped Providence, con= tinued to advance steadily; and every morning he looked on human misery with fresh eyes and tirelessly kept on creating new remedies for it. It is men like that who extend the king= dom of God, men who know that "new wine is not to be put in old wineskins," men who know have not come to terms with things as they are.

Such an attitude calls for courage; not merely the courage required to emerge from ourselves and our way of doing things, or the courage to remake ourselves continually without becom= ing attached to what we have loved and accomplished; but also the courage to show others the way, to win others over and rouse them to accept—or better still, to discover for them= selves—the new roads that have to be travelled. People expect us not to be timid. How many men of good will there are who, sometimes even without knowing it, would be eager to vol= unteer if they were only called upon! And how much bad will would melt away like snow in the sun if only the sun were hot enough—that is, if only the priest were an enthusiastic optimist radiating conviction and an infectious confidence in his cause!

The priest is expected to be filled with the charity of the gos= pel, the charity which St. Paul says "spurs us on," and to which alone we can look to produce the qualities just mentioned: the missionary spirit, zeal for souls, the anxious desire to do better, the daring of the saints. People want to feel that the charity of Christ is in the heart of the priest; and they want the priest's words, both public and private, to be an expression of his love. The main thing is, not that we should be good publicity men, alert to every opportunity, but that we should be men with hearts on fire, men in whom the Spirit of Pentecost continues to live on. That is why the people expect us to be one heart and one soul, as the first Apostles were. They look for us to be priests who love one another and understand one another, who live a community life, who carry on their apostolic work as one man.

Besides, when we take the trouble to investigate thoroughly the reasons why the Christian spirit has, in certain environ= ments and regions, proved incapable of resisting decline or cor= ruption, it becomes evident that in most cases the unhappy state must be traced to priests who were not up to the mark. Why, for example, do the great number of Catholics who come from a solidly Catholic region of our country abandon the prac= tice of religion as soon as they arrive in Paris? The reason is that their priests failed to give them a true Christian formation. Why do such people often prove more anticlerical than others? Because, before coming to Paris, they had the experience, in those Catholic regions, of a clericalism that proved oppressive.

A few examples might be welcome. A young priest has just sung his first Mass in his home parish. To celebrate the event, his boyhood friends have prepared a feast in his honor in the village square. The young priest, who has dined at the rectory and is uneasy at the thought that his friends have been kept waiting for him, asks the pastor for permission to leave. "My dear boy," answers the pastor, "now that you are a priest, you will have to learn to make people wait for you."

Passing by a church, a man from another parish decides to go to Mass there. On the bulletin board of the church he reads that Mass is at seven o'clock and, as it is already ten minutes after seven and there is no one at the altar, he rings the rectory doorbell. "Is there going to be a Mass today, Father? It is after seven and I don't see anyone." "My good man," replies the pastor from the window as he buttons his cassock, "it will be seven when I get there."

And anticlericalism is perhaps not the worst fruit of such bad principles and attitudes, for they have also produced formalism. If so many Catholics no longer have a genuine Christian mentality, may not the reason be that they were often expected to conform outwardly when they had received no interior formation? External actions and practices were demanded of them, and they were required to use formulas, yet no one gave them the ideas and convictions which originally gave birth to the formulas. External deportment was so stressed that it acquired the status of a virtue. Only recently, in a certain parish young girls were refused absolution for having taken to wearing hats instead of *coiffes* and for riding bicycles. We admit children to baptism without having had any conversation with their parents, without saying a single word to them; instead, we hurry as fast as we can through a sorry ceremony at the back of the church. When engaged couples come to arrange for a marriage, all we do is ask them how expensive a wedding they want and write down their answers to the prenuptial questionnaire (which, by the way, could provide us with an excellent missionary opening); then we require the young man to make a sacramental confession that will be a farce. We water down Christian obligations by agreeing to all sorts of compromises and concessions. Our demands are exacting only when it is a question of externals. And yet when the externals are those of our own priestly functions (celebration of Mass and administration of the sacraments), the faithful who attend see us show so very little reverence! Unless they have a very deep faith, how can they fail to conclude that all this is a sham and that religion has no real basis at all? What other explanation is there for such a state of affairs but that the faith of priests is not strong enough to be infectious and their life not interior enough to make them emphasize chiefly the things of the inte‑ rior? "We have too many," Cardinal Suhard used to sigh, "too many administrators and not enough priests."

The main task, therefore, the one that has priority over all others, is the making of good priests. When we say this, we are not for a moment forgetting the indispensable role which belongs to laymen in the work of spreading the gospel. But the two prob‑ lems are closely connected; and the problem of the formation of priests must obviously take precedence, for the priesthood of laity will never have a chance to be exercised if the priesthood of the priests is not strong enough to give the other impetus it must have. To form true priests and then to keep them up to the mark, to develop them and to make the fullest use of them—these are the principal tasks that confront us in our day.

What we ask of seminaries is this: a training devised and carried through with the idea of giving to Catholics—and non‑Catholics—the apostles they need, not individualist accus‑ tomed to thinking and praying and working in isolation, but teammates animated by the need of holding together and exert‑ ing influence as leaders. It is priests with really priestly souls that are called for, priests so conscious of the demands of the missionary ideal, priests so eager to do all they can, that they will never be likely to use a canon of the Code as an excuse for taking it easy.

When the young priest, just out of the seminary, is begin‑ ning his life in the ministry, with what care should he not be surrounded, if he is to keep and develop the apostolic fire indispensable for fruitful missionary work! How sad it is to see him so often placed in situations that can rob him of all his life and all his enthusiasm! It is regrettable that there are still only a few dioceses where this problem can be easily dealt with. We all know too well how the shortage of priests and the difficulty of filling vacancies crowd all other considerations off the stage.

But does this justify leaving young priests, at the beginning of their ministry, in an isolation that breeds depression? Does it justify transferring them even more frequently (one of our confreres has been in three different places within two years)? Without giving them a chance to get a start at serious work? And does it justify placing young priests under a pastor who is discouraging, sour, dictatorial, or else so indifferent that his assistants feel that they cannot count on any support in the tasks that face them?

In one of our dioceses, plans had been made for the establishment of a missionary deanery. Three priests had formed a team for the enterprise. A friend of theirs was ready to join them and was to be assigned to a parish in the deanery. But at the last moment the pastor who was to make room for him by moving to another parish backed down on the agreement, and the young priest was named to a chaplaincy... Customs may, of course, be so strong as to make it practically impossible to transfer a priest against his will. But this at least must be clear: that, in the first place, the priest who stubbornly stands in the way lacks real spirit of the priesthood; and that, in the second, such customs ought to be reconsidered, since they go against the common good.

We have already spoken about certain flaws which hinder the work of the apostolate. These flaws, it is worth pointing out, are to be blamed much less on the men involved than on the established customs. They are almost inevitable, as long as we do not form communities of priests who will give each other mutual support and assistance, and as long as we do not place together men who can do good work together.

It is all very well to say that the young priest must keep his spirit, his sacred fire. But if the present system continues, if three or four parishes are committed to a single priest instead of a team being placed in the center of ten or twelve parishes, how can anyone expect this young man, isolated and without support, to keep his zeal for long, when he sees himself alone to confront the indifferent mass of people he is supposed to rouse?

It is all very well to say that the young priest must do intellectual work, that he must read and reflect on his ministry, that
he must not slip into the rut of routine. But how is he to do
all this without a stimulus? He is hardly likely to find what he
needs at the deanery conferences, where from time to time he
will meet pastors whose basic orientation (if indeed they have
any) is quite different from his own. Often enough, he will find
quite the contrary and will go back to his solitude less strong
than before. He needs books and reviews which, in his poverty,
he cannot obtain for himself, but which a team could obtain. He
needs to be able to exchange views with priests engaged in the
same kind of work. He needs the advice of an older man with
whom he could do good work, finding in him both experienced
counsel and needed companionship. In a community life we
learn a great deal, since we are able to take lessons from one
another by comparing our ideas and confronting our projects.

And from the spiritual viewpoint, is there any substitute for
a common life in which men pray together and feel that they
are brothers with the same apostolic interests? Is it not true
that the Holy Spirit dwells in such communities?

Even on the material plane—as has been pointed out a hundred times but needs to be continually emphasized—it is quite
obviously a crushing responsibility for a priest to have to look
after so many things, which none the less he cannot eliminate.
There is his food, its preparation, the business of fuel and heat-
ing, his own needs and those of the church to be provided for,
including the needs of the parish activities—all those terrible
money problems which dog his every step. The formation of
communities will not, of course, do away with these; but it will
lighten them, because the burdens will be divided, and there will
be several priests to put their shoulders to the task. In this way,
too, it is possible to lessen the contrast between the so-called
"good" parishes, where a living comes comparatively easy, and
those where priests find it impossible to make ends meet.

Let us make no mistake about it: the power of priests to
maintain their missionary spirit, once they have begun their

ministry, depends to a very great extent on the way they are utilized, whether in isolation or in community.

It also depends on the degree of fatherly interest that they feel their superiors take in them. In some large dioceses, the administration spirit colors everything and takes precedence over everything else—even over the relationship which ought to exist between sons and fathers: between sons who can be free and open, and fathers whose benevolence is full of solicitude.

It is true that we must have administration; but let it be, as an old legal expression puts it, the administration of the father of a family. The priest ought to feel that he belongs to a family and that he is ruled by something more than decrees and statutes. *Dominus regit me et nihil mihi deerit . . . Virga tua et baculus ipsa me consolata sunt . . . et misericordia tua subse-quetur me omnibus diebus vitae meae . . .*

With good reason, all our dioceses are disturbed over the falling off in vocations to the priesthood. Yet religious com-munities today are attracting more vocations. What are we to conclude? That these young men (for generally it is not a question of boys, but of young, and sometimes even mature, men) are mistaken in thinking their vocation is to a religious community, whereas in reality it is to the diocesan clergy? Or that communities resort to excessive propagandizing and a method of recruiting that is out of order? Perhaps, in the case of one or the other modern community, such a reproach is justified. Perhaps even, now and then, there is a certain amount of self-deception in some individuals' infatuation for the reli-gious life. But it would be a much more serious self-deception to concentrate on such cases and fail to see further into the matter. In fact, the root reason seems quite certainly to lie in the way the young view the life of the secular priest. What the young want, when they are about to give themselves, is to do so completely and thoroughly. They are looking for a priestly life which is one hundred percent priestly. They take a look around and see the conditions in which many a secular priest is called upon to live. They notice how isolated he is;

and, knowing that they themselves are not made of iron, they fear that they could not live like that for a lifetime. It is easy to call them cowards or deserters. Much too easy. We ourselves know many who realize quite well that it is the parish priest who is called upon to fight the most important battle. We know that they would prefer to enter directly into the great work of the diocesan clergy, that at times they have to do violence to themselves in order to embrace the religious life with all that it implies. But they embrace it nevertheless, because for them the development of their priesthood takes first place. When they give their life, their only fear is that some day they may take it back again.

Who would dare to blame them? What most attracts the young is the example of an apostolic priest living in the present—that, and the assurance that their priestly lives will not be wasted, that they will have a chance to be real priests, that they will be given the training they require and, when the time comes, will receive both the appointment that suits their ability and the support they need. They never bother to ask themselves whether they will depend on the Pope through the intermediary of a bishop or of a superior general. What interests them is not whether the diocesan community is the sole priestly community of divine institution or not, but rather: where they will find a priestly community that is a reality. The drama enacted in their hearts is not one in which the terms "diocesan" and "non-diocesan" play the principal roles, and any attempt to make them look at the problem in this light is artificial and doomed to failure.

It is not much truer to say that some are looking for a particular form of the apostolate—say, preaching, teaching, or Catholic Action. They have their preferences, of course, and often enough these are for parish work. But, taking them all in all, they are expendable and will prove it later on by their docility to the direction of superiors. In point of fact, what they want above all else is the means of sanctification during and after their period of formation, the hope of teamwork, the warm and friendly atmosphere of a family. What they find most repugnant is the prospect of a priestly ministry degenerating into a merely perfunctory performance of official duties.

Let us once have a great many parishes where priests may live the communal life in its fullness; let us once see whole dioceses offer their future priests seminaries where they will be formed according to their spiritual needs and their life work; let us see dioceses offer their priests in the ministry the opportunity for apostolic and fraternal teamwork—then vocations to the diocesan clergy will once again he numerous. In a word: give them the possibility, the assurance that they will not be left alone but will be able to count on assistance all their life long, and you will not have to warn them against the seductions of the religious life. For many of them, the secular priesthood will be enough; but, to use a proverb, we must not put the cart before the horse and ask the young to sacrifice their legitimate aspirations in order to further reforms which could be initiated today.

Besides, it is obvious that this work is already being under= taken in many places and that it has already attracted many vocations, as in the case of the Mission of Paris. It is in this direction we must work—a direction which we would like to call "the reassessment of the priestly vocation."

Revolution in a City Parish has occasioned our receiving the confidences of a great many lay people. Most of them, sad to say, struck the same note: "Oh, if our pastor would only . . ." "If our pastor only understood!" "If our pastor would only get into it!" The same plaintive cry seems to go up on all sides. Sometimes it took another form: "I have no one to go to. There are many priests in the city, but I cannot find a spiritual director." Of course, we must be wary in apprais= ing such complaints. Yet it is also true that when we see the work there is to do, especially when we see how slow is the progress and how sometimes there is none, we cannot fail to reach the conclusion that it is the question of the priesthood that counts before everything else. Whether you discuss the problems of the apostolate with bishops or priests or laymen, with believers or unbelievers, with laboring or professional men, with intellectuals or with plain people, you always come back to the same point, the point with which you must start: "We need priests," they will all tell you, "many priests; but above all we need priests with the missionary spirit, priests working together shoulder to shoulder and in the charity of Christ."

One comes back from a trip abroad convinced that it is in France especially that there exists not only this desire but also the beginning of its fulfillment. We do not believe that any= where else such an admirable effort is being made to produce a missionary clergy, both secular and regular. Our readers in neighboring lands need have no doubt about this: the longings we are expressing are those of the great majority of the French clergy, and every day they are being translated into realities and in a way that gives us every reason to hope for tomorrow.

Our desire is that this effort may not be compromised by excesses and deviations. To these we shall devote the next chapter. ✢

✠[2]✠
On Certain Forms of the Pseudo=Missionary Spirit

"ACCEPT NO SUBSTITUTES."
All valuable things, from bank notes to superior brands of candy and biscuits, have their imitations. It is the same in matters of religion. The four authentic Gos= pels were succeeded by a swarm of apocryphal gospels. For one apparition of the Virgin that has all the marks of genuineness and is acknowledged by the Church, twenty are produced by the imagination and the Church has to disown them. The mag= nificent Thomism of the thirteenth century degenerated into the hairsplitting scholasticism of the fourteenth, and is again found (not easily recognizable, though still bearing the name) six or seven hundred years later in certain manuals for seminary use. All our dogmas have had their counterfeits, which we call her= esies. Every movement to renew the life of the Church—from the monastic movements to those of Catholic Action—has had its fanatics, its bigots, its dead weights, its eccentrics.

Ordinarily, loss of equilibrium is responsible for this phe= nomenon, emphasis being put on one aspect to the detriment of another, and generally on a secondary, external aspect to the detriment of the essence and of the spirit.

Corruptio optimi pessima. There is no sadder sight than the disintegration of something that was great and fine.

The missionary movement is not immune to this danger; but, if we are to protect ourselves against it, we must look it in the face, especially since the enemy is to be found not only in others. He is in every man and can be the ruin of anyone who is not on his guard.

In those whom we shall call "pseudo=missionaries," all the stock defects are to be found. There is the spirit of the Pharisee

("Thanks, Lord, that I am not like the rest of men . . . "); the spirit of rivalry and of criticism of those fellow workers of ours who will not adopt our pet ideas in their entirety; the spirit of independence towards authority; the spirit of taking the easy way (and therefore the spirit of laziness), which rests content with the slight effort required to apply recipes (the recipes being considered as cure-alls); the "nominalist" spirit, hypnotized by words; the superficial spirit, which would change everything except itself and which tends to take refuge from necessary tasks in dreaming. Every one of these is, of course, clothed with the finest "missionary" pretexts.

With the reader's permission, we intend to caricature these in our own way. The originals of our caricatures doubtless do not exist in the pure state, but this attempt exposes tendencies which are in all of us and which all of us must check.

THE RITUALISTIC SPIRIT

The man with the ritualistic spirit is very hard on the liturgical fanatics, whose horizon is limited to a network of rubrics. If you were to tell him that he is a rubricist without knowing it, he would be quite amazed. And still he too has his ritual—a ritual with its vestments, its magic words, its attitudes, its external actions.

What is the secret of being an apostle? It is really quite simple: you have only to wear a work shirt and a heavy belt, cultivate a military or a proletarian air, and take off the clerical garb, if necessary . . . Over a drink of wine, such an apostle calls a friend "Buddy," and thinks that he has won over every worker in the bar—who did not realize they were letting themselves in for this! . . . He makes his little mark as the priest of "the little people," quite proud of being ashamed of the bourgeois and never suspecting that the workers accept him only with a kind of sly amusement.

If he finds life in the parish boring or if he is at a loss to know how to make his services acceptable there, he is off to the factory. It is the fashion of the day. Excellent priests, those who have a head on their shoulders and know what they are doing, try this method for a definite reason, realizing its limited scope. Their object is, for example, to acquire a better understanding of the worker's mentality; or to bring into the factory a witness, which they know to be exceptional, of priestly brotherhood in work and poverty; or to install the priesthood of Christ in the midst of those who have no idea of what it is. Not so with our ritualist. He throws himself into the adventure with a light heart, although it is an undertaking for which he ought to have exceptional qualities both as a priest and as a man. He goes into it merely because he thinks it is the fashion: nowadays, there is no priest worthy of the name who is not a priest-workman. He has none of the spirit which has urged this difficult course on others; he has nothing but the external likeness. The criticism that he draws on himself, the setbacks he suffers, and then the bitterness and irritation he is sure to show, all do their share to throw discredit on an admirable cause.

He also has a genius for emptying of their meaning the words he takes over. Why does he take them over? Always for the same reason: they have an up-to-date ring to them; they go over; they are "the last word." He employs them at random, making them do duty in a hundred different causes; he puts his own private meaning into them, and it is amusing to see the surprising purposes he can make them serve. And so, little by little, discredit falls upon words which, when they were first employed by intelligent men, had a precise and valid meaning; words which, as embodying an inspiration, might have been very fruitful. But now they can be used no longer.

There was, for example, the word "conquest." The Jocists used to speak in 1930 of conquering their brothers, and they meant only that they wanted to win them for Jesus Christ—a meaning which seems to be just as valid twenty years later. But the word has taken on certain overtones which convey the disagreeable suggestion of an injudicious proselytism. Hence you may no longer use it. And the very individual who always had "conquest" on his lips will now give you a condescending smile, or an annoyed look, if you have the bad taste to do so. Then there was the word "Christendom."[1] We were going to make another Christianity. It was quite a simple thing the word was meant to express: the idea, namely, that the Christian spirit ought to permeate not only individuals alone, but institutions also, environments and social groups and laws insofar as possible. The word, however, also designated a social order which existed in the Middle Ages. Obviously, there was no question of returning to it. But what a temptation there was to glorify that typically Christian era as an ideal! The temptation was not resisted. As a result, the aim of those who wished to build another Christendom was disfigured, and they were made to appear visionaries.

There was also the word *"engagement,"*[2] with consequent talk of a brand of thinking that was *engagé* and of Christians who were *engagés*. There was nothing wrong with the word at all, since it meant only to express a preference for men who live in contact with real conditions and whose ideas are formed in such contact, rather than for theorists who live isolated in their studies. But along comes our ritualist to appropriate it. He sets himself up to judge the extent of his contemporaries' *engagement*, granting to one man the right to have his say because he is sufficiently *engagé*, while denying it to another because he is not *engagé* enough. *Engagement* is now the only topic of conversation. You have it forever ringing in your ears. The new word gives fresh life to the unending debates on the Christian's part in the temporal domain. You must, however, use the word *engagement*; otherwise, you are behind the times and have no right to be heard. It is so abused that, in the end, we grow tired of the word and then disgusted, and no one will use it any more.

---

1   The French here is *chrétienté*.
2   It has been thought better to italicize this word which is hardly at home in English in the sense in which it has lately proved so popular in French — that is, to describe the attitude of one who is not detached observer, but is willing to, and in fact does, commit himself completely to the causes and movements in which he believes.

But what of it? We can use "incarnation" in its place. At the moment, this is perhaps the expression which best typifies the spirit we wish to denounce the tendency, namely, to hypnotize oneself with words. The Incarnation, the Word of God made flesh, is a wonderful reality and one that opens up many ave-nues of thought: it helps the one who has to preach the word of God to see that, far from being content to expound theological abstractions, he must make the gospel message concrete, incar-nating it in everyday language; it helps the Christian to see that his whole life must express the whole of his Christianity; and so on . . . But it sends our friend into an ecstasy of delight. Here he is to tell us that we must become incarnate—even though, to all appearances, this is already a fact. Christ, he tells us, must become incarnate in us (he means that we should reflect the true image of Christ, but his way of saying so is abominable). And so it goes, on and on. In the end, you notice that you can no longer speak of incarnation without causing your companions to wince.

The same is true of the word "testimony." This book, for instance, will be called a "testimony." A testimony of what? Oh, of what the author thinks. What a discovery! Surely when a man has testimony to give, he does not speak of himself but of what he has seen and heard. And the same fate, alas! is in store for the "communitarian spirit" and the "missionary spirit."

Our ritualist transforms words into slogans. For him they are not the signs of realities which he has understood and assimilated; in his mouth they become the passwords and the catchwords of the modern world and the modern apostolate. He ends by making even the most apt and expressive words sound ridiculous, although we need them to spread ideas. This man has a dangerous talent for shrinking values.

We ask you not to confuse the ritualist and the true missionary. The latter will perhaps wear a work shirt, because he thinks it is more practical; he may not always use the best French, because of the environment in which he works; he may be a priest-workman, because this work has been assigned to him; when the situation calls for the words we have discussed, he will use them along with others that he coins himself. But he will never mistake all this for the essence of the missionary apostolate, and he will always put the spirit before the letter and the outward form.

THE PIONEERING SPIRIT

There was a time when Catholics imagined that the real mis= sionary was the man of the jungle and the bush, the man who lived in exotic lands and led a life of escapades, grappling with snakes and panthers, eating unusual food, running rapids in his canoe, and so forth. (To others he was a civilizer, an ambassador of France, an ethnologist. But that is another story). In the tales they told on returning, the missioners (to suit us, doubtlessly) delighted to dwell on the exotic character of the countries from which they had come back. If our memory of the talks we heard as youngsters does not betray us, little mention was made of the kingdom of God or of the means the missioners had discovered to open the minds of the natives to the gospel. We were no doubt too young to understand. The result has been that for quite a long time the missionary in China or Africa has been considered as an adventurer, and that he himself sometimes shared the idea and set out for the mission field filled with illusions as to what was in store for him.

It was the same story over again when there was the ques= tion of undertaking the "mission" here in our own country. We were greeted with descriptions of "pioneers" in the Red zone of Paris, these modern explorers being generally welcomed by the fierce inhabitants with a shower of stones. Père Lhande, with his picturesque and moving accounts, succeeded in awaking generous vocations to that very special apostolate. The seminar= ian who could not see himself at work in the ordinary priestly ministry, as well as the priest of not altogether stable character, found a new career; they felt called to this new work because it was out of the common run, and because in it they would have their freedom and would be doing what others are not. "Here life is monotonous, but there it will be full of excitement. And what heroism it calls for! how sensational it promises to be! and what tales there will be to tell in letters to friends!"

It is the kind of dream the romantic girl has as she finishes the beautiful novel in which the stenographer marries her employer... And how drab life seems to her when she goes back to her housework or sets out once more for the office!

Our missionary pioneer finds out even during his apprentice-ship that the red zone is appallingly like the fifteenth *arrondisse-ment*, that the things that make up a priest's life there are just as monotonous as they are elsewhere, and that the word "jun-gle" is only a metaphor, the image of the same spiritual reality that is everywhere, only more impenetrable. The adventurer type missionary must face the fact that adventure is not found on the street corner; and the reporter type must realize that he will uncover no sensational story to tell.

Amor novitatum is not the missionary spirit; a man is not called to be a missionary because he loves novelty for the sake of novelty or is always in search of new angles and original approaches or because he needs change for its own sake. The missionary in mission territory, like the apostle in Christian lands, has to do his work in the midst of the simplest realities. His first and foremost ambition is, not to change everything, but to bring Christ to this district, a district that is new only to the missionary himself. Only later will he know whether he must make changes, and then he will not make them as an adventurer would, but as a careful and patient planner, who is guided above all by love.[3]

---

3   We cannot do better here than refer to the allocution given by Pius XII to the pastors and preachers of Rome on March 23, 1949. "But always," the Pope said in part, "it will be necessary for the faithful to come together to assist at Mass on Sunday, and the sacraments will always have to be administered to them. And, when we speak of the ministry of souls, we are thinking especially of the sacrament of penance, which requires that the priest should lead an absolutely exemplary life and that he should have a sense of responsibility, clarity, and sureness of judgment, self-control, pru-dence, and tact. The poor and the needy, moreover, will always be knock-ing at the door of the church; there will always be sick people to assist and strengthen by means of the last sacraments; there will always be the deceased, whose funerals will have to be celebrated; the priest will always have to find time for personal conversations with his parishioners . . ."

THE PLANNING SPIRIT
Our next character, the planner or the architect, is at home in this age of the planning board. Recent years have seen the publication of a great number of plans to stabilize the finan= cial situation, to organize the food problem, and to promote world peace. The only thing that remains to be done is to apply them—unless, for having failed to keep in touch with reality, they have already proved themselves inapplicable.

Somewhat the same fate befalls certain desk missionaries. Although they are only second=rate intellectuals, they turn out endless schemes for spreading the gospel systematically. They construct a prefabricated mission without considering the ter= rain on which they will have to work. They know all there is to know about efficiency. We might represent them as follows: they start by buying the filing cabinet and index cards; then they decide what to write on the cards, only to find that they have nothing to write because they have no documentation on which to draw. Their plans are inapplicable because the authors, when devising them, were out of touch with real life; and above all, because life—especially spiritual life—laughs at plans, for life is the domain of human liberty. It is possible, to be sure, to draw up a four=year plan for equipping a country with airplanes; it is much more difficult to draw up a rational four=year plan of attack on a mission territory. Or rather, nothing is easier than to put such a plan on paper; but when it comes time to carry it out, you find that those for whom it was intended are not ready for it, and that the cooperation you counted on fails to materialize. Every missioner, of course, makes a plan of campaign and decides on a certain pattern of attack. But when he does so, he works on the basis of the concrete situation as he knows it by experience and on the basis of his knowledge of the road he has already travelled; moreover, he is ready, if the need becomes plain, to change his plans, because he does not attach undue importance to them.

Nor is our planner incapable of altering his views, provided only that he be permitted to remain in the realm of theory. The concrete situation is mobile and always eludes him, but he is even more mobile. What really interests him is drawing up plans. If the first plan does not work, it makes no difference: he will make another. The plans pile up, the actual work is never done. This planner of ours is afflicted with intellectual fidgets. He is continually sending his collaborators, laymen as well as priests, off in new directions, and he always has them panting for breath. After a while, he is amazed to see that there are none to follow him or carry out his orders; instead, following the wise slogan of the barracks, they wait for the orders to be countermanded. He grows impatient and wants to see immediate results. He forgets that many imponderable factors operate in the realm of the spiritual, that the harvest comes long after the sowing, that "one man sows and another reaps." He needs more humility, a greater readiness to adapt himself to reality, and fewer of these ambitious dreams.

The same type of missionary—or his brother, if you like—puts his talent for theorizing at the service of his likes and dislikes. Every man of action feels the need of principles to justify what he is doing. And, like the famous theologian who formulated a thesis and then sent his students to search St. Augustine for texts to support it, our missionary has no scruples about calling theology to his rescue and forcing her to approve his attempts to dodge distasteful work and devote himself to work he likes. If he does not care to visit the sick or his parishioners, to take his turn on duty or at preaching, or even to prepare a sermon, he will not hesitate to go to the Fathers of the Church and to the Scriptures for justification—when a humble examination of conscience would very quickly show him that his lack of mortification is the real reason.

Let us leave to the real thinkers, philosophers or theologians, the task of building up, disinterestedly, the doctrinal source for our work. At the present time, we have thinkers we can be proud of, who are in constant contact with men of action and who are giving us a pastoral theology that can be used by every missionary, no matter what type of work he is engaged in. We do better to go to them, bypassing the so-called intel-lectuals who will (on the basis of new data, new and ephemeral experiences, which they glean here, there, and everywhere) draw up a system on the spur of the moment. These too are architects; they have the best will in the world and are eager to help us. But they are a threat to us, for we may be misled by their incessant flow of plans that are hastily put together and quite insufficiently thought out.

We know them well, these charming confreres. Sometimes they are quite young. They have never put their hand to the plow. They have never really done the work of the ministry. Or, what is worse, they have spent a few weeks or months in it, and are going to live on that "experience" forever afterwards. Still, they have been given, or have taken upon themselves, the responsibility of doing the thinking for those who are actively engaged in the ministry. They listen to a discussion in which men of action, after struggling to see their way clear in the midst of endless complications, have to go home without hav-ing reached agreement. But it takes more than that to daunt our confreres. They enter the silence of their study, where their desk provides them with a field of action. Having com-pared the various points of view, they quickly reach a solution. They emerge triumphant to propose their views, and it never dawns on them that most of the time their discovery is at best a truism.

It must be understood once and for all that the conversion of the world is to be effected otherwise than by sitting down to a typewriter, with a telephone on your right and a filing cabinet behind you. Nothing is more useful than a parish file. Sometimes it is indispensable. Making such a file can afford an extremely valuable examination of conscience on the real state of the parish. But we must be on our guard: once this is completed (and it is never completed, but always in the mak-ing), the main thing still remains; and that is to begin the real work, the work of spreading the gospel.

THE SOCIAL-WORKER SPIRIT

Our next type is the man who confuses the role of the missionary with that of the social worker. He would like to make
religion popular and to reach souls by looking after bodies.
Hence he intends to throw himself into social work, to be an
organizer, to start dispensaries, to open placement bureaus, to
start a mutual aid society, to organize recreation, and so forth.

It is true that this kind of social work is indispensable. We
must have it. Institutions put their stamp on those they work
for, marking them with the spirit of the people who take them
in hand; it depends on what these people are whether the
institutions will prove a beneficial influence in the development of souls or will stifle their spirit. And so we must have
Catholics engaged in seeing to it that there is such a thing as
Catholic social work.

But is this kind of activity the work of a missionary? On
the intellectual plane, in the field of study and theory, it is
indispensable to have priests—theologians and historians and
even economists—collaborating with laymen in working out
a social doctrine (as, for example, in the case of "Economy
and Humanism," "Popular Action," the "Social Weeks," and
such works). In a diocese, it is normal for a priest to be specially assigned to advise lay people who are engaged in social
work. But the priest charged with the care of souls—is it his
work to engage personally in this activity? It is better for him
to leave this to the laity, whose work it really is—not their
only work, as we shall have occasion to point out later, but
nevertheless their work.

Otherwise, who is to keep the missionary spirit alive in the
parish? Who is to do the actual work of evangelization? Social
work is, as we know so well, an absorbing thing, and the man
who gives himself to it will soon have no time to announce
Christ. He runs the risk of having his activity become, gradually and unknown to himself, quite secular, and of deserting the spiritual for the merely profane. His dispensary will
be crowded; children will have been sent off to camp in the

mountains; his various activities will be in full swing. Thus he will imagine, too quickly, that his work is done, when in fact there will be so many things left to be done—so many things, or everything, because his real mission work, the work that is his special responsibility, will have yet to begin.

The man who is interested only in typical and rare cases (even in his priestly ministry) is another variety of the missionary-social worker, since his mentality is not unlike that of certain women social workers. He is always on the watch for something out of the ordinary; usual, everyday events and the common run of mortals do not interest him. But he has a passionate interest in difficult spiritual states and complicated spiritual problems. Our "architect" worked with ideas alone when he was drawing up his magnificent plans; but this man limits his activity to the pursuit of individual cases, and he is even capable of framing them to preserve their memory. For him, the ministry consists in gathering data or cases. Does he ever realize that deep down he is working for himself, and not for the good of God's children? He will have to give an accounting for all souls, not only for a few.

THE PROPRIETARY SPIRIT

Have you ever noticed the way the word "consolation" is mis- used in ecclesiastical literature? People tell a young priest that they hope he will have "many consolations" in his ministry. A prelate speaks of being "greatly consoled" by the fine results he has noted here and there. A pastor congratulates himself on the "many consolations" that a certain portion of his faithful flock gives him, and a big crowd at the Corpus Christi procession seems "especially consoling" to him.

Heaven help us! Do we really find the doing of God's work such a sad business that we need all these sweets to console us in our desolation?

Such must be the mentality of the pseudo-missionary, who is constantly fretting over results, always stealing a glance at his neighbor, and taking note of his success with a certain feeling of bitterness. He wears himself out watching the very slowly ascending—and sometimes descending—curve of his graphs. He would like to harvest, to store up his grain in barns. He is a miser.

Ego plantavi, Apollo rigavit, Deus dat incrementum. It is for God to grant the increase, today or tomorrow or the day after.

You see your neighbor's success, but you do not see the work he has done. You grow tired of your own ministry and you dream of changing places with him; but you never suspect that he too has his difficulties and that the secret of his success lies perhaps in the fact that he works unstintingly and does not worry over results.

When the seventy=two came back overjoyed because their ministry had gone so well, Jesus said to them: "Rejoice not in this, that the spirits are subject to you, but in this, that your names are written in heaven" (Luke 10:20). And you know the words of *Téméraire*:[4] "A man can undertake a task even when he has no hope, and persevere in it even when he has no success." It is true that we have to hope, but with that virtue of hope which envisages the undertaking *sub specie aeternitatis* and puts it in God's hands. We can get along without success, however, for we are called upon, not to succeed, but to work.

It may be providential that there is no harvest for you to reap. If you were to reap, you might perhaps be in danger of becoming set in your ways and of settling down to a life of ease. And that would be the end of everything.

You may dream of the happiness of forming once more a truly "primitive" community, in which you could breathe the very air of the early Christian community. A consolation, indeed, wor= thy of the name—the kind that appeals to the historian esthete! But if this is your aim and you achieve it and take pleasure in it, you are done for, because you will lose sight of the essential inspiration of the primitive communities: the insatiable desire to extend the boundaries of the kingdom of Christ.

When we search the Acts of the Apostles for inspiration in our missionary work, it is a spirit we are looking for, not

---

4   Charles, Duke of Burgundy (fifteenth century).

a formula to copy (like a Viollet-le-Duc, when he wanted to reconstruct the cathedral of the Middle Ages). And this spirit is the exact opposite of that proprietary spirit which insists on seeing the harvest. God is the sole proprietor, and He alone has the right to harvest. When we want to usurp God's role, we lose the missionary mentality. Christ reaped no harvest. We will have ours "on the last day when the Lord of the harvest comes." On the last day. Not now.

THE COMPETITIVE SPIRIT

There is another type of missionary in whom the missionary spirit is deficient: the man who lines up his work alongside his neighbor's in a spirit of rivalry. He may do good work in his own bailiwick, but in his eyes everyone else is a competitor, a thorn in his side, perhaps an enemy. When some question arises concerning the Chancery office or the management of parish activities, the district or national directors of the Catholic Action movements or the pastor of the neighboring parish, the religious whom he himself has invited to preach in his parish or the parishioner who has an interest in a supra-parochial movement, you always sense that he is instinctively hostile. He shows it by his conversation and bad humor. His territory is an enclosure where he has every intention of enjoying his extraterritorial rights. The souls in it belong to him. He looks upon himself as the owner of his parish, and his primary concern is that no one but himself should lay a hand on what is his.

He received considerable attention in *Revolution in a City Parish*; but our picture gallery in this present chapter, were we to omit him, would be incomplete—since this forgetfulness of the kingdom of God (which is implicit in the seeking of one's own kingdom) is the pseudo-missionary spirit in one of its most regrettable forms.

There is an enormous amount of work to be done, and on all sides it reaches beyond the limits of what we might call "our work." If it is to be done, we need the cooperation of every available worker, priest or layman, secular or religious, diocesan and extra-diocesan, local and national. When we have charge of this work in a particular sector, our charge carries with it the responsibility of promoting God's work there with all our strength, and therefore the duty of seeing to it that this work is not compromised by ill-advised or conflicting plans. But it does not give us any right to stifle the Spirit. "Test every spirit and retain what is good."

If our competitor would only read St. Paul again! He would find the Apostle repeatedly reprobating these *aemulationes* and *contentiones*, which are such an obstacle to missionary work precisely because they spring much more from self-love than from love of God.

Paul himself gives us a splendid example of disinterested-ness when, as a prisoner in Rome, he writes to the Philippians, among whom all sorts of apostles are working: "Some preach out of envy, to compete against me. They are prompted by a spirit of rivalry and think that they are increasing the sorrows of my chains. It matters not: in any case, whether through hypocrisy or sincerely, Christ is proclaimed. I rejoice in this and I will always rejoice in it."

THE PSEUDO-MYSTICAL SPIRIT

The pseudo-mystic is likely to be found among those who have already been in the active ministry for several years. He has tried everything (at least he thinks so!) and he has not suc-ceeded. Can it be that he has failed to grasp this fact: that the first thing to do is to reform himself, his ideas, and his life? He has devoted himself to the reform of externals, and the externals offered resistance. And now he is cynical.

There are different ways of being cynical. Sometimes a man becomes bitter and makes up for his disappointments by laugh-ing at others and being critical of their work; and he is a cause of discouragement to them.

The pseudo-mystic, though, has his own way. He canonizes his desire to escape from it all. "If I have not succeeded," he says, "it is because God does not want me to succeed. Now

I understand my vocation: it is to be a failure. There is no use saying anything. I will retire to a life of silence and prayer. There is no need for me to be upset: God is using my failure for His own ends."

There is no doubt the man means well. He speaks that way, but is he quite sure he is not making the will of God responsi‹ ble for his own mistakes in procedure, his own tactical errors, his own personal shortcomings, and now for the cowardly desertion which leads him to abandon a task that has become too heavy for him? How does he know that God wants to work through his failure? To be sure of it, he would have to have a personal revelation. If he restricts himself to the revelation that is the property of all—and is all that counts when you want to stay on the right track—God wants to work, not through his success, but through his labor.

As long as there is a breath of life in us, it is our duty to use it on the work we have to do. And that work is: the actual labor itself, a spiritual task of prayer and sacrifice and a task of thinking over and repeatedly reconsidering the form our activity is taking. Suppose we have failed—it is much too easy to say that God does not will our success, and much more likely that we have not gone about our work properly. We must retrace our steps, go back to the intersection where we probably took the wrong road, and have the courage to look for the new roads that are still open to us. That means we must observe what others are doing, and pay more attention to the needs of the people under our care and to the possible openings which the grace of God might find to enter their souls. Besides, it means we must pray more fervently for light.

THE PSEUDO‹ANGELIC SPIRIT

We have used strong language to denounce those priests who allow themselves to be absorbed by work which is not theirs, by manual work, by dramatic and sporting organizations, by administrative and financial activities. Hence we have the right to present the other side of the picture too.

There is a type who would over-spiritualize the apostolate and avoid any work which is not purely priestly and mission-ary. In the end, such a man loses sight of a certain number of things to which, whether he likes it or not, he must submit if he is to accomplish anything in this base world.

There is a principle that we should "do nothing that is not purely priestly." Our angelic missionary uses it for all—and more than all—that it is worth. With that to back him, he rises to such heights that he will no longer even touch the earth with his foot, nor will he stoop to raise, even with the tip of his little finger, the burdens which others (his fellow workers) will have to carry for him.

Woe to the pastor who has the bad luck to have such an assistant! The parish may be having a fair or a bazaar. Every now and then it may be necessary for someone to put a room in order for a catechism class, to arrange the chairs for an unfore-seen meeting, to start a fire, or to see to the transportation of the baggage when some group is going to camp. In an emer-gency it may be necessary to call upon someone to do some typing or mimeographing in order to prepare announcements for a meeting; someone may even have to take his bicycle and distribute them without delay. There are the decorations to be improvised for a popular feast, and the plans to be made for a liturgical ceremony. It is just too bad for his confreres, and for the success of the undertaking too, if anyone is counting on this assistant. This gentleman has declared that he will not waste his time on such things. It is up to his fellow assistants or to his pastor to look after them if they wish to.

Generally it is with disdain that he refuses to have any part in such things, but at times he may take refuge behind an argument which renders him invulnerable. In order to have the right to play the angel, he will have no qualms about playing dumb and warning you that he knows nothing at all about such things, that he is awkward and out of his element, that he would not know where to start. Nor will he hesitate, if it helps the cause, to intone a hymn of admiration for his more gifted associates, though it may only be a question of taking a broom to sweep out a room or of going into the church to see that all the people have their books.

And when his associates are doing their best to arrange schedules, plan decorations, and see to it that the services will go off well, he continues his spiritual occupations unmoved. His life is affected by Christmas Eve and Corpus Christi only to the extent that he has to spend more time in the confessional; but he is able to prepare his sermon in peace, while the others must prepare theirs in advance or try to do it in the rush of preparations for so many other things.

But you, his beloved associates, must not be downcast. You will have the comfort of seeing him come in at the last moment, his mind and face in repose, and quite surprised that the commotion is not yet at an end. Woe to you, however, if in the course of the ceremony or the meeting it turns out that you have forgotten something or failed to foresee some contingency. It is a safe bet that our angelic missionary will be the first to complain of your lack of foresight and to protest against your sad incapacity to cover it up.

It is true that we ought to leave the greatest possible share of the manual work to lay people when they can replace us. And when it is a question of work of this kind, we are justified in following the well-known barracks slogan: "Never do today what someone else can do tomorrow"—but on condition that the someone else is not an associate who has just as much work to do as we have.

Yet we should not forget that the faithful who are tied down by this material work are not doing the work of the apostolate any more than the priest would be. They, as well as we, can be seriously tempted to abandon the urgent and necessary work of Catholic Action to take refuge in occupations which require much less effort and self-mastery. When we use laymen for this kind of work, we are simply transforming them into church employees.

Nor should we forget that in an ideal, perfectly organized parish, the priests would not have to bother with these material affairs, or that a committee for church celebrations can assume much of the clergy's burden in such matters. But until the day comes when the priest has his eyes and his hands altogether free, he will inevitably have jobs to do which will force him to roll up his sleeves, dirty his hands, and sometimes tear his cassock. It is a fortunate pastor who has curates with courage to knuckle down to these jobs, ingenuity to do them well, and simplicity to do them with a smile.

If we went on with portraits of this kind (which we very well could do), we would meet the *journalist*, whose mind is on nothing but book reviews and convention reports; the *pontiff*, whose life work is to see that his dignity is respected; the *aesthete*, the *gourmet*, and many others. And even when we had pinned up our collection of specimens, we should not have exhausted the reality, since the weeds spring up all too easily in the poor soils of our souls. Why do we produce so many weeds? Can we explain it by the defective training given our young men? Are not these aberrations from the missionary spirit a reaction against repression? The young priest has heard so much criticism of fresh initiatives, he has been warned so often against dangerous tendencies, his aspirations have been so stifled, he has been under such pressure that he lets off steam wherever he can find an outlet. In his experience there have been too many ukases (arbitrary commands) and too many pro= hibitions, all of them laid down without sufficient explanation. All the deviations we have pointed out betray a lack of mis= sionary spirit and an absence of authentic missionary principles. But in certain forms of attachment to tradition and to things as they are, is there not the same lack of missionary spirit and principles? Drawing up a list of deformities and banning them does not cure them. You can cure them only by changing the spirit that begot them.

From the start of this book, we have insisted on drawing up an indictment of varieties of the pseudo=missionary spirit or of possible deviations from the missionary spirit. But the reader may be sure that we have done so not for the perverse pleasure of criticizing nor with any idea of making common cause with the complacent and the satisfied. We wanted to do it for two reasons. In the first place, to dissociate the missionary cause from those individuals who are discrediting it by their excesses and exposing it to condemnations unfair to the majority of missionaries. And in the second place, to warn our younger brothers (and ourselves first of all) of the pitfalls we shall all, to a greater or lesser extent, find in our path, because it is into these that we run the risk of falling.

Finally, at the end of this court trial, we may sum up its positive aspect. The thing to emphasize, always and endlessly, is the missionary spirit, which is nothing but the authentic apostolic spirit. We must never let ourselves be taken in by externals—by methods or words, attitudes or so-called consolations, results or theories or prestige. We must never seek ourselves, but only the kingdom of God and his justice, being constantly eager to serve, here where we are and with all that we are, in total submission to the guiding hand of Providence and the unfailing stimulus of charity. *Caritas Christi urget nos.* ✛

♦[3]♦
On the Need of Having Something to Replace What We Destroy

W E MIGHT HAVE sketched another portrait, entitled "The Wrecker," and added it to those in the preceding chapter. It would have represented the missionary who has but one ambition on arriving in a new locality—to make a clean sweep of everything his predecessors have done.

Some readers of *Revolution in a City Parish*, readers who went through the book in a hurry, picking out a paragraph here and there, may have imagined that this was the method we championed; they may accordingly have praised us for it and claimed us for their side; or, on the other hand, they may have charged it up against us.

After all, this age of ours is one of reconstruction, one that is so perforce because of the war bombings. Are we not accustomed to seeing reconstruction jobs getting their start everywhere by a demolition job? We take advantage of our misfortunes to rebuild on new lines; and, when needs be, we do not hesitate to tear down buildings that are still intact, in order to carry out a city plan providing for model neighborhoods.

We might even push the analogy further and remark that there is sometimes a danger for the tenants who happen to be involved in these splendid city plans and who, because of these plans, see the time when they will be decently lodged removed to the far distant future.

But let it suffice to say that souls must never be treated as if they were stones, nor the field of the father of the family as a lot on which we are to be continually rebuilding. The Lord does not send us to perform experiments, but to do His work. We have no right to make tests *in anima vili*, to see what the outcome may be, at the risk of making our parishioners suffer; we must not be like those unscrupulous doctors and surgeons who experiment on their hospital patients. Even in the hypoth= esis that our fellow workers would learn from our tests and derive profit from them, such tests are not permissible, because the end does not justify the means. The hypothesis, besides, is a purely imaginary one, because what proves a success in one place turns out a failure in another, and vice versa.

Missionary work is not done in the clouds or in the realm of a priori considerations. Our task is to bring our priesthood into a definite area which the Father has entrusted to us just as it is. We can visualize our parish as we imagine it will one day be, rather than as it really is; we can—but doing so is a bad mental habit. There may quite well be something wrong with the situation we find on our arrival; and, if so, we shall certainly have to make changes. But we must not decide in the abstract what these changes should be; we must begin rather with what already exists and proceed from there to make things better. What that "better" thing actually is will gradually become clear to us as we acquire a better knowledge of our people, their possibilities, the things they are most attached to, and their special needs.

We should like to take the liberty of borrowing some of the Marxist thesis on the historical process. We cannot make history, or influence its course, by attempting to impose pre= fabricated views on our contemporaries, without taking into account the existing historical situation. We must accept reality and take our place in it if we want to have an influence on its evolution. In other words, what we have to do is to inject a spirit into all the concrete realities and existing institutions which present themselves to us. Those that have life in them will absorb this spirit and serve as a vehicle for it; those that have seen their day will waste away of themselves, and others will take their place. Our job is not to destroy, but to build.

And the new structures we raise, if they are really what is needed, will make the old ones fall apart.

What we as priests have to do is to put God into a given part of this world. The only previous consideration which helps the priest in this task is his determination to love all his parishioners unselfishly, without excluding or favoring any of them—a determination, that is, to love them as Christ desires to love them through us. The main thing is not to organize a district according to our way of seeing things; the main thing is to make it an offering to God, while at the same time we ask Him to give us His light and His love so that we may be enabled to transform it in the way He wants it transformed.

This is all the more true because, when we do find in a parish something that has to be changed or that displeases us, although it may well be due to abuses or ignorance and ineptitude, it is much more probably due to historical, social, or geographic factors we are unaware of. At any rate, the parish, in the state we find it, both as regards the people and the activities, is our inheritance from those who have preceded us. The people are not to be blamed if their formation has been incomplete or faulty. Most of them have carried out in good faith the directions given them. It is not their fault if our predecessors asked too much or too little of them. Our duty is to accept the inheritance lovingly and with a grievance against no one, to accept it in order to make it bear fruit, not to destroy it. Furthermore, if we love persons and not institutions, souls and not our own kingdom, we shall have no difficulty in welcoming all of our people just as they are.

Some examples from parish life will illustrate our point.

CHURCH RECREATION CENTERS

Church nurseries are not, in our opinion, effective as a missionary method of reaching the children—a view which we explained at sufficient length in *Revolution in a City Parish*. As we see it, our priestly activity should not be primarily centered on the children, but rather on the adults.

Does this mean that we think there is no need to bother with the children, or that, on arriving in a parish, our first act should be to abolish the recreation center? God forbid!

In many parishes, the various recreational activities extend all the way from those for very small children to those for older girls. The only solidly established organizations in the parish, they have this at least in their favor—they exist. We need not look upon them as forever sacrosanct. Deep in our hearts we may definitely prefer other more apostolic and more fruitful forms of activity. But it will take time for these other forms to come into being, and in the meantime we must make use of these recreations—not with bad grace, letting everyone know that we are not interested and are going through with them simply out of a sense of duty and for lack of something better to do; no, but using them wholeheartedly and sincerely. If we bring a missionary spirit to this kind of work and succeed in injecting it into these activities, it is quite natural that the members of such groups will eventually hunger for something more, and the time will then have come for us to introduce new forms and new ideas.

Father Rétif has already explained in some detail the work he proposes to do with the children, both while they are attending catechism and afterwards.[1] We will mention briefly what is being done; it is certainly not definitive, but, like everything else in the missionary life, is being continually adapted.

Let us take our parish at Grand Colombes as an example. The priest in charge of the recreation center there soon noticed two things. First, that most of the children who kept up the practice of their religion did not come to the recreation center; second, that the center did not afford him the opportunity to have on the children an influence deep enough or priestly enough to satisfy him. He continued to spend his Thursday afternoons at the recreation center until the children began of their own accord to gather in small neighborhood groups, called

---

1   Cf. "Catéchisme et mission ouvrière" in the series *Rencontres*.

"gangs." There is already a considerable number of children in them. The priest has enlisted the aid of several of the young-sters, and now spends all day Thursday passing from one gang to another. That he never thought he should get the children off his hands is clear from the fact that he now gives them a greater part of his Thursday than he formerly gave to the recreation center. The only difference is that he has restricted his activity to what is essentially priestly.

And so too with the priest who works with the little girls. He has no recreation center, but the same system of small groups (called "circles" by the girls) certainly enables him to reach more children than did the recreation center.

The results are not ambiguous. Every year the number of those who turn out for both retreats (one at the beginning of the school year and the other at Easter) is very large in relation to the number of those making their solemn Communion. In one of the worst sections of our parish at Petit Colombes, for example, we observed that there was not a single deserter at the end of a year, and two or three at the most the following year.

From this, there can clearly be no question of abandoning the children; on the contrary, we must think of all and take in hand every soul in the parish as efficiently as possible.

We would never dream of giving up recreation centers and parish activities if we had nothing to put in their place. Our conscience would give us no peace if we did not see to it that the children as well as the adults were having the gospel preached to them.

THE QUESTION OF THE SOLEMN COMMUNION

The question of the solemn Communion illustrates even better what we have been saying. A great deal of criticism has been levelled at this ceremony. And rightly so. Generally everything connected with it is a lie: the words ("first," which is false, and "solemn," which is meaningless); the speeches, which pretend to believe in tomorrows that will never exist; the renewal of the baptismal promises made by children who are not old enough to make any commitments; the mentality of so many parents, who accede to our demands only for the sake of the family celebration in which the main thing is the meal, the costume, and the presents.

Since this is so, should we abolish the solemn Communion? Some think so, and it is precisely the love of truth that moti﹘ vates them. Father Remillieux, of whom we thought so much, was one of these.[2] Gradually he succeeded in replacing this ceremony with another of quite different form, a ceremony whose preparation permitted him a very interesting contact with the families of his parish.

If we disagree with this procedure, it is because we look at the situation from another angle. It has been our experience that the first solemn Communion is the only religious event left which, without our having to work up the interest of the people, creates a stir in the de﹘Christianized environments in which our work lies. This is the one time in the entire year that we do not have to attract the people; they come of themselves in such numbers that we never know where to put them. They come—all kinds: good Catholics and non﹘Christians, friends of the family and members of the parish. This is a fact. This is the real situation.

Of course, we accomplish nothing at all if, on this occasion, we simply fill ourselves with pleasant ("consoling") illusions and deliver sentimental sermons punctuated with insipid and unreal hymns. Do this, and we simply become ridiculous, to the detriment of religion in general and of those who attend the ceremony.

But before the first Communion takes place, it can be an occasion for us to visit the families of the children; to orga﹘ nize meetings of their parents, in the course of which we can touch on problems of living that are as important to the parents as to the children; and finally, to cultivate public opinion by preparation for the big day. That is an excellent opportunity for

---

2   Cf. "Notre﹘Dame Saint﹘Alban" in the series *Rencontres*, ch. IV.

missionary work. As for the day itself, there is nothing to pre≠ vent our looking upon it as a chance for a splendid introductory ceremony for the benefit of all those half≠Christians who will be with us morning and evening. There is nothing to prevent directing our sermon at them rather than at the children. The promise the children make at the evening ceremony will be nothing but make≠believe, if we encourage the pretense that it commits them for life. But there is nothing to prevent our cutting it down to their size and making it concern the more immediate future; nor is there anything to prevent our asking the parents to join in it.

Neither does this promise, adapted to the age of the children, in any way preclude the possibility of a more serious pledge several years later when, as adolescents, they will know what they are doing.

Let us suppose for a moment that this institution did not exist at all, and that we had neither the solemn Communion nor the instructions that lead up to it. What would be left to us, in most of our parishes, in the way of opportunities for giving religious instruction to the children or even for making contact with their parents?

Let us also suppose that somewhere in France (where, in the hypothesis, nothing of the kind existed) a pastor conceived an idea. It consisted in a yearly ceremony which enabled him to round up most of the twelve≠year≠olds, together with their parents and an army of relatives. Furthermore, it enabled him to have the children meet with him every week for three years with their parents' consent. Let us suppose further that this priest is clever enough to succeed in making this ceremony so much a part of life that it becomes a custom. The stores mark it by special displays; the public schools respect it; even the indifferent have come to look upon it with a certain sympathy. In short, let us suppose he does his work so well that this cere≠ mony becomes a social event. Every priest in the country would come to admire this ingenious pastor and to interrogate him, and everyone who wanted to be a missionary would copy him.

Now it is just such a situation that exists among us and has passed into the category of a custom. We must not overesti= mate it; we must never imagine that it has more value than it actually has. We must put life into it if it is showing signs of old age, but let us not destroy it for the pleasure of destroying.

Likewise, we have no illusions concerning the efficacy of the catechism, that famous catechism which we have to teach the children as preparation for first Communion.

We know very well that they will not retain one word of the catechism and that religion is not a subject which can be "taught" the same way as arithmetic. But, since we know this is so, why should we not take advantage of these years of prepa= ration to accomplish something at once more fundamental and more genuine?

On this point there is no need to elaborate, since Father Rétif has just published in this same series a work entitled *Catechism and the Worker Mission*, which treats the subject from every angle and to which we refer our readers.[3]

THE CARE OF THE SICK

Just as some question the value of the first solemn Communion, others question the current practice in regard to the sacrament of the sick.

"Here you have people," they say, "who have lived their whole lives outside the Church, people whose lives have been wholly uninfluenced by religion. Now their last hour has come. They are hardly conscious perhaps. In any case, they know nothing about the nature of the sacrament they are going to receive. And often they protest against the priest's visit. What am I supposed to do for them? I will have no part in this sham of administering a sacrament which will not mean anything."

This they use as a pretext for refusing to go see the sick who do not call them, putting forward the claim that they do not wish to exert any imprudent pressure on people and prefer to leave

---

3 "Catéchisme et mission ouvrière" in the series Rencontres.

the sick their liberty. They save themselves for people who are in the full flower of life and who are of so much greater importance.

We agree that we should never force the sacrament on anyone underhandedly, because this sacrament, like the others, has no magical or automatic power. Yet it is only when the sacrament has been explicitly refused that we are forbidden to administer it. Whenever there is a possibility that it is desired, even if there has been no sign of this desire, we are obliged to administer it.

With much greater reason—and this is the point we wish to stress—can we be charged with failing gravely in our duty if we neglect visiting the sick, even if we neglect only those who are not practicing Catholics or who are hostile to the Church. It is not a question of capturing them or of adding another name to our pious list of conquests. It is an obligation of our mission-ary apostolate which we have to the sick as to all, though our obligation to the sick is a more urgent one because they are so soon to appear before God. "Father, of those whom thou hast given me, I have not lost one." We must be able to say that to the Father when He asks us for an accounting; we must be able to say, "No one has been lost through my fault." The Lord has poured out His blood for this sick person who has lived so far from Him. We still have a chance to make him understand this, to let him glimpse that eternity which is now so close to him. We may not be able to give him the sacrament, but the words with which we prepare him for a good death may be the means of starting in him an imperceptible interior movement that will open up to him the arms of Mercy.

The true missionary is not fastidious about the exercise of his ministry: he grasps every opportunity that offers itself. And this work with the sick is obviously one of the most urgent tasks of the ministry.

THE PARISH MILIEU

The reader may recall the way we used this term in *Revolution in a City Parish*. It served to describe the parish as made up of the restricted circle of those Catholics who, though practicing and devout, have no missionary outlook at all, but are quite content with things as they arc and quite attached to their own way of doing things. They are a threat to the clergy because they tend to make the parish priests prisoners within their "consoling" and suffocating circle, isolating them from the great masses who are left to go about their business with no one to care for them.

We said, and at sufficient length, that the missionary had to fear being taken over by this narrow group, that he had to go beyond it and reach the rest of the people. Does this mean that we must cast these Catholics of long standing into the outer darkness or that we cannot bother with them? Must we tell them that their reign is over and that we have something else to do besides spending our time on them?

God forbid! To begin with, they have souls as well as anyone else—souls which we must look after. They constitute our inheritance, and it is our duty to pick up the work of our predecessors where they left off. Such people generally have the best will in the world; and, although it is difficult, it is not impossible to win them over to the missionary cause. After all, they are the first field of activity open to us. They are there—there, just as the Jews of the synagogues of the Dispersion were. And God knows how unwilling those Jews were to receive the new dispensation that Paul was preaching to them and how they threw all their weight against him in his resolve to convert the Gentiles. Yet, not only did Paul always begin with them, but he made many converts and found many useful collaborators among them.

The parish milieu has to be transformed, but it must not be neglected. How can we reach these people? The virtue of religion offers us a starting point. Since non-Christians are more easily reached through the evangelical and social aspects of Christianity, we can use these means to bring them around to the sphere of religion proper. Traditional Catholics, on the other hand, have a sense of piety, a realization of their duty to God. But God is the Father of every one of us; Mary is the Mother of the human race; Christ is the universal Redeemer. They have a great devotion to the Sacred Heart, even if it is not always as enlightened a devotion as it might be. All these facts represent so many avenues by which they may be led to an evangelical and social view of the world—provided we start with what is, if not very real to them, at least very familiar. If we can get them to see that their desire for the kingdom includes and implies the apostolate and that they cannot love God without loving their fellow men, we are doing missionary work.

Moreover, the parish milieu is not made up solely of fer= vent Catholics or even of Catholics who habitually practice their religion. On its fringes there is also an important group of people who once went to catechism, who made their Com= munion, were married in the Church, and who now send us their children. To them also Christianity has only one aspect: the "religious." The normal thing is for this group to give the mission its first conquests; it is among them that our visits first bear fruit and that our liturgically inspired ceremonies can count on winning sympathizers. Not that we are to concentrate on them exclusively, since this would cut us off very quickly from the pagan masses who are even more important. But we must do serious work among them. And once they are touched by grace, they have the mettle to make good leaders in the pagan environment to which they are closer than most other people.

When we speak thus, we are taking the risk of being a little too jubilantly approved by persons who have never broken out of the parish milieu and tried to reach those beyond that circle. So much the worse for those who understand us so! Now, more than ever, are we convinced that it is precisely those "others" who must be the preferred object of our missionary apostolate, since it is they who are the lost sheep. Now, more than ever, are we convinced that we must preach the gospel to the whole world, not just to a small group that is already organized. But it is "with Jerusalem, Judea, and Samaria" that we must begin; and these too, despite appearances, need to be reached by the missionary movement.

THE MISSIONARY HIMSELF

The conclusion is that the true missionary of Jesus Christ, when considering his work, ought never to think of what he has to destroy, but only of what he has to build.

Let us now take a further step. All the demands we make on him in his personal life, if it is to be that of a real mission‑ary, must be considered—not under their negative, but under their positive aspect—as demands that spring from the very depths of our priesthood.

There is, for example, the question of priestly poverty. The priest has to be poor. But why? So as not to shock the workers. So as to be in tune with his people, who are poor. This is the first reason that comes to our minds, and there is truth in it. But if this were the only answer, the whole answer—would it not be a kind of trick, this poverty of ours: a trick to curry favor? Moreover, as an argument it would be extremely feeble if our people happen to be for the most part middle‑class. The truth is that, if we must be poor, it is because Christ was poor, because the Apostles were poor, because the gospel beatifies poverty, because the very nature of our priesthood demands that we should renounce the goods of this world. We have to be poor in order to be free, free to be priests of Jesus Christ and nothing else, free to be available for every type of missionary apostolate.

Then there is the matter of the priestly community of life and work. Beyond a doubt, we champion the community as an indispensable means of sustaining our fervor and of support‑ing ourselves in our work. But here again it seems to us that community life and work are demanded by the very nature of the priesthood. If we read the Acts of the Apostles again, we will see that there are always several gospel preachers together. They do not act individually. It is a group that announces Christ. A body of assistants takes shape around the bishop, and this forms the core of the Church of such and such a place. The same phenomenon is reproduced again and again in the his‑tory of the first centuries. Communities of presbyters are the rule. And every time there has been a renewal of life in the

Church, a resurrection of community life has been part of it. St. Augustine is a case in point. Not that we are to copy or even transpose a way of life taken from the Acts of the Apostles or the Constitutions of St. Augustine — it is the spirit behind them that we have to discover and make our own. And what is that spirit? Nothing but charity and fraternal love, for this is the very essence of the missionary spirit.

Often enough we say that we must make the laity do their part, and not do everything ourselves. But our purpose should not be merely to give them something to keep busy with or to put them into the game so that they will feel useful, whereas we feel all the time that we could get along quite well without their help. If this is our attitude (like that of a mother who makes her little daughter quite proud by assigning part of the housework to her, though it will all have to be done over later), we are acting in that frame of mind which we have called neg‑ ative. We give the laity only such jobs as are purely material, and even then we keep an eye on them all the time. We mis‑ trust their initiative and are always on our guard to see that they do not take anything upon themselves. We treat them as perpetual minors. All in all, we give them dolls to play with while we are taking care of the serious business.

We have to get away from this paternalistic and clericalist attitude. When we say that we must make the laity our asso‑ ciates in the apostolate, we mean that they have a mission of their own in the Church. We mean that they have a part to play which derives from their very nature as persons whom baptism has made members of Christ the Priest. It is their "priesthood" we have in mind. They have a work of their own to do; it is not ours, and we must hand it over to them with complete readiness and confidence.

There is, in the first place, all that material work of which we as priests ought to free ourselves. We recall here the example of a cathedral pastor. He has divided the affairs of his parish into five categories (schools, vacation camps, secretarial work, and so forth), and has entrusted the management of each category to a committee. He started by entrusting to them the admin= istration of all *expenditures* in connection with schools: salaries, furniture, repairs, books, etc.; and automatically the *income* increased three hundred percent, so quick were the people of the parish to catch the idea.

But there is spiritual work for them too—the work, for example, of directing the liturgical ceremonies, of organizing neighborhood meetings, of directing activities in a workers' sec= tion. Again, there is the work of participating in a missionary campaign, as did the laity in the mission of Briey or la Creuse or l'Yonne,4 etc. It is obvious, of course, that we are never going to turn over to them the entire work of spreading the gospel, and that we must constantly supervise them in order to see that their teaching is sound and their methods prudent; otherwise, we would risk heresy and anarchy. But, on the other hand, we must never look on them as mere errand boys, and never refuse to allow them initiative or give them responsibility. The positive work of the priest in this matter consists in creating a laity. Were he to be content with making some concessions to them, his action would be purely negative.

The same principles apply in the ticklish question of politics. "No politics" is our advice to the priest; it is the advice of the entire hierarchy too. This advice, however, may be taken quite negatively; and, so understood, it would differ little from the ideal of the lay state. Politics is a field of human activity, and nothing that is human can exclude Christ altogether. This advice therefore means that no stand is to be taken in purely political questions in which men are free to make up their own minds, and that we should not, as priests, interfere in a domain in which the faithful have a right to their liberty. It is easy to see how far this transcends any cheap opportunism, which

4 In these three districts of France, there were recently conducted parish missions according to a somewhat new plan. All the parishes of a district, as many as thirty or forty, had a mission going on at the same time. Part of the plan was to bring the mission before the eyes and ears of the public by an extensive publicity campaign, and in this the laity played a prominent part.

would have us avoid offending anyone so that we might win everyone. The priest, by the very fact that he is a priest, is the father of all and belongs to all; it is inherent in the priesthood to be above human quarrels. Yet, at the same time, political activity is human activity; and the priest must constantly be forming men who will be capable of fighting as Christians in the state, so that through them the state may be the city of God.

We could give many more examples. But these will suffice to bring out our main thought: that the demands which the missionary priesthood makes on us should not be envisaged as a series of almost negative concessions to what is called for by the spirit and the conditions of our times, but rather should be thought of as springing directly from the priestly spirit itself. If we are to make the fullest use of our priesthood and bear the fruit we should bear, our priesthood must be poor and com= munitarian; it must have the laity as its associates; and so on. The most urgent work of all is to provide true priests—priests who will neither be content with things as they are without taking the trouble to reflect on them, nor, on the other hand, throw themselves into the apostolate with the crude notion of turning everything upside down; but priests who will be so conscious of their priesthood and of what God wants from them and from the world in which they live that they will instinctively discover how they ought to conduct themselves and what work they ought to take up. ✢

✤[4]✤
The Essence of the Missionary Spirit

WE HAD, AT first, to clear up false notions about the missionary and point out that his work is positive rather than negative. It is now time to pass to the main theme: to ask ourselves what the missionary spirit—as we envisage it—really is, and to draw up a general outline of a missionary spirituality.

We will start with the missionary spirit, which to us seems composed of a threefold vision: a vision of the world, a vision of the Church, a vision of the love of Christ.

VISION OF THE WORLD

To make ourselves better understood we are going to use a modern illustration and compare the missionary spirit with the spirit of a convinced Communist militant. But note that we are confining our observations to the field of psychology. We are making no comparison between communism and Christianity. Such a comparison, as we know only too well, is bound to do less than justice to the true nature of Christianity. Christianity is no socio-economic theory, but something else altogether, something so transcendent that we cannot lay it alongside human theories. Our comparison, therefore, bears on states of mind, and on these alone.

A MAN OF CONVICTION

It is a fact that the militant Communist, surrounded as he is by all sorts of opportunists with no convictions at all, bases his action on a philosophy (we came near saying "a theology") of the world, a philosophy which has breadth. His actions may give the impression that he is only a shortsighted politician, and he may seem to be constantly shifting his ground. But these changing positions have no effect on his creed. On the contrary, they are dictated by his creed—the Marxist concept of histor‑ical development. This is a development which is inescapably moving toward the establishment of universal communism; and universal communism is the condition of human well‑being and happiness. In the light of the historical materialism of Karl Marx and Lenin, the Communist sees the world of tomorrow which is even now in the making. He has his plan. He knows where he is going and where the world is going. His gospel has told him these things.

Let us be honest enough to admit that we cannot say as much of many Catholics or even of many priests. They are the custodians of a tradition, the formulas of which they discreetly repeat. Still, can it be said that they are carried away and almost entranced by a world vision that is their own? They are the heirs of a past; but they are not builders of the future, because they do not appreciate the full magnificence of Christianity. They preach a moral system; they even preach dogmatic truths; but they are not heralds proclaiming the only Word of God.

The real missionary is, if anything, just such a herald. He is the messenger of the living Word, whose name is Jesus Christ. He too has his view of history. To him history is the kingdom of God being born in pain and sorrow. To him it is not the story of a past for which he sadly longs, but the story of the Cross, its preparation, and its glorious reality: *stat Crux dum volvitur orbis.* He too has a solid body of doctrine as the cornerstone of his life; it is the gospel of Jesus Christ, and he is completely obsessed by it. For him, too, the world in general, and with all its ups and downs, is moving toward an end to which it is also carrying us. That end is the second coming of Christ, without which it is impossible to make sense out of the world and its movement. In his body of doctrine there are immense riches: the Mystical Body of Jesus Christ singing the praises of God; the divine life, which glorifies and elevates the life of men; the universal love that comes from the Father and goes back to the Father; the Easter message that the world is saved because the risen Jesus is ever moving through our midst and carrying us along with Him toward the happiness that is to be ours. And it is more than a message, for the God-Man is really living in our midst and inviting us to be united with one another in Him. What are objections and controversies, or even shortcomings and setbacks, in comparison to the Word of God Incarnate in Christ, that Word which never ceases to resound in the missionary's ears? He knows where he is going and where the world is going. He has been swept off his feet by the beauty and the magnificence of the universal salvation which it is his mission both to proclaim and to translate into reality. This, surely, is far removed from the didacticism of tracts and catechism and codes of moral precepts.

The psychological state of the missionary is that which St. John describes for us at the beginning of his first Epistle: "What we have heard, what we have seen with our eyes, what we have looked upon, what our hands have touched—and the life also has been manifested and we have seen it and we bear witness to it . . . we announce it to you also that you may be in communion with us. For your communion is with the Father and with his Son Jesus Christ. And we write these things in order that your joy may be perfect. . . . The news that we announce to you is that God is light . . . "

It is possible to read between the lines here and detect what an overwhelming experience it had been for St. John to come into contact with Christ, of whose life he was a witness. It had been an overwhelming experience for him that day when he first met Him who was the Messiah and who was bearing the sins of the world, that day when John first came to see the sins of the world through Christ's eyes. After that, he could no longer look at the world without thinking of its sins and without taking upon himself the burden of its sins.

It had been an overwhelming experience for him to hear Christ announcing the Beatitudes and telling the parables. After that, he was haunted by the need to preach those Beatitudes and to see them put into practice; he was dominated by the passion for the kingdom that lived in him both as an unfading dream and as the only worthwhile reality.

It had been an overwhelming experience for him to see Christ working miracles, and to know that he was in the presence of God and was touching God ("what our hands have touched"); but it had given him confidence in that divine power, which would not stop short of miracles, and the conviction that God would be with him when he was doing God's work.

It had been an overwhelming experience for St. John and the Apostles to witness Christ's Passion and death and to feel their own human lives falling to pieces along with Him. But the supremely overwhelming experience for him had been to see Jesus risen from the dead, to see Him ascend into heaven, and to receive the revelations of Pentecost. Yes, it was an over-whelming experience, one that struck him like a bolt of light-ning; but one that shed its light on everything, on his own life, on life in general, on the world. "The news is that God is light."

This is the ferment that gives the heart of the missionary no rest. This is the passion that agitates him. This is the vision he has of the world; and, once he has it, he cannot rest unless he is bringing to others that same light and power and vision.

A REALIST

Though his adversaries may consider his vision of the world Uto-pian, the militant Communist is a realist all the same. He has eyes for more than history and the general direction it is taking. He never takes his eyes off what is happening around him and in the world at large, and he sees that things are not what they should be. He is obsessed by the suffering of others, which for him is a reality. He sees injustice in the relative situations of both the underdog and the profiteer. He sees the injustice and he does not reconcile himself to it. He is not content with the things that are, as they are; in fact, every detail of things as they are is, in his eyes, an aspect of the evil he wants to do away with. If you invite him to conform, he answers you with facts. Facts, always facts—this is a characteristic of every communist argu⸗ ment. And it accounts in part for the strength of communism, because, while it is quite possible to discuss theories, facts are there in front of you, hitting you between the eyes. You must concede that they exist, before you can begin to interpret them.

It is a rather curious paradox that people who pride them⸗ selves on being the least Utopian are also the least realistic. But on second thought it is not surprising: they are not hungry, and so they are the first to have enough. Let us imagine an apostle who lacks the missionary spirit. He will be content to hold on at any cost to things as they are; at the same time, he will be very quick to say, "Let us have no exaggeration. It is not as bad as all that." If you tell him, "Look here! There are already four hundred Adventists in this little city of ours, and they are taking quite a few people from us," he will give you a smile of pity and reply, "At Easter our cathedral was crowded at all the Masses." He picks up a magazine and reads two articles, one of which sets forth the distressing figures showing the progress of de⸗Christianization, while the other lists the number of Easter communions in the *grandes Ecoles*.[1] The first article will shock him slightly when he reads it, but his memory will make a place only for the figures of the second article. Realities escape him—spiritual realities even more successfully than statistical ones. He fails to see what everyone else around him sees. He never knows the mood of his region or his parish. So when he speaks, how far removed from reality are his words! How remote from him is the life of all those listening to him! And when he acts, how many of his actions are ill⸗timed!

There is a real danger that we priests may fail to see the drama of the century (if we may call it that), the struggle being waged right under our eyes each day, the anxious material struggle for their daily bread in which all our parishioners are engaged. We ourselves have almost no experience of permanent

---

1 *Les grandes Ecoles*—the various types of schools which prepare men and women for the professions. Admittance is by competitive examinations for which the lyceums prepare the students.

insecurity of this kind, of permanent uncertainty, or of the stern realities of life. But there is another struggle, perhaps even a more bitter one: the struggle between God and sin. Nor do we sufficiently see it as the tragedy it is. Somewhere in his book, *The Lord*, Guardini says that the Passion is not a tragedy, because we know that the words of eternal life are in it. That is true enough, but it is a truth that may mislead us: it ought to be a source of great confidence for us and a light in days of distress; but it is also a threat to us, since it can give leave to a dangerous kind of tranquillity to gain entrance into our souls.

The missionary is, of course, quite certain that the Christian cause will triumph in the end. He entertains no doubt about the outcome of the struggle. But he also knows that, even if the history of the Church and of the world is not a tragedy in the sense that evil has any chance of coming out on top, the history of each individual and of every society is a tragedy. He knows that in this tragedy he has a part to play, a crucial part. His every movement and his every decision may have terri= ble repercussions; tremendous issues may be decided by his industry or his indolence. And for this reason the missionary is alert to the history that is being made; he knows what is taking place; he passes judgment on it; he evaluates it.

It should trouble our consciences to see how we sometimes abuse the highest truths in order to justify our peace of mind and go on living in an unreal world. We know, for example, that God's actions count for more than ours and that He can get along without us; and so we come to the point where our blunders no longer upset us and our failures no longer set us looking for their cause. Again, our liturgy carefully preserves rites that are eloquent memorials of our Christian past. They were the products of a vital atmosphere which is timeless. But if we fail to replace them in such a living atmosphere, our con= tact with them is only too likely to make ritualists out of us, to accustom us in our everyday life to use words unconnected with reality and to hang on to methods totally ineffective in our world of today.

We want to make it clear that a real missionary will never delude himself with words and statistics and methods. In his parish he will not spend his time and consume his energy in trying to keep life in those activities which he knows have seen their day and are now incapable of having any influence. Perhaps a handful of people use them and thereby find a way of spend= ing their leisure time. But he wants more than that. He has no time to lose in conserving museum pieces. When the intelligent shopkeeper inventories his stock or analyzes his sales, he does a thorough job of it; when the shrewd industrialist examines his income from the plant, he makes it a point to know the real returns from each shop and each workman. Neither one of them holds on to a useless annex, an unprofitable enterprise, or a piece of broken machinery. So it is with the true missionary.

He knows that the work is too much for him and that he cannot do it all. He therefore chooses the item which gives a good return, and in choosing he does his best to be uninflu= enced by sentiment, snobbishness, or routine.

When we carefully examine the activities in which priests are engaged, we are astounded to see how many useless things they continue to hang on to for no other reason than a kind of unconscious sentimentality. It is disconcerting to listen to two priests, two apostles, discussing new moves to be made or reforms to be introduced into their apostolate, whether the innovations concern church ceremonies or parish activities or Catholic Action. You can see at once that their decisions are based only on impressions pure and simple, and not at all on real situations which they have observed in the course of their own experience, or on the returns which they expect in view of such real situations. One will insist on the need for continuing one activity, while the other will lay down certain limits for his contemplated ventures; and neither of them has any compelling reasons based on figures or on real situations which he has closely scrutinized. Both, in fact, have nothing but vague motives dressed up as *rationes convenientiae*—*rationes*, however, that have nothing to do with reason.

In one parish, everything is concentrated on a particular activity; in another, a certain institution is stubbornly maintained at any cost. It takes everyone's time and energy and absorbs all the financial resources of the parish, but no one ever asks himself whether there might not be some better way, whether it might not be possible to accomplish a hundred times more by devoting more manpower and money to some other enterprise. In the meantime everything else is endangered, because all the waking hours of the pastor and all his energy is taken up by the one activity which, by habit or personal preference, he is resolved to maintain.

No missionary will be satisfied with a name or a plan. He will not think, for example, that all the children of his parish are being evangelized simply because he has a recreation center, nor will he continue the recreation center simply because he himself used to frequent one as a boy. He will not believe that the working class has been reached when each of his curates has a Jocist section under his wing. He will not imagine that the families in his parish are having the gospel preached to them because the Catholic Family Movement has been established. He knows only too well that recreation centers, Jocist sections, and Catholic family groups can all of them be sterile and lifeless things, nor is he tempted to feel that his work is done once he has begun to use a certain method or to follow a certain directive. He always wants to know exactly where he is. Whenever a problem comes up, he asks himself once more the question Foch used to ask himself: "What is our objective?" Our objective is not to have a Jocist section, but to evangelize the working class; not to have such and such an activity for the neighborhood children, but to see that Christianity plays its part in their lives.

When people see how certain parishes and institutions are run, they say to themselves that if an industrial concern or a business were run, so it would have gone on the rocks long ago. Perhaps, unfortunately, that is just what has happened. It is painful to see that the children of light are not so wise in the affairs of the kingdom of God as the children of darkness are in their own domain.

A true missionary realizes that God gives His grace to men for a purpose, to enable them to carry out His will; and he realizes that he himself is the instrument of that will. He is certain of final victory, and yet he knows that the winning of the victory depends in part on him. His vision embraces the whole world, and for that very reason he works in the concrete situation which has the dimensions of his parish, without sep≠ arating his parish from the world. It is because he is a realist that he devotes himself just as much to the small everyday jobs as to the broad reforms that are required.

AN UNEASY MAN

We described the militant communist as one who sees and does not reconcile himself to what he sees. This is a distin≠ guishing trait of his. Many, in fact, see and countenance what they see; many who live surrounded by misery are resigned to it, shrugging it off with a, "There is nothing we can do about it." The militant communist is in a perpetual state of anger. Everything stirs him to revolt: the household where the wages are exhausted before the week is up; the accident at work which means destitution in the home; the brutality of a foreman. Everything feeds his revolutionary fever; every≠ thing intensifies his reaction: "There must be a change." He is forever contrasting the reality he meets along his path with the dream he bears within him. And the further he advances on the path, the more intense his passion becomes.

Transpose this to another plane, without putting the com≠ munist altogether out of your mind, and you have the state of mind of the missionary. He is a man who is not on the side of evil and is not reconciled to it.

The reader may think this is self≠evident. Perhaps. But I remember the pastor of a small parish whom I once met. He said to me, almost lightheartedly: "Everything is going to the dogs here, you know. For the twenty years that I have been here things have been constantly going downhill. But, after all, it will have to end someday. When they reach the bottom, things will have to start up again." To him his parish seemed like a rubber ball. He was not uneasy. We grant, of course, that this is an extreme case; but how many priests are really uneasy? We do not mean with that timorous uneasiness which is always reckoning up catastrophes, for there are only too many of that type. We mean rather with the healthy uneasiness which keeps a man from going to sleep. The majority have grown used to the situation. They are well aware that four people out of five in their parish, and often less, never set foot in their church. But that is the way things are. Perhaps when they first arrived in the parish, they looked about with furrowed brows; but long ago, the situation ceased to worry them. Every now and then you will hear a pastor say: "Little John, who made his first Communion the other day, has no faith, I am quite sure." The pastor himself had given him permission to make it. A few minutes' reflection would show that the whole passive crowd of people sitting in church for Mass is not receiving its spiritual nourishment and does not understand what is going on at all. But it is better not to think of these things too long. Where there is good will—and there is plenty of that—some routine practices will be revised under the pressure of a universal movement; there will, for example, be a few timid attempts at the dialogue Mass. But because there is no personal uneasiness behind the changes, the results are scanty; and perhaps such half failures even give rise to a certain satisfaction, enabling the priest to say, "I told you so." In any case, the routine drags on in essence: there is no deep disquiet; there is the same incapacity to receive a shock.

The true missionary is always receiving shocks. A scandal breaks out; a horrible example of ignorance comes to light; a home breaks up; a child is morally abandoned; a leader deserts the cause; a baptism is a mockery—anything like this affects him, because he is vulnerable to everything. "If they only knew," he says to himself, "such things would not happen. And if they do not know, they have not been taught. They do not know what love is. They should have been told. Is it not my fault?" The true missionary has not lost the ability to be surprised or to become indignant. We are not thinking of the young priest fresh from the seminary and just discovering evil; it is natural that everything should surprise him, because he knew nothing of it before. We have in mind rather the missionary who has already been working a long time and has nothing more to learn, and yet is not blasé. He sees the same things occurring over and over again until they are familiar to him, but his priestly sensibilities are not blunted. Each fresh blow he receives only strengthens his conviction that there must be a change. It is no morbid love of novelty or inborn restlessness at the root of his uneasiness. It is the *caritas Christi urget nos;* it is the gospel, which is for him the ferment of perpetual renewal, the ferment of revolution. Have we not time and again in our lives said, "*Emitte Spiritum tuum . . . et renovabis faciem terrae*"? A renewal of the face of the world! The missionary is haunted by the thought of this renewal: it is a veritable passion with him. He is not afraid of it, as are so many others who, when confronted with reforms proposed to them or already under way, are always inclined to ask themselves where it is all going to end. He is too shocked by the wretchedness of the things that are, to consider their disappearance a loss. Hence, he is ready for any improvement and is ever on the lookout for something better. He projects his apostolic uneasiness on the whole world. That de-Christianization is such a widespread phenomenon is a perpetual source of pain to him. It is a fact which he keeps before his eyes so that he may never forget it, and before his mind so that he may keep looking for a solution.

We have already mentioned an international meeting we recently attended. It was noticeable that the laymen of the eleven countries there represented had observed the same phe-nomenon. According to them, there was a serious condition of de-Christianization (even—and, in fact, especially—in the reputedly Christian countries); and, at the same time, a clergy unconcerned about and ignorant of the true state of affairs.

Every fact and every failing that comes to the missionary is armed with a question mark. He cannot see or hear anything without asking himself what bearing it has on the missionary problem. Perhaps it is a new film or a newspaper article, a new social or philanthropic venture; it makes no difference, because he always thinks immediately of the good or bad influence it will have on his cause. That consideration is the scale in which he weighs everything.

He is consequently able to go out and make contacts without waiting for others to come to him. He is not a functionary working at his job for so many hours and no more; he is a missionary all the time, and he never misses a chance to impart his enthusiasm to others. You may catch sight of him in a sacristy talking to a young man who happened to come along; and perhaps in another corner an old priest, one of those who have grown used to things as they are, may be saying to himself, "Look at him! He can't see a young fellow without falling all over him." The old man has unconsciously hit the nail on the head. The missionary "falls all over" every soul that comes within his range. And when he comes face to face with misery and misunderstanding and suffering in all its forms, he feels the enormous distance between the reality and the dream that he is carrying within him. With his whole being he wants to lessen that distance and is more than ever determined that there must be a change.

Does this surprise you? "To be at ease is to be unsafe" (Newman).

A VICTIM

In this battle, it is not the immediate results that count. As everybody knows, one of the leading themes of the communist theory is that we have hardly begun to see the realization of integral communism. Several generations will have to be sacrificed before this objective is achieved. We will not see the results. We are working for a society that is still to come. The real communist leader, the type who has not lost the fire of his Communist faith, the type found especially among the rank and file—he is filled with this spirit.

It is certainly sad to see so much generosity misdirected in the service of a cause which will never satisfy the hopes it arouses, since it considers only man, and man cut off from God. But it is impossible not to admire the inner inspiration, which is an unconscious transposition from the very essence of Christianity.

Sine sanguinis effusione non fit remissio. Without the Cross, there is no redemption. The suffering Redeemer is on the pro-gram, and His provisional failure also. To human eyes the story of Christ is a failure, and His Passion a defeat. The harvest was to come afterwards, the never-ending harvest that was to crop up on the graves of the martyrs and of their brothers in sacrifice. Only with the eyes of faith do we know that the Cross is a victory; even after twenty centuries of history have strengthened our faith, we still need faith to see the Cross as a confirmation of our faith. Even the greatest Apostle of all, St. Paul, on the day of his death had to look to his faith for assurance that his life had not been spent in vain. "One sows, another reaps." If a man wants to reap everything he sows, it will only be a small garden he can cultivate. If you wish to be a missionary, you have to renounce success; you have to wel-come joyfully the words addressed to you: "May the kingdom of Christ move on over your body."

"He who would save his life will lose it, he who loses his life for my sake will gain it." This powerful proverb of Our Lord's, which is true in so many different ways, finds its most striking application in the apostolate. In the struggle which makes up the apostolate, victory goes to those who are willing to lose. Not to lose the battle (on the contrary, they are sure of winning it), but to lose themselves. Victory belongs to those who are willing to lay down their lives in the struggle without asking to see the victory. Ah! It is no doubt quite possible that they will sometimes speak like the communist militant who dreamed of the renewal of the world: "I would certainly like to live long enough to see the beginning of the new world . . . " But this desire is only a manifestation of their optimism and their faith in their cause. In fact, they will never say this seriously, for they know that the kingdom is not of this world. At the same time, however, they know that the kingdom of God is already in the making in this world, that it is in the making every day, that they must work without respite for it, that the victory is already won, but that they are the ones who must enable the multitude to benefit by it. *Adveniat regnum tuum!* It is coming even now; it is coming invisibly into every soul which allows itself to be won over by Love. It sometimes shows its face when a group or a parish gives proof of fraternity or devotion. But then you can be sure that the Cross is in the background. The kingdom of God does not come through a successful meeting from which the cry goes up, "Hail to Christ the King!" It does not come through a victory at the polls. It does not come through perfectly organized parish societies, nor even through magnificent ceremonies. All these things have their importance, greater or less as the case may be; but we must not let ourselves take them for the real thing, or mistake these successes for the victory of Christ. *Haec est victoria fides nostra.* There is no victory for Christ except where there is an increase of faith or of love.

This is the same distinction we made in *Revolution in a City Parish* and which seems to us of prime importance—the distinction between God's kingdom and ours. The missionary refuses to seek his own kingdom. He is even uneasy when he sees the beginning of a little kingdom of his own: *Non nobis, Domine, non nobis, sed nomini tuo da gloriam.* He has eyes for nothing but the kingdom of God, the kingdom which comes interiorly and which uses as its instruments all those who are willing to lose their life with Christ. And this is which, in the final analysis, explains why he is never discouraged. When a man looks for immediate results it is quite natural that he should be easily discouraged, just as it is quite natural that he should react to failure by pseudo-spiritual submission which

287

inclines him to give up trying to accomplish anything. The mis=
sionary does not "resign" himself to failure. He gives himself
through his failure, because he sees it as a kind of condition of
the final victory. He adds his own failure to the great stream
that is sweeping on to ultimate triumph. He knows he is a
victim, and that is what he wants to be.

VISION OF THE CHURCH

A world vision such as we have just sketched will give us a
missionary and even a Christian missionary, but not necessarily
a Catholic missionary.

A man can be a Catholic missionary only if his name is writ=
ten in a Catholic context. This Catholic context is the Church.
To be a Catholic missionary is to belong to the Church. The
vision of what the Church is and of what membership in the
Church entails will determine the missionary's whole outlook
and behavior, the whole tenor of his conduct and life.

The word "mission" evokes the idea of being sent. No one
sends himself. A mission is something one receives. "As my
Father has sent me, I also send you." We receive a mission
from Christ, from Christ living in His Church, to which He has
committed the duty of preparing the coming of His kingdom.

There was a time when the word "mission" was used exclu=
sively of apostolic expeditions which went beyond the frontiers
of Christendom. But that was an age in which there was a
Christendom. The word continued to be used thus long after
there had ceased to be a Christendom (though many were still
under the illusion that it continued to exist).

Today paganism is everywhere. There is now no longer any
danger of confusing the kingdom of Christ with the kingdom
of St. Louis or even with the Holy Roman Empire. Is this
something to be regretted? The invasion of paganism certainly
is. But it is all to the good that the mask has been torn away
from it and that it now appears in the open instead of veiling
its face. In any event, the Church has profited by this devel=
opment to the extent that she is again, as in the Apostolic age,

able to see herself as a ferment, as a leaven spread wherever the dough of humanity needs to rise. The mission today is *ad intra*. It is here in France, in Italy, in Spain, in South America, in the United States. It is in your own parish, even if your parish happens to be one of the so-called "Catholic" ones. The entire Church is in a state of mission.

That the Church is in a state of mission in a de-Christianized parish is only too evident; but it is also in the same state in the "practicing" parish. This is true because, first of all, only rarely does the practice of the practicing parish run as high as fifty percent, and no parish can forget the half of its members that are still to be won. It is true also because practicing Catholics, as well as others, are the object of a mission, the purpose of which is to make the charity of Christ take root in them. Finally, and above all, it is true because the rest of the Church needs the mission, and no Christian community can be without solic- itude for the rest of the body. No community, whether a parish or a religious community, can call itself Christian if it isolates itself and does not participate in the perpetual mission of the whole Church. All who really possess the spirit of the Church are animated by a missionary spirit, even if their environment is entirely Catholic.

This applies to every member of the community, to priest and layman alike—to the layman every bit as much as to the priest, since the layman too has received a mission from the hierarchy. It is not a matter of choice; it is bound up with one's status as a member of the community, for the community itself is a portion of the Church.

The reader may think we are laboring the obvious. It is true enough that all this has been said already and repeated countless times. But when you see the spirit which exists in so many of our "good parishes," you feel duty-bound to say it again. Those who are, or think they are, the *beati possi- dentes*, seem to look upon missionary problems as no concern of theirs. Even when you try to interest them in something vital to almost the whole Church, they do not hesitate to say that it does not concern them at all. "That does not concern us." What a small concept of "us" that implies! They have no qualms about planning their activities without giving a thought to the possibility of coordinating them with the work in other parts. This means a loss to the whole missionary movement and a loss to them as well. For they are thereby losing that dynamism which, before long, they will need more than they think; perhaps they already need it for the reconquest of what, without their knowing it, is now being lost to them.

We would even go so far as to say that these almost wholly Catholic parishes are the ones which ought to be the most mis-sionary. And we see at least two reasons why this should be so.

In the first place, they are Christian and therefore fully equipped to do Christ's work, to abide by the dictates of the Church, and to receive a "mission." Well and good. Now let us see how a political party, for example, wages an election campaign. What would we think of a party which, at election time, paid no attention at all to those districts where it has a majority, making no campaign there, and fighting only in those districts where it is certain to be defeated? The party must, of course, even without hope of immediate success, put up a fight in those localities where it is unknown or in the minority; but it must also work where its chances of success are good, and make sure of the victory which is within its reach. Or, again, take a businessman. Will you ever see him leave a market where business is good and go to one where there are no customers? Pardon these comparisons: they are not much to our liking either, but they illustrate our point well enough. It is obviously necessary to go after the one lost sheep. This we have said so often that our attitude ought to be known. But at the same time we also have to look for ways to enlighten the sheep that are beginning to wander off and look for the roads which lead to them. And surely it is eas-ier to inject the missionary spirit into a parish where there is goodwill and where everyone has the faith and is ready to heed the directives of the Church. Do we really appreciate what an increase in power would result, particularly for the Church in France, if all the Catholic regions were to acquire a real sense of their missionary obligation and act according to it? Is it not strange that certain dioceses with an ample number of priests find it so hard to part with vocations for the Mission of France or for religious congregations, although in the past it was these very dioceses which were the principal providers of vocations for the missions in China and Africa?

In the second place, the mission means, not propaganda, but testimony; and it functions much like the light on the bushel. What we need is to show the world real Christian living. The great need is to plant "witnesses" of Christ in society, community witnesses as well as individual ones. Imagine what a testimony to the truth it would be for the whole of France if our practicing parishes were truly Christian communities in which rectitude, justice, and charity were genuine everyday realities. What a testimony to the truth if we could say to our de-Christianized populations: "You want to know what Christianity is and what happiness it can bring into the world? Go to the Vendée, to Brittany, to Anjou, and see for yourself what life is like there, how the priests there act, and how the Catholics there live!" We are not asking for universal sanctity; still, we cannot help but think of the wonderful spectacle it might have been for the whole of France if there had been one province to which we could have pointed and said: "See that Catholic region! There is no black market there!"

The missionary spirit is a spirit of the Church; the spirit of the Church is a missionary spirit.

The missionary keeps his eyes fixed on this vision of the Church in the world: a Church on the march, a Church in the minority, a Church misunderstood, opposed and ignored.

He is interested in what happens to the Church, and not only in what is happening in his parish, his activity, or his movement. He thinks according to the dimensions of the universe. And what excuse could there be for thinking otherwise in our world? Every day, the newspapers and the radio bring us face to face with world problems and make us see how the whole world is affected by events which occur anywhere on the face of the globe.

The missionary thinks this way and, because he does, he also realizes that he is a man of the Church, that his actions constitute a commitment for the Church, that he represents her, that he is responsible for her, that he either helps her to advance or handicaps her. This is true of every priest, and indeed of every Catholic layman as well—at least of every‐one known as such. Whether we like it or not, whether we find it a nuisance or not, this is a fact, and a fact none of us can ever afford to forget: my attitude, my words, my smile, or my forbidding appearance, the way I offer my hand, the way I judge, the way I administer the sacraments and the way I enter into the Mass—this and everything else I do results in a favorable or unfavorable judgment being formed of the Church of Jesus Christ.

It must not be imagined that the missionary feels like pat‐ting himself on the back when he hears someone say: "You, sure, you're all right. You aren't the same kind of priest as the others; but why aren't the others like that?" He has no desire to be an exception. Far from it. But such a remark surprises him, because he is convinced that he is doing only the most elementary things. On the other hand, it is a pity that anyone should have to admit such a remark is true. Unfortunately, it is true. When an individual Catholic or an individual priest is a real witness, that is a good thing. When a group or a parish community gives witness, that is even better. Our witnessing, however, will be as effective as it should be only when it is the mass that witnesses: Christians and priests as a whole, our parishes as a whole. It will, in fact, be effective in witnessing when it is the witnessing of the Church, or at least (since we are writing in French) of the Church of France. Love for the Church should make it impossible for any Catholic leader or any member of the clergy to isolate himself from the mission‐ary movement.

The fact that we are making commitments for the Church forces us to think twice before making any move or taking any step, but it also serves as a stimulus to us and an invitation to go forward. It makes us realize that we are not marching alone. When we ourselves have to bear painful opposition and incomprehension from those around us, it helps to know that in other places, and in more places all the time, the mission-ary movement is going ahead. Furthermore, it helps to know that this missionary movement is essential to the Church, and that we are in the right, as against every form of stagnation and routine.

Thus, to the missionary it is of the utmost importance to see that his work is carried out in union with the whole Church. He does not take to the road alone or set out to do battle alone. The ground he covers is put down as part of the whole forward movement of the advancing Church. He will therefore be careful to keep in contact with the Church—a need which entails many obligations.

His first obligation is to keep his leaders informed. Our lead-ers make no claim to be like the heroes of Molière's comedy: "We, men of quality as we are, know everything without ever having learned anything" Our leaders know quite well that there is no one more isolated than a superior whose subjects, in an attempt to please him, tax their ingenuity to draw a rose-colored curtain of pious optimism between him and real-ity. Our leaders are more like Foch when he said to a liaison officer: "Do not tell me what you think will please me, tell me what is true." They have the assistance of grace and of the Holy Spirit, but they need to be kept informed. And they can be kept informed only by the priests and laymen who are in actual contact with the great masses of the people, believers and unbelievers. The Vatican and the diocesan chancery are like ourselves: they can work no more than fifteen or sixteen hours a day, and in this time they cannot acquire a personal knowledge of everything. The Pope sees only what is brought to his attention. The bishops hear only what they are told. It is the missionary's duty to give them an exact picture of the temper of the times as he knows it, of the needs of his people, of the precise degree of their ignorance, and the reason for it as he sees these things. It is his duty also to let them know what the people are thinking and saying; to tell them the story of his own experiences, what he hoped to accomplish and how far he has succeeded; and to suggest possible remedies for par= ticular situations.

Sometimes we hear bitter remarks about the failure of supe= riors to understand the real situation. Do those who make such remarks do anything to clear away the misconceptions of their superiors? Have bishops been able to get a clear picture of the true state of affairs from some of the reports that are made at the time of the pastoral visitation or from the accounts that appear in the religious bulletin of the parish? Whose fault is it that bishops are sometimes poorly informed? Who put them on the wrong track? We all know that it requires a certain amount of courage to tell the truth, much more courage than to describe conditions in a way that will be pleasing and flattering. If we lack this courage which our leaders expect us to have, we are not the kind of missionaries we should be.

There is also the matter of loyalty, the loyalty we owe our superiors and the loyalty we owe those under us. Every minor superior, indeed every man who is entrusted with even the smallest responsibility, is an intermediary between the one who gave him his mission and those to whom he is sent. The priest as an intermediary has this responsibility to a greater degree than others. By his very nature, he is the bridge that joins men to God, and the faithful to the hierarchy of the Church. He is not only the representative of the hierarchy before the faithful; he is also the representative of the faithful before the hierarchy. He is the pastor of the faithful; their souls have been placed in his care; and it is his duty to see that his leaders know the sufferings and the needs of his people. Often enough, the faithful, especially if they are ordinary people, will experience needs and sufferings and difficulties without knowing how to formulate them or without daring to express them, at least to those in high places. Perhaps the idea of making them known to their leaders will never even occur to them, or, if it does, they will lack the courage; and sometimes, they will be unable to express their sentiments even to themselves. Who will be their spokesmen, if not we, their pastors? When we see and hear things and keep them to ourselves, when we come face to face with problems every day and lack the courage to make them known to those above us, whose responsibility for these masses is greater than our own, we are at one and the same time betraying our leaders and our sheep.

The missionary has another obligation which is even harder to live up to: adjusting his pace to that of the Church. All agree that we are supposed to lead. The Church counts on us to go ahead, and so we have at times to assume responsibilities which not everyone can assume. But at the same time, we have to remember that we are part of a great fighting body, one which is not only spread out over today's battlefield but which also extends far back into history, one which has its traditions and is conditioned by its past. The term "vanguard" (avant-garde) is one that most of us are very tired of hearing used for everything and for nothing—to designate, for example, those who are experimenting with audacious methods as well as those who are only restoring things that should never have been allowed to disappear (and who are, in fact, only the vanguard of the rear guard). But since people insist on calling us the vanguard, we will not make a fuss about it. In any case, if we are the vanguard, we will have to keep in mind that the vanguard has no right to cut itself off from its bases and set out in search of adventure. Should it do so, it would be putting itself in danger of being wiped out and would be deserting the main body of the troops. Let us drop the metaphor. Only at the price of exposing the faithful to bewilderment and of bringing on divisions and regrettable reactions can any one of us, no matter who he is, launch any innovation, unless it has been approved by higher authority. We must, of course, be clear about what constitutes a dangerous innovation, and not call as such those things which ought to be the rule for every pastor who is really concerned for the welfare of his flock. An explanation of the ceremonies at a funeral or a translation of the prayers, to take an example from the domain of liturgy, is not a dangerous innovation. But there are other innovations for which there is no real need: the creation of new forms of Catholic Action movements, the holding of inopportune meetings which may interfere with an action of the whole hierarchy, the celebration of Mass in the vernacular by a priest in public, and so on. The common good of the Church is at stake in every new step we take. We may never take such a step without considering its effects on the common good and its repercussions on the community as a whole; and, if it is an important step, we must first propose it to the authority responsible for the common good.

In the parish community itself the same holds good. Here also there must be no reckless pushing ahead heedlessly of the main body of troops. It is the simplest thing in the world to start a missionary movement into which a small number, those most easily led, will enter enthusiastically. But what good does it do to record an advance of this kind when no one else follows? It is the whole parish that ought to be missionary, not merely the few; the whole parish has to be a missionary unit in its liturgy, its teaching, its activities. Some will, of course, be more dynamic than others, and it is they who will have to set the pace. But a man who is supposed to set the pace is of no use to his companions when he streaks off several miles ahead of them. He must never lose contact with them.

The transformations and advances of the parish must affect all the parishioners; and therefore, to achieve more universal results, we will at times have to slow down our pace. Suppose, for example, I want to have my people sing. It would be rela= tively easy to form a *schola cantorum* of twenty young ladies; everyone would be happy; after a year or two, such a choir would be quite credible. But no one else would have the cour= age to join in with it. If you think you need a *schola cantorum* to guide the rest, you must, at the same time form it, do all in your power to get everyone to sing. It is the same with the Jocist section which gets off to such a brilliant start that it soon leaves the mass of young workers far behind. Perhaps a word of warning is in order here. We can already see some of our readers seizing upon these words of ours, convinced that they justify stagnation and getting ready to sing once more their favorite refrain: "Let us not go too fast." Before they settle back in their comfortable chairs, let us make it clear that, just because it is much harder to get a whole parish moving than a select group, we must set about it at once and keep at it all the time.

This same solicitude for the Church calls for the teamwork about which we shall have more to say later. Since all of us (we priests and our lay people with us) belong to the Church, we cannot work in isolation at parallel tasks; we are yoked together to do the same work, and that work is the work of the Church.

For the same reason, we shall do our best to adjust our pace to that of the neighboring parishes, the national organizations of Catholic Action, and the religious Orders. The Church militant is a collaboration on a grand scale in the service of the same Leader; this means that there will be different tasks to be carried out, but that all will be directed to the one end under the inspiration of the same Spirit, the Spirit of Love.

Certain parishes, certain groups, certain individual missionaries will perhaps be called upon to bear witness in a distinctive way and to blaze trails. They will be "on a special mission," so to speak, and will serve as a leaven for the rest; but they must not forget that they belong to the Church and that they have an obligation to serve the community as a whole.

This is the kind of missionary spirit that has always been proper to the Church. Every time the Church has allowed it to take a concrete form, she has had to take a risk. There is a risk involved today as there was in the past, but there is no added reason to fear the risk. The Church sent her missionaries, as she is still sending them, to far off lands. She was not unaware of the risks involved: the risks to their bodies, because of the climate and the hostility of the people; and the risks to their souls also, because isolation can bring on discouragement and because there were other temptations to which they would be exposed. Still, she did not hesitate to send them.

When today the Church sends her missionaries into facto≠ ries, she is not unaware of the dangers of another kind which lie in wait for them; but, all things considered, there is no more reason to worry over the priest you send into the factory than over the one you send into tropical regions where he is surrounded by people of loose moral standards. The Church's inclination to expand has always enabled her to overcome such fears and put to one side the motives that would bid her lie still.

We must, however, hold firmly to two principles. The first: the more advanced the post you are holding, the more necessary it is that you should have been given it by lawful authority; the individual ought not to choose his role in the Church, and least of all when there is danger of bringing discredit on her. The second: the more advanced the position the missionary holds, the more necessary it is for him to be in communication with the center of the Church, with a community, and with his bishop.

When he is thus linked to the Church, through his man≠ date and his fidelity, the missionary will be certain that he is doing God's work and that he is accomplishing something worth≠while for God's kingdom.

VISION OF THE LOVE OF CHRIST

But the missionary spirit will be a truly Christian spirit only if its consuming and overpowering motive is that of making the Person of Christ known and loved and served. We are, of course, heralds of a Church; but not of a Church as an orga≠ nization, nor a Church that stands for order above all else, nor yet a Church that is primarily a temporal institution. It is the Church of Christ that we preach, the Church that is the society of God's children gathered together in Christ, the Church that is the Body of Christ. We preach the Truth, but not a theory or a Christian philosophy or even a theology; the Truth we preach is the Word of God, the Word made flesh: "I am the Truth, I who speak to you." We announce the gospel teaching, but not only the message (as we might if we were in the Old Testament): it is the Messenger Himself that we announce.

Since Harnack's time some have been more or less inclined to say that charity is "the essence of Christianity." It is not so. The essence of Christianity is a living Person; the essence of Christianity is Christ. It is not a moral system, however lofty and beautiful, that we have to proclaim. We proclaim Christ, the Incarnation of a God who is love. The worship we offer is Christ: Christ praying and Christ offering Himself through our hearts and voices and hands. And the cause for which we want victory is the cause of the Person of Christ; we want to see Christ known to all, in order that all may love Him.

The priest becomes a real missionary only on the day that the vision of Christ as center of the world's history takes hold of him, the day that he begins to see Christ as the One who gathers together the scattered children of God, as the human manifestation of the Father's love for men, as the crown of all creation, as the adorer of the Father, as the choirmaster of humanity's adoration, as priest, and as victim. On that day, he stops preaching theses which leave most men cold, and he begins to reveal the moving mystery of the God who so loved men that He gave them His only Son.

The missionary is not an exegete, a controversialist or a philosopher; he is the herald of a fact. He proclaims that God became man and dwelt in our midst. He holds up the Cross and tells men what it means. He recounts the story of Jesus, how the prophecies and events of the Old Testament prepared the way for Him, how He lived here on earth, suffered, and died, rose again and ascended into heaven. He declares that Christ is present in the Church and in the Eucharist. He announces that Christ is to come back again, and that we are on our way to meet Him. A discussion may leave us neutral; but a man—we take sides for or against him. The missionary announces the Man-God and invites men to declare themselves.

The men of our age, in spite of all their protestations against dictators and dictatorships, are quite ready to allow themselves to be guided and led by a man. The contradiction is only an apparent one. They are looking for a great leader whom it is safe to follow, a leader they can admire and obey—above all, a leader they can love. The missionary's work is surely made easier by this characteristic aspiration of our times. It is, in fact, quite easy to point to Christ as the true leader, the One who did not come to enslave others but to serve them, the only one who does not make use of others, but gives Himself for them. But it is easy only if people can see that we are sincere, and only as long as they do not spy the ghost of clericalism lurking behind the Cross of Christ the King.

There is one more point. If you wish to make a leader loved, you must love him yourself, love him passionately. But first of all you must know him intimately. When a man can say of a great human leader, "I know him: I have seen him," everyone who trusts the speaker is reduced to silence. We must therefore have a personal knowledge of Christ, a knowledge which is not bookish or speculative or affected. We acquire it through a loving familiarity with Holy Scripture and with the Gospels in particular. We acquire it also through prayer and through the Mass, in the very heart of our prayer and of the Mass, filled as it is with the Scriptures and the Gospels illuminated by the unique light of the Paschal mystery which we are celebrating and commemorating as we offer Christ in person.

As far as the missionary himself is concerned, there is no substitute for a close contact with the Bible. The missionary is by his very nature a bearer of the Good News, and he must speak in the name of a Person whom he has some experience of hearing and seeing.

There is for us, therefore, a distinct method of studying the Bible. If we have a complaint to make against our seminary professors, it is that they did not teach us to read the Bible and to look in it for the one and only Christ. They taught us exegesis, but did not teach us to look at the Psalms, the Prophets, the Gospels, and St. Paul with the fresh and keen and mobile eyes a man needs when he is looking for the counte= nance and the thoughts of Jesus Christ our Lord, for His inten= tions and His love. We know a seminarian who was severely reprimanded because he tried to construct from the Gospels a picture of Christ's appearance and character. He was accused of "naturalism." It is still more painful to recall the structure of a Catholic, strongly tempted to turn to Protestantism, who said to us, "In Protestant churches, they speak of nothing but Jesus; in Catholic pulpits, they speak of nothing but moral conduct." This is, of course, an exaggeration; but, if our lips are to speak out of the abundance of our hearts, we must become familiar with Jesus Christ in our studies and meditations and prayers. We will never succeed unless our spirituality is more than a mere "moral" spirituality, unless it is a meeting with Christ and an unaffected intimacy with Him.

Strictly speaking, there is no such thing as a missionary spir= ituality. Men live and teach many spiritualities, among which none is especially indicated for the missionary, just as none is forbidden him. Yet it is true that the missionary needs to live in a close and personal union with Christ, and that his need is greater than that of any other Christian. "For I am determined to know nothing among you except Jesus Christ, and him crucified." ✠

✠[5]✠
Some Materials for a
Missionary Spirituality

S PIRITUALITY IS A big word, and we want it to be clear from the outset that we are using the word only because it is the best one we can think of. The various forms of spirituality were never so much discussed as in our day. The traditional spirituality has been confronted with the modern spirituality; comparisons have been made between the various forms: Benedictine, Franciscan, Dominican, etc. Some have advocated a spirituality for the laity; some have attempted to define a spirituality for the priest; and some have even ques-tioned the very existence of these various spiritualities.

It is not our purpose in this chapter to have our say about such controverted matters. When we speak of a missionary spirituality, we have no intention of comparing it with any other kind; and the idea of introducing a new spirituality is even further from our thoughts. Our purpose is much more modest. Convinced as we are that there must be a variety of the interior life which is characteristic of the missionary, we are simply ask-ing ourselves what it is. It is to this characteristic variation of the interior life that we give the name "spirituality." Now we can let the authorities proceed with their disputes about the term.

The reader will not, therefore, expect to find here a treatise on spirituality, or even some elements of such a treatise. We have nothing to offer him in the way of theories worked out at a desk. We are simply taking a position from which we can observe a reality—a reality made up of the mission work to be done, the priests called upon to do it, their failures and their successes in the domain of the interior life, and our own experiences as well. When we observe this complex reality, we feel that we have something to say, that we have a word of advice to help our younger brethren avoid mistakes and find what we are searching for along with them.

"MISSIONARY"?

Often enough—much too often, in fact—has it been our experience to hear laymen or fellow priests calmly bestowing on us or on themselves the title "missionary," but it has never failed to set our nerves on edge. To their way of thinking, it is to be taken for granted that the Christian world can be divided into two parts or, so to speak, into two states: the static state and the missionary state. You make your choice between the two according to your tastes, or you are definitively assigned to one or the other by a mandate of the hierarchy.

But "missionary" is not a title one should be quick either to assume or to bestow.

And when you "are a missionary," you are not therefore entrenched in a definitive state or situation. You are a missionary to the extent you are a saint. You tend to become a missionary as you tend to become a saint. The missionary state is an ideal of the priestly life which Christ places before our eyes. To call oneself a missionary is as ridiculous as to call oneself a saint. It is nothing we can lay claim to, but only something we can tend to.

There is an effort to be made, a constant advance to be achieved, an ideal to be realized. All of these—the making of the effort, the achievement of the advance, the realization of the ideal—must spring from love and must develop our love. And precisely for this reason there is room for us to look for a spirituality in the full development of our being as missionaries.

To be a saint, to be a missionary—for us, these two are the same thing, for two reasons. The first is that, the present state of the Church and the world being what it is, it seems to us impossible that a priest once engaged in the apostolic ministry should find any other way of sanctifying himself than by becoming more and more missionary, by spending himself completely in the immense work to be done, and by forgetting himself that the work may be done through him. The second reason is that the man who wishes to mount towards God can find in his mission‹ ary zeal everything he needs in the way of genuine mortification. We explained this point in *Revolution in a City Parish.*

The Church has in the past found room for many other types of sanctity, and she will do so in the future. Yet it seems to us unlikely that even the contemplative can grow to his full stature in the love of God unless he too catches a touch of the "missionary fever." In any case, the sanctity of a priest appointed by his bishop to any kind of post in parish work must be a missionary sanctity. The demands of the work to be done impose on him the form of sanctity which God expects of him. The struggle for perfection and the missionary effort are not two parallel entities: they are so intimately intertwined that they are but one thing.

It might be a good thing to try inverting the terms of an expression we frequently use. We are often told: "Be holy, and you will surely be a good priest or a good missionary." Would it not be more correct to say: "Be a real priest or a real mission‹ ary, and in the effort to become one you will become a saint"? Sanctity does not pre‹exist as a reality from which missionary work might come forth as a fruit. The fact is rather that, in our search for the fullness of the missionary spirit, we are enabled to discover the sanctity that is ours.

MORTIFICATION THROUGH THE MINISTRY OR THROUGH SPIRITUAL EXERCISES?

We all know that spiritual writers traditionally divide the spir‹ itual life into the three ways: the purgative, the illuminative, and the unitive—or mortification, the practice of the virtues, and union with God. All the saints tell us, by their example as well as by their words, that mortification is absolutely necessary for anyone who wishes to strive after perfection.

Could it not be that the time‹honored mortifications, as we find them described in devotional books, have proved so discouraging to some people in our day that they have come to slight the very notion of mortification, considering it either impossible or unnecessary? "Times have changed." "Our health cannot stand up under that sort of thing." "We have too much work to do." Lay people say, "To work is to pray;" and priests, "A man can find God in his ministry."

Besides, is there still a place in the apostolic life of today for the "spiritual exercises" as they were taught to us in the seminary? Would it not be advantageous to replace them by contact with souls and by the discovery of God which we make at every moment we are giving Him to souls? If it is true that the more missionary we become the closer we approach to sanctity, is it not enough to give oneself once for all without so much concern about the rest?

As the statement we made might, in fact, give rise to an illusion, we must dispel that illusion immediately. The fact that a man thinks he is a missionary does not mean he is on the road to sanctity. Let us repeat what we said before: it makes no more sense to call oneself a missionary than to call oneself a saint. The missionary state is a thing to which we tend. It consists in an unceasing effort, and this is like every other effort in that it needs a stimulus and a discipline. Its rhythm is that of two steps ahead and one back, with periods of weariness following on periods of generosity. There never comes a time when one can give up working on oneself.

The story of this struggle may be the story of a man's holiness. It may be possible to outline broadly a missionary spirituality after we have reached some firm conclusions based on many kinds of missionary experience. But we have no intention of doing that here. It is only as friends and brothers that we wish to speak, as friends and brothers who may enable others to see some things in a new light and who are glad of the chance to mention some of their own misgivings.

Some of our fellow priests are, to judge by their words, laboring under a serious misconception in the matter of holiness, a misconception which might seriously detract from their effectiveness as apostles.

It is clear that every type of spirituality aims at putting the soul in contact with God. It is equally clear that we can find God present in those around us and that our ministry affords us many opportunities to discover in souls the work of God—or God in person. How often have we not left the confessional, deeply moved by the confession someone has just made or by the resolute purpose of amendment manifested! How often, in the course of our priestly lives, have we not felt forced to over‑come ourselves, to check up on ourselves spiritually, by our very struggle to rescue a young man from his bad habits or to save a home from shipwreck! And our own experience of adminis‑tering the sacraments, of preaching and of time spent meeting people in the sacristy or rectory, all has proved to our satis‑faction that these too can be excellent means of sanctification.

We would even go so far as to say that the ministry in itself presents continual opportunities for mortification, and that it is a grave defect in the training of seminarians that they are hardly taught to look for mortification in the exercise of their future ministry. In *Revolution in a City Parish,* we did not spare our praises of this properly missionary asceticism—an adapted asceticism, granted, but one no less crucifying than our time‑honored ascetical practices. It comes into play in the close watch we have to keep on our various apostolic movements; in the painful submission we must make to the demands of God's work; in the insistent demands charity makes on us, giving us no rest, refusing us any interior rest or feeling of satisfaction. *Sacerdoce oblige.* The priesthood has its obligations, and at times we have to pay an enormous price to live up to them. They may take us as far as the mortifications of the Curé of Ars, who immolated himself for his parish; but in ordinary everyday life they will regularly take the form of tiresome work, humble acceptance of reverses, abandonment of our own ideas for the good of the common work, surrender of things dear to us, and renouncement of our comfort and our habits.

It is a mortification not to choose one's work in a parish, but to take on any work at all according to the need.

It is a mortification for a priest to be confined to the con‑ fessional during an entire afternoon and be prevented from spending his time on the direction of a promising individual. Such direction has its place, no doubt; but the long wait in the confessional also has a place, and a more important one.

It is a mortification to learn how to listen to those who consult us, to see their problems as realities, suppressing our exasperation and smashing the shell of our indifference, which is the offspring of our self‑love.

It is a mortification to keep our good humor when we have to deal with unreasonable people, if we do it because we know that every contact with a priest should leave a visitor with the memory of a door opened to the charity of Christ.

It is a mortification to take criticism to heart instead of turn‑ ing up one's nose at it; it is the way we can learn what there is in us that grates on others and interferes with our service of them.

It is a mortification to be forever anxious to do better, and therefore to be always asking people (especially our own parish‑ ioners) for their opinion, in order to make adjustments and improvements and to give greater service.

It is a mortification not to linger with those who are fond of us, in order to keep our hearts and our time at the service of all. It is not an easy thing and it requires a detachment which hurts. Our fatigue, our isolation, and the affectionate solicitude of our friends are all leagued together against us, inviting us to let ourselves be surrounded and monopolized. Soon, we would no longer be "all things to all men." We must know the secret of tearing ourselves loose.

It is a mortification to be conscientious about the prepara‑ tion of our sermons, our catechism classes, and the talks we have to give to groups, instead of indolently trusting to our glibness. This is a very trying mortification when our days are fully occupied and it seems to us that we could get by with a lesser effort.

It is a mortification to force ourselves to prepare carefully for, and to celebrate reverently, the sacraments of baptism and matrimony, funerals and the parish Mass, without ever doing anything negligently, without ever rushing through anything, being always careful to use the tone of voice and to give the explanations which will remind all that they are coming in contact with God. And it is especially a mortification to do this when we would prefer to be using our time otherwise (in visiting our district, for example), and to do it when only a few people attend—none of them leaders. But we must do it because we are at the service of the parish and because our brother priests will have to do what we refuse to do.

It is a mortification, and in no way an outmoded one, to be punctual in celebrating Mass and other ceremonies. We owe it to the faithful to be on time. There comes to my mind the case of a teacher in an Alpine village: on weekdays she used to walk several miles to assist at an early Mass, and some‑ times after an hour's wait she had to leave without hearing Mass because the priest was not ready. Fortunately, this is an extreme instance; but there are others which, if not so extreme, are greatly to be regretted.

This effort to be punctual, as all the other things we have just mentioned, constitutes an "exercise," an *ascesis* in the full‑ est sense of the word. It is not the *ascesis* of the monk, but it is the one that our vocation of priest and missionary requires of us. Will anyone maintain that it is not as purifying, and sometimes as crucifying, as any other form of asceticism?

We recorded our views on this point in our earlier book, but we felt it necessary to repeat them here. Otherwise, what fol‑ lows might lead the reader to think we had changed our mind.

There is need, in fact, to sound a warning. We must beware of concluding—on the pretext that the ministry, the apostolate, and priestly work are sanctifying activities—hat have done everything once we have given ourselves to these activities. The temptation to do so may be very strong. It is quite right, for example, to say that to find God all we need to do is carry out our ministry perfectly, our entire ministry as priests and mis‑ sionaries. But are we sure that we are carrying it out perfectly?

Carrying it out with the right spirit? Are we absolutely certain that we are not rather seeking ourselves and our own satisfaction in it? That we are not following our own impulses rather than the will of God? Are we certain that we are doing our work from motives that are sufficiently supernatural and disinterested? It is the quality of our work that is at stake, and it is in relation to quality that the matter of the other means of sanctification has to be considered.

Certain means of sanctification were proposed to us in the seminary—meditation, spiritual exercises, spiritual direction; but they sometimes prove very difficult to keep up in a life engrossed in the thousand and one parochial activities. Fatigue and nervous exhaustion are always there threatening to render meaningless the moments set aside for prayer. These means of sanctification were presented to us so solemnly, as bastions to be held at any cost, almost as if they were the essential element in the priestly life; and here we find ourselves with duties so pressing that we can no longer see any way of being faithful to the exercises, or at least to the letter of them. In a word, we do not know what to make of it all.

Then there is this. At the very outset of our priestly lives everything is so new to us that it captivates us, and our first contacts with souls are extremely rewarding and very apt to rouse in us an immediate response of generosity and thanksgiving. The young priest, overflowing with his seminary meditations and with the fervor of a neophyte, experiences no difficulty in having a motive of charity in every word and every action.

Everything goes so well with him that, almost before he knows it, he finds himself tempted to say: "What good are all these bothersome exercises when the ministry itself provides me with everything I need in order to find God? There is no need for me to seek Him by means of formulas which have their value for seminarians, nor in definite times of meditation. I am meeting Him everywhere, all day long, in the people I am meeting and in the work I am doing."

Where does the fallacy lie? To us it seems to lie in mistaking the starting point for the goal. We would be glad of the chance to tell others that they hold up the traditional exercises to us as ends, whereas they are only means; but do not we ourselves too quickly believe that we are beginning to catch sight of the end, although we are neglecting the means?

"I have no need of anything but souls to find God." Very well indeed, brother priest of mine! But suppose a young Benedic-tine or Trappist novice declared to his Father Director: "Father, I want to know nothing but the unitive way. I am finding God in my prayer. The road you point out to me, which is the one the others are taking, with its controls and ascetical practices and counsels, is too long for me. I am taking a short cut." What would you say of him?

The contemplative has the obligation to seek God in his prayer. Freed as he is from other concerns, he spends his whole life long seeking God directly; but he *seeks* Him, and (as everyone knows) he can be the victim of many an illusion. What sensible spiritual director does not smile when he hears the declarations of certain splendid souls who think they have arrived at the highest forms of the mystical life? Those around them would have no difficulty reminding them of the most elementary laws of industry, considerateness, and patience.

Are you not making the same mistake, brother priest? You claim to be finding God directly in souls. This should certainly be your aim. It is the perfection of your holiness. The contem-plative must reach God through his whole life of prayer, and you must reach Him through your ministry. In the final analysis, both of us have to be contemplatives: to see God in souls is a kind of contemplation, and to serve Him through activity is perpetual adoration. But to both of us, to the monk as well as to myself, God is invisible and difficult to access; He desires to be sought after, and at times it is along dark roads that He wants us—groping and sometimes falling—to seek Him. If a man is to do this, he must have training, and this entails "exercises;" above all, he must go to the sources, where alone it is possible to drink in the light and strength of the Spirit. Otherwise, he runs the risk of deceiving himself, of seeking himself under the guise of seeking God—and of finding only himself, not God.

If you are attached to the exercises for their own sake, you are deceiving yourself; but if you regularly omit them, I greatly fear that you are presumptuous, unless you are simply letting your-self do anything you like. We are so made that we act a certain way, continue until it is a habit, and then justify our conduct by a theory concocted for the occasion. It is the easiest thing in the world to create a theology of oneself and one's whims, But this "theology" of whims, of the easy way, fills me with dread, when what we are looking for is a form of missionary life. There are always *rationes convenientiae* and high principles which, when decked out in the latest phrases, will cover a multitude of things. We do not believe the reader will accuse us of being inclined to conformism. We have fought hard enough against the tendency to rely on methods just because they are old, as well as against shams and cheap contrivances of every kind, to have the right to voice our alarm when we see others throwing overboard restraints and ascetical practices and spiritual exercises under the impression that they are following out our ideas.

Since we are in the active ministry, and not in the seminary, you will allow me to make an appeal to you on behalf of souls. If you throw yourself recklessly into activity (even though it is highly spiritual and apostolic) and make no place in your life for sacrifice and for concentrated periods of meditation, your work will lose its vitality and it is souls that will be the first to suffer. You will, no doubt, use the same words as true missionaries; you will speak as well, perhaps even better; and your acts will possess the same external reverence. But there will be under-tones and indefinable qualities missing along with the lack of a true interior life. And without these you will not ring true.

Let us take an example from the experience of all of us, whether we are young or already well advanced in years. Let us recall the period after a fervent retreat or after a meditation which was better than usual; surely we can remember what our visits to the sick were like then, and our advice in the confessional, our words in spiritual direction, and even our welcoming smile in the sacristy. Now let us compare this with our behavior in similar situations a long time after the retreat or when we were spiritu⸗ ally at a low ebb. What should we conclude? Certainly that we must never allow ourselves to be taken in by the fact that from time to time—when we were least deserving, and from the most unexpected sources—have things happened to us which, like wonderful actual graces, served to give us the shock we needed. We must not count on having them happen all during our lives.

Let us be reconciled to the fact that we have to take the long, dark, and hard purgative way, with all the restraints and exercises that it entails. Afterwards, and only afterwards, will we be able to find God in the activities of our ministry. But "afterwards" is inexact, for we have no intention of defining a chronological order. First of all, we have no choice. We are in the apostolic life and it is in it and along with it that we must conduct ourselves in our search for God. Moreover, God gives Himself gradually, according to His good pleasure. And, above all, we shall never know whether or not we have arrived at that "afterwards:" it is always possible to deceive ourselves. Never, and at fifty no more than at twenty⸗five, is a man definitively established in total union with God; self⸗distrust and self⸗denial, therefore, will always be necessary, and at no time will it be possible to dispense with the ordinary means to that union.

Let us go further, even though some who are anxious to be rid of all restraints may think we are overdoing it, and say that the nature of the modern apostolate itself requires us to keep a stricter watch over our interior life than ever before. To be closer to those we wish to reach, we want to be with them wherever they are, wherever they live and act; we want to be with them in their neighborhood and in their recreations, and even at times to share their life at work. We are not content to remain tucked away in our sacristy or rectory, nor to be the prisoners of a priestly routine on the pretext that any other course is danger⸗ ous. We refuse to change our course merely because it may be dangerous, and we are right. But, still, we must see that it is dangerous; we must not be blind to the fact that the atmosphere of the secular life into which we intend to go as priests does rep‹ resent a threat to us and might end by "naturalizing" us. When we set out on these paths under the orders and supervision of the hierarchy, it is clear that the graces of our state will not be wanting to us if we ourselves are faithful. Some priests, however, have a very keen desire to join in this or that form of recreation, to dress as laymen even when there is little reason for it, and to adopt the standards of laymen. Is not this eagerness the mani‹ festation of an unconscious naturalism? Even when it is under obedience that we are to try some bold experiment, this is but an added reason for bringing to it the most intense interior life possible. We recall hearing young seminarians describing the period they had spent in a factory. Some told us how easy it was for them to remain united with God all during a day of manual work in the midst of noisy machines and the humming activity of an industrial plant. "True enough," some of the older priests said to them, "but look out. You are still alive to the need to fill the void you find in this completely material life, and this is a new and startling experience for you. But wait until you get used to it. Then you will be no time in finding that the material and materializing life is threatening to invade you through every pore of your skin, unless you take pains to counteract it by a stronger interior life and to provide yourself with the support of an intense team life."

We want to avoid artificial occasions of meeting our people and to capitalize on all the natural occasions of doing so, and this is all to the good. But we have to be careful not to delude ourselves with words, not to give such a high‹sounding word as "contacts" to what are only idle conversations, nor to speak of giving spiritual direction to families when we are satisfied with being invited to a meal or with passing a pleasant eve‹ ning in a home.

It is a good thing to wish for an increasingly "spiritual" apos‹ tolate and to give it the preference over work which does not properly belong to the priestly ministry. But in that case we need to be highly spiritual men. Unless we are, we will no longer be accomplishing anything at all, neither the material tasks we have abandoned nor the spiritual work for which we find ourselves unqualified.

It is true that some predecessors of ours have fallen into a bourgeois existence, have succumbed to an official routine or settled down into an easygoing life. But at the same time let us not forget that in them this was the result of tendencies which are inherent in human weakness and are a threat to us too. If a priest turns into a bourgeois or a mere official, or if he becomes indolent, it is not the methods which are at fault, but the way he uses the methods. The same natural inclinations can lead us into the same aberrations, even though our starting point and our ambitions are so opposed to them. It hurts us, for example, to find in our parishes many a venerable activity and many a confraternity no longer in line with today's mentality, just as it hurts us to see some of our fellow priests limiting themselves to a few of the faithful and faithfully tended sheep. But, on the other hand, it is not altogether uncommon to see a priest of another type doing much the same thing. He considers himself to be at the opposite pole from these last representatives of an outmoded spirituality, yet he himself gives all his time and solicitude and affection to some little conventicle of leaders whom he is visiting and cultivating all the year long. He streaks out ahead, as we mentioned previously, with a few souls who are more gifted or more capable of understanding him, and he forgets all about the rest. He does not suspect that he is succumbing to the very same temptation as his elder brothers, but for him, too, happiness consists in having a small circle of devoted disciples. It requires self-denial, and a great deal of it, to keep ourselves from acquiring a taste for such spiritual desserts and to preserve our appetite for more substantial and less delicate food. We can never dispense with self-distrust.

In a word, we think it impossible for a priest to maintain his spiritual tone unless he finds a place in his life for meditation (to which we shall return later), for spiritual reading, for contact with the Scriptures, and for a real visit with Our Lord in the Blessed Sacrament during the afternoon. Only when he has the stimulus of such a preparation will he be able to celebrate his Mass with due fervor. We fear that even his breviary will become a burden= some routine unless the priest very frequently goes back over what he has read and gives himself the time to meditate on it.

Apart from the element of formalism, we believe that the traditional exercises do not sin by excess, but by defect. We can also understand why so many priests doubt their effec= tiveness. In the first place, there has been too much insistence on these exercises being kept up at any cost, and too little effort put into teaching priests how to live these exercises in the concrete circumstances of their ministry. Nothing harms a priestly life more than a formalistic fidelity to exercises which sets a man's conscience at rest without stirring it to life. In the second place, these exercises have been taken over unchanged from the monastic or seminary life and may be ill=suited to an active life. They need adjustments, and their shortcomings must be filled by something else. We shall have more to say on this later when we speak of the sabbatical rest and, later still, the spiritual life of the team.

It is very difficult to keep up the traditional exercises in a priestly life, and some of them ought to be completely revised; but, in addition to this, it is absolutely essential to realize that many priests neglect these exercises as not providing the needed sustenance and support. Until we take steps to enable the priest to receive support from the very framework of his life, his spiri= tual exercises will prove inefficacious most of the time. That is why we refer the reader to the sections which treat of the peri= ods of renewal and the pooling of the team's spiritual resources.

MEDITATION

What must we do to be in continual union with God? What is the secret of being able to find God everywhere and always, without deceiving ourselves? How can we manage to be constantly charged with a true spiritual dynamism? There is, as far as we know, only one answer: arranging our lives so that there will habitually be room for what we have called intense or concentrated periods of meditation.

Many words have been expended on the question of "dif=fused" meditation or prayer. At the risk of perpetrating a bad pun, we cannot resist saying that "we should be on guard lest our prayer be only confused," while we are ready to consider it "infused."

We have, of course, no intention of proposing a method of prayer. In fact, we are quite convinced that the prayer which is best for us is the one which is personal to us, the one we have discovered after much groping and many failures and new starts. To us it would seem a mistake to consider the time given to prayer as a debt to be paid to God, a debt we could consider paid after we had put in the prescribed number of minutes or quarter hours. There is no such thing as a time of prayer after which we are free to go about our business with our minds at rest because we know we have taken care of our praying. No, it is the whole day which ought to be a time of prayer, and the vision of God ought to color everything we do. What we customarily call meditation is simply an exercise whose function it is to turn us Godward and enable us to see our whole day in a divine perspective. But it must, we repeat, be an intense period, intense enough to make its influence felt throughout the day.

And so we believe it is indispensable to set aside, every day, a short period of recollection and silence. This will be an oppor=tunity for our minds and hearts to recuperate their strength, to take their bearings, and to open up to the grace of a greater intimacy with God.

When are we to make our meditation? It is quite hard to say. The first thing in the morning is the natural time for it; but we must take into account the weariness which remains from the previous evening, the drowsiness we feel when we have not had enough sleep, and the need of being in readiness near our confessional. To spend a half hour in church doing nothing does not mean we have made our meditation, for we cannot subscribe to that definition which makes meditation a half hour during which you do nothing else. In this matter, above all, we must determine to be realistic and to have no traffic with soothing illusions. Let us not be afraid to admit that there are periods when, for mornings on end, our minds are so lazy that we finally fall into a half-dreaming state which is simply a prolongation of the slumber nature insists on having. If we need to—no matter how old we are—let us have the courage to pick up a book, and, if this does no good, to take our breviary and recite it conscientiously. It sometimes requires more courage to force ourselves to say our Office well than to let ourselves fall into a prayer of quiet which has nothing in common with the peace of the soul lost in its Lord.

Why not postpone this period of concentrated prayer to a time when we will be better disposed for it—say, later in the morning or even the middle of the day? We at Colombes have found the period from noon until twelve-thirty a very good time for the whole team to meditate. We can easily prepare our meditation in the morning if we fail to do so the night before, and this midday meditation puts a stop to our activities and enables us to renew our strength.

What we are to do during this time will be sure to vary with temperaments and the graces God gives to individuals. We must not, however, forget that ours is an active life, this being a fact which our prayer should not fail to take into consideration. Unfortunately, it is a fact which often affects our meditation in ways we do not like. How can we be recollected when the problems of the previous evening are still passing through our heads, when we realize that we will have to spend the entire day trying to solve yesterday's unfinished problem or to undo yesterday's mistake? But is it so essential that our minds be completely free from such things? If our life is constantly over-whelming us with distractions, why should we not use these distractions as the subject of our meditation?

Let us suppose, for example, that we received a crushing blow last evening, causing us such shock and anxiety that we could not close our eyes the whole night long. In such a case, a very strong-willed individual may succeed in imposing interior silence on himself, but for a great many this is impossible. They should look at this wretched affair with God's eyes and speak to our Lord about it, asking Him for His light and, in their nearness to Him, finding the strength to face their problem. There is a story about a priest who made his meditation by taking up his agenda every morning and going over in God's presence everything he was planning to do that day. There is obviously a danger, and no slight one, of getting out of the atmosphere of prayer altogether; but, with a little good will, it is better for us to try to incorporate the troubles of the day into our prayer than just to put up with them, since it is likely that our minds will drift to them anyway.

On the other hand, there will be many days when our pre-occupations will not be so absorbing and our minds will be free to seek solid nourishment. Have we not the Gospels? Will the time ever come when we shall have exhausted them? Meditating on the inspired text, we sometimes go too rapidly and devour a whole paragraph or a whole page, when a single sentence would give us enough nourishment for the day. There are days when we cannot get anything out of our reading and are unable to make a meditation out of it; but we must not minimize God's part. We may have nothing to say to Him and may be unable to find anything by ourselves, but surely He has something to say to us. Why not ask the Holy Spirit what special message He has placed for us in a verse or passage of Scripture? Only to a very slight extent is meditation a reasoning process: primarily, it is prayer, and the prayer of abandonment is the most valuable prayer of all.

Have we the good sense to force ourselves to do spiritual reading so as to provide nourishment for our meditation? We purposely say "spiritual" rather than "intellectual," for we are thinking of the kind of reading which nourishes the heart as well as the mind. The very act of reading is in itself an excel⸗ lent stepping stone to meditation, because it introduces into our active lives a time of calm, a time of concentration of our interior faculties—provided, of course, that our reading is not limited to worldly or purely intellectual matters.

Then we have our Mass with all the riches of the Missal texts, and our breviary with the inexhaustible treasures of the Psalms! It is perhaps in these that we can most easily find suit⸗ able subjects of meditation, for the meditation themes in them are already clothed in the form of prayer. Taking our subject of meditation from them has the added advantage of helping to unify our whole life of prayer and of enabling us to celebrate our Mass and recite our Office more fervently.

One more thing. We must not hide the fact that fidelity to meditation in our pastoral ministry requires a severe discipline of the will. But let us state just as emphatically that it will be even harder for us to say that our lives are a continual prayer if, in fact, we begin by capitulating when it is only a few necessary acts of the will that are required of us. If we find it impossible to impose on ourselves the brief period of silence which would enable us to find God, how can we possibly say we are able to find Him in the moments when we are very busy?

FAITH

If the priest is really to live the gospel and bring it to the mod⸗ ern world, it seems to us that he must really live the theological virtues of faith, hope, and charity.

In *Revolution in a City Parish* we stated that our people, especially working class people, no longer place any faith in logical argument. The best argument in the world leaves them unimpressed. But they are impressed by the man who speaks with conviction. The moment they can see a man is convinced of what he says, they show some sign of the respect and sym⸗ pathy they feel. What they admire in him is nothing else but a faith that is really lived. We ourselves need the faith that made the Apostles say, "We cannot but speak." And the people need to feel this sense of urgency in us. It must shine through when we preach, for in no other way will we win the allegiance of the workers' world.

Let us not confuse this power of conviction with any special way of preaching. Even without a powerful voice or effective gestures a man can sound sincere. An individual may be thor⸗ oughly at home in the pulpit and quite unimpressive in private conversation. This is not faith. Faith shows itself as an interior fire which burns always and in all circumstances. Our Catholics, and even more our non⸗Catholics, should be able to discover that we really believe merely by observing us act.

A young man comes to arrange for his marriage. He begins by asking about fees and the difference between the various types of weddings. In reply the priest tells him that it is not the fee nor the kind of wedding that counts but his Christian preparation for marriage, and he adds a word to the effect that religion is not a matter of money. The young man replies at once: "In that case, Father, we can go right ahead; since you are doing this for us, I can see that you really believe in it."

How many priests are like that? They have the faith, of course. Péguy was exaggerating when, after stating what he believed in, he wrote to Lotte: "The maddening thing is that we can't trust priests. They have no faith at all, or very little. It is among the lay people that faith is still to be found." And yet, when we realize what was in his mind, can we say that he was entirely wrong? Is it not true, for example, that at Lourdes the fervor and courage of the people often put to shame the indifference of too many ecclesiastics? This blunt judgment of a young man can give us food for thought: "From the time of my first Communion I had nothing to do with the Church. Then someone gave me the Gospels to read, and I said to myself, 'This Jesus Christ is the real thing. But priests, what are they? When they are the real thing and are more like Jesus Christ, then we will follow them. They leave you with such a strong feeling that they are only doing a job.'" Many sermons are given without conviction, so indifferently that they remind you of a lesson

being repeated. We cannot but be uneasy when we consider the impressions Jacques Rivière confided to Claudel: "Do not believe that I have not tried at all. This morning I went to Mass. I tried to get hold of myself and pray. The Our Father is almost the only thing I remember now. I said it over and over again, but without succeeding in becoming attentive and without any fervor. I was not able to visualize God as being present. There are so many things you have to try not to see! Why does the priest confine himself to reciting the Mass instead of consummating the sacrifice? He was going so fast that he sputtered."

A real faith, the kind of faith that testifies to a personal experience of Jesus Christ, would produce very different results.

The missionary believes in the gospel, believes in it with his whole heart and soul. To him it is really a message of good news. To him the Sermon on the Mount is the only true map of happiness.

The missionary lacks confidence in indirect methods of reaching souls, and prefers the direct apostolate and the immediate contact, which allows him to speak to men of God. He prefers it because he believes in supernatural methods and the attractiveness of Jesus Christ when He is presented as He really is.

It is in his own contact with Christ that he himself finds the light, which shows him the way and fills him with joy. When, therefore, he goes to bring Christ to others, he goes with the certainty that he has the greatest possible riches and the finest possible present to offer them. He is so happy and proud to bear such a message that he does not feel any need to apologize for his insistence. And his happiness is more contagious and effective than a skillfully conducted discussion.

Since he believes in the transcendence of Christianity, hostile systems do not disturb him, nor does he feel it necessary either to refute them by argument or to offer sensational and provocative counter-attractions. Not that he is afraid of a fight. The idea simply does not interest him: to believe in fighting means to believe in its methods; and he believes only in Christ's methods, which are to state the truth and present the message. There is an intrinsic power in the truth and the message which makes its own way into souls.

"He really believes that it happened." Precisely. He believes in the Incarnation, in Christ the Redeemer, in the Resurrection; he believes that God, and the man who is God's instrument, can do what is impossible to mere man. People may smile at him, but in the end he makes an indelible impression on them and succeeds in conveying his own convictions to those whom he meets. Pascal said he found it easy to believe in the stories of witnesses who laid down their lives to prove their truth. All men are like Pascal. They find it easy to believe in the man of faith, who is himself convinced of the reality of the invisible world. They find it easy to believe in the missionary whose words and deeds prove that he is a witness of Jesus Christ. Is there a single one of us who has never been entrusted with the secret of the tremendous impression made on another by the radiating conviction of such a man? [1]

It is this spirit of faith which attracts others. It is the only thing that will enable us to speak out of the abundance of the heart. It will express itself in ways that we may find hard to define, but these are precisely the ways which prove convincing.

Is it not this very spirit of faith which will keep us from becoming functionaries and routine administrators?

Again, to have a profound faith means to believe in the attrac= tive power of our religion in itself. Many men of faith have, of course, devised indirect methods of the apostolate, means that we shall presently call ersatz. Apostles whom we all admire have not hesitated to use external pleasures and worldly attrac= tions as bait to gather around them a crowd of people to whom they might preach the gospel. But if we are to imitate them, eventually we must really preach the gospel to the people.

---

1   In Douai there are some religious who are workers. Two delegates of the C. G. T. (the Communist National Labor Union) were exchanging their impressions of them one day. "Have you talked with them?" one asked his companion. And he (the secretary of the Union) replied, "My friend, you don't have to talk with those fellows; you see the way they live, and that is enough."

Besides, the reason we try dressing up the gospel in all kinds of human frills is all too often that we do not believe that souls are hungry and thirsty for Christ and the gospel as such. We do not believe in the drawing power of our religion and the need of faith which is innate in the souls of men. Why do we not believe in these things? Because our spirit of faith is not what it should be and because we ourselves do not live sufficiently in the perspective of our faith. Why does a convert have no hesita‹ tion about telling people of his discoveries? Because he himself is intensely alive to them, because he appreciates all the light which the faith has brought him, and because he is sure it holds the secret of happiness for others too. It is a lack of confidence in the magnetic power of our faith itself which makes us use sports and outings to attract the young. The same lack of confidence leads us to invent a whole array of external activities to enable us to keep in touch with families. We are convinced that no one will come to us unless he is brought by some material interest.

It is, on the contrary, the opinion of the author that our priestly lives are far too short to answer the needs of the men who are thirsting for nothing but truth and prayer and charity. If we do not hear them crying out to us, it is because our own faith is not strong enough. If they do not find in us the answer to their anxiety, it is because there is not enough conviction in our gospel preaching and in the very sound of our voice.

In the midst of the attacks made on our Church and our beliefs today, why do we so often assume the attitude of a victim or of a whipped dog? Is it not because We ourselves are not quite sure that our faith must triumph despite all this chaos, amid all this chaos, and even by means of this chaos? *Haec est victoria, fides nostra.* We are not sure enough of success. Some give up in discouragement after a timid effort—often the very ones who are at the same time busy on a personal spiritual system in which failure represents the ideal.

The missionary is prejudiced in favor of his brother priests. Because they have the same priestly character as himself, are animated by the same apostolic ambitions, and share with him the same priestly grace of Christ, he is inclined to judge their undertakings favorably even before he sees them in operation. Some individuals are always on the lookout for reasons to justify their suspicions and their condemnations, but the missionary finds things to admire and encourage everywhere. The suspi= cious critic has, in reality, but little faith; and, once he gets beyond the region of mechanical fidelity to a few formulas and traditions, he feels himself lost, and the Church with him. He takes his own theology for dogma, his rubrics for the liturgy, and his personal system for the Church. He has faith, but more in his own intellectual theories than in revelation or the gospel of Jesus Christ.

The man with real faith believes that Christ is always living in the Church. He believes that our Catholic treasures, the *nova et vetera*, contain inexhaustible riches. He believes that one and the same tradition has (according to the needs of the time) given birth to, carried along for a time, and then abandoned a great number of intellectual expressions, none of which was for a single moment synonymous with tradition. Of course, there can be no question of denying that the hierarchy must keep a very close watch over the orthodoxy of all those who preach or act or write. We want only to express a decided preference for an attitude of fraternal understanding over one of suspicion and criticism among priests who are fighting in the same cause, because the very faith which all unanimously profess is on the side of the former attitude.[2]

---

2   Cf. Cardinal Suhard, *Growth or Decline*, p. 49–52: "We must not confuse integrity of doctrine with the preservation of its passing forms of expression ... Undoubtedly, we must scrupulously maintain the defined dogmatic formulas. But must we identify revelation with theological systems and schools? [The Church has made the doctrine of St. Thomas her official teaching.] Must we conclude that St. Thomas has said everything, and that his thought has exhausted and equaled the revealed deposit? Must we now stop thinking? Obviously not. As Lacordaire expressed it: 'St. Thomas is a beacon, not a terminal.' His light should clarify an ever=increasing investigation of the two sources of faith: Scripture and tradition ... Tradition is by no means simply the mechanical transmission of an inert 'thing.' Rather it is the living

We must not let ourselves imagine that the faith of our brother priests is in danger the moment they seek to establish contact with the ideas of unbelievers. We must have enough confidence in their faith to admit that they can enter into dis⸗ cussions with unbelievers and mix with them, neither making concessions nor endangering the vigor of their own belief. If our faith is strong enough to surpass the convictions of men who lack the true light, why should not the faith of these priests be strong enough to do so?

If we have a deep faith, we will also have the missionary optimism which springs from it and which enables us to detect the action of the Spirit in our lay Catholics—for the Spirit is very often at work in them, even in the roughest of them. Since it is in this "multiform" Spirit that we put our faith and not in ourselves, and since we have St. Paul's admonition to "test every spirit and hold fast to what is good" (I Thess. 5:21), we will be on the alert for the directions of the Spirit wherever they

communication and the progressive manifestation—under the infalli⸗ ble control of the Magisterium—of a global truth of which each age discovers a new aspect . . . The same holds true for the discipline and the action of the Church in the moral order and in institutions. Should we identify tradition, which is life, with routine, which is death? . . . To preserve life, modernism sacrificed forms; to preserve forms, integralism sacrifices life . . . Excessive traditionalism forgets one of the factors of the problem, and thus ends up in the same contradiction as modern⸗ ism. While the latter made a norm of every value of today, the former makes of yesterday's forms the ideal of the present. This is a serious mistake of which Catholics should be doubly careful, first because this negative attitude of distrust of legitimate changes hampers the forward march of the Church, delays its penetration of the world, and risks furnishing pretexts for inaction to the average faithful; but especially because this habit of suspicion, if it assumes a systematic form, would not be Christian. It would add a subtle danger of private interpretation to a lack of intellectual charity. For is not anticipating the hierarchy in its judgments, or even criticizing it for the initiatives it authorizes, a transfer of competence of which the least one can say is that it is not in order? Certainly it is not to this defensive retreat that the Church calls the faithful. Supremely exacting in all that concerns orthodoxy, ready for every sacrifice when it is a question of what comes from God and the apostolic tradition, she does not forget, however, the spirit which animates her interiorly. 'Extinguish not the spirit,' says St. Paul, 'but prove all things; hold fast that which is good!'"

are to be detected, even when at first they are only stammered out. The bruised reed can become strong again, and the wick with still a spark may once more burst into flame. We have no illusions: we know only too well how feeble the faith of many is. But, at the same time, we believe in the power of Him who gives light to whom He wills; we will not agree to "sacrifice" anyone, to permit anyone entrusted to us to perish.

The virtue of faith in the missionary of Jesus Christ man⸗ ifests its presence by the need he feels to communicate his faith to others.

HOPE

We must cultivate the virtue of hope too. Quite obviously, the missionary spirit is based on it. Almost as obviously, the reason why many lack the courage to undertake missionary work, or lose heart once they have begun, is because the virtue of hope is not there to give them courage.

Since childhood we have been reciting our act of hope. "O my God, I firmly hope that through the merits of Jesus Christ You will give me Your grace in this world...." What is that "grace in this world"? It is the grace to assist us in working out our personal salvation, and we believe in it. But do we not also expect to receive the grace to assist us in doing God's work in this world and in bringing salvation to those entrusted to us? Do we not believe that God is more interested in our efforts than we are, and that it is always God who takes the initiative? How, then, do we ever manage to become cynical? "My dear young man," a pastor said to his assistant, fresh from the semi⸗ nary and full of enthusiasm, "you will get over it. In four or five years you will have lost your illusions...." Was it not rather the pastor who had the illusions? For the assistant was full of the virtue of hope and, therefore, an integral realist. St. Paul said, "I can do all things in him who strengthens me." Should we not say the same? The grace of Christ is all⸗powerful, and with Christ's grace, I am all⸗powerful too. The love of God can overcome the most recalcitrant of men and rouse the dullest of them; and I am the instrument of this love. Christ died for all; hence there are unlimited possibilities everywhere.

God is the prime mover in everything we do; still, that does not mean that He does everything without us, nor that hope can justify our indolence. Hope is not a passive virtue. It goads us into activity. It makes many demands on us. It is based on the Cross. Since we can do nothing without the Cross, we can= not be satisfied with setting it up by the roadside: we have to carry it. It is through the Cross and under the Cross, in spite of our falls and our failures, by getting up again after our falls and by making good our failures, that we do the work we have to do. Missionary hope is essentially hope in the Cross. We need only to go back over the story of our own apostolate to prove it, to be able to see in dim outline, behind the failures and the crosses, the redeemed souls we thought we were pursuing in vain. After a setback we will feel all the more energy to get to work—that is, to take a fresh approach to the work entrusted to us—for we will know by experience that the Cross is in it.

To believe that God is acting in us and through us is to believe in Providence and to be sure that God will never aban= don us, even in purely material matters. The chapter in *Revolu= tion in a City Parish* which seems to have created the greatest stir is the one on money. It has earned us protests of every sort.3 "But where are we to get the money to support the

---

3   A few remarks on the question of money in our two parishes of the Sacred Heart and SS. Peter and Paul at Colombes may be in order here. We would like to point out that we have no secret source of revenue to call upon, and that we have to fulfill obligations at least as great as other parishes in regard to the diocesan funds. The reader must keep in mind that there are two types of parishes in Paris: parishes whose priests are in part supported by diocesan funds, and self=sustaining parishes (those which support their priests without outside aid). Sacred Heart parish belongs to the first class, SS. Peter and Paul to the second. This has enabled us to try out our system of eliminating fees and providing solemn ceremonies for all without charge in both types of parishes. At SS. Peter and Paul, however, we still receive something for funerals: we give the same solemn ceremonies to all, but those families which pay the undertaking establishments often make the offering which corre= sponds to the undertaker's class which they choose (though the offering

priests, our various activities, our parishes?... It is madness
to give up assured revenues." But this is to forget there is a

---

made never goes beyond that for the sixth class). When we undertook
to eliminate the system of classes at Sacred Heart, we made an agree‹
ment with the diocesan authorities whereby we would never ask the
Chancery Office for an increase in our annual allowance, which was at
that time 60,000 francs. Since then, the other parishes have had their
allowance increased and now receive the additional amount required
for the upkeep of their clergy. Sacred Heart parish alone continues to
receive the same allowance, although there has been a continual devalu‹
ation of our money. In the case of SS. Peter and Paul, when we decided
to abolish fees altogether, we made an agreement to continue the same
contribution to diocesan funds for weddings, which was established by
taking the average contribution of the preceding years. Our average
contribution per wedding corresponded to the sixth class, and so for
each wedding celebrated in our church we contribute to the diocesan
funds the amount that it would have a right to from a wedding of the
sixth class. Thus, we have contributed the following amounts to the
diocesan funds in the years 1947–1949:

	Diocesan Coll.	Church Tax	Stole Fees
1947 (with fees)	71,576 francs	75,639	79,364
1948 (without fees)	134,230	133,558	120,874
1949 (without fees)	256,199	156,623	140,242

The increase in our Church Tax has been greater than these figures
show. The actual amount of our 1948 Church Tax was 130,000, but the
archdiocese established a ratio on the basis of the contribution of the
parish in 1938, and the parish was allowed to retain the surplus. Our
total income from collections has increased at the same time that we
have been reducing their number. The Church Tax used to be taken up
every month. At present we mention it only once a year, and the first
year it went up 400%. This year, 1949, the increase continues, the total
being 460,000 francs. The other collections, which are not prescribed
and from which nothing goes to the diocese, show a similar increase.
In 1948 these brought in 414,788 francs; in 1949, 504,014 francs. The
reader may wish for some information as to our means of support. 1.
We have no list of benefactors and no benefactors from outside the par‹
ish. 2. We hold no bazaars or charity sales. 3. There is some assistance
at Sacred Heart from the sale of publications, but this brings in much
less than a bazaar or a charity sale. 4. In our first year we published
nothing and had no income from royalties. All we have done is acquaint
our parishioners with the financial situation and ask them to assist us
directly rather than indirectly through a charity sale. They responded
to our appeal. We should add that in each of our communities the
number of priests and clerics is considerably in excess of the number
of assistants for whom the diocese grants an allowance. Sacred Heart

Providence. This is to forget that Providence will not fail to
see that we and our parishes are supported, should it prove
necessary or advantageous for the good of souls to suppress
compulsory fees. Would this be the first time we lived on help
sent us by Providence? We must not be Pharisees. If we can
preach so eloquently on abandonment to Providence, let us at
least have the courage to practice what we preach.

A young mother already has three children. When the last
one was born, her already precarious health became further
endangered. The doctor assures her that another pregnancy
may prove fatal. Her pastor, when she tells him about it, advises
her to trust in God's Providence, and with great courage she
accepts the idea of the risk. But in another conversation with the
pastor, the subject of abolishing classes and eliminating fees for
ceremonies happens to come up. "That is a fine thing," she says.
"It should be that way everywhere." "True enough," the pastor
answers, "but it is a somewhat Utopian idea. After all, a man has
to live." The woman, when she was telling us about this incident,
remarked, "What do you think of that? My pastor preaches to
me on abandonment to Providence when it means risking my life,
and he is not willing to run a much slighter risk for God's work."

We must be careful not to let any plan for increasing our
apostolic effectiveness serve as a pretext for placing our hope
in anything but God. It is in God, and not in human means,

---

has one seminarian; SS. Peter and Paul has one seminarian and two
deacons. Thus, it is evident that our obligations are heavy. Where does
the income we need come from? We can only say that Providence is
evidently working through the normal sources of the revenue of a parish,
the Sunday collection, and the box in which the people may, if they
choose, place offerings for the ceremonies which are provided without
fee. Our books are open to any of our brother priests who desire more
information. We are very anxious, however, that all should know the
deep Impression made by our change in policy. Even those who have
least contact with the parish have been impressed. It has been a subject of conversation in every factory and place where men work, and
it is still being talked about. It has won the unfailing sympathy of the
people for the clergy of the parish. We could quote hundreds of facts
and proofs. If it were necessary, we would go down on our knees and
beg our fellow priests to consider the idea of abolishing fees.

that we must hope. People deceive themselves when they trust in things which they consider a source of strength, but which in reality are unsteady and unreliable. They hope in God, of course; but in the final analysis they are eager to have the backing of political power, the security money gives, the favor of powerful friends, the prestige of a well-turned phrase, and the strength that derives from solidly established activities.

When they have to get along without these advantages in which they have put their faith, they are upset, afraid of the future, desperately determined to recover them. Yet none of these advantages can do anything to convert a soul, to lay the foundation for God's work, or to produce the slightest move= ment of love. Something has gone wrong with their hope, for the Christian virtue of hope should have the opposite effect: making us appreciate the insecurity of everything which is of this world. The time for us to start feeling uneasy is when all the worldly signs are favorable to us and we enjoy the pro= tection of the powerful and the financial support of the rich. *Deposuit potentes de sede et exaltavit humiles.* "The *foolishness* of God is wiser than men and the weakness of God stronger than men" (I Cor. 1:25).

It is hope that enables us to take our place alongside the mass of common people. For what is the great drama of the workingman's life, and the ever=present source of anguish in the workingman's home? The insecurity which is always with him. Our people are at the mercy of the slightest incident or acci= dent: a prolonged illness, a crippling injury, a strike, a period of unemployment — and the whole family is in want. At the beginning of the year there is never any assurance that the chil= dren will not be going hungry by the end of it. A workingman's life may begin in comfort and end in destitution. But with us priests it is different. There are some of us who have never known what insecurity is, and we have too little experience of real privation. We are always saying that we have chosen the better part. We should not forget that these words, as Our Lord used them, had reference to contemplation and attachment to God alone, and no reference at all to the anxious concerns of Martha. I am not forgetting the destitution of many priests in the country, but it is not these who refuse to abolish fees (which in their case constitute a very small part of their meager income). Why are others, who have never done without any-thing, so averse to abandoning themselves to God's Providence? If we were to accept the same insecurity as our people, would it not bring us closer to them in their suffering?

Let us continue with our act of hope. "My God, I await with a firm confidence . . . eternal glory with You in the other life." Without doubt, it is the next world which counts, and people often reproach us for thinking only of Paradise and forgetting this life. We know the familiar slogan about religion being the opium of the people. But there is another side to the picture. All our efforts to reach a better world really enable us to estab-lish contact with the aspirations of all our people, for they too are searching, with uncertainty and in the darkness, for what is to come, for a new world.

If the missionary whose work lies in the workers' world is complacent or resigned, he has no chance at all of understand-ing that world or of being accepted by it. He will find it easy enough to win a hearing from people who are complacent in their lives and ways, but he will not succeed in killing their complacency, and thus will do no good to them. The workers' world is anything but complacent. It is in constant movement. There may be alternating crises of hope and despair, but through them all there runs an obstinate and unchanging aspiration for a great change to take place and a new world to arise at long last. It is all too easy to laugh it off and say. "Of course, they long for the day when all the poor will be bourgeois; and, when that day comes, their desires will be satisfied." It is true enough that many of them want only a life a little less tormented or a little more comfortable. Would anyone think of blaming them for that? But the man who really knows the workers' world realizes that there is more than this in their aspirations. Even when they are not personally its victims, injustice revolts the workers more than other people. They are haunted by the dream of a state in which all will be brothers. When anyone speaks to them of justice and brotherhood, and on a world-wide scale, he is always sure of moving them.

There is little, if anything, in this world of ours that is per= fectly pure; and these aspirations of the workers are, of course, sometimes tainted with materialism. But if we cannot see that these longings represent hope in an obscure form and consti= tute a good soil for Christian hope, then we do not know our business. These people are yearning for a better world. What is it our mission to announce, if not this? What did Christ come to bring us, if not this? "We announce to you a great joy: a Savior is born to us." "And there will be new heavens and a new earth." We have no idea of indulging in double talk: it is not our mission to announce an ideal economic sys= tem, a "Christian" technique of social life or happiness here on this earth. Just as we do not dream of restoring medieval Christendom considered as the supreme ideal of the organiza= tion of nations under papal direction, so we have no idea of establishing a social system in which everyone would be happy because society would be in conformity with the gospel. We know that such a temporal triumph of the gospel—which in itself would be the ideal, since it would surely stamp out war and injustice—will always be thwarted by the selfishness of men. We also know that Christ never promised it to us.

Yet we do hope in and announce "the kingdom of God." What does this mean? To all Christ's followers it means, in the first place, the City of God in heaven, where there will be no more tears or suffering, but only unending joy in love. Yes, it is heaven we hope in—and so much the worse for unbe= lievers who scoff and speak about the opium of the people. Our conscience bears us witness that we are not preaching resignation to injustice when we say that injustice will one day be vanquished and that those who have believed in love will know happiness, whereas all oppressors will suffer eternal defeat. We know that with the same words we are preaching both the interior kingdom and the happiness on earth which is the experience of all who consent to carry their cross and follow Christ. We preach the Beatitudes promised to the children of God, and at the same time we believe that it is the peacemakers, the meek, those who hunger and thirst after justice, and the pure of heart who will be at once the happiest of men and the architects of happiness for others, even in suffering and opposition. Finally, we proclaim as a doctrine, as the teaching of the Gospels and St. Paul and the Popes, respect for every human person, the solidarity of all men as the creatures of the same God and the brothers of the same Christ, the precedence of brotherly love and the common good over individual interests.

A social evolution, contained in germ in the message of Christ, has slowly come about under the influence of this teaching. No historian would deny the pre-eminent importance of Christianity in humanity's forward march toward a more just and human social order. Lacordaire spoke of it as "the progress of humanity under the light of the Cross." It has gone on in spite of opposition and even of temporary relapses; for there are obstacles to this progress and deviations which reverse the trend for a time, but they are all derived from doctrines or movements opposed to the gospel. We are therefore justified in hoping that the more there is of the spirit of the gospel in the world, the more firmly the "kingdom of God" is established in the souls of Catholics; and the more fervent Catholics there are, so much the more will this earthly city of men reap good results, even temporal ones. Since we are animated by such a hope, there is no reason why we should not plant it in the workers' world whose evangelization is in our hands; indeed, there is every reason why we should. This workers' world has been fooled by false prophets a thousand times, and yet it is still hoping that tomorrow will be better than today. It is simply unthinkable that we should meet such a world with an attitude of scoffing scepticism or with a pseudo-supernatural indifference. Perhaps the future holds no better living conditions for them, but justice and love are ours to give them, and these are never called into play without leading to a better life for men. A missionary, if he is alive to the legitimate longings for the better life which fill the world, will make them his own and include the people's hopes in his hope.

It is our duty to announce the gospel, that is, "the good news." We have retained the word "gospel," though it almost seems as if we had agreed that it is no longer to mean "the good news." Listen to catechists and preachers, and see whether or not you feel that they have news to announce — or whether they have not that tone of voice which warns you their news is sad rather than good? Are our parishes and our Sunday con﹤ gregations "good news"? You would describe them better as stale or out﹤of﹤date or stereotyped news. It all seems so dull and dreary, as if you had seen and heard it a thousand times before.

To show the ambassadors of John the Baptist that He was really the Messiah, Jesus pointed to this proof: "Tell what you have seen: The lame walk, the deaf hear, the dumb speak, and the poor have the gospel preached to them." Could we say the same of our parishes? We would be more likely to say: "The people who come here cannot hear any more; they cannot speak any more; they are completely paralyzed. And as for the poor having the gospel preached to them, alas! alas!"

What is it we need to make us missionaries? What is it our little group of Catholics needs? It is this virtue, this tiny little virtue of hope, as Péguy would call it — a virtue which ought to make us at once poor and confident, and give us the power to have the song of the "good news" always on our lips.

CHARITY

We could, taking charity as a starting point, cover all the pas﹤ toral problems with which a missionary has to deal. And we can say without exaggeration that it is impossible to imagine a missionary without charity. The missionary mentality is, in fact, the result of the stimulus provided by the twofold command﹤ ment: "Thou shalt love God with thy whole heart, and thy neighbor as thyself." These two commandments are similar — a fact we never see more clearly than when we analyze the mis-sionary mind, which is the child of the first commandment as well as of the second. Some plunge into the missionary life because they cannot bear to see God's love disregarded; others, because they cannot bear to see their brothers in darkness.

The missionary must foster this charity, which will make him expendable at all times. It would be true to say that, if his heart is filled with charity, the other virtues will be given him as well; but true only if his charity is the real thing—that is, love. Priests speak of charity being a virtue, but some of them would perhaps hesitate to speak of love being a virtue. Our ecclesiasti-cal language should not make us forget our native tongue. This is not a mere matter of words; like other words, these are signs of realities. In the efforts to give us a spirituality at the semi-nary, it is hardly love which receives the greatest notice. And when love is mentioned, we are left with the impression that it is something quite distinct from—love! We are not told often enough that we are loved, that we have been chosen through love, that the choice which singled us out (*Ego elegi vos*) is an entirely gratuitous act of predilection, of which love alone is the source. We are not told often enough that we have been chosen to love, that it is our mission to love, that a priest without love makes no sense. We are not told often enough that it is just as illusory to love God without *really* loving the people in our care as it is to pretend having a priestly love for men with no love for God. We cannot exercise the priesthood in its fullness unless we love those whom Jesus loves and unless we have a burning zeal for the welfare of those to whom we are sent.

It is strange that this zeal could appear to be lacking in a priest: that people could be with him and not sense a heart full of love and solicitude, but find him cold, distant, heartless, and rarely moved by anything but administrative difficulties or theoretical discussions. Yet this phenomenon exists, and much more frequently than it should. Parishioners can live in a parish for twenty years and never see a priest come into their home or the home of any other workingman. A young worker, only sixteen, can go to Mass every Sunday for more than a year and never be contacted by the priest in charge of the Jocists. Important high schools and large public elementary schools can have assigned to them as chaplains priests who are unable to do the work. A sermon can be a frigid instruction or a piece of unctuous nonsense without a breath of life in it. Ninety percent of the people in a parish can stay away from church, and the talk and the preoccupations of the rectory be entirely unaffected by it. Are these not signs which indicate that zeal is not the dominant virtue of some priests?

And yet Jesus has chosen us. It is His will that His love should reach certain of His sheep through us. He has given us His heart in order to love them. It is in us that some men must find what Christ came to bring them—above all else, His burning charity. Had we His look, the look with which He regarded the people at the multiplication of the loaves, "and seeing these people, he was moved with compassion for them because they were harassed and exhausted like sheep with‐ out a shepherd," would we not be moved with compassion too? There are the sheep condemned to die of hunger because they do not know where the pastures are, nor the road leading to them. There are the sheep born for the immense riches of Christ, and not even knowing that Christ exists. There are the little ones, the weaklings, looking anywhere for nourish‐ ment, looking even to deceivers for it, and letting themselves be imposed upon and exploited. And they are all sheep that belong to Jesus personally. He is there in the midst of them, but they do not know it. It is on us that He is counting; we might say that He is counting on us alone to show them this, to enable them to see Him looking at them with real affection. Unless He reaches them through us, they will not be reached at all. This is a tremendous responsibility. If we looked at them with His eyes, could we be listless and indifferent? Could we act toward His people as did the Apostles before Pentecost, calling down fire from heaven on the towns that would not receive them, or keeping people away from Jesus lest their loud appeals annoy Him? Or could we re-enact the priest and the Levite passing by the wounded man of Jericho as quickly as they could? It is now the period after Pentecost. We too have received the Holy Spirit, the "sacred fire." What are we doing with that fire? It ought to send us out of our cenacle, just as it sent the Apostles out of theirs. Our habits constitute our cenacle; so does our narrow-mindedness and the fine company that surrounds us, for none of these has anything to do with love. If we have the fire, it ought to make us spontaneously prefer looking after the "sheep without a shepherd." When the missionary is animated by the charity of Christ, he identifies himself with Christ, as Christ intended and still intends him to do, and to such an extent that he loves the sheep as if they were his own. Yet the same reason prevents him from seeking to keep them for himself and helps him efface himself in order to bring them into contact with their only Shepherd. He feels a real need of going out to others, and to those who have the least. It is a need that gives him no rest: *irreguietum cor.*

We must understand that the people of today's world have no more belief in love than they have in God. They believe in selfishness, in every-man-for-himself, in the instincts of self-preservation and self-defense. Our poor people see themselves trapped in a jungle from which there is no escape. It is the law of the jungle which holds sway, with everyone snatching as much as he can from the claws of the rest. When we show our people that we love them — that we really love them, individually and unselfishly — we have already given them their first taste of revelation. If we are to reveal to them the existence of a God who is Love, the first step is to love them in His name in order to let them discover that they are loved by us. Especially with people who are so thoroughly materialistic to begin with, no Platonic love will do it, but only a charity that is effective and that makes itself felt in practical life. Only this charity will show us that in our parish there are people poorly housed and undernourished, suffering people of every kind; only this charity will let us see every case, not as a case to be filed away in our records, but as a personal case on which we are going to work with all our heart until we have seen it through.

It should now be clear what we mean by "charity." It is a fire stronger than anything, the same fire that Christ came to start on earth. It is the very thing which characterizes the heart of God. We have received the heart of God, the very love He has for men, the love which carried Him even to the sacrifice of the Cross. "There is no greater love than to give your life for those you love." This love ought to make us desire the good of those we love—and every sort of good, temporal as well as supernatural. This, and nothing else, is apostolic charity. This is also the missionary spirit. We are missionaries to the extent that we are "charity," as Christ Jesus was.

Those who mistrust the missionary movement as not interior enough, and those who depreciate it as "activistic," fail to understand that it is above all a movement from within, the same thing that St. Paul's life and letters are filled with: the *caritas Christi urget nos*. Like every other love—but more than any other love, because it is the greatest of all—the charity of Christ drives us ahead, spurs us on, insists, demands. But it demands not only that we run after the sheep, but also that we do whatever else this entails in the way of humility, selfdenial, service, poverty, common life and, above all, union with God.

It is by such charity that the mission idea will take hold of us interiorly, will come to rule us, to dominate our every thought and moment and instinct, to take complete possession of us.

We may conclude that there is no better way for the missionary to cultivate the spirit of his mission in himself than to develop the three theological virtues. But this conclusion is no mere point in a seminarian's meditation. It contains the very foundation and the indispensable demands of the missionary life. If our seminaries are not sending forth as many apostolic souls as we would like and if our clergy retreats fail to kindle the missionary flame in many priests, the reason is that these virtues are preached for their own sake, and not from the viewpoint of the mission life and the problems of the day.

A CARDINAL MISSIONARY VIRTUE: GRACIOUSNESS

In *Revolution in a City Parish* we attempted to show the importance of welcoming people, of meeting them with a smile, and
of making all those who come to us feel at home. We also tried
to show what a decisive influence the welcome which people
receive in the sacristy may have on them. At Colombes we
always speak of the priest "on welcome" rather than of the
priest "on guard."[4] It is more than a mere matter of words. At
any rate, we want to make it clear that this virtue of graciousness is not just a matter of external deportment or an art of
treating well the parishioners who come to us; it is even more
than a good means of reaching their souls; it is a virtue, and
one that our priesthood itself requires of us.

Under a different name (possibly *amicitia* or *affabilitas*), St.
Thomas would probably have classified it as one of the subdivi-
sions of justice. Would he also have seen certain characteristics of
charity in it, and perhaps some features borrowed from the intellectual virtues as well? At least, it is certainly not found under
this name in the traditional classification. But we have made it
plain that we are not writing a treatise on spirituality. In looking
over missionary life, we discover that this ability to welcome
people is something quite distinct from a method of the apostolate. We see it as a kind of supernatural instinct which opens the
priest's heart and mind, renders him receptive and understanding,
and makes him a door, a *porta coeli*, through which all human
values can find their way to God. It is in this sense that we call
it a virtue and, by analogy, a cardinal virtue, for it seems to us
that it is one of the hinges of our priestly spirituality.

We would be glad to have a theologian help us when we look
at God to see what basis there is in Him for this virtue of graciousness. What is the Holy Trinity but one Person constantly

---

4   These are literal translations of *"prêtre d'accueil"* and *"prêtre de
garde."* The term *accueil* is the new virtue which is the subject of this
section and which is here sometimes translated, for lack of a better
word, "graciousness."

welcoming the others? Might not God, as He stoops to His creature, be called the "One who welcomes"? He has brought creatures into being so that they might return to Him; He became flesh that they might have a way by which to return. He has placed in His creatures an appetite for Himself, to guide them in their gropings toward Him, the Supreme Good. In the Parable of the Prodigal Son He represented Himself as the One who waits, who receives, who holds His arms open. In the Gospels and in the Apocalypse He is the "One who returns," whom we are on our way to meet. He made man and therefore knows what is in man. He knows that every man is infinitely original, although all are created in the likeness of the only God. He knows that men do not come off a production line, but that each one is a unique phenomenon in the history of the world. And that is why there are many mansions in His household. He made us free and He respects our freedom; He treats us as friends to be invited, not as slaves to be forced.

These expressions of the divine psychology (St. Thomas would say the *mores divini*) and these comparisons which invite us to fathom God's mind, help us to see the attitude God's minister should have toward souls. The minister is not greater than his Master. He should not appropriate souls to himself, nor lord it over them. He is not to worry them or turn them away, but to welcome them with the same impulse of love which is at the origin of Creation and Redemption, the love which is expressed in the gospel destined to be announced "not only to you, but to all those who are afar off, even to all whom the Lord our God calls" (Acts 2:39).

It follows that a priest has to be gracious and friendly. But not only because this is a wise and prudent policy, such as a man might adopt if he failed to understand the true value of souls and yet had to respect them if he wanted to win them. No, it is love that imposes this graciousness on the missionary. God loves every soul. Every soul is infinite in value; and we ought to love every soul in spite of its wretchedness—and, indeed, even because of its wretchedness, since it was because the souls of men were so wretched that the Redeemer poured out His blood. The priest should often make his meditation on this point, keeping his whole flock before his mind or dwelling on one or two individuals whom he might be tempted to neglect or who seem to him less well disposed.

If every Christian ought to be a unifying influence, a "cata=lyzing agent," wherever he is, what are we to say of the priest? By the very fact that his is the priestly office he is a shep=herd, a man of the flock, a man who belongs to all. He has been "ordained" for the salvation of his fellow men—that is, appointed to see that they are saved.

The word "pastor" makes no sense except in relation to a flock. The pastor must provide himself with a soul big enough to embrace all his flock. His heart must beat in unison with the flock. He must, for the sake of the flock, nourish himself that he may be able to nourish the flock. He must be able to feed himself by feeding them. It would not be going too far to say that the flock will be healthy only if he is healthy.

Let us take Sunday as an example. To every Christian, Sun=day is the Lord's Day, the day of the Resurrection, the day of joy. Now, for the pastor, the feast consists in being there in the midst of his flock, not in getting away from the flock to find a more recollected atmosphere. His Mass is his prayer. Whether he celebrates it himself or helps his people assist at it or is merely present at it in their midst, the Sunday Mass is his joy and the full flowering of his prayer. In our opinion, it is even quite right for him to forget his purely pastoral work on this day. Let him leave visits and catechism and societies for the rest of the week, and on Sunday renew his strength by permitting himself the joy of being with all his people. The idea of his isolating himself in his office, once he has said his Mass, on the pretext that there is nothing more for him to do in church, is altogether appalling. If he does this, this is not the Sunday of a true shepherd.

The shepherd ought to live with his whole parish. He has not the right to slice off a choice portion of it for himself.

The pastor, as we have already said, must beware of leaving the main body of troops behind as he streaks out ahead with an advance platoon; he must realize that it is only as a unit that the parish will be missionary.

The pastor must also be careful not to impose his own brand of spirituality on the parish. This is a danger especially to the young missionary, to the one inclined to the esthetic and the esoteric, the snares of which we have already pointed out. Why must we avoid doing this? The reason is that the parish embraces all kinds of spiritualities and even many people who seem to have none at all. The reader will remember what we said in the third chapter about "old Catholics." We have to make allowances for the differences in souls, for their differences in temperament, and for the fact that some find it easier than others to follow a new lead and that some go ahead faster than others. There is the lady, for example, who is president of the Perpetual Rosary Society; even in a parish we might call evolved, she will be part of the existing reality and count for something. There is the group of graduates of the parish recreation center; even if it seems to be a nucleus of resistance to change, it is part of the parish and each of its members has a soul.

We have to think of such people, listen to them, and take their existence into account when there is question of the parish making some step forward; nor should we regret having to give them such attentions. It is not a waste of time for us now and then to try to take their pace. Sometimes this may be hard, humiliating and discouraging, but it is always a hardship for a young man to adjust his pace to that of the old man with whom he is walking. Is this not still another missionary mortification?

Being gracious will often mean knowing how to wait, not being impatient to gather in a successful harvest, to register a conversion too soon, for example, or to bring a soul back to the sacraments before the time. "When grace does not come by the direct road, it comes by a roundabout way. When it does not come from the right, it comes from the left. When it does not spring up like a fountain, it may, if it chooses, come like the water which secretly oozes out under a dike on the Loire" (Péguy, *Clio*).

When an engaged couple comes to us and the young man is not baptized, it is being gracious to ask why he wants a reli‐ gious marriage and, if he asks for baptism, to point out to him that there is no obligation for him to be baptized in order to be married in the Church. It is being gracious to set people free from an obligation which the Church herself does not impose. It is not uncommon for young people to come back later and ask us to prepare them for baptism or First Communion. "If you had insisted on this before marriage," they say, "I would have done it simply because you required it, but I would not have been sincere in the least. Now I am coming to you by my own free decision."

The Church, as Father Congar says, is a building which is constructed both from above and from below. How can it ever be built from below unless the priest graciously welcomes the observations and inspirations of the laity, of all the laity without exception?

Graciousness is not a passive virtue, but fundamentally an active one. From the standpoint of our actions, it means that we must not only welcome people when they come to see us in our office, but that we must also go out after them. And likewise from the standpoint of our mentality: it is not enough to listen to people; we must also try to know them as well as possible, put ourselves in their place, live their life, share their sufferings, go to them in order to be with them—not to "catch" them. The reader will recall the scene in the movie *Monsieur Vincent* which shows St. Vincent in the presence of the Car‐ dinal who wants to appoint him Chaplain General. St. Vincent answers him: "Leave me with my poor. I no longer know the face of a single poor man, the name of a single poor man." It is this personal knowledge of people that is the important thing.

Being gracious means knowing what the people who speak to us can do and what they cannot be expected to do, and tak‐ ing this into account. As we become more experienced in the direction of souls, a serious danger threatens us: the danger of believing we have seen everything, and so of acting by analogy and of placing the person we are dealing with in a category we have already met. People sense this, and it hurts them. It is not possible to classify human beings and personal dramas in this way. The life of every individual, and every period of it, is a drama which is his alone. Every individual is a creation and he has no duplicate.

For the man who has a general responsibility, for the pastor especially, there is still another danger. He is all taken up with the broad aspects of his charge and the general interests of the parish, and is therefore inclined to neglect individual cases, to treat them as negligible quantities, and to consider those who seek his help as so much business to be got through with. But unless this graciousness of ours enables us to enter sympathetically into individual cases, what good is it?

To be the pastor and guide of souls is a wonderful calling, and by appreciating our role we will avoid these dangers. Our role is not to dictate the policy to be followed, as we would have it, but to conform ourselves to the will of the Holy Spirit. It is to listen, to discover, to aid each soul and the whole parish to follow the inspirations of the Holy Spirit. We must not get in the way of the Spirit. "The Holy Spirit," as Father Varillon expresses it figuratively, "does not generally blow in the pipes that are prepared for Him in advance." We must believe that; our experience will often bear it out.

And thus our virtue of graciousness is not limited to the gracious welcome we give to souls; it is even more important to give a gracious welcome to God.

A Prayer of the Abbé Godin

For all the brothers and sisters and little children, for all
  those sons and daughters of Yours
That You have entrusted to me, O Lord, with their lovely
  and noble souls,
And for the knowledge of You that I owe to them,
I thank You, O Lord, and I praise You.

For all the souls redeemed by Your blood, O Christ, who
  have come into my life,
To whom I failed to give the message You gave me for them,
I ask Your pardon, O Jesus.

For all the men and women You put in my path,
Whom I abandoned, because I was indifferent or too busy,
Like a bad shepherd who does not know his sheep,
Have pity on me.

And for the good seed which You once sowed,
Which grew up slowly,
And which will go on growing to the end of the world,
Every day I pray to You, O Lord Jesus.

For all the men and women the Lord Your Son has given me,
With a prayer and a plea I turn to You, O Worker
blessed among women, nurse of all souls, Light of all mornings,
O Our Lady!

AN EXERCISE TO ADD: THE SABBATICAL REST

Perhaps there are too many exercises in the list presented to
us in the seminary—we are not competent to say. But at any
rate we are proposing still another exercise, which we call *the
sabbatical rest.*

In Genesis we are told how God obliged men to rest one
day out of every seven. There is no reason to think priests are
exempt. There may be priests who waste their time. But there
are certainly many others who would be happy if they could
have, not an eight-hour day, but simply an eight-hour night.
We think that for them it is necessary and even indispensable
to rest one day in the week. Certain priests, for having entirely
lost sight of this fact, now find themselves handicapped by bad
health as well as by weakened morale.

It is worthwhile while observing that, in general, we think
too much in terms of the day and the rhythm of the day. Modern life is measured rather by the week than by the day. In
regard to the workingman, for example, we no longer speak of
an eight-hour day, but of a forty- or forty-eight-hour week. In

345

regard to the priest too, although we often forget it, life with all its complications and variations spreads out over the whole week. The priest's daily schedule no longer allows him to get adequate rest: often, there is no such thing as the evening period of relaxation; the night's rest is curtailed; the day's intellectual work is disturbed; and the morning meditation is frequently broken into. The priest must therefore see to it that he gets a *weekly* period for physical rest, intellectual work, and meditation; nor is this so difficult as it might appear at first sight.

To be more specific: there has been, as we mentioned earlier, a great deal of discussion concerning the value and opportune= ness of the spiritual exercises in the traditional sense. Some have indicted them on the charge of having been transplanted from life in the monastery to life in the world, deeming this enough to condemn them. Some have accused them of being too burdensome, incapable of fitting into our modern life. We observed, however, that these practices sinned by defect rather than by excess, and by that we meant precisely that the exer= cises of the sabbatical rest needed to be added to these daily exercises. The daily exercises may be all that the monk or the scholar needs, because the monk or scholar can go directly to study or to the recitation of the Office or to meditation with a mind at rest. He lives at all times in an atmosphere of peace and intellectual life. Our lives, however, are full of agitation, and we go to prayer or study with our heads crammed with worldly or even apostolic concerns. We have just finished attending to two or three matters, and we know that our presence will soon be required elsewhere. Thus, the few moments we have managed to save, with great effort, for renewing our interior life are as full of agitation as the rest of the day, and it is sometimes easier for us to count the times we have been without distractions than to count our distractions themselves. But since this is not so in the weeks following our annual retreat, it is clear that what we need is, not time, but rather a soul attuned to study and meditation.

If so, why should we not take one whole day of rest every week? Let us get away from the parish altogether beginning

Sunday evening—and I say Sunday *evening* intentionally, because the night is as important as the day. Let us take refuge in a religious house where we will not hear the rectory doorbell or the voice of our good housekeeper, and where we will not know whether or not someone is asking for us. Before Monday evening comes. we will be able to give ourselves the rest our system needs and to renew ourselves intellectually and spiritu= ally. We have hardly any idea what such a day of relaxation can mean to a man who is wholly absorbed in the active life, or how much *time* there is in a daytime in which to get things done, not time to "kill." It is incredible how much a man can accomplish between morning and evening when he is left in peace.

This weekly exercise seems to us the most important of all, and we hope that seminary rectors and spiritual directors of priests will do their best to see that priests make it part of their schedule. If all the other commandments of Genesis do no more than codify the natural law, whereas this one alone is a positive precept, may it not be because this precept comes closer to being a natural law than we had imagined?

On this day of rest, after a good night's sleep, we will be able to spend two solid hours in meditation and reading; we will have the joy of reciting our Office in peace, and will still have plenty of time to plan our week and outline the following Sunday's sermon. On this day we will write whatever we may have to get ready: articles, conferences, reports. We will set out for home again with peace in our souls, our minds alert once more; and our work the rest of the week will be ten times more effective, thanks to the sabbatical day.

If we pastors allow ourselves this day of rest, clearly we must allow it to our assistants too. We think it is not enough to allow them to have it: in many cases, we shall have to insist upon it. There is no reason why in larger parishes we should not draw up a regular schedule of sabbatical rest for the priests. The faithful will very soon learn that Father N. is not in on a certain day of the week, but they will understand also that their priests take the time to think over the problems entrusted to them.

Several months ago at Colombes, the question arose among ourselves whether some of us at least should not go to work in factories. To be as certain as possible that we would make no mistake, we asked several of our finest lay militants what they thought of the idea. Most of them favored the principle of our going to work; but one felt differently and explained his view as follows: "We laymen are wholly taken up with the preoccupations of material life, and we have not enough time either to pray or to think. So we want to work hard and contribute our money to enable you priests to think and pray for us, to allow you to be free from work and material worries in order that you may study and give us the benefit of your studies." This man was not far wrong in the way he envisaged our life, nor would he think we were failing in our duty if we allowed ourselves a day a week for the purpose of renewing ourselves spiritually and intellectually.

A sabbatical rest every week. Do we not also need a *sabbatical week* at least once a year? We do not mean a week's vacation. Vacations, if they involve travelling (no matter how beneficial it may be), often leave us exhausted. Nor do we mean the priests' retreat, which is of course indispensable. What we mean is a week devoted to reviewing the year that is past and to preparing for the year to come. It would be good for us, with all our assistants or with the priests of the deanery, to take a week in which to relax together and study the main directions of our parish apostolate. Nothing as stiff and formal as a meeting or a session behind closed doors, but rather a week of relaxation in common. At the end of it we should be closer in hearts and minds: an atmosphere of joy is always a great help when there is serious work to do.

We believe in the sabbatical week, and even more strongly in *the sabbatical year*. Life is continually sapping our strength, and in the ministry it is all too easy to lose our intellectual habits. Moreover, one generation is not the same as the next, and the great intellectual interests change, while we are fighting at close quarters with pressing difficulties. Now and then we wake up to the fact, always a surprise to us, that we no longer understand the young people and that they no longer understand us. It would be good if this happened to us more often. It proves that we need to take our bearings carefully again and apply ourselves once more to some serious study.

How are we to do this? The Jesuit Fathers have their "third year," during which they return, in principle at least, to the scho-lasticate, after having been some time in the ministry. The Mis-sion of France is thinking of making it possible for its members to have a "third year." Why could we not allow ourselves a sab-batical year three or four times in our lives—every ten years, for example. Perhaps we could arrange for it before assuming a new post. For such a year, there would be the need of a house suited to the purpose, with a good library, a superior who understood his role, and a rule—but a rule framed for priests who have been engaged in the ministry. All the residents of this house would be there by their free choice. Perhaps it would not be easy to obtain such a house; but it would be worth the trouble even if only ten or twelve priests experienced in apostolic work came there every year, priests who could pool their experiences and make them available for scholarly research and who would have a chance to prepare themselves for a new stage in their lives.

Finally, we shall have to read the first chapter of Genesis once more. After six days, when He had finished His work, God rested. There is in that a hint for us from God, a hint that we too should stop when we have done all we can do. This means: a day will come when we ought to realize that all the good which can be expected of us has already been drawn out of us, that it is time to retire and leave the field to others. To have the sense to retire in time, to give in one's resignation in time, is to observe another law of nature. Alas! how many fail to do so. Let us have the good sense to give ourselves this rest, our last rest on earth. Let us do so in order to prepare ourselves for the day of the Lord, but also as a charity to our brothers and as a sacrifice for the common good of the faithful. We will serve them best by handing them over to others. ✚

✦[6]✦
The Absolute Need
of Teamwork

IN *REVOLUTION IN* a *City Parish* we devoted a good deal of space to the idea of teamwork. It might therefore seem unnecessary to reiterate our strong belief in the advantages the team offers us or to expound once more the functioning and the details of team life.

But the years have passed, and time enables us to test many things. It leaves some institutions crumbling or covered with ashes, others more solid. Some ideas develop; some acquire depth. In our earlier book we advanced many ideas on various subjects, but we can say unhesitatingly that it is the idea of the team which has struck the deepest roots in us and done the most to prove itself. At that time, we suggested quite a number of new directions, but team living now seems to have proved itself the best by far. Indeed we have never once questioned its value. More and more we are coming to look upon it as fundamental to missionary life. The longer we are in the ministry, the more it seems that every time we run up against a difficulty or have to solve a problem, the team always and without fail holds out possibilities which, had we been isolated, would have been out of the question. Whenever we have had occasion to envisage the general problems of the apostolate in France, and even outside of France, and to admit its shortcomings, we have at the same time had the feeling that there was only one remedy: team living. Whether it is a question of the control we have to keep over our-selves or others, of striking out in new directions, or of assuring continuity in our work, the answer is always the same: see to it that there is a team. Nothing will slip past its collective vigilance; its judgment guarantees greater security; its permanence will protect our work from being disconnected and disrupted.

It is probably an incurable weakness of humanity to look for easy methods and ingenious contrivances. We often have priest visitors who expect us to supply them with such appliances for their apostolic work. At times they tell us in detail about their difficulties and the impossible situations they are in. We always reach the same conclusion: it would be easy to solve the difficulties if there were a team.

For us, therefore, it is no longer a question of simply put= ting forward the idea of the team. We did that four years ago somewhat timidly, for one is always timid when one speaks of something for the first time. We can now state the conclusion we have come to with the passing of the years. It is this: there is no substitute for team living and teamwork; nor are these merely an indispensable means of getting much more work done and making it much easier for the priest to develop his spiritual life; they are indispensable almost by a natural neces= sity, like a biological entity inherent in the authentic life of our priesthood and pastoral ministry.

THE THEOLOGICAL BASIS

We presume permission to make two statements, the one based on theology, the other on history, even though we have no inten= tion of writing a tract on theology or history to substantiate them. The first is that the priesthood is not something personal to each one of us, but is inconceivable except as a participation in the priesthood of the bishop. The second is that the "presby= terium" was originally a team participating in the priesthood of the bishop and giving expression to it by its activity.

To be more concrete: when several priests are working in one parish, it is absolutely necessary for the faithful to have a clear idea of the unity of their priesthood. It must be made possible for them to abstract from the individual priests and to see their priesthood as one thing—one thing in space and in time. But we all know only too well that such is not the case. In how many parishes is it a reality? Rather, everyone singles out one priest as the center of influence and credits all the success to him. "I am for Paul, I am for Apollo." It is not a new phenomenon. The very first contribution a genuine priestly team makes to a parish is to show the people that it is useless to try to monopolize Father X or to make a hero out of Father Y. Fathers X and Y will not stand for it, nor will the other members of the team. The people of the parish must learn one lesson so well that it becomes an instinctive reaction: they have at their service, not several priests, but a team. This does not, of course, mean that the priests will not have their special tasks, nor that a person who wishes to consult the priest of his choice on a matter of conscience will be denied his right to do so. But it does mean that no priest is going to be excessively monopolized.

On our arrival in our new parish of SS. Peter and Paul at Colombes, we chose the priesthood as the first subject to preach on. This we did to enable our Catholic people to see the purely spiritual role of the priest in its true light and to grasp the fact that the priesthood of the team was one priesthood. "We really feel," one of the girls said to us, "that it is a team which is at work in our parish; and we find it reassuring to know that, if one priest or another leaves us, we are not on that account going to be abandoned." And since then we find our parishioners them= selves constantly speaking of the team. It is always: "Does the team agree on this?" "Has the team thought of that?" and so on.

That is what we meant by the unity of the priesthood in space. Unity in time is even more indispensable. We do not remain in our parishes forever, and very often the departure of a pastor or an assistant brings on a disaster; when he dies or moves on, it means the end of every activity which revolved around him, of everything he started or directed. But this can hardly happen when there is a team in the parish instead of individual priests working independently. The team lives on and, through it, the priesthood. There will perhaps be dark moments now and then, when a member of the team has to move and his personal qual= ities are missed, but this will never mean a complete disaster.

Here, from our own experience, is an example of this "peren= nial" nature of the priesthood. When half of the team, the pastor included, left Sacred Heart to go to Grand Colombes, there was no faltering because the pastor was leaving or because others were accompanying him. The parishioners were aware that the team was still there, and they said so.

On the other hand, we remember the pastor who was assigned to another parish and wrote, for the last issue of the parish bulletin before his departure, a message to this effect: "The following twenty-two projects I had decided to carry out in the parish. So far I have been able to translate only two of them into reality." His poor successor has his hands tied, and will be in danger of losing the respect of his parishioners unless he can manage to see eye to eye with his predecessor on all twenty-two points!

THE ADVANTAGES FOR US PRIESTS

For us priests, the team has this essential advantage: it helps us realize that it is our priesthood which counts, not our person. The team obliges us, if we may use the figure, to pass our priesthood through a filter and rid it of every element not proper to it.

In connection with our spiritual exercises, we spoke of the great danger there is of their being omitted or losing their value unless we have the reciprocal control and example which the team gives us. We must explain ourselves more fully here. We are becoming more convinced every day that the spiritual exercises cannot have the effect they should have apart from the favorable atmosphere the team provides. Our team life has flowered since the first five years at Petit Colombes. There was, to begin with, a community of action and thought, and this has brought us quite naturally to a greater community of soul. Every member of the team—or of both teams, as we shall say hereafter—is now much more aware of what is taking place in the souls of his brother priests. All have taken responsibility for each of the members. When there is a falling off in fervor, or an increase, it is common to all. When we meet now, it is no longer merely to plan our work or to pray. It is quite common for members of the team to confide their spiritual difficulties to one another or to pool their spiritual resources. There is a perpetual exchange among us, and a constant reciprocal enrichment. In addition to the parish council meeting at which we study the problems of the ministry, we also hold a weekly meeting con= cerned with the spiritual life at which every member of the team acquaints the other members with his actual spiritual condition. Sometimes we discuss a subject previously agreed upon, and each man strives to make the greatest contribution he can. Sometimes, when one member is more qualified for a particular question, he gives the rest of us the benefit of his study and experience. It is obvious that such a meeting is worlds removed from those sessions in which one man holds the floor throughout, and the rest have only to listen—for the fact that a man is the superior of a house does not necessarily mean that he is qualified to preach the gospel to the rest. In our meetings everyone has something to say; to be more precise, the Holy Spirit is given an opportunity to speak to all through the par= ticular graces given to the individuals. In this way, a common soul is forged, and we come to feel the solidarity of the team.

This seems the right place to answer a question which a num= ber of priests have put to us. Some confreres of ours, whose good intentions are obvious, ask us if it would not be right to begin by pooling the *spiritual resources* of a group in this way. It is true enough that the team which, at the beginning, planned to restrict the team's activities to mere *work* done in common, would be in a very insecure condition. But it is impossible to divide a living thing in that way. Both things are necessary, and provision must be made for both. Yet we cannot disregard the laws of life. We should begin by living together, and the first thing we should ask ourselves to accept is the mortification of team life. Later on, and almost naturally, the "spiritual life" of the team will strike deeper roots. Some priests think that the members of a priestly team spend their time in mutual contem= plation of one another. This is not so. The life of team members is like the life of friends: it does not consist of stopping to look at one another, but in marching ahead together toward the same goal. And it is by our marching together, sometimes after having journeyed the whole day, that the evening brings us an experi= ence like that of the disciples at Emmaus: "Was not our heart burning within us while he was speaking to us on the road?" The team helps us intensify our spiritual life. We are con= vinced that the team is also a great help in intellectual work. At the seminary we were told that we must not think our education was finished once we were in the ministry, but that we must continue our intellectual work. Almost the only means suggested was reading. But we must realize that many priests are so heavily burdened by their duties that they have little time to read. If many activities tend to dissipate the life of the soul, they have the same effect on the life of the mind. It will perhaps be said that a man has but to do himself a little violence and adhere to regular periods of reading if he really wants to further his edu= cation and continue developing his mind. This is obviously an excellent method of enriching the mind. But let us be honest with ourselves. Men of action are not to be treated as if they were scholars. It would be close to the truth, we think, to say that men of action keep up their intellectual life quite as much by listening and speaking as by reading. We have no time for exten= sive reading, and all the exhortations in the world are not going to change this situation in the least. Even if we did have time, there is no guarantee that extensive reading would necessarily raise our intellectual level. We know priests who spend long hours in their studies, who devour all the reviews and follow the latest developments even in the field of abstract thought, but who seem to do little more than passively take it all in. It provokes no reaction in them. The reason is that they lack the life that comes from the spoken word, and especially the ability to react that comes through exchanging ideas with others. For some priests who are isolated in their country rectories a personal intellectual life is out of the question, often because they can see no sense in storing up ideas and knowledge which they will never use, but more often because—with no opportunity to exchange or compare or discuss or refine their ideas—the ideas they derive from books come into them as exhibits into a museum.

It could be that the remedy lies in giving priests opportunities, not so much to read books, as to hear specialists who really have something to give them. One of the good points of the team is that it can invite to the common table men whose conversation is extremely rewarding. In the course of an hour's conversation, an author will often give us the substance of his book; and later, when we have time to read its three hundred pages, we will derive much more profit from them because of the stimulus his presence gave to our minds. We can talk and discuss a subject with such a person; and, after he is gone, we team members can go on with the discussion. More often, we members can take turns reporting on our reading, putting it into the common stock for all to discuss; this is a great help and a precious timesaver.

In a word, though it is good to insist on our keeping up our spiritual and intellectual life, it is no less necessary to devise means of enabling us to do so. Those hitherto suggested fall short of the mark and most often prove failures. If we are to supplement them and make them effective, we need help. We believe that team life can help us as nothing else can.

We can already hear an objection: "But you just mentioned our brother priests in the country. Do you not think team life is out of the question for them? Are you not afraid that what you say will discourage them?" It is true that our experience has been mostly in the city, nor do we deny that it is much more difficult to start priestly teams in the country than in the city. Yet Canon Boulard, in his *Missionary Problems of Rural France*,[1] pointed to a number of priestly communities and teams which were already functioning in rural districts. We ourselves know that there are such teams in almost every part of France; and we know also of a number of deaneries in which the priests, without living together and without ordinarily being able to

---

1 *Problémes missionnaires de la France rurale.* The reader of this English translation may be interested in knowing that in many respects this book parallels *Revolution in a City Parish*, although the factors that are responsible for the decline of Catholicism in the countryside are somewhat different from those to which it is usual to trace the loss of faith among the working classes in the cities.

work side by side, have found ways of meeting frequently and of forming a real work team.

We do not say it is necessary to live in community, but we do think it is absolutely necessary for the priests of the same dean= ery or the same region to pool the resources of their apostolic, intellectual, and spiritual life, which cannot possibly be kept up to the mark with the minimum of meetings the deanery confer= ences represent. Though the team is obviously not a universal remedy for all the weaknesses of the missionary movement, it is an indispensable factor in missionary work. The very existence of such a little community of thought and prayer and work will overcome many of our defects, many of our troubles and failures.

As we go on living this team life and seeing what it enables us to accomplish in our parishes, we are constantly meeting evidence which proves that such team life is almost a physical necessity.

We aim to make our parishes real communities. But the more closely we examine the missionary problem, the clearer it becomes that we cannot make converts (especially in a workers' milieu) unless there is a community for them to join, no matter how small. Our parishes have to become communities with some warmth about them, and the warmth must radiate. We believe that parishes cannot achieve this transformation unless they have at the center a priestly nucleus to animate them. There is a comparison which seems to fit the subject exactly. Our parishes are like the cells of an organism, which, if they are to live, must have a vital nucleus at the center. Without such a nucleus, they consume themselves; they live on their reserves for a time, then they waste away. They continue in existence, but in an existence without life. It has been our lot to hear the grievances of many priests, both pastors and assistants. They have told us they were helpless to do anything to revitalize their parishes in view of the resistance either of parishioners who form a block to protect the stagnation with which they are satisfied or of their fellow priests who refuse to move at all. Now, these priests lack neither zeal nor intelligence nor energy. Their only fault is that they are alone, with no one to share in their plans and their actions. What do they need? They need that sense of vastly increased strength which the combined efforts of several priests would give them; they also need to feel that there is one will animating the actions of several men; but even more, they need something which it is impossible to define exactly in words or even in thought. We may perhaps be satisfied with calling it the radiating influence of a small community on a larger one, and it is like the power of a living thing to create new life.

We might find it useful to continue the analogy in the matter of multiplying teams.

When we are called upon to infect a parish with the mis‹ sionary fever, the task ahead of us is not easy. To undertake this work, which requires exceptional prudence and initiative, we have to form many teams; and, in making them at once bold enough and reliable, we have to suffer many a headache. There is the problem of choosing the captain and the members of the teams, whether these are chosen by the members of the team or associated with it by authority. Once the team is established, there is the difficulty the members have in getting to know one another and in agreeing on principles and their application. All this takes time, and the time consumed in the clash of temperaments and ideas may test our patience to the limit. But the worst is yet to come, for it still remains to be seen how the parish will react to the decisions the team makes. The parish's reactions are of the greatest importance and value, but we must know how to interpret them correctly and distin‹ guish superficial resistance from serious opposition. Priests of different backgrounds and mentality, if they have only recently been formed into a team, do not find it easy to draw the same conclusions from the reaction in the parish. They may all be willing enough to undertake a certain new work; but if they go about it timidly, because it is new to them all, the project may come to grief at the first obstacle it meets. This would not happen if there were at the center of the group several members who had already carried through such an undertaking elsewhere and were able to give the team the benefit of their experience.

We are sure to encounter all these difficulties if, when we seek to form new teams, we insist on sending into the parish where missionary work is to be started priests who are new to teamwork and to one another. Whether it is a new pastor in the midst of old assistants or a whole team composed of new elements, the result will be the same. It is like sowing seeds. Such priests will require time to learn the parish and to decide on the steps they must take. They can easily fall prey to doubts. There will be the doubts, for example, of each individual con= cerning his own ability or the ability of the others, doubts on the meaning of the parish's reactions, doubts concerning the team's power to survive. There will be much indecision, many discussions, and also—if we are willing to face the facts—many failures. We know only too many of these experiments which died almost as soon as they were initiated. Yet they began with the best intentions and all the good will in the world.

Are such fumbling and uncertain methods inevitable? Would it not be possible to avoid them by propagating new teams from existing ones? Obviously, what we are suggesting here is not the only possible method. For a long time to come, it will be neces= sary to start teams with members, all of whom are new to the life. A start has to be made. But surely, the moment it becomes feasible, the solution we propose is more in accord with the laws of life and better adapted to the special difficulties of the modern apostolate. We are not proposing it as an untested theory. It is the fruit of the experiment we tried when we divided the team at Sacred Heart in order to take over SS. Peter and Paul. Part of the team went to Grand Colombes with the author, and the rest stayed on at Petit Colombes under the direction of a former assistant who became the new pastor. Both teams were brought up to the required number by aggregating new priests to them.

When the Cardinal Archbishop of Paris asked us to take this second parish, he did so with the idea of enabling us to apply the same missionary methods to a whole section of the city. There are many advantages in such combined work, but they were not immediately apparent. We have had to wait for both parishes to arrive at the same stage of development, and that stage has not yet been fully reached. Still, from the begin= ning we had one advantage on which we had not counted: we discovered that in the second parish we had the support of a team which had previously grown to maturity as a unit. At the heart of the new team there was a nucleus formed by years of living together and working together. From the outset we could see what a great source of strength this was: we were spared a great deal of groping and were able to see openings right away. There was no temptation to try experiments which had failed at Petit Colombes. This held true both for the community life and for the work of the parish. We had the immediate impression that, with no extra effort, we would be able to cover the same ground in half the time. We can truthfully say, for example, that we have done as much in two years to make the parish into a liturgical community as we accomplished in five years at Sacred Heart. It is obvious that, with so much work to be done on all sides, we are not making such rapid progress in other forms of apostolic work — getting to know our territory and our people or starting communities of lay people. And yet even in this field we have benefited, for we set to work at once on the basis of our previous experience, and up to now it seems quite clear that the parish has gone ahead more rapidly. The lay people have been much quicker to grasp their role. If there is a delay, the fault lies with us priests who have too much to do. The lay Catholics are not lagging behind, nor are they offering us any opposition.

Not that we should ever go into a parish like heavy=handed colonizers eager to apply ready=made methods and ingenious con= trivances transplanted from other fields. But it is easy to see how great a help such a unit can be for the new members of the team and for the entire parish, for it is a real unit, whose members have the same ideals and ways of life, and between whom there is reciprocal trust. The parish sees and realizes that its priests are united by the life they lead and by their love for one another, and it is around this nucleus that the whole parish community will be formed. We repeat that this is not the only way teams can be multiplied. But might it not be more generally applied? Only a large team can propagate itself in this way; a small team cannot afford to split off a group to provide a nucleus for a new team in another parish. But there is nothing to prevent us from putting in a parish twice the number of priests needed and leaving them there for four or five years, after which a division could be made for the purpose of taking over a new parish.

The number of priests this requires may cause some to pro= test vehemently: "How are we to do it, when we are so short of priests that we cannot even provide them for all our parishes?" We do not admit the justice of the protest. On the contrary, we think this system is the best answer to the present situation of the clergy and the parishes. Over and above the advantages of this system which we have already pointed out, there are others which might result from increasing the number of priests in certain parishes: 1) where there is real missionary work to be done, and 2) where there is a desire to provide young priests with a good school of apprenticeship.

ADVANTAGES FOR MISSIONARY WORK

The process of dechristianization is so far advanced that superfi= cial remedies cannot really cope with it. You cannot cure tuber= culosis with poultices or cough drops. Parish missions lasting three weeks or a month do produce good results; they have been, and they still are, effective when it is a question of stirring up parishes that are still Catholic. When there is a mission in such parishes, everyone is aware of it; and, as they all have the faith, it is enough to shake them out of their indifference and to lead "sinners" to conversion. But with our working class, posting up notices of the opening of the mission is not sufficient. The people will pay no attention. To our knowledge, several parish missions in Paris failed to attract as many peo= ple as the Sunday Masses. Even in such cases, of course, the mission serves to wake up the faithful Catholics and to make a few "conquests." But, if we really wish to accomplish some true mission work. we have to give time to it, as much as several years perhaps. Preaching is not enough. There is need for work at all levels. And the work will have no lasting effect until a Christian community has come into being and all the lay people have put their shoulders to the task, with the priests teaching them to understand their role and inspiring them to assume responsibility for the whole neighborhood.

It is obvious that even a few priests will accomplish some≠ thing; but they will do so at a very high price and at the risk of losing their health, their spirit, and their enthusiasm.

Do we see what will inevitably happen if we let things go on the way they are going? It is reasonable enough to wish to provide every place with a priest, and we all shudder at the prospect of leaving any village without one. Nevertheless, we must face the facts, no matter how unpleasant they are. If we go on trying to fill all the needs, what will the outcome be? Priests will be overburdened and will be able only to look after the "dispatch of current business." In the rural areas the situ≠ ation is especially critical. It is impossible for the priest even to provide Mass and teach catechism in all the districts for which he is responsible. Tired out from long trips by bicycle or motorcycle, his legs and feet aching, he is not in the right frame of mind to be able to welcome people smilingly or to give them the support they should have. What is worse, the priest burns himself out bodily and spiritually. His health succumbs to overwork, and he becomes disheartened. Have we not too often seen young priests full of spirit and with high ideals lose their enthusiasm and their buoyancy after a few years of such a life? Should we be surprised when we recall the crushing burdens they have been called upon to assume?

If these priests were living in a community, the situation would be very different; if there were a number of them together, they would be able to do something more than superficial work. They would have time to accomplish real missionary work, to make lasting contacts, and to engage in some genuine study. At the beginning of this book we mentioned the need of taking very special care of the "priestly instrument." If a kind of paralysis seems to creep over the lives of so many priests and they appear to be constantly losing their dynamism, where are we to put the blame? In part, perhaps, on their personal shortcomings, but much more on the conditions in which they have to live.

The bishops are fathers to us. They are understanding enough to see in this list of grievances nothing more than the plaint of one of their priest sons. The words come from a priest who has often seen his brothers break down and cry, and who now has the boldness to speak aloud—but with respect and love—of the suffering he has so often witnessed.

All of us tremble, and with good reason, at the thought of sending priests to work in factories or mines. It is certain that they will have to face many dangers. And yet they are on fire with apostolic zeal as they take up the work, and there is good reason to hope that the contrast between the materialism of the life they see and their own high ideals will give them a healthy shock. Furthermore, these priests generally form part of a community, for good care is taken to see that they are not left alone.

What do we think will happen to the young assistant who, after two or three years in the priesthood, is sent off to a deserted region far from any priest colleague and with almost no truly spiritual work? How is it that we do not fear much more for him than for the priest workman, since we have seen so many of the former lose heart or enthusiasm in such conditions—and sometimes much more than heart or enthusiasm?

The present state of affairs even causes loss of vocations to the priesthood. What he has before his eyes is what attracts a boy to the priesthood. Now, the sight of priests all taken up with business and material concerns is not one to fill a boy or a young man with a longing to do what he sees them doing. Let us suppose that an assistant is removed from a good parish and not replaced, because an abandoned region needs one more pastor. Who is the more likely to stimulate vocations—the young assistant who is full of enthusiasm or the pastor who is on in years and far too occupied with administration? Nor should we expect vocations from neglected parishes, but from

Christian communities, where piety and the faith of parents and children provide the proper soil for these choice plants to thrive.

We ask pardon for these remarks. We could not speak thus, were we not convinced that our present policy condemns us to move in a vicious circle, whose radius, unfortunately, is likely to become smaller and smaller.

The system we are suggesting does indeed require the sacrifice of whole areas, and this is painful to consider. Besides, the system does not promise immediate large-scale success. But when there is too much to do, is it not the rule to begin at one end and not try to do everything at once? When we try to do something everywhere, we end by doing nothing permanent anywhere.

A GOOD SCHOOL FOR APPRENTICES

The forming of teams would offer priests, especially young priests, the advantage of an excellent school of apprenticeship.

We all realize the importance of the first years in the ministry. The seminaries are often blamed for failing to prepare seminarians adequately for the difficulties they are certain to meet. In some instances the criticism is undoubtedly justified. At the same time, almost all young priests, when they come out of the seminary, are full of generosity and zeal and the will to give themselves. How is it that, after four or five years in the ministry, far too many of them lose these qualities? It seems to us that we can explain it only by admitting that a young priest's very first contacts with pastoral life may get him off on the wrong foot. The influence of his first pastor and the example received from his older brothers are of primary importance in forming the mentality of the young assistant. There is great danger that his youthful enthusiasm may not prove strong enough to withstand the baneful effect of the sacristy slogans, the hasty statements, and the deanery conference criticisms to which he is subjected. When you take his surroundings into account, you come to believe that the result was inevitable.

We must also bear in mind that the first contacts with the ministry are often very trying. Unless the young priest is understood and enjoys the companionship not only of a good pastor but also of other priests hardly older than himself, his first year is an intensely painful experience, as he lives through his dark days alone and solves his problems without knowing to whom to appeal for advice. The mere change from the regulated activity of the seminary to the liberty of being able to organize his personal activity tends to make him fritter away his days and at the same time be convinced that he is overwhelmed by his duties. We have seen young assistants killing themselves and bemoaning the fact that they were doing nothing, and we know how much they suffer. What better remedy could there be for this than to have parishes which could absorb young priests and gradually initiate them into the secrets of pastoral work, parishes in which they would find real missionary work to do instead of the wearisome round of parish societies and administrative tasks?

In other days there were "priest schools." Their accomplish≠ments in the way of intellectual formation are perhaps question≠able. At any rate, they were an excellent means of providing an initiation to pastoral life, for the candidates had opportunities to visit the sick, to receive people at the rectory, to teach catechism, to look after the church, and so on. At the present time no pastor could assume responsibility for such a "priest school," but there is no reason why a team might not become a school for apprentices.

And then there are the religious communities. Up to now they have furnished most of the missionaries for parish mis≠sions. Could they not now come to the aid of the secular clergy? Would this not be a modern way of giving a mission? As their contribution, the religious would offer their habits and tradi≠tions of community life, and the seculars would teach them how to make real contact with the masses. Nor is this a mere paper plan. It is already a reality in Marseilles, in Paris, and in Colombes, where religious from different Orders and secular priests trained in different seminaries are living a true commu≠nity life and closely cooperating as a team in their work. If we mention the fact, it is, as usual, simply because we desire to make a contribution from our own experience in the hope that we may throw some additional light on our common problems.

It is only our personal experiences that have given us the courage to write as we have written here. We are filled with embarrassment at the thought of it, for we have touched upon questions of policy which it belongs to the diocesan or religious authorities to formulate, and not to us. We beg them to par= don us for our audacity. "One has always," according to Father Doncoeur, "the right to weep before a father."

But we had little intention of weeping, and none at all of remonstrating with authority—for we realize only too well the impossible situations which our fathers, the bishops, have to cope with. And the affectionate respect we bear them enables us to suspect something of their suffering and solicitude in the face of problems for which it almost seems there is no solution.

Thus, it is not to them that we had any intention of speaking. Indeed, the Holy Spirit used Balaam's ass to point out to the prophet the way he was to go, but we do not think of ourselves as filling even that lowly role. Some priests have, however, seen fit to confide their difficulties to us, and we have to admit that the obstacle they encounter when they desire to undertake something or to start off in a new direction is sometimes the very wall of priestly opposition. How can priests be expected to form a team if they have not been trained with this in view, if they have never had any experience of this life or even any thought of it? How can we bring priests in undermanned par= ishes to accept the idea of a certain parish being given more priests than are actually required for the parish work?

It was because we had priests in mind that we felt it was our duty to let our ideas be known. The priests we have in mind are those of our brothers who are actually in the priesthood and the seminarians who will one day live that same life. It is for these, for these alone, that we have spoken. We must create a strong current of priestly opinion; we must change the outlook of priests; we must make the best use of all the resources at our com= mand—for then, and only then, will it be possible for our fathers, the bishops, to make the decisions they judge opportune. ✢

Catholic Action
and the Parish

❖

✢[I]✢
The Meaning of "Parish" and "Vocation"

THE WORD "PARISH" covers everything from towns in Brittany or eastern France to some section of a province, a zone of Paris or a suburban community Can the priests in such different localities have the same outlook? Will a pastor in Vendée have the same views, plans, worries and projects as one in Argenteuil or Kremlin=Bicêtre? Canon Law imposes the same rules on both men. Still, can peo= ple and things look the same to the village priest who knows there is a family of practicing Catholics behind every door and the city priest who is not too sure what door to knock on? Is it possible that these two men, whose work is designated by the same term though it is so dissimilar and is performed under diametrically opposed conditions, are of the same mold? Both of them are pastors and the two spheres entrusted to them are currently described by the one word "parish."

In country districts, "parish" is easy to define. Its limits are those of the community; it is territorial as well as personal. Look at the map; where one parish ends, another begins. There is no question of continuity. When, on the contrary, a suburbanite speaks of "my parish" or "the parish" in general, you have to listen for a moment to see whether he means those who practice the faith or those who happen to live within the parish limits.

In this connection, does the expression "a de=Christianized parish" make sense? If it refers to an area where the people, though baptized and possessing the faith, no longer live accord= ing to the gospel or fulfill their religious duties, the expression is correct since it denotes a parish which was Christian once but is no longer so. But if the term is applied to a place where a fervent community of believers dwells in the midst of a larger group who, for the most part, have never had the faith, then it is difficult to see who or what can be labeled "de-Christianized." Could it be the faithful? No, because they are fervent—perhaps more fervent than they would be in a Christian country, where social pressure often forces one to go to church. Could it be the non-believers, those who do not frequent the sacraments? Hardly, since they have never been Christians at all.

Shall we, then, have to give a precise meaning to the word "parish" as used in this book? To be logical, we should choose one definition and stick to it; but that is exactly what we do not want to do. Always mindful of suburban parishes, we would rather not restrict the term "parish" to the Christian commu-nity any more than we would want to equate it simply with the confines of a parish.

We are glad that the word designates both believers and the multitude of half-believers or total unbelievers. We are glad that it focuses our attention and thought on those who "come to church" as well as on those who do not, for the simple reason that we do not want to abandon one group or forget the other.

We do not wish to choose, because choosing means sacrific-ing something and the true shepherd of souls cannot consent to that. We are glad that the word "parish" reminds us of all our pastoral duties at once and that the very mention of it conjures up both the joy and the anguish of a shepherd of souls.

The word "parish" is dear to us because it is synonymous with being drawn and quartered. When I say "my parish," the "my" is not a possessive pronoun; much like a personal pronoun, rather, it expresses the utter gift of myself—all that I am and have—which I must make to the parish entrusted to me. As for this task to which I must devote myself, I want it to serve two ends: to help faithful souls draw near to God, and silently to call all who do not and cannot know of Him, those I constantly desire to reach.

The Code of Canon Law has often been criticized for legislat-ing for dechristianized countries as if they were still Christian, and we in the ministry have frequently deplored the lack of a spiritual code to follow in mission territory. Yet is that not proof of great feeling on the part of the Church, who refuses to brand definitively as infidel the vast domains of early Christendom? She cannot bring herself to call "pagan" those countries where the material cross of Christ still stands and which not only belonged to the Church but were the Church for so many centuries.

The Church is both the far-flung lands where missionaries go and the faith-fed lands whence missionaries come. The Church is the community of Christians whose divine and human dynamism leavens the whole dough of mankind; and because of that, the parish—which is essentially a part of the Church, which is the Church in a given territory—can no more choose between believers and unbelievers than we can choose between yeast and dough and forsake one to concentrate on the other.

We regret having to spend so much time splitting hairs but it so happens that, from the very beginning of our little book on the pastoral and religious vocation, the word "parish" assumes the power of a symbol and a standard. In its several connotations it summarizes our whole call: a call to be shepherds and missioners, a call to arouse and bring the community together, a call to be ready for any task and accessible to everyone.

"My parish"—the expression makes me think immediately of the huge crowds entrusted to my care, whom I do not know, and, doubtlessly, shall never know because it would be humanly impossible to do so. But I want the words to summon up each and every soul I have charge of, regardless of class or social standing, the Meaning of "Parish" and "Vocation" regardless even of beliefs; and at the same time I want to say they are "mine"—even those who hate me, and those on the furthest fringe of the parish morally or territorially.

When I say "my parish," I want to remember that group of the faithful—small as it may be—which surrounds me with its faith, prayer and activity. I want to recall every adolescent and adult, every home, every sodality. I want to evoke the atmosphere of Sunday Mass and each tiny community in the neighborhood which is striving to live the gospel throughout the week. I want to include those who knock at my door and sit waiting for a word of cheer. It is not enough for me to remember that community, whether large or small, afire or just kindling. No, I must understand that it is the scene of my labors; it is where I can work like yeast in dough; it is the life cell I have to nourish since it is in and through that community that the greater part of the work must be done. What I count on is that group and the numberless ways it can amplify and supplement my work as keeper of souls. Only in and because of it—since it is the Church and therefore the body of Christ—can I look at the vast field around me without being crushed by the job to be done.

"My parish" means the best I can discover among the treasures Christ has given me to distribute, all I can give, and all the inspiration I can find living among those who understand; but it also includes the ceaseless sorrow I feel for those who do not know and do not want to know. Giving life to my parish means living Christ, living His life, His teaching, His apostolic love.

"My parish" sums up all my sufferings and joys, my cares and my hopes. It expresses all I willed when, as a young man, I glimpsed the priestly calling: celebrating the mysteries, preaching the word, and spreading the kingdom of God.

That is why any attempt to limit the sense of "parish" would rob it of its missionary implications, and, by that very fact, of all that makes it meaningful to us. It would be killing the word, the way you kill a Living thing by mutilating it or depriving it of those stimuli it needs for growth.

We have refused to restrict the meaning of "parish," then, for fear of narrowing our outlook. Let us now try to see what this outlook, this perspective, is. Occasionally we find a boy who likes to re-enact church ceremonies at home, makes himself an altar, candelabra and vestments, and officiates at the services. People predict he will become a priest, and when questioned he avers, "Yes, I will say Mass some day."

Can any of that mean he has a real calling? Is it a sign of a vocation? An expert at recruiting seminarians once replied, "Surely. It's a sign he's called to be a sacristan."

Nevertheless, many vocations have come to light during this sort of play-acting. The young celebrant, now an altar boy, has become familiar with the real ceremonies; he loves the ritual, public prayer and all the feasts. The thought of consecrating his life to this, warms his heart and he enters the seminary, where the call and his response to it grow deeper as he gains a broader understanding of the life and labors that lie ahead of him as a priest. Thus does an altar boy's dream develop into a genuine missionary vocation.

It would be unfortunate if a priest, especially a pastor, saw merely the liturgical aspect of his duties; for, after all, parish life means more than worship or the administering of the sacraments. We agree that the Mass, especially Sunday Mass, is the precious leaven that lets a parish rise and take shape and grow strong. We agree, too, that the parish is the real "home" of the sacraments, that one of its most urgent tasks is to teach the people how great and vitally necessary each sacrament is, and that pastors and assistants are at the disposition of anybody who asks to receive one. Never can we priests prize these channels of grace at their true value or administer them with too much love. I pity the priest who is not happy in his church. I pity the pastor or the curate who does not feel at home with his congregation; who fails to experience the deep joy of the Lord's Day spent among the praying and singing throng; who cares little to officiate at ceremonies, conscious of being responsible for the fervor of all; and who cannot taste the tremendous thrill of giving Communion, No priest can forget the long hours spent in the confessional. The priest must be happy in everything related to the sacraments, and, indeed, "everything related to the sacraments" is an extremely important part of his work in the parish.

Still, it is only a part and not the whole story. His activity, his mission, is not limited to that. The parish is the agent that awakens, animates, guards, broadens and deepens Christianity in a given territory, in relation to which territory the parish is a part of the Church and has almost as broad a mission as the Church.

Some seem to think that, in a parish, the Church's mis=
sion is restricted to the liturgical life. We would be seriously
tempted to say with Bishop Blanchet, "A parish that has only
been preserved' is one that has yet to be won over. At any rate,
the Church's mission is far broader and more complex in areas
which are predominantly unbelieving.

For the parish—which is part of the Church on the
march—does that mean simply some sort of adaptation, more
or less difficult according to locality, more or less successful
according to the capability of the clergy? Can a parish be said
to have the missionary spirit merely because it is the scene of
a few minor revolutions or of ceremonies so designed as to be
accessible to the masses and especially the common people?

We may say Mass facing the congregation, with explanations
and hymns in the vernacular. We may reorganize sodalities
and make them appealing to the young. By looking around
and evaluating them we may discover and successfully use
methods and formulas which have proved efficacious elsewhere.
Our parish will then be a combination of societies which will
periodically renew their source of appeal but always continue
to group together, under the guidance of the parish clergy (as
completely and actively as the clergy's intelligence and zeal war=
rant), the few souls who want to feed on the choice food set
aside for them, and, in return, agree to remain faithful.

Yet, can that group be called a parish, a living parish, a mis=
sionary parish, or, more exactly, a part of the Church? A parish
is that portion of humanity which lives within the area assigned
to a pastor; and his responsibility, his essential mission, is to
insure that this portion of humanity sees a genuine witnessing
to the gospel in its midst. His work is not over when he has
tended to parish business or taken care of the faithful. His work
is something more than that: something indefinite—not only
what he gives, what he is or does; but a spoken or unspoken
sermon, the very life, activity and demeanor of the parish he
quickens. His work is not done until that witness, like the
yeast which imparts its strength to the lump of dough, is

brought to the most destitute and errant, the most indifferent and hostile of men.

Understanding the vocation of the parish and of the parish priest means understanding the urgency and the scope of their work; understanding it not as a utilitarian need of our times but as the very power of Christ for the salvation of the world; understanding that it is the deep-down growth and the vital force of that mustard seed sown on earth two thousand years ago; understanding that that seed is none other than the word of God which has called us and still calls all Christians and ceaselessly troubles "every man who comes into this world."

But the question is precisely this: Can parish work still bear witness to the gospel? Can the parish be a field where the seed of Christ may grow? After seeing the near-lethargy of certain parishes and the amorphous I groups of worshipers in some churches, we can well ask whether parishes have not become bloodless bodies or sapless branches no longer capable of receiv-ing life. It is an undeniable fact that the sight of such paralyzed parishes presents a serious problem to the young man who wants to work in the vast fields the Master says are ripe for the harvest. He has reason to ask himself with great concern, "Is that where, having dedicated myself unreservedly, I can best answer Christ's call and do really effectual work for Him?"

We shall try to answer that question in the next chapter. Before doing so we must say this: If, in judging the effective-ness of parish work, we consider only lifeless parishes, we already know the answer. But it would be almost as surely dis-couraging to judge from the failures or seeming ineffectiveness of certain parishes which have done everything they could to produce results. They made, or thought they were making, all necessary adjustments, nor did they hesitate to use any means that seemed good. They even gave a new life to the community. But they did not give it its full share of power or let it grow to its proper dimensions. They used methods and systems and imposed them in such a way as to wear them threadbare and make them forever useless for anyone else.

The explanation lies in a lack of synthesis, of something to serve as a keystone to the whole edifice—which keystone may very well have been that final wholehearted welcoming of the common man, that final thoroughgoing spirit of daring and enterprise.[1] Because there was no synthesis there was no seed; because there was no keystone there was no edifice. But that does not prove that the seed cannot exist and mature elsewhere or that the building cannot be built in some other place. ✛

---

[1]   We should like to give a few examples of ineffective changes. *As regards the liturgy:* To give life to the various services, some churches read and comment on the text used; but not everyone in the congregation has the same text. Other churches provide missals for the faithful but do not consider whether the translation is adapted to their intellectual level, intelligible and interesting; or they simply give them books to use as best they can. Still others read and comment, but in such a hieratic fashion as to remedy the situation not a bit. And in many parishes it is the curate, or the pastor alone, who is trying to effect the minor revolution. Such cases betray ignorance of the problem. What is needed is a profound transformation–changing a drowsy congregation into a fervent community. There is so much laziness to be overcome that the change cannot be wrought by external means or without the united effort of the various militant groups within the parish.

As regards the money question: With the best intentions in the world, a pastor may abolish budget envelopes but expound the problem of money to individuals and families so insistently that they feel obliged to give more than they reasonably should. Another no longer exacts a fee for the first Holy Communion ceremony, but on his desk he places a box in which the parents may place a "voluntary" offering. A third one has gone further and does not even use the box; yet the greater part of his Sunday sermon is devoted to studying the parish's financial situation. In any case, the results—apostolically speaking—are negligible.

We could mention other matters—accessibility, the apostolate, Catholic Action—and give examples of half measures. Even though the work to be done in one sphere has been clearly comprehended and accomplished, the fact that nothing has been done in some other sphere is enough to render the best intentions fruitless. Our trouble, it seems, is that we do not see, feel or think for ourselves. We are afraid to act.

⁘[2]⁘
Cures, Not Sinecures

THE GREATEST DANGER a parish priest runs is that of being locked within a little circle of practicing Catholics, trapped by his very priestly activity on behalf of a group of the faithful who monopolize his time, his person, his labors and may lead him to think that the life of the whole world is conditioned by and modeled on the life of this tiny cell.

Such groups have been called artificial, but they are not. If they were, they would be harmless because artificiality is soon routed by the exigencies of life and practical living. The truth is that these milieux are restricted. But society is full of little groups which draw a magic circle around themselves and avoid others as sedulously as others avoid them. Like all such cliques, these pious ones live after the manner of microcosms; and that is exactly what is wrong with them, for their isolation is diametrically opposed to the gospel ideal which should animate them. As we have said, a truly Christian community exists — and exists in a particular manner — solely because it is the yeast in the dough and must lose its life to find it anew with the masses. Usually, however, the coteries in a parish shut themselves off, become self-sufficient, and devote all their attention and activity to their own interior perfection.

It is easy to see how this spirit and its sclerotic effects might frighten a seminarian as he reflects on parish work and wonders whether he too will have to narrow his life and his dreams down to such dimensions and time them once for all to such a sleepy rhythm. On entering the seminary, a young man keeps vivid recollections of what he saw in the world. Only yesterday he was living like all his friends, sharing the same work and studies and pastimes. He grew up among country people, factory workers or students; and if called to priesthood relatively late, he may have been an engineer or a doctor, a merchant or a mechanic. There is a sudden, drastic change between his life in the world and his life in the seminary.

Now, he has answered the call to the priesthood precisely because he wants to evangelize that part of humanity whence he comes. Having sensed its moral and spiritual wretchedness and measured the dreadful distance separating his old compan‹ ions from the Church and Christ, he has willed to consecrate his entire life to bringing the Church and Christ back to them. The sight of the deep moat that estranges the modern world, and especially the working class, from Christ, and the desire to work with all his might to bridge it—these two things con‹ stituted for him his missionary vocation.

Is it surprising, then, that when contemplating parish work he is afraid—afraid of being snapped up and imprisoned or at the very least cramped by the environment in which he would enter? He goes to the seminary, not to forget the place he comes from, but rather to think of it all the more, to think of it all through life. He has dreamed of being a contact man between that milieu and the Church, and now he is afraid of becoming a sort of high priest isolated in the sanctuary.[1]

This fear seizes not only the candidate who enters the sem‹ inary late in life. Unless quite chloroformed by their mode of living, so many of those who have spent years in juniorates and minor seminaries look with wide‹open eyes upon the world around them and are overwhelmed by that same dread: "What shall we do. If our whole life is to be spent on the parish tread‹ mill?" How many major seminarians and young priests are alarmed at such a prospect!

A few decades ago, earnest seminarians would spend several weeks of their vacation helping the pastor conduct summer schools or camps. They became very enthusiastic over this type

---

1 In the original French this sentence contains an untranslatable play on words: "He has dreamed of being a bridge (pont) between that milieu and the Church, and now he is afraid of. becoming a pontiff isolated in the sanctuary." (Translator's note.)

of work—and, fortunately, many still do. Knowing nothing else, they conceived their whole future ministry in terms of groups and teams to be organized. Every one of them had worked out his own theory—a very definite one, too and seminary walks were loud with tireless discussions on this method and that.

Until forbidden to do so by Rome, seminarians used to take advantage of vacation time to acquire experience in agriculture, industry, commercial fishing, newspaper hawking and many other fields where they discovered immense throngs who had yet to be evangelized since they were quite outside the parish's scope of influence.

For it is a fact that present-day living has divided life itself into zones which are by no means territorial. Some sections of the working class resemble the company which was building a dam in the mountain village where I remember going to say Mass one Sunday. Chatting with the parishioners after Mass, I asked how many practicing Catholics there were in the parish.

They answered, "Everybody here goes to Mass, and the pastor keeps in touch with all of us."

"And is he welcome when he visits the company sheds?"

"Oh," they blurted in amazement at my question, "he doesn't go there. Those people never come to church, and Father doesn't go to see them. They're not part of the parish."

There is an example of a parish ignoring a group of laborers. And what about parishes that stand in their midst and yet drive them away? A huge mill opens in some town and draws all hands from the surrounding countryside. The management builds them a little world of uniform houses and creates everything in it—co-operatives, social centers, and even a church. It goes further and places a "pastor" at the entire disposition of the workers. This looks like a magnificent piece of work, and it may be; but it may also make the worker look upon the "parish" as a creation of the management and consequently as something which is not for him.

Hospitals, especially sanatoriums, training centers and agricultural schools wall off life into definite compartments. There are even vaster sectors of thought which eventually become sectors of life, little worlds all by themselves: the world of the movies, the theater, and others as remote as they are inaccessible to us. When discussing work and leisure with a casual acquaintance, we have often been astonished to find him living with others in a completely engrossing—and, to us, quite unknown—world of occupations and thoughts and feelings and interests.

Now, all these sectors, because they constitute very special milieux, are totally and almost necessarily beyond the influence of any parish. It is becoming clearer and clearer that plans for apostolic and social action must transcend the hierarchical map= ping out of the Church. We must think and act in terms of cities, geographical regions and nations. The fact that there are several parishes in a country town may facilitate assistance at church services, but does it facilitate activity on a wide scale? At every step specialized Catholic Action comes up against parish boundaries. The workingman's world knows no such boundaries and middle=class families pay even less attention to them in their social dealings. Neither can civic and munic= ipal business take account of them. If Catholics, then, want to campaign for proper housing, peace, or anything else, why should their efforts be restricted to the boundaries or the active members of one parish rather than another? Should not the whole town work together? In some sections any apostolic labor has to be organized from the regional viewpoint. With regard to a country as a whole, obviously such work can hardly be fitted into the artificial molds of dioceses. By the very fact that specialized Catholic Action must adapt itself to the various phases of life which it seeks to affect, it has highlighted these problems and made us realize that we must solve them.

As everyone admits, specialized Catholic Action is essential to the development of Christianity today. We may even say it is the authentic form of that development. This is nothing new. There has long been a universe of private worlds—for instance, the world of commercial fishermen—which have nothing to do with territorial limits. Still, in the past, that did not keep such men, drudges though they were, from thinking of themselves as belonging to a parish, basing their Christian life on it and gladly returning to it to fulfill their duties as good parishoners, Father Lowe reminds us that the dockers he met in Marseille seem to have preserved that parish-feeling. But, he adds, most of them were Maltese, Italians and Portuguese who still had a bit of faith—at least a few habits and practices. Unfortunately, there are many others who do not even give a thought to Christian life and practices.

Is it not one of the consequences of our age's materialism that it so wraps man up in his work and his pleasure that they become his sole interest, his whole life? Such "worlds" become all the more impenetrable as they are cut off from the spiritu- ality of the Church or of some broader ideal which could cut through the materialistic walls of his environment and unite him to his fellow man. Accordingly, we feel justified in drawing this conclusion: these segments of life and the means to reach them means we must never disregard but study ever more atten- tively—indicate that the territorial concept of the parish must now be cast aside as powerless to evangelize the modern world.

We can never overestimate the force which groups exert upon the minds and the lives of individuals. It seems that life today is designed, like some frightful machine, to melt enormous blocs of society together.And among all those blocs the working class is the one that thinks most "Collectively."

Of course, we should not exaggerate; oversimplification would make us forget even the elementary laws of psychology. Despite the pressure brought to bear upon them, thank God, human beings can still find satisfying outlets in this world of ours. Many people think and react according to the pattern prevalent where they work or go for relaxation. Many wait for the press or the radio to hand them ready-made opinions. On the other hand, many revert to their own personal way of thinking when they reach home, reacting quite differently now that they are with their family, friends and neighbors.

Family and neighborhood create two very real environments. Even in our day, every human being is indelibly marked by the family which formed him and the family which he forms. The influence of one's neighborhood, though generally harder to detect, is none the less sure. There are some districts where priests can be certain of a hearty welcome, and others where they are considered kill-joys; some where the young can remain good without too much trouble, others where it is almost impossible; some where Catholic youth organizations recruit members year after year, and others where never a worker can be found or a team formed; some where it is customary, though no less spontaneous, for the people to help each other, and some where it is just as customary to squabble.

But the family and the neighborhood are precisely the two spheres in which the parish can operate. The parish can act upon persons because it deals with them at every stage of their development within the family—childhood, adolescence and maturity; and it does so by influencing not only individuals but also the family, and, in a more general way, the mentality of the neighborhood.

Indeed, the chief accomplishment of the parochial apostolate today seems to be its influence upon the home and the awakening of numerous small communities. As a result, the preaching of the word is no longer confined to the pulpit and many more people benefit by spiritual direction. The ideal of perfection is no longer one of individual advancement. The leaven has been put where it belongs. The parish priest now arouses and assembles the community, starting from the basic cell (which is the home), reaching the entire community (which is the parish), and including all the other more or less sporadic and enduring smaller communities formed to answer some particular need. Eventually these groups become centers whence good influences radiate, and points where human personality is no longer cramped but enabled to reach its full development, morally and spiritually as well as materially.

All these communities—and therefore the parish—contact the individual exactly when he has the best chance of shaking

off the yoke of the collectivity and the crippling weight of materialism. A man rediscovers himself on coming home after a
day's work. There he finds his love, his cares, his personal
problems; and if he does not lend an ear to the religious question at that time, he never will.

We should not, of course, foolishly imagine that present-day
wages, housing and home conditions are ideal for the development of personality. In fact, the housing shortage is one of the
worst social problems of our times. Still the fact remains that,
in his own home and neighborhood, a man can draw deeper
draughts of purer air. Family and neighborhood are the most
fertile soil for the word of God—a fact which experience has
pretty generally confirmed so far, especially with regard to the
working class—and we must acknowledge that the best work,
though slow and limited, has been done in these last few years
and starting with the parish.

Though organizations like the *Jeunesse Ouvrière Catholique*
have often tried to unite workingmen into groups, such groups
have rarely seen the light of day and even more rarely lived
through the night. It is difficult just to get the workers together
before or after their day at the factory; even union meetings
have the same problem. The proper psychological atmosphere
is lacking. Militant Catholic Actionists can do much to improve
those around them even while actually at work. But where
shall they find the time and the means to replenish the springs
of their activity? When and where shall new members be
recruited if not during leisure time and in the little communities formed by the various "sections" outside of working hours?

The answer to those questions brings us to the role of the
parish, since it is a fact that the most active and firmly established Catholic Action and Jocist teams are those which were
created, nourished and sustained by parishes. Others, we might
say, are rather more like makeshifts and stopgaps—though God
knows how often and how badly they are needed because of
shortcomings on the part of some parishes. As far as Catholic
Action is concerned, there are whole sections which resemble

deserts and where some sort of federation is the only thing that affords militant persons (often the self-taught products of spontaneous generation) a chance to work together and find for their spiritual life the nourishment their respective parishes cannot provide. Only too often do we meet splendid Catholics, eager warriors for Christ (conceived by some unaccountable power and admirably trained by no one save the Holy Spirit), who complain: "Our priests give us no encouragement whatever, no help at Sunday Mass, no solid food in their sermons, and no chance to meet with other parishioners."

Consider these all too common complaints, the precarious existence of Catholic Action units which get little or no support from the clergy, the lamentable deficiencies of parishes—consider all these and see whether it does not prove that the harvest is ripe, the task is urgent.

The *Jeunesse Ouvrière Catholique* has made astounding progress since its earliest members first made themselves heard in the workman's world. Yet, we remind ourselves of the resistance and the misunderstanding, not to mention the contradiction often endured at the hands of parish priests. We remember the many branches set up haphazardly only to round off the list of parish activities. We recall the sorrow apostles have expressed to us at not finding competent spiritual directors in their home parish, and we wonder at the great work this movement might have accomplished had it come upon the atmosphere, the fertile soil and the priests it had a right to expect in every parish. We wonder at the scope it would have taken on, the good it could have done had each unit in each parish only been recognized and supported as a *real* unit. The sight of such magnificent results obtained despite a lack of co-operation from parishes makes us ask, not whether parishes can be effectual, but how very effectual they can be if only they do their job properly.

The working class seems an infrangible bloc, unfamiliar with the religious problem; and we can well repeat, like Cardinal Suhard, that it is cut off from the Church by a thick wall or, like Abbé Godin, that it is avast mission field. For a pastor to think or say otherwise proves he has never dared look out from his bourgeois ivory tower or has systematically forgotten or deformed what he has seen.

All the same, we may say that a seven-league step has been taken since the start of the *Jeunesse Ouvrière Catholique* and that, being the first, it was the hardest step of all. No matter how arduous the work done by missionaries and how slow the progress made by the Church in subsequent years, it is always the first step—arriving in a country and setting up the first center of Catholicism—that is the most difficult.

Catholic Action in France may appear to have made little progress since 1927. It may not have spread far and wide but it certainly has struck its roots deep. Militant members have arisen just about everywhere. The genuine Christian may still be an exception in his shop but he is no longer an anomaly. This victory makes us look forward to greater victories to come. This first step proves that other steps can and will be taken. The only danger is, not that the reapers may become overconfident, but on the contrary that they may give up in despair. Here as elsewhere, people who work with constancy and enthusiasm have no illusions—illusions being nothing but the so-called realistic views of the bored or the impulsive, who value their work according to the quick and brilliant results they obtain.

Let each parish and each parish priest fully recognize his duties with regard to Catholic Action, especially toward the working class, and we shall soon see that the "illusions" of those who believe in it and in the parish are the least illusory of all.[2] We say "Catholic Action" and "parish" in the same

2   We wish, however, to make this point clear: in attributing such efficacy to the parish, we are not in the least underestimating the need of action on a broader scale. We feel, instead, that the work done in any parish must go hand in hand with that done by regional and national organizations. Everything we said about the immense sectors of life and thought makes this necessary. Militant laymen should be able to get together in order to map out a course of action and present a united front. If they are to take part in other movements for the temporal betterment of mankind, they will need chaplains, appointed by the

breath because we insist that Catholic Action must receive its impetus from the parish and that both go together.

More than anything else, our age needs that every corner of it be illuminated by an authentic and broadscaled witnessing to the gospel of Christ. Words persuade only insofar as they echo sincere conviction; example leads people on only if it is more than an external attitude. People distrust whatever smacks of propaganda, hypocrisy and self-interest.

Now, the plain truth is that in all the worlds which make up our modern world we do not see the leaven of the gospel exert its power. Moved and informed by other philosophies and dynamic concepts, they seem totally ignorant of Christian thought. The latter must be carried right to their very door, and the urgency of the task has given rise, of late, to any number of undertakings, some of which do the work of paratroopers behind the wall of materialism.

It would be ridiculous to expect immediate and tangible results from these undertakings. Asking a priest-worker whether he has seen the fruits of his chosen way of life is like pulling up newly planted shrubs every night to see whether they have taken root. Regardless of the orientation and the scope given to such movements (as, for example, the Mission Ouvrière mentioned by the French hierarchy when asking the priest-workers to modify their program), we know very well that those movements will not be enough and will not take up all of a priest's energy and devotion.

To hear certain people talk, you would think that the parish ministry was something outmoded, something engaged in temporarily to satisfy diocesan authorities and performed without enthusiasm as if their real work lay elsewhere.

In this matter, too, rigidity can lead one into error. Why must apostles always feel they are contradicting one another

hierarchy, to help them do the work of the Church on every level and in every field. We have insisted that the parish is indispensable for the mustering and animating of militant members, but we have not thereby lessened the need of other kinds of activity, for without them the activity of the parish would be sporadic anti ineffectual.

whereas they are complementing one another? You would think that one undertaking immediately precluded all others and that everything was outdated because of à new discovery in the apostolate. Though a certain area is illuminated by a beacon, there may be obstacles within the area that cast shadows and therefore must be lit from behind. Even so, it is expedient and urgent that the light of the gospel be enkindled behind the wall which separates the working class from Christ and the Church.

What does that mean concretely? It means that those spheres which seem impervious to Revelation must be shown an authentic example of the Christian life which will teach them the value of that life and lead them to imitate it. It means, furthermore, that Christ must be introduced where His Church cannot be, that His gospel must be lived where He cannot be adored, and that a little charity must be practiced where the gospel cannot be preached in its entirety. But we should not forget that charity, the gospel, Christ and the Church are one and the same thing and that there can never be a genuine rev=elation without an explicit revelation of Christ and His Church.

Some cannot bear the full brightness of the light and others, in their search, do not think they can find it in the visible Church. Unfortunately, many of our most sincere contempo=raries experience difficulty in seeing the fascinating Christ in the clergy; they find it hard to hear a faithful echo of the gos=pel in our Sunday sermons; and they have even more trouble recognizing modern parishes as the descendants of the early Christian communities.

Must we for that reason abolish all parishes, eliminate all sermons and dismiss all the clergy? Would it not, instead, be wiser and more expedient to restore to them their truly Christian savor? Revealing the Church means, not so much camouflaging it, but showing it as it ought to be and is in the mind of Christ, and making it what it should be.

Whether we like it or not, the Church, for our contempo=raries, is the hierarchy and each parish church, together with those who run it and those who live around it. Especially of the crowds is it true that their contact with the Church is made through the parish; they see the Church and deal with it through the parish. When they say "clergy," they mean the pastor and the curates who work in their midst. When there is an official religious act to be performed, they go to their parish church. Whether arranging for baptism or the publication of marriage banns or enrolling their children in a Christian doc‹ trine class, they go to the sacristy or the rectory. It may be a wedding or a funeral, but everything revolves around the parish church. Even the laborer who has been greatly impressed by the example of a fellow workman or a priest‹worker must some day ring the rectory doorbell or assist at a church service. Now, suppose he has been drawn there by the ideal of the gospel and, coming in during the sermon, hears nothing but a talk on money and collections. Suppose he has been led on by his need for a sense of community and finds only a shapeless, loosely knit group of worshipers at high Mass. Or suppose he has conceived a lofty notion of Christian charity and is received in the sacristy just as if it were a business office. If such things happen, you may be sure that any lesson put across at home or at work by priest or layman will be dangerously overshadowed by the almost official contradiction met with at church.

It would be ridiculous, however, to make the parish's func‹ tion something purely negative when it, too, in every phase of its life and activity, can bear glorious witness to the gospel. Let a parish do away with class consciousness and price‹lists, for instance, and not only will the faithful few be impressed by the change—they may even be the last to appreciate it—but it will soon be the topic of conversation in every factory. To take another example; a young couple come to the rectory and make arrangements for their wedding. They cannot help think‹ ing seriously of more important matters if the priest, instead of explaining a complex scale of rates for carpets, music and decorations, dwells primarily and exclusively on preparation for their entire married life. If Christians everywhere showed real brotherly love for one and all, and if it were a matter of course to find the spirit of Christ in cities or wherever there is a job to be done, a problem to be settled, or a cause to be supported, such examples of charity would not redound to the praise of one man's convictions and devotedness but would make people look to the very source of that general spirit.

For such witnessing to be genuine and effective in the world of today, it cannot be the work of a few. No, every single Catholic has to understand his duties toward the very life of society and react in every place and circumstance according to the doctrine of the gospels. Naturally, we have to make allowances for human weakness (and our contemporaries are quite understanding on that score), but until Christians as a whole will not be showing the world the true likeness of Christ. There are two alternatives: either everything that bears the name of Christian will live up to its ideal and thus enlighten the world, or it will fall short and sporadically flame and flicker.

Now, in our mind, the agency chiefly responsible for this united action is the parish; first, because the parish is the center where Catholics meet in a body, and then because the essential work of parish priests is to summon and sustain apostles.

From a purely utilitarian and even from a tactical viewpoint, the most elementary strategy requires that the apostolate depend upon the parish. We need paratroopers, as we have said; still in all, the spreading of the kingdom is the work of the masses: Though it is only too true that our good Catholics, as a whole, are often torpid, we should not declare them hopeless and accuse them of every crime. After all, they are people who have remained faithful to the Church, and, in our modern world, that fact alone bespeaks a certain amount of good will, moral stamina and love of Christ. Their stamina may not always have been well developed or properly oriented, but is that a reason to let it remain unused any longer? As soon as we make them want to act, they say, "Tell us what we should do." It would be better, no doubt, if they had enough initiative to discover it for themselves and knew how to reduce their ideal to practice; but it is none the less true that many of them are ready to give themselves unsparingly, to assist the clergy, to let their belief shine out over the world.

We must confess at the outset that the job is a tremendous one, bigger than all of us. Any priest who tries to stimulate souls to action, be they youths or whole families, soon gets a feeling of helplessness before the magnitude of the task and in no time exhausts his store of time and energy. No one can hope to influence more than a relatively small group of his fellow men; but the more a priest does, the more he finds to do—a fact which can easily make him flit from one thing to another or sink into discouragement. There can never be enough priests to fill the need and it would be a serious mistake, almost a heresy with regard to Catholic Action, if there were. Priests are not supposed to take the place of militant laymen but rather must they find and develop such laymen. Never numerous enough to be everywhere, priests must be posted at strategic points. But if in their parishes they act, not as administrators but as awakeners, they will find many souls who can apply their own limited activity to an indefinite number of concentric spheres. This work will progress slowly, and we will never live to see the masses converted. Actually, these masses are like a country which can be conquered only yard by yard. This does not mean, however, that the purely apostolic work inspired and guided by the parishes is less effective than the many paratrooping missions organized independently of any parish.

Moreover, conversion work, fascinating as it may be for any Catholic, is not the most urgent of our present duties. The important thing, as we have said, is that every Catholic should live his religion to the full. What we need is mature lay Catholics, and not somewhat childish ones who possess good will but are afraid to move without orders from their pastor. But this again is the lookout of the parish. Clearly, parishioners will remain immature just as long as pastors are content to lead them from on high like almighty Jupiters. That kind of leadership does not call for supermen; but to develop initiative, to work with the whole parish as a team, to remain in the background and let the parishioners assume their own respon‡ sibilities, that calls, for real leaders and not adjutants. Never will we have a mature laity until our parishes have priests of this caliber in tactical positions. To want to use them elsewhere is, in our opinion, a grave mistake.

If the situation in a parish needs changing or improving, that is all the more reason for rallying around. The transformation cannot be wrought by ignoring facts, and even less can the job be entrusted to such as refuse to see or change anything. This work is delicate, difficult, and it requires open minds and ready devotedness. Must all the valor and dynamism of our young clergy spend itself on projects and techniques that have nothing to recommend them but their newness, and cast aside as unimportant the basic, essential work which alone can keep them from building on sand?

The fact of the matter is that nowadays, when other duties seem more spectacular and allow for no end of versatility, parish work appears dull and definitely short on glamor. And there is a lot of truth in this view, for, as a priest once said to me, "It is easy to turn a cure into a sinecure." If a priest, however, realizes how much there is to be done, if he tirelessly studies ends and means, and concentrates on them without, for all that, closing his mind to new problems and methods, he will spend many a sleepless night and at death will doubtlessly bewail the fact that his work is still unfinished. The job of the parish priest is a difficult one, long‡drawn‡out and often monotonous. It takes patience and calls, not for such as love to draw up tidy reports and collect laurel wreaths, but for humble workers who have the will to tackle a tough job and do it well. ✛

⊹[3]⊹
All Things to All Men

THE INCONSTANT ARE not drawn to parish work since, for reasons just explained, it is not their cup of tea.

A pastor does the work at hand as it is; or, more correctly, he does the work handed him to do, being at the disposition of superiors who send him where he is needed, not to work a while and move on, but to effect the slow but sure transformation of his parish.

His primary duty is to see the situation as it is, and not as he would want it to be. That constitutes his first major problem, for we all tend to call good what we wish to retain and bad what we can easily change. It is always a great temptation to say that our predecessor accomplished nothing and to strike out in exactly the opposite direction, as if to build ourselves a pedestal on the ruins of his work or to assert ourselves by discrediting him.

A pastor must see things as they are because he has no right to pick and choose only the jobs that suit him. He may prefer one aspect of the ministry—working with children or adolescents, for instance, or perhaps with adults. He may have a special liking for confession or an aptitude for preaching. He may be so drawn to the poor that if he listened to himself he would spend all his time visiting them and solving their problems. Perhaps he would rather work among the sick. Or again he may be ideally suited to serve as chaplain for some Catholic Action group. The truth is that all his qualifications can help him in the ministry but that he may not concentrate exclusively on any one of them or even be dominated by one.

A pastor must be able to do everything. He undertakes whatever task awaits him with all the attendant circumstances of person, time and place, and sees it through to the end without being carried away by whims or weighted down with weariness.

He takes charge of children's summer schools, young people's sodalities, social clubs or family groups exactly as they are, since it is not he who has chosen them. He may find docile, devoted, intelligent workers in some quarters and gaily medio‚ cre ones in others. Yet all of them have been entrusted to him in the same way and he does not know which ones the Lord will eventually call to be His chosen apostles. He is not dealing with hypothetical characters but with the real people God has placed in his care. His mission does not consist in forming or perfecting a splendid Catholic Action unit, but rather in tending the flock he finds in the pasture turned over to him.

Even though he does everything in his power for such units, he should expect deceiving ups and downs and new difficulties each day. At any time he may encounter a youngster who shows signs of ill will, find that someone he was counting on has suddenly gone away, or sense some unaccountable hostility which may well undermine all his labors.

At certain moments, no doubt, he will have to assert his authority, yet his authority is not like that of an executive or even of a professor. He has no right to get rid of people, simply throwing them out because they bother him; and before deciding on such a course, he has to weigh the matter with infinite care.

No, the pastor cannot be a creature of whims. Neither can he put his work aside when it becomes tedious. Quite the contrary: he grows old with his flock and his heaviest cross often consists in seeing no improvement in it. How can he tell whether his efforts have borne fruit over the years? Some parishes make promising beginnings, but lasting success is no surer for all that.

With time, they may seem ready to scale the heights. Still the shepherd of souls should not grow complacent or rest on his laurels. Instead, he must ever keep his eye on what has yet to be undertaken, perfected, transformed.

Only those who have been engaged in parish work can appre‚ ciate what it is to have heart and soul constantly whipped and crucified by the problems it poses. To get some idea of their difficulties, we need only try to imagine the details connected with merely visiting the sick or with planning a feast which will draw the crowds and have missionary significance. Is it surprising, then, that at times priests are sorely tempted to turn to some type of work that allows for more freedom and variety?

And yet is there a more eminently priestly work than this? The pastor does not choose what he wants to do; he has to do everything.

He is an educator, but his pupils represent every social condition and all ages—children, adolescents and especially adults. By "children" we mean all the children in the parish, the children of common laborers as well as those of the rich. And by "adults" we mean, not a group, but all of them as far as possible, individually or collectively, directly or indirectly.

In his parish the priest is specifically a teacher of spirituality. He can be an educator even though he does not spend the better part of each day teaching some science or secular art; in fact, the more he endeavors to work on a spiritual plane, the better he will accomplish his task. Without pretense he can be a religious educator his whole life long; for he is a priest, and solely a priest.

He may have a special love for the poor. Well, they will not be lacking in any parish—all kinds of them: those who come to the rectory, the real poor or the professional beggars (and how poor *they* are!), and those who will not come and whose plight you have to guess and relieve secretly.

Could such a priest possibly dream of devoting his life to relief work? If he did, he would have to choose one type of case and specialize in it; then if someone came who did not fit into his particular line of work, he would have to say, "Sorry, but we can't do anything for you." One day in the sacristy will prove to anyone that each parish presents every possible kind of prob= lem. Then there are strikes, shutdowns and housing shortages, and, above all, those unforeseen, exceptional cases which are always the most tragic and the hardest to solve. Such is the lot of every priest who keeps both his heart and his eyes open.

We have not mentioned the spiritually poor, and yet how often parish priests hear people say, "I don't go to church and I have no faith; still I come to see you and I tell you things I couldn't tell anyone else."

More than any other priest the shepherd of souls has to be a preacher of the word. It is impossible to overestimate the power of sermons when pastor and curates take pains to make them instructive, timely and appealing. The vitality of a parish, as well as the inspiration given Catholic Actionists and the nour= ishment afforded the spiritual life of all the faithful, depends to a large extent on the quality of the preaching done there. To communicate the life in the word of life, the pastor and his assistants must know how to speak and hold the interest of their listeners. In passing, we should like to say that any priest can learn to deliver interesting and worth while sermons if only he works and practices in collaboration with his fellow priests. But that subject would lead us too far afield.

The parish priest, more than any other, must be a preacher and a good one. Unlike professional speakers, he is beset by this difficulty; he has to preach every Sunday, on every feast, and at every meeting held in the parish. Though he has been rehashing his sermon outlines for the past five or ten years, he must continue doing so not only because someone may remem= ber them but because there is so much to say and because time and the human mind march on. He cannot repeat; rather, he must ever renew his matter and his manner of presenting it. Practice should make him perfect but not give him that glibness which turns sermons into a wearisome waste of time and makes parishioners very clever at avoiding them. On the other hand, if his sermons are vital and make demands on the congregation, you will find everyone in the parish telling his neighbor he considers them an integral part of his week and could not get along without them.

Who can deliver a more effective sermon than a shepherd of souls? Who is in a better position than he to know his hearers, their needs and reactions, to know what he should say and how he should say it? Is there any other preacher who can follow his charges as closely as he in the progress they make and the changes they undergo, through all their anxieties, their temporal and spiritual cares? No one, therefore, is better qualified to talk their language and be understood by them, to teach them how to react and embody spiritual values in their whole life. But that requires observation, thought, work, and it is a difficult job.

We hope no one will be surprised to hear us say that the parish priest is, more than anyone, a chaplain for Catholic Action units. We have already said how indispensable the parish is for the functioning and progress of Catholic Action. We may go further and state that it is the very source of Catholic Action. What do we mean when we say that the pastor has been entrusted with the care of souls? We mean it is his mission to enkindle the Christian spirit in everyone confided to him. And that he can best do by making his parishioners conscious of their responsibilities. For too long now we have narrowed those responsibilities down to individual prayer and personal morality. But in this age, when everything takes on a social and cosmic meaning, Catholics have to work together at common tasks; and it is doubtlessly because preceding generations failed to do so that they allowed the world to grow pagan in every sphere. A Catholic is not someone who goes to church on Sunday and receives at Easter, contributes to the support of the Church and marches in all the processions. A Catholic is someone who, everywhere and in all circumstances, strives to live according to the gospel. A Catholic is someone who loves Christ, is proud of Him, wants Him to be known and loved, and tries to establish His kingdom of love throughout the world. Now, people do not think of these things spontaneously or, if they do, they soon forget them in the rush of egoism and daily living. But that is precisely where the pastor can do something; for he is the mandated spiritual director of his entire parish. As such, it is his duty to preach the gospel in season and out — not some vague, impractical gospel but one suited to the concrete circumstances of twentieth-century life; it is his duty to reprove, to denounce the sin of the world, and preach a crusade against it. What does that mean, practically, if not the conversion of Catholics into militant Catholic Actionists? We try to get apostles, not because we want to keep Catholic Action alive and growing, but because all Christians are called to be soldiers of Christ and have to answer that call. Where are those Christians? And who is in such daily contact with them, who knows them as well, visits and follows them as closely, and is as solicitous for their perfection as their pastor? If he fails to inspire and sustain them, those who have to do so in his stead can only fill the deficiency as well as contacts and circumstances allow. Pastors and curates are the only ones to do this work and until they do it, specialized Catholic Action will not reach its full stature, Christians Will be unchristian, the dough will fall flat, the Church will not really be the Church.

More than any other priest, the parish priest is a chaplain of specialized Catholic Action—not only in one place but every-where. In a parish where there are several curates, one may devote himself especially to workers, another to key men, and so on; yet in the sector entrusted to him each priest meets people from every rank and walk of life. In any case, parish work as a whole—the full mission of the priest—embraces each and every milieu, so that the shepherd of souls is, so to speak, a chaplain whose specialty is Everyman.

Here again his task is a hard one because it lies in a field which has yet to be tilled. Unless he is a realist, he will fail, since obedience to reality is the basic law of successful Catholic Action. That law applies to the level of organization which we may call Catholic Action units. But the parish is anterior to the unit, for it is there like a fertile field even before a unit has sprung up. The chaplain of a unit may find it already formed; but the parish priest finds only the field which his parish is, and, even when a unit already exists, the rest of the parish still stretches all about him like a vast fallow-ground. He cannot stop once a unit has been set up; he must keep on until the whole parish has become a body of specialized Catholic Action. Now, this field to be plowed and sown — that is reality, the reality whose laws, and whims sometimes, he must know and love or miserably fail.

And now for a remark made with malice toward none. A national director can launch new ideas, propose novel techniques, and suggest goals as fast as he dreams them up; and if he is clever at all, he will usually find enough enthusiastic followers throughout the country to put his ideas into practice. Needless to say, we cannot recommend such procedures to a national director. The parish priest, on the other hand, need not even be warned against them. If he has illusions, cold facts will soon make him come down to earth in spite of himself. He cannot move without contemplating his parishioners and asking himself what he has to work with, what sort of people they are, what they have to offer, and what they can do. Let him act otherwise, and he will fail.

The very factors which make parish work long and hard also guarantee its effectiveness. Here the demands made upon a priest betoken success. His task is difficult because it leaves no room for fancy; and it leaves no room for fancy because he must perform it, not in the clouds or in the realm of abstract thought, but in the midst of the most objective, immediate and gripping reality.

Time is no respecter of things wrought without regard for it, whereas those done in accordance with its laws are likely to be solid and lasting achievements. The fundamental rule for parish ministry is: Know and be known. Christ puts it even more plainly when describing the Good Shepherd: "I know mine and mine know me." Mutual knowledge of this sort takes time, grows ever more intimate and is never over; the deeper it is, the more possibilities it offers.

The shepherd knows his sheep. In a rural parish the pastor can get around to visiting every family in a few months' time. He soon recognizes every face and even starts to sense the sympathy, indifference or hostility hidden behind it. Still his knowledge will grow with the months and the years. Grad-ually he comes to know every family's problems for having heard about them or having been asked to help solve them. He becomes familiar with the difficulties of individuals too. Of course, many mysteries will never be explained to him, but no priest can spend years among his people without learning the story of this or that family, this or that piece of good or ill fortune. Over the years, he not only knows but lives out everyone's story. There is always one generation he baptized, one he prepared for first Communion and others which are growing old and passing on. The longer he lives, the more he knows and the more everyone realizes it. He knows his parish and his parishioners.

A city pastor, on the contrary, cannot get to know every-one. There are many people of whose names and existence he must ever remain ignorant. In large suburban or city parishes the majority will be strangers to him, and broad areas of life and thought will escape him. That is a fact he must face but never cease to bewail. Yet, who can know this multitude better than he — or better than they, since priests work together as a team? Every day a priest meets more families and receives new callers. With each priest exploring on his own the area assigned to him, entire districts are eventually discovered, and, if not wholly illuminated, at least brought within the range of the Light. Each priest can then acquaint his team mates with what he has learned and those he has met, though it is by no means necessary for each single priest to know everything and everyone personally. As was stated earlier, the "shepherd of souls" is not only the pastor or the curates but all of them together, and it is essential that the collective shepherd have a true and vital concept of what his parish is.

Finally, the city priest, almost as well as his brother in the country, comes to know the reactions of his flock. He bears them within himself and lives them, lives their life. He senses what has to be said or left unsaid. He realizes that he can count on some and must be wary of others. He foresees the possible results of what he says and undertakes. Not only can he preach or preside over a meeting without being advised, but if he has any tact and experience he knows spontaneously how best to get his message across. He is ever mindful of his parishioners, their way of life, their likes and dislikes. He speaks their lan= guage and has a better chance of being understood. Seen in the right light, this knowledge appears, not as another new technique, but as a source of power hard to overestimate.

The shepherd of souls knows his sheep and his sheep know him. In the rectory or the sacristy, the church or the street, the priest is at the disposition of the faithful from morning till night. He should be and he is always available, and that is how most people think of him. At first even this idea of him is superfi= cial, but gradually it grows deeper as circumstances justify it. People who come to see him find him gracious. They feel that here is someone who is trying to understand their problems, someone who bears their burden with them. They tell him not only their spiritual difficulties but all sorts of worries and cares. They notice that he listens, thinks, answers and, over and above answering, takes matters in hand as much as he can, sheds light in darkness, and takes the necessary steps to remedy a situation.

If he does these things, the entire flock will soon know its shepherd, for those who know him will be telling others about him. Slowly but surely he becomes a figure in the eyes of his parishioners. And that is where he can give his most telling testimony; that is where he must reproduce as closely as possible the likeness of Christ—good, understanding, gentle and firm at the same time. "It's a great, thing to have a good priest in a district," a peasant once said to me while describing the local pastor in a voice full of admiration for his genuinely priestly ministry.

People do not ask their pastor to be an intellectual giant, a brilliant organizer or an intrepid fighter. No, they want him to be first and foremost—and exclusively—a priest. Even those who approach him for material assistance pay special note to the way he receives them. Though their business be secular, what they are looking for is the charity of Christ. Let us not forget that the priest, more than anyone else, is considered the witness par excellence to the Church. For all practical purposes we can say that in the mind of the faithful he and his fellow priests *are* the Church.

It may be objected that we have painted too idealized a picture of the country priest, and indeed the situation in densely populated suburbs is not as romantically perfect as sometimes pictured. When you consider a priest in any large city, you are struck first of all, not by the thought that he is well known, but rather that hardly anyone can possibly know him. Still, as we have pointed out, that priest is not one man; he is part of a team, and we should not undervalue the power of it.

In this matter of "learning" a parish, teamwork is a process of multiplication, not mere addition. What matters far more than the sum of the findings of individual priests is the views of the team, its ideas, and its joint efforts. If they are the product of constant co-operation, those views will be doubly sound, those ideas broader and deeper, those efforts more pertinent and effective. Far from being a mere research group, a team of this kind is a cell living in the midst of the faithful, trying to understand their reactions better, checking and correcting their opinions. It is, furthermore, a smaller and more earnest community which prays at the center of that larger community, the parish, We must not think of it as a committee studying problems of sociology or psychology. To put the matter briefly, a team is a single soul, a single heart, trying to beat and live in unison with the parish. It is a source of power, and of power that has not yet been guessed.

A team, moreover, consists not only in a group of priests but soon includes those who, in their own small or big way, regularly or intermittently, take part in the parish apostolate. When clergy and laity join forces to study their parish, it is obvious how greatly the laity can help. It will supply names, addresses and personal information, but especially it will express viewpoints and value judgments closely bound up with everyday life. As the priestly team keeps doing its work, the lay half of the team takes shape, adheres to it, encircles and grows with it.

Time is the big factor here. No passing force can ever have the impact of a team knit more closely together with every day. Our failure to appreciate this reservoir of strength has kept us from getting the best out of our parishes. As a result, they have lost their vigor and paralysis has set in. A parish has many means of carrying on its apostolate, all of which work better the more we know about men and their environment; and if only we realize this fact, we can then gauge the possibilities of the basic means.

Of those means we should like to list just a few. The pastor has at his disposal a pulpit and a congregation which he does not have to call together; and since he knows his sheep, it depends entirely upon him whether he will or will not be heard. By "pul‹ pit" we mean not only his preaching of sermons but his teaching of catechism classes attended by many or most of the children in the parish. There is no generation which he does not influ‹ ence. God alone knows how often he can reach parents through their children if only he knows how to make the most of every opportunity. The pulpit, again, is the remarks he makes at every meeting. It is the parish bulletin and all types of publications.

In addition, we could mention the many societies and orga‹ nizations, social and charitable, which have sprung up in the last few decades. These groups and undertakings represent many different corners of the parish. Granted that they have developed rather haphazardly, they are none the less a strik‹ ing proof of all the human and material resources the parish holds. And, we repeat, if they were seconded by a, thorough knowledge of the people and their environment, many withered branches would doubtlessly have to be left for the fire, but ever so many more could be given a new life and made to bear fruit.

One glance at this wealth of material, moral Jund spiritual resources, and we need no longer ask ourselves, "Is there any‹ thing the parish can do?" but rather, "Why isn't it doing more?"

No nation-wide movement and no political party can boast of so many supporters from all quarters, so many enthusiasts totally dedicated to their cause (we are thinking, for example, of all the nuns who assist parish priests), or such a variety of ways and means as can that nation's parishes as a whole. What we lack is, not possibilities and methods, but men—men with enough zeal to care and work without ceasing, men with enough humility to face the facts and see each problem as it really is, men who are so united with God that it is always He who is working through them. With such men in a parish, we no longer have to worry about it: it will march on confidently, progress and discover new possibilities at every turn.

We do not realize how much could be accomplished by parish work if it were always genuine parish work. ✠

✠[4]✠
The Sons of Charity

*H*ISTORY SHOWS US that the religious life has been of extraordinary benefit to the Church.

Some consider the religious life as a means of enhancing their priestly consecration, of stabilizing their spiritual life or of enlarging the scope of their apostolate. Some deem it an ideal in itself. But in dedicating themselves both groups are seeking the glory of God. By utterly surrendering their heart and their will, all that they are and all that they have, they are saying, "Lord, this one act is the homage we want to offer You, by our whole life and the use we make of it, for our life and everything You have given us."

Consecrating oneself to God means undergoing a long and arduous preparation in order to attain a peak of fervor and then trying to remain there, adjusting one's whole life to that level—burning one's bridges behind one, in a manner of speak-ing, so as to find oneself stripped of everything and locked in the arms of God.

That is the goal of the religious life. It is what everyone on profession day wants to reach, somehow or other. For exam-ples of bridge burning consider the hermits who went into the desert to live a life of contemplation, the monks who surrender their will into the hands of their abbot, and the girls who shut themselves off from the world behind cloister and grille. Freed thus from the temptation of going back on their word, they can try to keep their eyes fixed on God alone.

Though the religious life was at first contemplative, over the years this perfect consecration to the service of God came to be prized as a marvelous instrument in the service of the Church. As urgent and difficult, not to say heroic, tasks confronted them, men of good will understood that those very tasks could be a means of consecrating themselves to God. They knew such work required dogged perseverance and not just a short-lived enthusiasm, and they saw that the religious life was their best guarantee of steadfastness.

If people can renounce the world to give themselves up wholly to contemplation, why can they not push fear aside to ransom captives, leave their family to evangelize the natives of far-off countries, and forget their comfort when duty bids them assist the poor? Whenever zeal and charity have found a new objective, it has become a means of asceticism for souls who wanted to give themselves completely to Christ. In this way the religious life offered its followers a chance to serve God and neighbor and to consecrate themselves entirely to His glory, at the same time spreading that glory throughout the world and practicing in every detail of daily life the twofold commandment "Thou shalt love the Lord thy God with thy whole strength, and thy neighbor as thyself for the love of God."

Nowadays no one who longs for the extension of God's king- dom can help being preoccupied with the tremendous problems presented by the evangelizing of the working class. It is like a vast untilled field: the further we walk through it, the more we realize how much must be done before it can be reclaimed.

For many years now, excessive industrialization has been making throngs move from the country to the city. Every year villages are deserted and whole generations are swallowed up by the suburbs of large manufacturing centers. Just as these droves come to offer their physical and intellectual assets to industry, so must others from among them also look toward the city, and follow them there to live among them as the priests they will need.

Bringing the gospel to the masses is an enormous and dif- ficult job. And now is the hour when a specialized body must rise up within the Church and be dedicated by vocation and vow to the evangelizing of the working class.

Young men in the Middle Ages dreamed of combining the life of a religious with that of a knight and dying on the battle- field in the service of God. How, then, can the youth of today help wanting to unite the service of God and the service of their fellow men, the love of the Church and the love of the working class? The crying need of the times must make them decide to live a life of poverty like their working brethren; they must make that poverty the substance of their religious asceticism and the pledge of their dedication to the evangelizing of the modern world.

To be ever more truly priests, they should put aside every= thing that could assure them an easy life, comfort, success and promotions; and, having done so, they might join a religious family and devote themselves for good and all to the exclusive apostolate of the working=man. For, surely, young men called to the priesthood may aspire to linking their whole life and future to the fate of the working class. And, surely, in view of such a gigantic and thankless task, that could be the goal of a normal congregation within the Church.

The truth is that more and more aspirants to the priesthood yearn solely to bring the gospel to the working class. Never before have they seen the multitude of problems involved so clearly or desired so vehemently to solve them. Yet the very number and variety of jobs to be done presents a danger. There is so much to catch their eye that, guided by their own likes and dislikes, they may choose their own mission. Vocation and mis= sion, however, are two different things. God calls a person, and, so that he may know he is called, gives his certain signs, such as attraction, aptitudes and circumstances, which mean some= thing only when evaluated and accepted by proper ecclesiastical authority. It remains true, of course, that a vocation is detected to a great extent by the person who hears the call. Once he has heard it, furthermore, he can answer it or not at his own risk.

Not so a mission. No one assumes a mission; he receives it. He may have a chance to ask for one, but the task he is doing becomes a mission only when he is sent, only when he has received his orders. Normally, he has a vocation first and receives a mission later, and the mission often makes the voca= tion more specific by concretizing it. When a person realizes .

he has a missionary vocation, he feels that he has been called someday to receive a definite mission in an area which has never had the faith or has lost it. Going to the ecclesiastical authority in that area, he says, "Here I am. I am ready to receive a mission from you in your territory."

To repeat, it is only natural that many young men today should want to volunteer for all the tasks and missions which the evangelizing of the working class entails. It is only natural, too, that the Church should see a specialized body rise up within itself wholly devoted to parish work, and to parish work among the laboring class.

His awareness of present-day needs and the desire for some form of real religious life led Père Anizan to conceive the idea of the Congregation of the Sons of Charity. His dream was to combine parish life and religious life, to practice poverty by living among the poor and the workers, to spend himself in the service of God by spending himself in his priestly ministry. With the intuition of a genius and thanks to his long experience in the apostolate, he understood the primacy and the efficacy of priestly work. Sensing the high mysticism and the essential realism of the twofold vocation, he invited his followers to live the life of pastors and curates within the framework of the religious life.

It is easy to see all the advantages to be derived from such a specialized group entirely given over to its particular work; from a body of men recruited from all corners and every walk and station in life, and united by the wish, the will, to do the same vital work.

When they meet, they do not have to start a conversation. They pursue the one which began in the soul of their founder and in their own soul when first they glimpsed the task that lay ahead of them. At each meeting they only go on with the same dialogue. Strangers yesterday, they speak the same language today. They are now united into one family by a common denominator, by the same spirit; and the variety of their temperaments, characters and qualifications will only increase the value of their common resources.

Everything helps to unify their efforts. Their ascetical life and their studies are cut out for them by their mission and their ministry. When the time comes for some to specialize—and it will come—they will be guided, not by personal preferences and momentary interest or weariness, but by their own fitness as judged by their fellow workers and especially by their supe‹ riors in view of the needs of the group.

The decisive factor is the work to be done rather than a lik‹ ing for it. You join a religious community so that its work may be done and not so that you may have the pleasure of doing it yourself. You join a missionary society so that the mission‹ ary work may be accomplished and not so that you may give yourself a mission. It is the same with a young woman who enters a nursing congregation: she comes that the sick may be cared for, not necessarily that she may care for them herself. The only thing that matters is the work itself. You come only to lose yourself in it, to give yourself to it body and soul. You are not looking for success or personal satisfaction, but you are irresistibly drawn on by every challenge the times offer. The work may rack and drive you mercilessly. You may be judged a worthless instrument and even cast aside. More exactly, you will be lost in the mass of workingmen and never ask yourself what you may get out of it all. The main concern is that the harvest be plentiful and that each reaper work hand in hand with his companions and not worry about getting credit for the bit he does.

In view of their special qualifications, efficient organization may make secretaries or treasurers out of a young girl who yearned to nurse the sick and a young man who dreamed of converting the natives in some distant land. They must, there‹ fore, be convinced that that is how they can best carry on the work in their own humble way. Joining a religious institute dedicated to the apostolate of the poor and the working class does not automatically mean a man will take over the job of Christianizing a certain neighborhood or pioneer a new phase of endeavor. But it does grant him the far more comforting guarantee that he will share, anonymously and selflessly, in a much broader realization of the general goal.

The various members of such a congregation can meet on common ground and help one another because they share the same views, but especially because they are united by their religious profession and must strive every day of their lives to attain their ideal, not by means of abstract ideas or emotional contemplation, but by a pooling of all their energy and labors.

A specialized body of this type will have to study the problems that stand in its way. That calls for meetings, for discussions and teamwork both within the parish and within the bigger team constituted by such a religious society. Thus will everyone benefit from the knowledge and initiative of individuals. Inspired as it is by their deep and undivided devotion to their work—the parish and the apostolate of the workingman—their specialization will be highly effective and proof against the dangers it might otherwise contain.

The amazing power of a religious congregation comes from the fact that its members, who join it in the springtime of life, are constantly shielded against the desire to take back their offering, conscious that they are not laboring alone but are backed up by other men who have consecrated themselves to work for the Lord with the same fervor and tenacity of purpose. Many a young man who wants to become a priest and is considering parish work balks at what he sees around him. It may be a country pastor who has lived so close (in one sense) to his people that he is now nothing but a rustic himself. The only difference is that he says Sunday Mass. Apart from that, his bees and his garden get as much attention as the spiritual welfare of his parishioners. Again, it may be a city pastor who has an easy time of it, free from care and snugly ensconced in the lap of ease—if not of luxury. How can the plight of the poor and the workingman ever break through the walls of his ivory tower and touch him? Parish life as lived by certain priests seems altogether too comfortable and business-like.

"Since we are giving up the world and consecrating ourselves to God, let us do so as wholeheartedly and generously as we can." These words of Emile Anizan's on leaving home voice the sentiments of so many young men on the threshold of the priesthood. They want to give their life up to God—but not so as to take it back or let it become sclerotic; not so as to enjoy the comfortable life their priesthood may eventually afford them. Consequently, they are afraid of parish work. Unwill= ing to become "pastors"—and the word as they use it has a pejorative meaning—they shun parish work even though they realize it is the most important of all. At any price they want to avoid the pitfalls into which they have seen others disappear.

The truth is, and we must admit it, that the parochial min= istry as generally conceived and carried out today holds some real dangers. Naturally, they are not inherent to that ministry, and, thanks be to God, many priests manage to overcome them and live as true priests and apostles in their parish.

Let us, however, be realistic. Isolation, a sort of sclerosis, the acquiring of a bourgeois mentality, routine and the more unfortunate effects of growing old all appear on such a large scale and cramp so many priestly lives as to seem the result, not of personal shortcomings, but of general laws. We may liken them to a set of circumstances which eventually win out over the best of intentions.

Consider a young curate who has spent himself unstintingly for three or four years, always finding the days too short to answer the endless demands his work made upon him. When suddenly named pastor of a rural parish, can he help looking with fear upon the isolation in store for him? From now on, he will be alone day in and day out; alone to think, to feel, to plan and undertake everything; alone in those inevitable moments of weariness; alone to pray in his church through the week; alone in his parish, since there is no one in whom he can really confide and the nearest priest is miles away. Too often the years spent in this solitude will wall him in a shell which his enthusiasm and generosity cannot break through. After ten years or so in country parishes, too many priests look back upon their dreams of long ago and feel like calling them illusions. Fortunately, teams have been organized in many deaneries and frequent conferences help to save the situation.

It is our fervent wish that the young priests who long for community life and teamwork may keep that longing alive till the end and be ever on the lookout to make their dream an actuality. We could hope too that the element of chance in the assignment of priests to various parishes might not dissolve existing teams or preclude fruitful meetings.

At first glance, there would seem to be less danger of isola=tion in the city, but the facts prove otherwise. Let us not even mention those priests who live quite alone in their quarters. We can only wonder at how completely the idea of the priestly community—as it existed in the days of Saint Augustine, for example—has been lost in the course of the centuries.

Isolation is a real threat even to priests who share the same life, gather around the same table and live under the same roof; for what we should fear most is, not physical or spatial, but moral isolation. Though they live together and work in the very same vineyard, many priests get so that they never discuss any=thing serious or exchange views on spirituality or the apostolate. Under such conditions, they almost necessarily lose their savor and their dynamism, and they surely lack the prodigious power they would derive from the backing up of a team.

On the other hand, mere membership in a religious con=gregation does not shield a priest from moral isolation. Nei=ther does profession automatically immunize him to all the defects, the selfishness and the pride which may plague him later. Kneeling together on the same kneelers, harkening to the same bell and calling themselves brothers is no guarantee that a group of men will share one dream, live the same spiritual life and work together. Nevertheless, it is true that, from its very foundation, every religious family and institute is haunted by a desire for the ever closer brotherhood and unity that come from sharing not only material possessions but also those gifts of mind and heart which God bestows on everyone. And until that community of life is achieved, their dream torments them and stands before them as a reproach,

Though past generations may not have understood this ideal of community life or seen the need of it, it seems that the younger men of today cannot ignore it and will find no rest till they have achieved it. In assigning pastor and assistants to a given parish a bishop may be thinking only of putting the right man in the right place, whereas the prime concern of a religious superior is to insure harmony among his subjects. Of course, he too can place his priests where they are most needed, but he should never forget his duty of making "one single, loving family," as Père Anizan said, out of the communi= nities committed to his care.

Now more than ever before, our young men are afraid of becom= ing bourgeois. And they have reason to be, since the temptation and the opportunity to settle for stuffy security dogs priests at every step. Rectories are often among the most comfortable and well=appointed houses in the neighborhood. Young curates start by buying a desk and often go on to fill their rooms with easy chairs, ottomans and knick=knacks, and sometimes with the kind of furniture you would expect to find in the home of a dowager.

The collections in certain parishes are quite gratifying—so much so that a priest may be tempted to set his heart on those parishes, and, once there, to benefit by the collections. Then, too, there are many ways of making people offer one a gift. We all know of such priests who live a life of great ease and lack nothing.[1]

---

1   We would not forget the many priests—pastors and curates, in the country and in the city—for whom the material side of life is a serious and harassing problem, Many of them have to do without a housekeeper because they can neither pay nor feed her. They live a life of poverty harder than religious know, a life that crucifies them day after day. Missionary priests sometimes come to a dechristianized

Despite everything we have said about it, there is something worse than this bourgeois love of comfort and material
well-being. Indeed, it is often a sign of bourgeois attitude of
heart. Priests who used to have time for all their parishioners
soon find it pleasanter to chat with the more cultured and educated, and much more enjoyable to deal with the well-to-do
than with the poor of the working class. Eventually, they keep
state or at least draw an enchanted circle within which they
practice their ministry.

Never would they have consented to such a state of affairs
in the beginning, but they soon found a host of good reasons
and excuses to justify attitudes that would have shocked them
a few years before. Aided and abetted by weariness and their
new-found "wisdom," they spend their time on whatever is
easiest and most eye-catching in the ministry. They represent
the bourgeois priest at his worst.

Religious poverty has been defined as the certitude of never
lacking anything, and there is perhaps as much truth in the
definition as there is danger attached to the vow. Freedom from
worry about shelter and food and clothing may very well be an
evangelical ideal, but it can also be an unmistakable effect of
laziness and egoism. Never having given a thought to material
problems throughout his adult life, a religious may too easily
forget how vexing such problems are to those who must wres-
tle with them.[2]

It is none the less true that all his life long poverty curbs
the desires of a faithful religious and keeps him from making

---

parish and ask for the pastor only to be told, "He must be at the rectory.
We haven't seen him for quite a while." On reaching the run-down,
deserted-looking rectory, they knock and, receiving no answer, walk
into an empty room where piles of cans and jars are the only sign of
life. In the next room they find the pastor sick in bed, too sick to get
up and tell someone and too completely forgotten for anyone to inquire.
He has been living alone for years. The cans and jars all about hint at
his poverty and solitude. No religious congregation knows such cold,
stark poverty as this.
2   The danger is far less serious for pastors and curates because of
their familiarity with all phases of parish work.

miserly calculations and setting something aside for a rainy day. We would find it hard to appreciate the freedom he enjoys in his every thought and deed from the simple fact that he never has to make provision for illness or old age. Should someone in a community be tempted to make things too cozy for himself, he is soon deterred by the superior and especially by his brethren. Should that someone be the superior himself—one who tends to ease the rules and makes life too comfortable—he can be stopped by the ideal that burns in the hearts of his subjects, for even the young religious have their say in the community chapter and are always there to cry out and keep the common will from growing slack.

Priests may be bothered by other temptations, more personal, more painful, and far more perilous. The life of many a priest has been utterly ruined by some lapse which came as a complete surprise in view of his past record and his present attitude. When a subdeacon offers himself to God, he gives himself with all the ardor of his young heart and is quite convinced he will be faithful to the end. He knows trials and temptations will assail him, but he trusts that with God's grace he may keep his word. Yet, how can he be sure that his bright hope, his fervor and the profound peace which his will and God's grace have wrought will last forever?

Sooner or later there are periods when one's interior life grows weak, when it may even sink temporarily into a dangerous lethargy. When the love of God wanes in one's heart, other loves creep in and claim it for themselves. Fatigue, too, harassing ministerial worries and late hours poring over problems set one's nerves on edge. Then again there are hours of discouragement, weariness and all sorts of trials. At such times a thoughtless word or action can be like the pebble which falls into a placid pool and breaks its surface into ever-widening waves of agitation. One unhappy word, spoken or heard, and the priest's heart feels its peace give way to a profound restlessness which will not be stilled. Sometimes temptation pounces upon him suddenly and brutally. Sometimes it gains admittance into his heart imperceptibly; and that is especially true of someone engaged in the care of souls, since his life is sedentary and consists largely of visits made or received. If weariness or spiritual anemia have deadened his will, he may wake up too late. At times, temptation comes from without, and it may be that his will is not strong enough to resist.

As could be expected, solitude, one of the worst temptations in its own right, only makes matters worse. In the dark night of isolation certain heartaches become too big to fight. At times one lacks the will and the strength to go seek help, or one loses all hope of finding it. And here again it will often be too late when one realizes the danger or, in a burst of energy, tries to clutch at some weapon to ward it off.

It is an incontestable fact that in these matters religious profession is no magic wand. The vow does not confirm a soul in virtue for good and all. On the other hand, religious life affords one an atmosphere, bounds, a superior and brethren, and these are most important in the hour of temptation.

Until the very end the framework of the religious life protects one imperceptibly against one's own weakness. Negatively, it offsets all manner of dangers. Positively, the whole spirit of a religious house helps by sustaining one's fervor. Sometimes, however, that is not enough, and there is no use pretending it is. In that case superior and brethren are an inestimable help. Take the superior, for instance. He is not just a pastor. Besides seeing to it that his parish functions properly, he must remember that his assistants are his sons and that he is largely responsible for their welfare. Then take one's fellow religious. The warmth that pervades a family is still one of the greatest safeguards against temptations of mind and heart. The very casualness and informality of brethren rubbing elbows day in and day out is a protection and a bulwark.

Some may smile and shrug their shoulders at these exterior means; some braggarts may rush into danger, sure they will emerge unscathed. But we do not think any priest's work has ever been seriously hindered by the use of such safeguards, whereas we do know that much good work has been definitely compromised because these helps, these supports, were not available or had been cast aside.

Should a priest fall into sin—and, alas! it is possible—the family we call a religious congregation proves an incomparably simple, immediate and sure means of salvation. A court-like or purely administrative approach to his plight could frighten him. Difficult as it may be, a conversation between superior and subject will always be that of father and son; whatever is said, the solution to the problem will be as merciful and efficacious as possible and their interview will end on a note of reconciliation and encouragement. We can hardly refrain from mentioning cases where priests might have been lost forever had not a single confidential talk with their superior put them back on the right road.

Besides isolation and discouragement, which are dangerous because they are temptations, there is another danger which is not a temptation but a law common to all men. We refer to growing old. All of us age imperceptibly. With every day we lose some of our physical energy, notice it and tell others; our minds grow duller and dimmer too, but we notice it less and tell no one. Our best qualities—versatility, courage, ini-tiative—give way to a sort of unconscious complacency at the sight of our achievements and of traditional ways of acting. For prudence we substitute timidity.

No one can escape this law. We need only look around to see how many parishes suffer from the effects of it. Once active and enterprising but now short-winded, many a pastor ends by suffocating the parish into which he had once breathed life.

What can be done about it? Canon Law says that the pastor of any parish, whether in Christian or in pagan lands, is irre-movable. Unless guilty of some serious offense, he may stay at his post till death. Thus we sometimes see huge city parishes which would tax even the strongest remain in the hands of octogénarians. Why, not a single grocery store could survive with such an old manager as these parishes have!

A religious, on the contrary, is not irremovable. Rather, he is at the disposition of his superiors, secular and religious, and not only does Canon Law not grant him any rights but his whole religious ideal keeps him from even desiring any. Free from ridiculous dreams of advancement, he knows he need not make a career for himself, Consequently, when age makes him inefficient, there is nothing to keep his superiors from giving him a less responsible position or sending him to a smaller parish. Many of us who were pastors are now curates once again—and without any bitterness. It is reassuring for a young man to know that as soon as he overrates himself and his responsibilities, as soon as self-love threatens to outstrip his zeal, his superior will step in and keep him from becoming useless or prejudicial to the cause.

Never for a moment would we think of drawing a parallel between the life of a secular priest and that of a religious. Never would we extol the religious life at the expense of the other, attributing a special virtue to it or calling it a safe harbor while criticizing the life of a secular priest as being full of danger. We are not boasting or patting ourselves on the back. All we are saying is this: we have réalized both our own weakness and the problems and perils that beset us, and, unwilling to live our entire priestly life amid the fluctuations of an unending war, we have chosen the religious life as a protection, as a staff to support us, and especially as a means of maintaining in our hearts the fervor of our youth.

We must finish our inventory, however, before exposing at length the essence and the glory of the religious ideal. Let us consider the many ways in which a congregation helps its members live their priesthood to the full. First of all, there is the novitiate—a difficult period of testing, a serious preparation for the priesthood. It is a time of chiseling and polishing which finally fashions the workingman's priest.

Far from being purely negative and austere, the novitiate is a group of young men, strangers till yesterday, who know at first sight that they have all shared the same dream and want to dedicate their whole life to it. They are in the novitiate, not only to study as in the seminary, but to develop their character and strengthen their will together. For an entire year they work hand in hand, with the tools of prayer, penance and meditation, to become more and more like their ideal. Emulation for them looks beyond scholastic or technical achievement to moral per= fection and union with God. Together they try to increase their love for the poor and the working class and to equip themselves for the mission awaiting them.

Almost beyond imagining are the benefits to be derived from a year of spirituality (either before or after the regular seminary studies) which they discuss among themselves, think out anew, and above all apply to their daily lives. At every step of their ministry, in years to come, that particular training will assist them both in giving spiritual direction and in preaching retreats and days of recollection. That year will be fruitful from even a purely practical viewpoint.

The novitiate reaches its consummation in the vows, which stand like guards strategically posted at the three most vulner= able approaches to the human heart. Indeed, the temptations to amass riches, yield to the flesh, and become proud and inde= pendent assail a priest his whole life through; and though the vows, we repeat, do not confirm a religious in virtue, they do serve as three points on which superior and subject may focus their attention and concentrate their efforts.

After our Lord Jesus Christ had fasted forty days in the desert, the devil tempted Him. The temptations Christ under= went before entering upon His ministry have been recorded in the gospel, not by chance, but because they illustrate so well the three chief temptations that beset the apostle, and, specifically, the apostle of today. It seems as though Christ, full of justice and virtue, thought immediately of those who would continue His mission, and willed to warn them at the very beginning of the gospel against the major pitfalls that lie in their path.

"Since thou art hungry, bid these stones become loaves of bread." Just as Satan tempted Christ to use His power in order to satisfy His hunger, so may an apostle, and particularly a pastor, be tempted to use his ministry as a means of acquiring, over and above the necessities of life, things that will afford him comfort and ease.

"Cast thyself down from the temple and, if thou art the son of God, angels will come to hold thee up." Again, just as Satan tempted Christ to do something spectacular in order to win over the rabble, so may a priest be subtly tempted to leave the beaten path and strike out on his own, to be different and even seek a bit of adventure, to concentrate on the unusual and the striking on the pretext of spreading the kingdom of God.

"I will give thee all the kingdoms of the world it only thou wilt fall down and worship me." Satan thought he could dazzle Christ with earthly kingdoms. Christ, of course, was above that, but many of His disciples are sorely tempted to seek their own little kingdom instead of His. They make the parish their court and gather about themselves a circle of penitents, followers and admirers.

Setting aside the vow of chastity, which holds for secular as well as for religious priests, we see that the other vows, poverty and obedience, are ever-watchful sentinels set about the apostle's heart to rout temptation.

Furthermore, since resolutions and promises and even vows are not proof against time, religious have their rule to help them remain faithful till death. Naturally, there is a world of difference between a sincere quest for the spirit of the rule and a slavish adherence to the letter of it. The ideal, in any religious institute, does not consist in duplicating the found-er's achievements literally; it consists in finding out and doing whole-heartedly what he would do if he were living today. Still, we should not look down our noses at strict obedience and conscientious observance of details. The rule is always there to urge religious on when fervor has cooled and when, alone, they would not see clearly or have the courage to go further.

Among the many provisions of the rule, some monthly and yearly retreats, for example—are especially useful and enable a religious to get his bearings periodically. In a religious congregation such retreats are not optional and nothing about them is left to the choice and good will of the retreatants. The silence, the reaffirming of ideals by the superior, the whole atmosphere of the retreat house—all these are. carefully calculated to make a religious face essential facts and to cast a new light on things which may have grown dim in his mind during his year's ministry.

Even more deep-rooted and all-pervading than the rule is the common ideal that unites the members of any congregation. Obviously, they did not all join it with the same identical outlook, and they invest that ideal with a variety of tints and hues. Though time may even alter particular points of view, yet it is quite true that in every congregation there is a spirit which takes shape and lives on. If born of self-sufficiency and pride, that spirit may well prove a paralyzing agent; but if it is to animate the apostles our modern world needs, it must be conceived and constituted by young souls, strong, noble and daring.

On certain days, when our work is difficult and we keep reaping disappointment, discouragement dogs our steps. If at such times we see a team at work around us and remember that the older men have known the same trials and that the younger ones are looking ahead to them confidently, plunging into the fray with enthusiasm, we will very likely be able to fight off discouragement. Alone, a man may be a prey to discouragement; surrounded by his brethren, he can conquer it.

Chronologically, the last advantage a congregation offers is a home where old or sick priests may retire. Some may smile to hear us call it an advantage, a prop, an encouragement; and the young will surely say, "We'll see about that."

Certain professions offer their members the prospect of such a home as a haven of rest. That is not what we are doing; we do not invite young men to join our Institute so they may sit back and relax some day. But we do say this: it is difficult to imagine what a blessing such a house can be throughout life.

As we stated earlier, a religious need not worry about the future or provide for his old age. If he works and spends himself without reserve, God, through his superior, will take care of the future. This certainty makes it easier for a priest to submit his resignation when he knows the time has come.

Some may look scornfully at these old priests and make irreverent remarks that approach blasphemy. Yet what a warm, comforting atmosphere surrounds a gathering of tired apostles who have labored at different phases of the same work! How many old warriors in these houses look with joy at what the young are doing, applaud their undertakings, and fall asleep happy in the peace of the Lord because they know the work will go on!

May our Institute provide ever greater power and dynamism for the coming generations so that more generous, enlightened and loving apostles may rise up among the poor and the working class. Our Institute is only a means, but may it be the efficacious means of promoting the kingdom of God among all the outcasts. ✣

ABOUT THE AUTHOR

GEORGES MICHONNEAU was born in 1899, and at the age of 23 was ordained priest at Niort, in the diocese of Poitiers (France), after which he was appointed curate in the town of Châtellerault. Four years later, in 1926, he joined the Fils de la Charité (Sons of Charity), a religious congre‐ gation founded in 1918 in Paris for the evangelization of the urban working class. Soon after he was sent to be curate in Clichy, an outer suburb of Paris. From 1939 to 1947 he was parish priest of nearby Petits Colombes, during which time he wrote *Revolution in a City Parish*, a seminal text of the French parish missionary movement, in which he was a leading figure. From 1947 to 1956 he was parish priest in neighbouring Colombes. His last appointment was to Bel‐ leville, a more central working‐class suburb of Paris, from 1956 to 1966. Apart from the many works he authored about missionary parishes and priestly ministry, many of which were published in English translations, he was also author of the *Missel communautaire*, which ran to many editions over several decades, beginning while he was *curé* at Petits Colombes. This small, inexpensive hand missal was intended to foster communal participation in worship among his largely working‐class congregation, with the Mass texts and hymns translated into French and photos to add visual emphasis to the texts. He died in 1983.